PUCK

"Lord, what fools these mortals be!" says Puck in *A Midsummer Night's Dream*. But these immortal lines of Shakespeare were meant as a gentle, rather than a sardonic, criticism of humanity. For as Mark Van Doren writes in the Introduction to the *Four Great Comedies:* "Shakespeare loved the world as it is. That is why he understood it so well, and that in turn is why he could make it over again into something so rich and clear.

"While we read a play of Shakespeare's we are in it. . . . Once we are there we are enclosed. That is the secret of Shakespeare's power. . . . He denies his reader nothing."

FOUR GREAT COMEDIES

by

WILLIAM SHAKESPEARE

Cambridge Text and Glossaries
Complete and Unabridged ·

Edited by   WILLIAM ALDIS WRIGHT
Introductions by   MARK VAN DOREN
Synopses by   J. WALKER MCSPADDEN
Illustrations by   FREDERICK E. BANBERY
Designed by   MAXWELL MARXE

A
Midsummer Night's
Dream

As You Like It

Twelfth Night

The Tempest

 SPECIAL SCHOLASTIC BOOK SERVICES EDITION

WASHINGTON SQUARE PRESS, INC.
NEW YORK

FOUR GREAT COMEDIES BY WILLIAM SHAKESPEARE

A *Washington Square Press* edition

1st printing.......................August, 1948
28th printing.......................March, 1966

A new edition of a distinguished literary work now made available in an inexpensive, well-designed format

L

Published by
Washington Square Press, Inc., 630 Fifth Avenue, New York, N.Y.

WASHINGTON SQUARE PRESS editions are distributed in the U.S. by Affiliated Publishers, a division of Pocket Books, Inc., 630 Fifth Avenue, New York 20, N.Y. and in Canada by Pocket Books of Canada, Ltd., Richmond Hill, Ontario.

ACKNOWLEDGMENTS

From SHAKESPEARE by Mark Van Doren by permission of the publishers, Henry Holt and Company, Inc., and George Allen and Unwin, Ltd. Copyright, 1939, by Mark Van Doren.

From SHAKESPEARIAN SYNOPSES by J. Walker McSpadden by permission of the publishers, Thomas Y. Crowell and Company. Copyright, 1902, 1923, by Thomas Y. Crowell and Company. Copyright, 1930, by J. Walker McSpadden.

Table of Contents

TABLE OF CONTENTS

Introduction

I HAVE imagined the reader of this book to be a person already acquainted in one degree or another with the poems and plays of Shakespeare, and willing now for the first or hundredth time to consider them as human documents and as works of art. The knowledge I have assumed is a reading knowledge, since that is the kind we habitually have. Further knowledge in a theater is finally necessary, but the interest of the plays as they stand in print would appear to be without end, and I have counted on that. I have made each chapter as brief as I could, my endeavor being always, with neither novelty nor convention as my guide, to say the things that seemed to me essential. The quotations, many as they sometimes are, have been kept as short and few as possible. They will need attention even when they are familiar, for they carry the discussion; but I have assumed in the reader an awareness that Shakespeare was never writing quotations, and that the force of anything he said was in a peculiar sense relative to the force of other things. As a whole can be greater than the sum of its parts, so a complete poem is richer than the sum of all the things that can be said about its passages. Twice as many quotations as I have used, and ten times as much critical wisdom as I may chance to possess, would still provide no substitute for Shakespeare.

I have ignored the biography of Shakespeare, the history and character of his time, the conventions of his theater, the works of his contemporaries, and, with respect to the plays themselves, most questions having to do with their text and authorship. These matters are important, but it was more important for my purpose, and more practical, to proceed on the theory that the interest of the plays as they have come down to us exceeds the interest either of the individual who wrote them or of the age that produced him. That he was an individual I have no doubt, but he exists for me wholly in the work he did, and I often fail to recognize him in pictures painted of his time. He had too much poetry, and—the same thing for him—too much sense, to be the slave of fashions in human being. He is typical of any world that can be understood, and he is the kind of story-teller who can be judged by the most general standards we have. The *Poetics* of Aristotle will explain him more readily than the unique literature of his age will explain him. It is difficult enough for such literature to explain itself; nor does Shakespeare seem to call for explanations beyond those which a whole heart and a free mind abundantly supply.

I have no other theory about Shakespeare unless further ones appear, as doubtless they will, in the chapters that follow. I have none at any rate about the order in which the plays were written. I have followed an order, violating it here and there for convenience in discussion, but I do not insist upon any chronology. Dogma in these matters is difficult in view of Shakespeare's variety, and it is absurd when it depends upon conjectures about his moods. I seldom assume that I know what those were, and I always assume that he was greater than they, both as artist and as man.

If the plays of Shakespeare had not been easy to write they would have been impossible. If their solutions had once been problems they could not have been arrived at in a dozen lifetimes, let alone one lifetime in which two or three plays were often the output of a single year. The great and central virtue of Shakespeare was not achieved by taking thought, for thought cannot create a world. It can only understand one when one has been created. Shakespeare, starting with the world no man has made, and never indeed abandoning it, made many worlds within it. Some of them are more interesting than others, and a few of them are merely sketched; but each of them tends to be internally consistent, immediately knowable, and—at the same time that it is familiar—permanently fresh and strange. He may never have said to himself that this was what he had done, and if he talked to himself at all there were other excuses for congratulation. As a poet, considering the term in the narrower, verbal sense which is its commonest meaning now, he had written so well that any kind of poetry and any kind of prose can be found in him at its best. This has its lasting importance, being one of the reasons that the words he used have become so widely known. But a reason of deeper importance is the context of those words in the worlds they helped to make.

How these worlds came into being cannot be plainly said. If it could be, the criticism of Shakespeare would at once reach an end. Criticism grows desperate from time to time and denies their existence. Shakespeare was merely a poet, a word-magician; or merely a carpenter of plays; or merely an Elizabethan; or merely a man who wrote for money. He was all those things and more things like them, but to be satisfied with saying so is to be thrown off the scent of his distinction. At the opposite extreme criticism grows fanatical in the definition of devices by which the miracle of creation was performed; performance assumed, the investigator looks for tricks. The styles of Shakespeare are studied—the styles, for it is true that he had no style, no special way of writing beyond the way of writing well, and that he is not to be imitated except by one who will say things both as clearly and as interestingly as he did. But his success is not a matter of devices; or if so, they are secondary to a larger method which ordered them instinctively to the ends of unity and delight. The unity of any play is not alone a matter of images, though the coherence of its metaphors may be amazing; or of diction and syntax, though the monosyllables of *Julius Caesar* and the involutions of *The Winter's Tale* have much to do with the natures of their respective universes; or of atmosphere, though the difference between the environment of *Lear* and the environment of *Antony and Cleopatra* is so palpable that one may well become lost in the exercise of feeling it; or of character, though Shakespeare's people live forever; or of plot, though he is inimitable at story-telling. Beyond all these, worthy of study and praise as of course they are, there is in any of the successful plays a created or creature life, a unity of being which reveals itself with every step of our progress into its interior.

It is literally true that while we read a play of Shakespeare's we are in it. We may be drawn in swiftly or slowly—in most cases it is swiftly—but once we are there we are enclosed. That is the secret, and it is still a secret, of Shakespeare's power to interest us. He conditions us to a particular world before we are aware that it exists; then he absorbs us in its particulars. We scarcely say to ourselves, this world exists; nor do we pause to note how consistent each thing in it is with every other. Our attention is on the details, which we take in as details should be taken in, one at a time. Meanwhile there is for us no other world. The great world is not forgotten—Shakespeare indeed knows best how to keep us reminded of its greatness—but it is here confined to a single mode of its being. He is not telling the whole truth in any play, nor does he do so in all of them together, nor could he have done so had he written ten thousand. But the piece of truth with which he is occupied at a given moment is for that moment eloquent both of itself and of the remainder. It seems to be all. It is satisfactory and complete. With each new line a play of Shakespeare's lights its own recesses, deepens its original hue, echoes, supports, and authenticates itself. The world is not there, but this part of it is so entirely there that we miss nothing; it is as if existence had decided to measure itself by a new standard. And the secret of that standard is shared with us. Shakespeare, who denies his reader nothing, denies him least of all the excitement of feeling that he is where things are simply and finally alive.

Only a remarkable artist could have done this, and only a remarkable man—a man, moreover, in whom the balance was well-nigh perfect between understanding and observation, between intellect and instinct, between vision and sight. It has long been recognized that his characters, while irreducibly individual, partake of that nature which belongs to all men, and seldom desert the types in whose terms they were conceived. Hamlet is young, melancholy, courteous, brilliant, and moral. Falstaff is old, fat, drunken, untruthful, and witty. None of those traits is new, and it would almost appear that nothing in either man had been invented by Shakespeare. Each, however, has his unique carriage and voice, and will not be mistaken for any other man on earth. He is first of all a member of the human race. After that he is himself, saying things which Shakespeare knows how to envelop in a silence so natural that for the time being we hear no other sound than that of his discourse. Yet the act of being himself never takes him beyond the range of our understanding. We hear him with our ears and we see him with our eyes, but he is most valuable to us because we can think about him with all the mind we possess. He is not that monstrous thing, an individual undefined, any more than Shakespeare's worlds are irresponsible constructions, or any more than Shakespeare's poetry is idiot-pure. Sometimes this poetry struts on cumbrous wings when it should go by foot, but seldom is it being written for its own sake, as if poetry were the most precious thing in the world. To Shakespeare it was apparently not that. The world was still more precious—the great one he never forgot, and the little one in which he knew how to imprison its voice and body. What he dealt in was existence, and his dealings were responsible, high-hearted, and humane. The reader who places himself in his hands will not be protected from any experience, but he will be safe from outrage because he will always know his bearings. What is supposed to happen in Shakespeare's plays does happen; and what has happened anywhere cannot be finally hated. Shakespeare loved the world as it is. That is why he understood it so well; and that in turn is why, being the artist he was, he could make it over again into something so rich and clear.

MARK VAN DOREN

A Midsummer Night's Dream

INTRODUCTION TO

A Midsummer Night's Dream

BY

MARK VAN DOREN

A Midsummer Night's Dream shines like *Romeo and Juliet* in darkness, but shines merrily. Lysander, one of the two nonentities who are its heroes, complains at the beginning about the brevity of love's course, and sums up his complaint with a line which would not be out of place in *Romeo and Juliet*:

> So quick bright things come to confusion.   [I, i]

This, however, is at the beginning. Bright things will come to clarity in a playful, sparkling night while fountains gush and spangled starlight betrays the presence in a wood near Athens of magic persons who can girdle the earth in forty minutes and bring any cure for human woe. Nor will the woe to be cured have any power to elicit our anxiety. The four lovers whose situation resembles so closely the situation created in *The Two Gentlemen of Verona* will come nowhere near the seriousness of that predicament; they will remain to the end four automatic creatures whose artificial and pretty fate it is to fall in and out of love like dolls, and like dolls they will go to sleep as soon as they are laid down. There will be no pretense that reason and love keep company, or that because they do not death lurks at the horizon. There is no death in *A Midsummer Night's Dream*, and the smiling horizon is immeasurably remote.

Robin Goodfellow ends the extravaganza with an apology to the audience for the "weak and idle theme" with which it has been entertained. And Theseus, in honor of whose mar-

3

riage with Hippolyta the entire action is occurring, dismisses
most of it as a fairy toy, or such an airy nothing as some poet
might give a local habitation and a name (v, i). But Robin
is wrong about the theme, and Theseus does not describe the
kind of poet Shakespeare is. For the world of this play is both
veritable and large. It is not the tiny toy-shop that most such
spectacles present, with quaint little people scampering on
dry little errands, and with small music squeaking somewhere
a childish accompaniment. There is room here for mortals no
less than for fairies; both classes are at home, both groups
move freely in a wide world where indeed they seem sometimes to have exchanged functions with one another. For these
fairies do not sleep on flowers. Only Hermia can remember
lying upon faint primrose-beds (I, i), and only Bottom in the
action as we have it ever dozes on pressed posies (III, i). The
fairies themselves—Puck, Titania, Oberon—are too busy for
that, and too hard-minded. The vocabulary of Puck is the
most vernacular in the play; he talks of beans and crabs, dew-
laps and ale, three-foot stools and sneezes (II, i). And with
the king and queen of fairy-land he has immense spaces to
travel. The three of them are citizens of all the universe there
is, and as we listen to them the farthest portions of this universe stretch out, distant and glittering, like facets on a gem
of infinite size. There is a specific geography, and the heavens
are cold and high.

OBERON.   Thou rememb'rest
            Since once I sat upon a promontory,
            And heard a mermaid on a dolphin's back
            Uttering such dulcet and harmonious breath
            That the rude sea grew civil at her song,
            And certain stars shot madly from their spheres,
            To hear the sea-maid's music?
ROBIN.   I remember.
OBERON. That very time I saw, but thou couldst not,
            Flying between the cold moon and the earth,
            Cupid all arm'd. A certain aim he took
            At a fair vestal throned by the west.

And loos'd his love-shaft smartly from his bow,
As it should pierce a hundred thousand hearts;
But I might see young Cupid's fiery shaft
Quench'd in the chaste beams of the watery moon,
And the imperial votaress passed on,
In maiden meditation, fancy-free.
Yet mark'd I where the bolt of Cupid fell.
It fell upon a little western flower. . . .
Fetch me that flower, the herb I shew'd thee once. . . .
Fetch me this herb; and be thou here again
Ere the leviathan can swim a league.

ROBIN. I'll put a girdle round about the earth
In forty minutes.

[II, i]

The business may be trivial, but the world is as big and as real as any world we know. The promontory long ago; the rude sea that grew—not smooth, not gentle, not anything pretty or poetical, but (the prosaic word is one of Shakespeare's best) civil; the mermaid that is also a sea-maid; the direction west; and the cold watery moon that rides so high above the earth —these are the signs of its bigness, and they are so clear that we shall respect the prowess implied in Robin's speed, nor shall we fail to be impressed by the news that Oberon has just arrived from the farthest steep of India (II, i).

Dr. Johnson and Hazlitt copied Addison in saying that if there could be persons like these they would act like this. Their tribute was to the naturalness of Shakespeare's supernature. Dryden's tribute to its charm:

But Shakespeare's magic could not copied be;
Within that circle none durst walk but he

has an identical source: wonder that such things can be at all, and be so genuine. The explanation is the size and the concreteness of Shakespeare's setting. And the key to the structure of that setting is the watery moon to which Oberon so casually referred.

The poetry of the play is dominated by the words moon and water. Theseus and Hippolyta carve the moon in our

memory with the strong, fresh strokes of their opening dialogue:

THESEUS.   Now, fair Hippolyta, our nuptial hour
Draws on apace. Four happy days bring in
Another moon; but, O, methinks, how slow
This old moon wanes! She lingers my desires,
Like to a step-dame or a dowager
Long withering out a young man's revenue.

HIPPOLYTA.   Four days will quickly steep themselves in night;
Four nights will quickly dream away the time;
And then the moon, like to a silver bow
New-bent in heaven, shall behold the night
Of our solemnities.

This is not the sensuous, softer orb of *Antony and Cleopatra*,
nor is it the sweet sleeping friend of Lorenzo and Jessica. It is
brilliant and brisk, silver-distant, and an occasion for comedy
in Theseus's worldly thought. Later on in the same scene he
will call it cold and fruitless, and Lysander will look forward
to

Tomorrow night, when Phoebe doth behold
Her silver visage in the watery glass,
Decking with liquid pearl the bladed grass.   [I, i]

Lysander has connected the image of the moon with the
image of cool water on which it shines, and hereafter they
will be inseparable. *A Midsummer Night's Dream* is drenched
with dew when it is not saturated with rain. A film of water
spreads over it, enhances and enlarges it miraculously. The
fairy whom Robin hails as the second act opens wanders
swifter than the moon's sphere through fire and flood. The
moon, says Titania, is governess of floods, and in anger at
Oberon's brawls has sucked up from the sea contagious fogs,
made every river overflow, drowned the fields and rotted the
green corn:

The nine men's morris is fill'd up with mud,
And the quaint mazes in the wanton green
For lack of tread are undistinguishable.   [II, i]

Here in the west there has been a deluge, and every object still drips moisture. But even in the east there are waves and seas. The little changeling boy whom Titania will not surrender to Oberon is the son of a votaress on the other side of the earth:

> And, in the spiced Indian air, by night,
> Full often hath she gossip'd by my side,
> And sat with me on Neptune's yellow sands,
> Marking the embarked traders on the flood.   II, i]

The jewels she promises Bottom will be fetched "from the deep" (III, i). And Oberon is addicted to treading seaside groves

> Even till the eastern gate, all fiery-red,
> Opening on Neptune with fair blessed beams,
> Turns into yellow gold his salt green streams.   [III, ii]

So by a kind of logic the mortals of the play continue to be washed with copious weeping. The roses in Hermia's cheeks fade fast "for want of rain" (I, i), but rain will come. Demetrius "hails" and "showers" oaths on Helena (I, i), whose eyes are bathed with salt tears (II, ii); and Hermia takes comfort in the tempest of her eyes (I, i).

When the moon weeps, says Titania to Bottom, "weeps every little flower" (III, i). The flowers of *A Midsummer Night's Dream* are not the warm, sweet, dry ones of Perdita's garden, or even the daytime ones with which Fidele's brothers will strew her forest grave. They are the damp flowers that hide among ferns and drip with dew. A pearl is hung in every cowslip's ear (II, i); the little western flower which Puck is sent to fetch is rich with juice; and luscious woodbine canopies the bank of wild thyme where Titania sleeps—not on but "in" musk-roses and eglantine. Moon, water, and wet flowers conspire to extend the world of *A Midsummer Night's Dream* until it is as large as all imaginable life. That is why the play is both so natural and so mysterious.

Nor do its regions fail to echo with an ample music. The mermaid on the promontory with her dulcet and harmonious

breath sang distantly and long ago, but the world we walk in
is filled with present sound.

THESEUS.   Go, one of you, find out the forester,
For now our observation is perform'd,
And since we have the vaward of the day,
My love shall hear the music of my hounds.
Uncouple in the western valley, let them go.
Dispatch, I say, and find the forester.
We will, fair queen, up to the mountain's top
And mark the musical confusion
Of hounds and echo in conjunction.

HIPPOLYTA.   I was with Hercules and Cadmus once,
When in a wood of Crete they bay'd the bear
With hounds of Sparta. Never did I hear
Such gallant chiding; for, besides the groves,
The skies, the fountains, every region near
Seem'd all one mutual cry. I never heard
So musical a discord, such sweet thunder.

THESEUS.   My hounds are bred out of the Spartan kind,
So flew'd, so sanded, and their heads are hung
With ears that sweep away the morning dew;
Crook-knee'd, and dew-lapp'd like Thessalian bulls;
Slow in pursuit, but match'd in mouth like bells,
Each under each. A cry more tuneable
Was never holla'd to, nor cheer'd with horn,
In Crete, in Sparta, nor in Thessaly.
Judge when you hear.   [IV, i]

Had Shakespeare written nothing else than this he still might
be the best of English poets. Most poetry which tries to be
music also is less than poetry. This is absolute. The melody
which commences with such spirit in Theseus's fifth line has
already reached the complexity of counterpoint in his eighth
and ninth; Hippolyta carries it to a like limit in the line with
which she closes; and Theseus, taking it back from her,
hugely increases its volume, first by reminding us that the
hounds have form and muscle, and then by daring the grand
dissonance, the mixed thunder, of bulls and bells. The passage sets a forest ringing, and supplies a play with the music
it has deserved.

But Shakespeare is still more a poet because the passage is incidental to his creation. The creation with which he is now busy is not a passage, a single effect; it is a play, and though this one contribution has been mighty there are many others. And none of the others is mightier than bully Bottom's.

Bottom likes music too. "I have a reasonable good ear," he tells Titania. "Let's have the tongs and the bones." So does he take an interest in moonshine, if only among the pages of an almanac. "A calendar, a calendar!" he calls. "Find out moonshine, find out moonshine." When they find the moon, those Athenian mechanics of whom he is king, it has in it what the cold fairy moon cannot be conceived as having, the familiar man of folklore. Bottom and his fellows domesticate the moon, as they domesticate every other element of which Shakespeare has made poetry. And the final effect is parody. Bottom's amazed oration concerning his dream follows hard upon the lovers' discourse concerning dreams and delusions; but it is in prose, and the speaker is utterly literal when he pronounces that it will be called Bottom's dream because it hath no bottom (IV, i). Nor is the story of Pyramus and Thisbe as the mechanics act it anything but a burlesque of *Romeo and Juliet*.

> O night, which ever art when day is not! . . .
> And thou, O wall, O sweet, O lovely wall,
> That stand'st between her father's ground and mine!
> Thou wall, O wall, O sweet and lovely wall.   [v, i]

Shakespeare has come, even this early, to the farthest limit of comedy. The end of comedy is self-parody, and its wisdom is self-understanding. Never again will he work without a full comprehension of the thing he is working at; of the probability that other and contrary things are of equal importance; of the certainty that his being a poet who can do anything he wants to do is not the only thing to be, or the best possible thing; of the axiom that the whole is greater than the part— the part in his instance being one play among many thinkable plays, or one man, himself, among the multitude that populate a world for whose size and variety he with such giant strides is reaching respect. Bully Bottom and his friends have lived three centuries to good purpose, but to no better purpose at any time than the one they first had—namely, in their sublime innocence, their earthbound, idiot openness and charity of soul, to bring it about that their creator should become not only the finest of poets but the one who makes the fewest claims for poetry.

The Story of the Play

ACT I

THESEUS, Duke of Athens, after conquering the Amazons in battle, is in turn conquered by the charms of their queen, Hippolyta, and plights troth with her. To speed the time until their wedding night, he orders amusements to be put on foot. Actuated by a spirit of loyalty, Bottom the weaver and other tradesmen prepare a play for the Duke.

Egeus, an Athenian, brings his daughter Hermia and her two suitors before Theseus, praying him to command Hermia to wed Demetrius. Hermia pleads to be allowed to marry the one she loves—Lysander. The Duke orders her to obey her father under penalty of death or of a conventual life. Hermia and Lysander bewail the harsh decree, and secretly agree to meet in a wood near by and flee to another country. They tell their plans to Helena, a jilted sweetheart of Demetrius, and she, to win back his love, goes straightway to inform him of the design.

ACT II

IN THE FOREST is great commotion among the fairies. King Oberon and Queen Titania are at odds. Oberon bids Puck procure a love-juice to pour upon Titania's eyelids when she is asleep, in order that she may love the first thing her waking eyes behold. Just then Oberon perceives Demetrius, who has sought out the trysting-place of Lysander and Hermia, only to meet Helena, much to his distaste. The lady's distress at her lover's coldness softens the heart of Oberon, who bids Puck touch Demetrius's eyes also with the love-juice, for Helena's sake, while he himself anoints the eyes of Titania. Meantime Lysander and Hermia arrive, and Puck in error

11

anoints Lysander's instead of Demetrius's eyes; so that Lysander, happening to awake just as the neglected Helena wanders by, falls in love with her, to the abandonment of Hermia.

ACT III

THIS same enchanted spot in the forest happens to be the place selected by Bottom the weaver and his companions for the final rehearsal of their play. The roguish Puck passes that way while they are rehearsing, and decides to take a hand in the proceedings. He crowns Bottom with an ass's head, whereupon the other players disperse terror-stricken. Then he brings Bottom to Titania, whose enchanted gaze fixes upon the human ass as her heart's love.

Meantime the four lovers come into great bewilderment. Oberon finds that Puck has anointed the eyes of Lysander instead of those of Demetrius, which he himself now takes occasion to touch. When Demetrius awakes he sees his neglected Helena being wooed by Lysander. His own love for her returns, and he is ready to fight Lysander. Helena deems them both to be mocking her; while Hermia is dazed by the turn of affairs. The fairies interpose and prevent conflict by causing the four to wander about until they are tired, when they fall asleep. Puck repairs his blunder by anointing Lysander's eyes, in order to dispel the illusion caused by the love-juice.

ACT IV

TITANIA makes love to Bottom, till Oberon, whose anger has abated, removes the spell from her eyes. To Bottom is restored his natural form, and he rejoins his comrades in Athens. Theseus, on an early morning hunting-trip in the forest, discovers the four lovers. Explanations follow; the Duke relents and bestows Helena upon Demetrius and Hermia upon Lysander.

ACT V

A WEDDING-FEAST for three couples instead of one only is spread in Duke Theseus's palace. Thither come Bottom's players to present the comic tragedy of "Pyramus and Thisbe," which is performed in wondrous fashion. After the company retires for the night, the fairies dance through the corridors on a mission of blessing and good-will for the three wedded pairs.

J. WALKER McSPADDEN

List of Characters

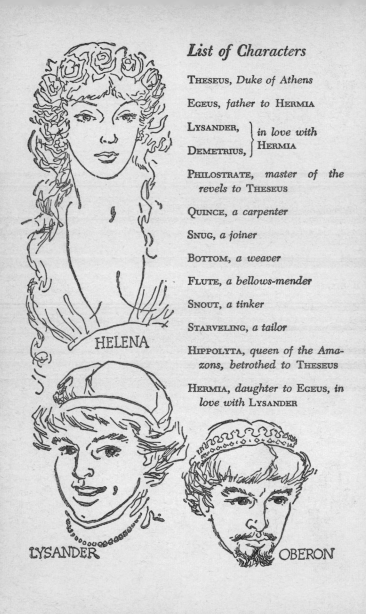

THESEUS, *Duke of Athens*

EGEUS, *father to* HERMIA

LYSANDER,
DEMETRIUS, } *in love with* HERMIA

PHILOSTRATE, *master of the revels to* THESEUS

QUINCE, *a carpenter*

SNUG, *a joiner*

BOTTOM, *a weaver*

FLUTE, *a bellows-mender*

SNOUT, *a tinker*

STARVELING, *a tailor*

HIPPOLYTA, *queen of the Amazons, betrothed to* THESEUS

HERMIA, *daughter to* EGEUS, *in love with* LYSANDER

HELENA

LYSANDER

OBERON

PUCK

TITANIA

HELENA, *in love with*
DEMETRIUS

OBERON, *king of the fairies*

TITANIA, *queen of the fairies*

PUCK, *or* ROBIN GOODFELLOW

PEASEBLOSSOM,
COBWEB,
MOTH,
MUSTARDSEED,
} *fairies*

Other fairies attending their
King and Queen. Attendants
on Theseus and Hippolyta

BOTTOM

A Midsummer Night's Dream

Scene — Athens, *and a wood near it.*

ACT I

Scene I — *Athens. The palace of* Theseus.

Enter Theseus, Hippolyta, Philostrate,
    and Attendants.]

theseus. Now, fair Hippolyta, our nuptial hour
  Draws on apace; four happy days bring in
  Another moon: but, O, methinks, how slow
  This old moon wanes! she lingers my desires,
  Like to a step-dame, or a dowager,
  Long withering out a young man's revenue.
hippolyta. Four days will quickly steep themselves in night;
  Four nights will quickly dream away the time;
  And then the moon, like to a silver bow
  New-bent in heaven, shall behold the night
  Of our solemnities.
theseus.   Go, Philostrate,
  Stir up the Athenian youth to merriments;
  Awake the pert and nimble spirit of mirth:
  Turn melancholy forth to funerals;
  The pale companion is not for our pomp.
                   [*Exit* philostrate.
  Hippolyta, I woo'd thee with my sword,
  And won thy love, doing thee injuries;
  But I will wed thee in another key,
  With pomp, with triumph and with reveling.
Enter egeus, hermia, lysander, *and* demetrius.]
egeus. Happy be Theseus, our renowned duke!
theseus. Thanks, good Egeus: what 's the news with thee?

16

EGEUS. Full of vexation come I, with complaint
    Against my child, my daughter Hermia.
    Stand forth, Demetrius. My noble lord,
    This man hath my consent to marry her.
    Stand forth, Lysander: and, my gracious duke,
    This man hath bewitch'd the bosom of my child:
    Thou, thou, Lysander, thou hast given her rhymes,
    And interchanged love-tokens with my child:
    Thou hast by moonlight at her window sung,
    With feigning voice, verses of feigning love;
    And stolen the impression of her fantasy
    With bracelets of thy hair, rings, gawds, conceits,
    Knacks, trifles, nosegays, sweetmeats, messengers
    Of strong prevailment in unharden'd youth:
    With cunning hast thou filch'd my daughter's heart;
    Turn'd her obedience, which is due to me,
    To stubborn harshness: and, my gracious duke,
    Be it so she will not here before your Grace
    Consent to marry with Demetrius,
    I beg the ancient privilege of Athens,
    As she is mine, I may dispose of her:
    Which shall be either to this gentleman
    Or to her death, according to our law
    Immediately provided in that case.

THESEUS. What say you, Hermia? be advised, fair maid;
    To you your father should be as a god;
    One that composed your beauties; yea, and one
    To whom you are but as a form in wax
    By him imprinted and within his power
    To leave the figure or disfigure it.
    Demetrius is a worthy gentleman.

HERMIA. So is Lysander.

THESEUS.   In himself he is;
    But in this kind, wanting your father's voice,
    The other must be held the worthier.

HERMIA. I would my father look'd but with my eyes.

THESEUS. Rather your eyes must with his judgment look.

HERMIA. I do entreat your Grace to pardon me.

I know not by what power I am made bold,
Nor how it may concern my modesty,
In such a presence here to plead my thoughts;
But I beseech your Grace that I may know
The worst that may befall me in this case,
If I refuse to wed Demetrius.

THESEUS. Either to die the death, or to adjure
For ever the society of men.
Therefore, fair Hermia, question your desires;
Know of your youth, examine well your blood,
Whether, if you yield not to your father's choice,
You can endure the livery of a nun;
For aye to be in shady cloister mew'd,
To live a barren sister all your life,
Chanting faint hymns to the cold fruitless moon.
Thrice-blessed they that master so their blood,
To undergo such maiden pilgrimage;
But earthlier happy is the rose distill'd,
Than that which, withering on the virgin thorn,
Grows, lives, and dies in single blessedness.

HERMIA. So will I grow, so live, so die, my lord,
Ere I will yield my virgin patent up
Unto his lordship, whose unwished yoke
My soul consents not to give sovereignty.

THESEUS. Take time to pause; and, by the next new moon,—
The sealing-day betwixt my love and me,
For everlasting bond of fellowship,—
Upon that day either prepare to die
For disobedience to your father's will,
Or else to wed Demetrius, as he would;
Or on Diana's altar to protest
For aye austerity and single life.

DEMETRIUS. Relent, sweet Hermia: and, Lysander, yield
Thy crazed title to my certain right.

LYSANDER. You have her father's love, Demetrius;
Let me have Hermia's: do you marry him.

EGEUS. Scornful Lysander! true, he hath my love,
And what is mine my love shall render him.

And she is mine, and all my right of her
I do estate unto Demetrius.

LYSANDER. I am, my lord, as well derived as he,
As well possess'd; my love is more than his;
My fortunes every way as fairly rank'd,
If not with vantage, as Demetrius';
And, which is more than all these boasts can be,
I am beloved of beauteous Hermia:
Why should not I then prosecute my right?
Demetrius, I 'll avouch it to his head,
Made love to Nedar's daughter, Helena,
And won her soul; and she, sweet lady, dotes,
Devoutly dotes, dotes in idolatry,
Upon this spotted and inconstant man.

THESEUS. I must confess that I have heard so much,
And with Demetrius thought to have spoke thereof;
But, being over-full of self-affairs,
My mind did lose it. But, Demetrius, come;
And come, Egeus; you shall go with me,
I have some private schooling for you both.
For you, fair Hermia, look you arm yourself
To fit your fancies to your father's will;
Or else the law of Athens yields you up,—
Which by no means we may extenuate,—
To death, or to a vow of single life.
Come, my Hippolyta: what cheer, my love?
Demetrius and Egeus, go along:
I must employ you in some business
Against our nuptial, and confer with you
Of something nearly that concerns yourselves.

EGEUS. With duty and desire we follow you.

                    [*Exeunt all but* LYSANDER *and* HERMIA.

LYSANDER. How now, my love! why is your cheek so pale?
How chance the roses there do fade so fast?

HERMIA. Belike for want of rain, which I could well
Beteem them from the tempest of my eyes.

LYSANDER. Aye me! for aught that I could ever read,
Could ever hear by tale or history,

The course of true love never did run smooth;
But, either it was different in blood,—
HERMIA. O cross! too high to be enthrall'd to low.
LYSANDER. Or else misgraffed in respect of years,—
HERMIA. O spite! too old to be engaged to young.
LYSANDER. Or else it stood upon the choice of friends,—
HERMIA. O hell! to choose love by another's eyes.
LYSANDER. Or, if there were a sympathy in choice,
War, death, or sickness did lay siege to it
Making it momentany as a sound,
Swift as a shadow, short as any dream;
Brief as the lightning in the collied night,
That, in a spleen, unfolds both heaven and earth,
And ere a man hath power to say 'Behold!'
The jaws of darkness do devour it up:
So quick bright things come to confusion.
HERMIA. If then true lovers have been ever cross'd,
It stands as an edict in destiny:
Then let us teach our trial patience,
Because it is a customary cross,
As due to love as thoughts and dreams and sighs,
Wishes and tears, poor fancy's followers.
LYSANDER. A good persuasion: therefore, hear me, Hermia.
I have a widow aunt, a dowager
Of great revenue, and she hath no child:
From Athens is her house remote seven leagues;
And she respects me as her only son.
There, gentle Hermia, may I marry thee;
And to that place the sharp Athenian law
Cannot pursue us. If thou lovest me, then,
Steal forth thy father's house to-morrow night;
And in the wood, a league without the town,
Where I did meet thee once with Helena,
To do observance to a morn of May,
There will I stay for thee.
HERMIA.   My good Lysander!
I swear to thee, by Cupid's strongest bow,

By his best arrow with the golden head,
By the simplicity of Venus' doves,
By that which knitteth souls and prospers loves,
And by that fire which burn'd the Carthage queen,
When the false Troyan under sail was seen,
By all the vows that ever men have broke,
In number more than ever women spoke,
In that same place thou hast appointed me,
To-morrow truly will I meet with thee.

LYSANDER. Keep promise, love. Look, here comes Helena.

Enter HELENA.]

HERMIA. God speed fair Helena! whither away?

HELENA. Call you me fair? that fair again unsay.
Demetrius loves your fair: O happy fair!
Your eyes are lode-stars; and your tongue's sweet air
More tuneable than lark to shepherd's ear,
When wheat is green, when hawthorn buds appear.
Sickness is catching: O, were favor so,
Yours would I catch, fair Hermia, ere I go,
My ear should catch your voice, my eye your eye,
My tongue should catch your tongue's sweet melody.
Were the world mine, Demetrius being bated,
The rest I 'ld give to be to you translated.
O, teach me how you look; and with what art
You sway the motion of Demetrius' heart!

HERMIA. I frown upon him, yet he loves me still.

HELENA. O that your frowns would teach my smiles such skill!

HERMIA. I give him curses, yet he gives me love.

HELENA. O that my prayers could such affection move!

HERMIA. The more I hate, the more he follows me.

HELENA. The more I love, the more he hateth me.

HERMIA. His folly, Helena, is no fault of mine.

HELENA. None, but your beauty; would that fault were mine!

HERMIA. Take comfort: he no more shall see my face;
Lysander and myself will fly this place.
Before the time I did Lysander see,
Seem'd Athens as a paradise to me:

    O, then, what graces in my love do dwell,
    That he hath turn'd a heaven unto a hell!

LYSANDER. Helen, to you our minds we will unfold:
    To-morrow night, when Phœbe doth behold
    Her silver visage in the watery glass,
    Decking with liquid pearl the bladed grass,
    A time that lovers' flights doth still conceal,
    Through Athens' gates have we devised to steal.

HERMIA. And in the wood, where often you and I
    Upon faint primrose-beds were wont to lie,
    Emptying our bosoms of their counsel sweet,
    There my Lysander and myself shall meet;
    And thence from Athens turn away our eyes,
    To seek new friends and stranger companies.
    Farewell, sweet playfellow: pray thou for us;
    And good luck grant thee thy Demetrius!
    Keep word, Lysander: we must starve our sight
    From lovers' food till morrow deep midnight.

LYSANDER. I will, my Hermia.   [Exit HERMIA.
                Helena, adieu:
    As you on him, Demetrius dote on you!   [Exit.

HELENA. How happy some o'er other some can be!
    Through Athens I am thought as fair as she.
    But what of that? Demetrius thinks not so;
    He will not know what all but he do know;
    And as he errs, doting on Hermia's eyes,
    So I, admiring of his qualities:
    Things base and vile, holding no quantity,
    Love can transpose to form and dignity:
    Love looks not with the eyes, but with the mind;
    And therefore is wing'd Cupid painted blind:
    Nor hath Love's mind of any judgment taste;
    Wings, and no eyes, figure unheedy haste:
    And therefore is Love said to be a child,
    Because in choice he is so oft beguiled.
    As waggish boys in game themselves forswear,
    So the boy Love is perjured everywhere:

For ere Demetrius look'd on Hermia's eyne,
He hail'd down oaths that he was only mine;
And when this hail some heat from Hermia felt,
So he dissolved, and showers of oaths did melt.
I will go tell him of fair Hermia's flight:
Then to the wood will he to-morrow night
Pursue her; and for this intelligence
If I have thanks, it is a dear expense:
But herein mean I to enrich my pain,
To have his sight thither and back again.   [*Exit.*

SCENE II — *The same.* QUINCE'S *house.*

Enter QUINCE, SNUG, BOTTOM, FLUTE, SNOUT,
      and STARVELING.]

QUINCE. Is all our company here?

BOTTOM. You were best to call them generally, man by man,
    according to the scrip.

QUINCE. Here is the scroll of every man's name, which is
    thought fit, through all Athens, to play in our interlude
    before the duke and the duchess, on his wedding-day at
    night.

BOTTOM. First, good Peter Quince, say what the play treats
    on; then read the names of the actors; and so grow to a
    point.

QUINCE. Marry, our play is, The most lamentable comedy, and
    most cruel death of Pyramus and Thisby.

BOTTOM. A very good piece of work, I assure you, and a
    merry. Now, good Peter Quince, call forth your actors by
    the scroll. Masters, spread yourselves.

QUINCE. Answer as I call you. Nick Bottom, the weaver.

BOTTOM. Ready. Name what part I am for, and proceed.

QUINCE. You, Nick Bottom, are set down for Pyramus.

BOTTOM. What is Pyramus? a lover, or a tyrant?

QUINCE. A lover, that kills himself most gallant for love.

BOTTOM. That will ask some tears in the true performing of
    it: if I do it, let the audience look to their eyes; I will move

storms, I will condole in some measure. To the rest: yet my
chief humor is for a tyrant: I could play Ercles rarely, or a
part to tear a cat in, to make all split.

> The raging rocks
> And shivering shocks
> Shall break the locks
>   Of prison-gates;
> And Phibbus' car
> Shall shine from far,
> And make and mar
>   The foolish Fates.

This was lofty! Now name the rest of the players. This is
Ercles' vein, a tyrant's vein; a lover is more condoling.

QUINCE. Francis Flute, the bellows-mender.

FLUTE. Here, Peter Quince.

QUINCE. Flute, you must take Thisby on you.

FLUTE. What is Thisby? a wandering knight?

QUINCE. It is the lady that Pyramus must love.

FLUTE. Nay, faith, let not me play a woman; I have a beard
coming.

QUINCE. That's all one: you shall play it in a mask, and you
may speak as small as you will.

BOTTOM. An I may hide my face, let me play Thisby too, I'll
speak in a monstrous little voice, 'Thisne, Thisne!' 'Ah Pyramus, my lover dear! thy Thisby dear, and lady dear!'

QUINCE. No, no; you must play Pyramus: and, Flute, you
Thisby.

BOTTOM. Well, proceed.

QUINCE. Robin Starveling, the tailor.

STARVELING. Here, Peter Quince.

QUINCE. Robin Starveling, you must play Thisby's mother.
Tom Snout, the tinker.

SNOUT. Here, Peter Quince.

QUINCE. You, Pyramus' father: myself, Thisby's father: Snug,
the joiner; you, the lion's part: and, I hope, here is a play
fitted.

SNUG. Have you the lion's part written? pray you, if it be, give it me, for I am slow of study.

QUINCE. You may do it extempore, for it is nothing but roaring.

BOTTOM. Let me play the lion too: I will roar, that I will do any man's heart good to hear me; I will roar, that I will make the duke say, 'Let him roar again, let him roar again.'

QUINCE. An you should do it too terribly, you would fright the duchess and the ladies, that they would shriek; and that were enough to hang us all.

ALL. That would hang us, every mother's son.

BOTTOM. I grant you, friends, if you should fright the ladies out of their wits, they would have no more discretion but to hang us: but I will aggravate my voice so, that I will roar you as gently as any sucking dove; I will roar you as 'twere any nightingale.

QUINCE. You can play no part but Pyramus; for Pyramus is a sweet-faced man; a proper man, as one shall see in a summer's day; a most lovely, gentleman-like man: therefore you must needs play Pyramus.

BOTTOM. Well, I will undertake it. What beard were I best to play it in?

QUINCE. Why, what you will.

BOTTOM. I will discharge it in either your straw color beard, your orange-tawny beard, your purple-in-grain beard, or your French-crown color beard, your perfect yellow.

QUINCE. Some of your French crowns have no hair at all, and then you will play barefaced. But, masters, here are your parts: and I am to entreat you, request you, and desire you, to con them by to-morrow night; and meet me in the palace wood, a mile without the town, by moonlight; there will we rehearse, for if we meet in the city, we shall be dogged with company, and our devices known. In the meantime I will draw a bill of properties, such as our play wants. I pray you, fail me not.

BOTTOM. We will meet; and there we may rehearse most obscenely and courageously. Take pains; be perfect: adieu.

QUINCE. At the duke's oak we meet.

BOTTOM. Enough; hold or cut bow-strings.   [*Exeunt.*

ACT II

SCENE I — *A wood near Athens.*

Enter, from opposite sides, a FAIRY, *and* PUCK.]

PUCK. How now, spirit! whither wander you?

FAIRY. Over hill, over dale,
    Thorough bush, thorough brier,
Over park, over pale,
    Thorough flood, thorough fire,
I do wander every where,
Swifter than the moon's sphere;
    And I serve the fairy queen,
    To dew her orbs upon the green.
    The cowslips tall her pensioners be:
    In their gold coats spots you see;
    Those be rubies, fairy favors,
    In those freckles live their savors:
I must go seek some dewdrops here,
And hang a pearl in every cowslip's ear.
Farewell, thou lob of spirits; I 'll be gone:
Our queen and all her elves come here anon.

PUCK. The king doth keep his revels here to-night:
Take heed the queen come not within his sight;
For Oberon is passing fell and wrath,
Because that she as her attendant hath
A lovely boy, stolen from an Indian king;
She never had so sweet a changeling:
And jealous Oberon would have the child
Knight of his train, to trace the forests wild;
But she perforce withholds the loved boy,
Crowns him with flowers, and makes him all her joy:
And now they never meet in grove or green,

By fountain clear, or spangled starlight sheen,
But they do square, that all their elves for fear
Creep into acorn cups and hide them there.

FAIRY. Either I mistake your shape and making quite,
Or else you are that shrewd and knavish sprite
Call'd Robin Goodfellow: are not you he
That frights the maidens of the villagery;
Skim milk, and sometimes labor in the quern,
And bootless make the breathless housewife churn;
And sometime make the drink to bear no barm;
Mislead night-wanderers, laughing at their harm?
Those that Hobgoblin call you, and sweet Puck,
You do their work, and they shall have good luck:
Are not you he?

PUCK.   Thou speak'st aright;
I am that merry wanderer of the night.
I jest to Oberon, and make him smile,
When I a fat and bean-fed horse beguile,
Neighing in likeness of a filly foal:
And sometimes lurk I in a gossip's bowl,
In very likeness of a roasted crab;
And when she drinks, against her lips I bob
And on her withered dewlap pour the ale.
The wisest aunt, telling the saddest tale,
Sometime for three-foot stool mistaketh me:
Then slip I from her bum, down topples she,
And 'tailor' cries, and falls into a cough:
And then the whole quire hold their hips and laugh;
And waxen in their mirth, and neeze, and swear
A merrier hour was never wasted there.
But, room, fairy! here comes Oberon.

FAIRY. And here my mistress. Would that he were gone!

Enter, from one side, OBERON, *with his train;*
        from the other, TITANIA, *with hers.*]

OBERON. Ill met by moonlight, proud Titania.

TITANIA. What, jealous Oberon! Fairies, skip hence:
I have forsworn his bed and company.

OBERON. Tarry, rash wanton: am not I thy lord?

TITANIA. Then I must be thy lady: but I know
When thou hast stolen away from fairy land,
And in the shape of Corin sat all day,
Playing on pipes of corn, and versing love
To amorous Phillida. Why art thou here,
Come from the farthest steppe of India?
But that, forsooth, the bouncing Amazon,
Your buskin'd mistress and your warrior love,
To Theseus must be wedded, and you come
To give their bed joy and prosperity.

OBERON. How canst thou thus for shame, Titania,
Glance at my credit with Hippolyta,
Knowing I know thy love to Theseus?
Didst thou not lead him through the glimmering night
From Perigenia, whom he ravished?
And make him with fair Ægle break his faith,
With Ariadne and Antiopa?

TITANIA. These are the forgeries of jealousy:
And never, since the middle summer's spring,
Met we on hill, in dale, forest, or mead,
By paved fountain or by rushy brook,
Or in the beached margent of the sea,
To dance our ringlets to the whistling wind,
But with thy brawls thou hast disturb'd our sport.
Therefore the winds, piping to us in vain,
As in revenge, have suck'd up from the sea
Contagious fogs; which, falling in the land,
Have every pelting river made so proud,
That they have overborne their continents:
The ox hath therefore stretch'd his yoke in vain,
The ploughman lost his sweat; and the green corn
Hath rotted ere his youth attain'd a beard:
The fold stands empty in the drowned field,
And crows are fatted with the murrion flock;
The nine men's morris is fill'd up with mud;
And the quaint mazes in the wanton green,
For lack of tread, are undistinguishable:

The human mortals want their winter here;
No night is now with hymn or carol blest:
Therefore the moon, the governess of floods,
Pale in her anger, washes all the air,
That rheumatic diseases do abound:
And thorough this distemperature we see
The seasons alter: hoary-headed frosts
Fall in the fresh lap of the crimson rose;
And on old Hiems' thin and icy crown
An odorous chaplet of sweet summer buds
Is, as in mockery, set: the spring, the summer,
The childing autumn, angry winter, change
Their wonted liveries; and the mazed world,
By their increase, now knows not which is which:
And this same progeny of evil comes
From our debate, from our dissension;
We are their parents and original.

OBERON. Do you amend it, then; it lies in you:
Why should Titania cross her Oberon?
I do but beg a little changeling boy,
To be my henchman.

TITANIA.   Set your heart at rest:
The fairy land buys not the child of me.
His mother was a votaress of my order:
And, in the spiced Indian air, by night,
Full often hath she gossip'd by my side;
And sat with me on Neptune's yellow sands,
Marking the embarked traders on the flood;
When we have laugh'd to see the sails conceive
And grow big-bellied with the wanton wind;
Which she, with pretty and with swimming gait
Following,—her womb then rich with my young squire,—
Would imitate, and sail upon the land,
To fetch me trifles, and return again,
As from a voyage, rich with merchandise.
But she, being mortal, of that boy did die;
And for her sake do I rear up her boy;
And for her sake I will not part with him.

OBERON. How long within this wood intend you stay?

TITANIA. Perchance till after Theseus' wedding-day.
If you will patiently dance in our round,
And see our moonlight revels, go with us;
If not, shun me, and I will spare your haunts.

OBERON. Give me that boy, and I will go with thee.

TITANIA. Not for thy fairy kingdom. Fairies, away!
We shall chide downright, if I longer stay.

[*Exit* TITANIA *with her Train.*

OBERON. Well, go thy way: thou shalt not from this grove
Till I torment thee for this injury.
My gentle Puck, come hither. Thou rememberest
Since once I sat upon a promontory,
And heard a mermaid, on a dolphin's back,
Uttering such dulcet and harmonious breath,
That the rude sea grew civil at her song,
And certain stars shot madly from their spheres,
To hear the sea-maid's music.

PUCK.   I remember.

OBERON. That very time I saw, but thou couldst not,
Flying between the cold moon and the earth,
Cupid all arm'd: a certain aim he took
At a fair vestal throned by the west,
And loosed his love-shaft smartly from his bow,
As it should pierce a hundred thousand hearts:
But I might see young Cupid's fiery shaft
Quench'd in the chaste beams of the watery moon,
And the imperial votaress passed on,
In maiden meditation, fancy-free.
Yet mark'd I where the bolt of Cupid fell:
It fell upon a little western flower,
Before milk-white, now purple with love's wound,
And maidens call it love-in-idleness.
Fetch me that flower; the herb I shew'd thee once:
The juice of it on sleeping eye-lids laid
Will make or man or woman madly dote
Upon the next live creature that it sees.

Fetch me this herb; and be thou here again
Ere the leviathan can swim a league.

PUCK. I 'll put a girdle round about the earth
In forty minutes.   [*Exit.*

OBERON.   Having once this juice,
I 'll watch Titania when she is asleep,
And drop the liquor of it in her eyes.
The next thing then she waking looks upon,
Be it on lion, bear, or wolf, or bull,
On meddling monkey, or on busy ape,
She shall pursue it with the soul of love:
And ere I take this charm from off her sight,
As I can take it with another herb,
I 'll make her render up her page to me.
But who comes here? I am invisible;
And I will overhear their conference.

Enter DEMETRIUS, HELENA *following him.*]

DEMETRIUS. I love thee not, therefore pursue me not.
Where is Lysander and fair Hermia?
The one I 'll slay, the other slayeth me.
Thou told'st me they were stolen unto this wood,
And here am I, and wode within this wood,
Because I cannot meet my Hermia.
Hence, get thee gone, and follow me no more.

HELENA. You draw me, you hard-hearted adamant;
But yet you draw not iron, for my heart
Is true as steel: leave you your power to draw,
And I shall have no power to follow you.

DEMETRIUS. Do I entice you? do I speak you fair?
Or, rather, do I not in plainest truth
Tell you, I do not nor I cannot love you?

HELENA. And even for that do I love you the more.
I am your spaniel; and, Demetrius,
The more you beat me, I will fawn on you:
Use me but as your spaniel, spurn me, strike me,
Neglect me, lose me; only give me leave,
Unworthy as I am, to follow you.

What worser place can I beg in your love,—
And yet a place of high respect with me,—
Than to be used as you use your dog?
DEMETRIUS. Tempt not too much the hatred of my spirit;
For I am sick when I do look on thee.
HELENA. And I am sick when I look not on you.
DEMETRIUS. You do impeach your modesty too much,
To leave the city, and commit yourself
Into the hands of one that loves you not;
To trust the opportunity of night
And the ill counsel of a desert place
With the rich worth of your virginity.
HELENA. Your virtue is my privilege: for that
It is not night when I do see your face,
Therefore I think I am not in the night;
Nor doth this wood lack worlds of company,
For you in my respect are all the world:
Then how can it be said I am alone,
When all the world is here to look on me?
DEMETRIUS. I'll run from thee and hide me in the brakes,
And leave thee to the mercy of wild beasts.
HELENA. The wildest hath not such a heart as you.
Run when you will, the story shall be changed:
Apollo flies, and Daphne holds the chase;
The dove pursues the griffin; the mild hind
Makes speed to catch the tiger; bootless speed,
When cowardice pursues, and valor flies.
DEMETRIUS. I will not stay thy questions; let me go:
Or, if thou follow me, do not believe
But I shall do thee mischief in the wood.
HELENA. Aye, in the temple, in the town, the field,
You do me mischief. Fie, Demetrius!
Your wrongs do set a scandal on my sex:
We cannot fight for love, as men may do;
We should be woo'd, and were not made to woo.
                                        [Exit DEMETRIUS.

I'll follow thee, and make a heaven of hell,
To die upon the hand I love so well.   [Exit.

OBERON. Fare thee well, nymph: ere he do leave this grove,
  Thou shalt fly him, and he shall seek thy love.
Re-enter PUCK.]
  Hast thou the flower there? Welcome, wanderer.
PUCK. Aye, there it is.
OBERON.   I pray thee, give it me.
  I know a bank where the wild thyme blows,
  Where oxlips and the nodding violet grows;
  Quite over-canopied with luscious woodbine,
  With sweet musk-roses, and with eglantine:
  There sleeps Titania sometime of the night,
  Lull'd in these flowers with dances and delight;
  And there the snake throws her enamell'd skin,
  Weed wide enough to wrap a fairy in:
  And with the juice of this I'll streak her eyes,
  And make her full of hateful fantasies.
  Take thou some of it, and seek through this grove:
  A sweet Athenian lady is in love
  With a disdainful youth: anoint his eyes;
  But do it when the next thing he espies
  May be the lady: thou shalt know the man
  By the Athenian garments he hath on.
  Effect it with some care that he may prove
  More fond on her than she upon her love:
  And look thou meet me ere the first cock crow.
PUCK. Fear not, my lord, your servant shall do so.   [*Exeunt.*

SCENE II — *Another part of the wood.*

Enter TITANIA, *with her train.*]
TITANIA. Come, now a roundel and a fairy song;
  Then, for the third part of a minute, hence;
  Some to kill cankers in the musk-rose buds;
  Some war with rere-mice for their leathern wings,
  To make my small elves coats; and some keep back
  The clamorous owl, that nightly hoots and wonders
  At our quaint spirits. Sing me now asleep;
  Then to your offices, and let me rest.

SONG.

FIRST FAIRY. You spotted snakes with double tongue,
    Thorny hedgehogs, be not seen;
    Newts and blind-worms, do no wrong,
    Come not near our fairy queen.

CHORUS.

    Philomel, with melody,
    Sing in our sweet lullaby;
    Lulla, lulla, lullaby, lulla, lulla, lullaby:
      Never harm,
      Nor spell, nor charm,
    Come our lovely lady nigh;
    So, good night, with lullaby.
FIRST FAIRY. Weaving spiders, come not here;
    Hence, you long-legg'd spinners, hence!
    Beetles black, approach not near;
    Worm nor snail, do no offense.

CHORUS.

    Philomel, with melody, etc.

SECOND FAIRY.   Hence, away! now all is well:
    One aloof stand sentinel.
        [Exeunt FAIRIES. TITANIA sleeps.

Enter OBERON, *and squeezes the flower on*
    TITANIA's *eyelids.*]
OBERON.   What thou seest when thou dost wake,
    Do it for thy true-love take;
    Love and languish for his sake:
    Be it ounce, or cat, or bear,
    Pard, or boar with bristled hair,
    In thy eye that shall appear
    When thou wakest, it is thy dear:
    Wake when some vile thing is near.   *[Exit.*

Enter LYSANDER *and* HERMIA.]
LYSANDER. Fair love, you faint with wandering in the wood;
    And to speak troth, I have forgot our way:

We 'll rest us, Hermia, if you think it good,
And tarry for the comfort of the day.

HERMIA. Be it so, Lysander: find you out a bed;
For I upon this bank will rest my head.

LYSANDER. One turf shall serve as pillow for us both;
One heart, one bed, two bosoms, and one troth.

HERMIA. Nay, good Lysander; for my sake, my dear,
Lie further off yet, do not lie so near.

LYSANDER. O, take the sense, sweet, of my innocence!
Love takes the meaning in love's conference.
I mean, that my heart unto yours is knit,
So that but one heart we can make of it:
Two bosoms interchained with an oath;
So then two bosoms and a single troth.
Then by your side no bed-room me deny;
For lying so, Hermia, I do not lie.

HERMIA. Lysander riddles very prettily:
Now much beshrew my manners and my pride,
If Hermia meant to say Lysander lied.
But, gentle friend, for love and courtesy
Lie further off; in human modesty,
Such separation as may well be said
Becomes a virtuous bachelor and a maid,
So far be distant: and, good night, sweet friend:
Thy love ne'er alter till thy sweet life end!

LYSANDER. Amen, amen, to that fair prayer, say I;
And then end life when I end loyalty!
Here is my bed: sleep give thee all his rest!

HERMIA. With half that wish the wisher's eyes be press'd!
                                         [*They sleep.*

Enter PUCK.]

PUCK.   Through the forest have I gone,
               But Athenian found I none,
               On whose eyes I might approve
               This flower's force in stirring love.
               Night and silence.—Who is here?
               Weeds of Athens he doth wear:
               This is he, my master said,

Despised the Athenian maid;
And here the maiden, sleeping sound,
On the dank and dirty ground.
Pretty soul! she durst not lie
Near this lack-love, this kill-courtesy.
Churl, upon thy eyes I throw
All the power this charm doth owe.
When thou wakest, let love forbid
Sleep his seat on thy eyelid:
So awake when I am gone;
For I must now to Oberon.   [*Exit*.

Enter DEMETRIUS *and* HELENA, *running*.]
HELENA. Stay, though thou kill me, sweet Demetrius.
DEMETRIUS. I charge thee, hence, and do not haunt me thus.
HELENA. O, wilt thou darkling leave me? do not so.
DEMETRIUS. Stay, on thy peril: I alone will go.   [*Exit*.
HELENA. O, I am out of breath in this fond chase!
The more my prayer, the lesser is my grace.
Happy is Hermia, wheresoe'er she lies;
For she hath blessed and attractive eyes.
How came her eyes so bright? Not with salt tears:
If so, my eyes are oftener wash'd than hers.
No, no, I am as ugly as a bear;
For beasts that meet me run away for fear:
Therefore no marvel though Demetrius
Do, as a monster, fly my presence thus.
What wicked and dissembling glass of mine
Made me compare with Hermia's sphery eyne?
But who is here? Lysander! on the ground!
Dead? or asleep? I see no blood, no wound.
Lysander, if you live, good sir, awake.
LYSANDER. [*Awaking*] And run through fire I will for thy
    sweet sake.
Transparent Helena! Nature shews art,
That though thy bosom makes me see thy heart.
Where is Demetrius? O, how fit a word
Is that vile name to perish on my sword!

HELENA. Do not say so, Lysander; say not so.
  What though he love your Hermia? Lord, what though?
  Yet Hermia still loves you: then be content.
LYSANDER. Content with Hermia! No; I do repent
  The tedious minutes I with her have spent.
  Not Hermia but Helena I love:
  Who will not change a raven for a dove?
  The will of man is by his reason sway'd
  And reason says you are the worthier maid.
  Things growing are not ripe until their season:
  So, I being young, till now ripe not to reason;
  And touching now the point of human skill,
  Reason becomes the marshal to my will,
  And leads me to your eyes; where I o'erlook
  Love's stories, written in love's richest book.
HELENA. Wherefore was I to this keen mockery born?
  When at your hands did I deserve this scorn?
  Is 't not enough, is 't not enough, young man,
  That I did never, no, nor never can,
  Deserve a sweet look from Demetrius' eye,
  But you must flout my insufficiency?
  Good troth, you do me wrong, good sooth, you do,
  In such disdainful manner me to woo.
  But fare you well: perforce I must confess
  I thought you lord of more true gentleness.
  O, that a lady, of one man refused,
  Should of another therefore be abused!   [*Exit.*
LYSANDER. She sees not Hermia. Hermia, sleep thou there:
  And never mayst thou come Lysander near!
  For as a surfeit of the sweetest things
  The deepest loathing to the stomach brings,
  Or as the heresies that men do leave
  Are hated most of those they did deceive,
  So thou, my surfeit and my heresy,
  Of all be hated, but the most of me!
  And, all my powers, address your love and might
  To honor Helen and to be her knight!   [*Exit.*

HERMIA. [*Awaking*] Help me, Lysander, help me! do thy best
  To pluck this crawling serpent from my breast!
  Aye me, for pity! what a dream was here!
  Lysander, look how I do quake with fear:
  Methought a serpent eat my heart away,
  And you sat smiling at his cruel prey.
  Lysander! what, removed? Lysander! lord!
  What, out of hearing? gone? no sound, no word?
  Alack, where are you? speak, an if you hear;
  Speak, of all loves! I swoon almost with fear.
  No? then I well perceive you are not nigh:
  Either death or you I 'll find immediately.   [*Exit.*

ACT III

SCENE I — *The wood.* TITANIA *lying asleep.*

Enter QUINCE, SNUG, BOTTOM, FLUTE, SNOUT,
        and STARVELING.]

BOTTOM. Are we all met?

QUINCE. Pat, pat; and here's a marvelous convenient place for
  our rehearsal. This green plot shall be our stage, this haw-
  thorn-brake our tiring-house; and we will do it in action as
  we will do it before the duke.

BOTTOM. Peter Quince,—

QUINCE. What sayest thou, Bully Bottom?

BOTTOM. There are things in this comedy of Pyramus and
  Thisby that will never please. First, Pyramus must draw a
  sword to kill himself; which the ladies cannot abide. How
  answer you that?

SNOUT. By 'r lakin, a parlous fear.

STARVELING. I believe we must leave the killing out, when all
  is done.

BOTTOM. Not a whit: I have a device to make all well. Write
  me a prologue; and let the prologue seem to say, we will
  do no harm with our swords, and that Pyramus is not killed
  indeed; and, for the more better assurance, tell them that I
  Pyramus am not Pyramus, but Bottom the weaver: this will
  put them out of fear.

QUINCE. Well, we will have such a prologue; and it shall be
  written in eight and six.

BOTTOM. No, make it two more; let it be written in eight and
  eight.

SNOUT. Will not the ladies be afeard of the lion?

STARVELING. I fear it, I promise you.

BOTTOM. Masters, you ought to consider with yourselves: to
  bring in,—God shield us!—a lion among ladies, is a most

dreadful thing; for there is not a more fearful wild-foul than your lion living: and we ought to look to 't.

SNOUT. Therefore another prologue must tell he is not a lion.

BOTTOM. Nay, you must name his name, and half his face must be seen through the lion's neck; and he himself must speak through, saying thus, or to the same defect,—'Ladies,'—or, 'Fair ladies,—I would wish you,'—or, 'I would request you,' —or, 'I would entreat you,—not to fear, not to tremble: my life for yours. If you think I come hither as a lion, it were pity of my life: no, I am no such thing; I am a man as other men are'; and there indeed let him name his name, and tell them plainly, he is Snug the joiner.

QUINCE. Well, it shall be so. But there is two hard things; that is, to bring the moonlight into a chamber; for, you know, Pyramus and Thisby meet by moonlight.

SNOUT. Doth the moon shine that night we play our play?

BOTTOM. A calendar, a calendar! look in the almanac; find out moonshine, find out moonshine.

QUINCE. Yes, it doth shine that night.

BOTTOM. Why, then may you leave a casement of the great chamber window, where we play, open, and the moon may shine in at the casement.

QUINCE. Aye; or else one must come in with a bush of thorns and a lantern, and say he comes to disfigure, or to present, the person of moonshine. Then, there is another thing: we must have a wall in the great chamber; for Pyramus and Thisby, says the story, did talk through the chink of a wall.

SNOUT. You can never bring in a wall. What say you, Bottom?

BOTTOM. Some man or other must present wall: and let him have some plaster, or some loam, or some rough-cast about him, to signify wall; and let him hold his fingers thus, and through that cranny shall Pyramus and Thisby whisper.

QUINCE. If that may be, then all is well. Come, sit down, every mother's son, and rehearse your parts. Pyramus, you begin: when you have spoken your speech, enter into that brake: and so every one according to his cue.

Enter PUCK *behind.*]

PUCK. What hempen home-spuns have we swaggering here,
So near the cradle of the fairy queen?
What, a play toward! I 'll be an auditor;
An actor too perhaps, if I see cause.

QUINCE. Speak, Pyramus. Thisby, stand forth.

BOTTOM. Thisby, the flowers of odious savors sweet—

QUINCE. Odors, odors.

BOTTOM.—odors savors sweet:
So hath thy breath, my dearest Thisby dear.
But hark, a voice! stay thou but here awhile,
And by and by I will to thee appear.   [*Exit.*

PUCK. A stranger Pyramus than e'er play'd here.   [*Exit.*

FLUTE. Must I speak now?

QUINCE. Aye, marry must you; for you must understand he
goes but to see a noise that he heard, and is to come again.

FLUTE. Most radiant Pyramus, most lily-white of hue,
Of color like the red rose on triumphant brier,
Most brisky juvenal, and eke most lovely Jew,
As true as truest horse, that yet would never tire,
I 'll meet thee, Pyramus, at Ninny's tomb.

QUINCE. 'Ninus' tomb,' man: why, you must not speak that yet;
that you answer to Pyramus: you speak all your part at once,
cues and all. Pyramus enter: your cue is past; it is, 'never
tire.'

FLUTE. O,—As true as truest horse, that yet would never tire.

Re-enter PUCK, *and* BOTTOM *with an ass's head.*]

BOTTOM. If I were, fair Thisby, I were only thine.

QUINCE. O monstrous! O strange! we are haunted.
Pray, masters! fly, masters! Help!

[*Exeunt* QUINCE, SNUG, FLUTE, SNOUT,
and STARVELING.

PUCK. I 'll follow you, I 'll lead you about a round,
Through bog, through bush, through brake, through brier:
Sometime a horse I 'll be, sometime a hound,
A hog, a headless bear, sometime a fire;
And neigh, and bark, and grunt, and roar, and burn,
Like horse, hound, hog, bear, fire, at every turn.   [*Exit.*

BOTTOM. Why do they run away? this is a knavery of them to make me afeard.

Re-enter SNOUT.]

SNOUT. O Bottom, thou art changed! what do I see on thee?

BOTTOM. What do you see? you see an ass-head of your own, do you? [*Exit* SNOUT.

Re-enter QUINCE.]

QUINCE. Bless thee, Bottom! bless thee! thou art translated.
[*Exit.*

BOTTOM. I see their knavery: this is to make an ass of me; to fright me, if they could. But I will not stir from this place, do what they can: I will walk up and down here, and I will sing, that they shall hear I am not afraid. [*Sings.*

> The ousel cock so black of hue,
>   With orange-tawny bill,
> The throstle with his note so true,
>   The wren with little quill.

TITANIA. [*Awaking*] What angel wakes me from my flowery bed?

BOTTOM. [*Sings*]

> The finch, the sparrow, and the lark,
>   The plain-song cuckoo gray,
> Whose note full many a man doth mark,
>   And dares not answer nay;—

for, indeed, who would set his wit to so foolish a bird? who would give a bird the lie, though he cry 'cuckoo' never so?

TITANIA. I pray thee, gentle mortal, sing again:
Mine ear is much enamour'd of thy note;
So is mine eye enthralled to thy shape;
And thy fair virtue's force perforce doth move me
On the first view to say, to swear, I love thee.

BOTTOM. Methinks, mistress, you should have little reason for that: and yet, to say the truth, reason and love keep little company together now-a-days; the more the pity, that some honest neighbors will not make them friends. Nay, I can gleek upon occasion.

TITANIA. Thou art as wise as thou art beautiful.

BOTTOM. Not so, neither: but if I had wit enough to get out
  of this wood, I have enough to serve mine own turn.

TITANIA. Out of this wood do not desire to go:
  Thou shalt remain here, whether thou wilt or no.
  I am a spirit of no common rate:
  The summer still doth tend upon my state;
  And I do love thee: therefore, go with me;
  I 'll give thee fairies to attend on thee;
  And they shall fetch thee jewels from the deep,
  And sing, while thou on pressed flowers dost sleep:
  And I will purge thy mortal grossness so,
  That thou shalt like an airy spirit go.
  Peaseblossom! Cobweb! Moth! and Mustardseed!

Enter PEASEBLOSSOM, COBWEB, MOTH, *and* MUSTARDSEED.]

FIRST FAIRY. Ready.

SECOND FAIRY.   And I.

THIRD FAIRY.   And I.

FOURTH FAIRY.   And I.

ALL.   Where shall we go?

TITANIA. Be kind and courteous to this gentleman;
  Hop in his walks, and gambol in his eyes;
  Feed him with apricocks and dewberries,
  With purple grapes, green figs, and mulberries;
  The honey-bags steal from the humble-bees,
  And for night-tapers crop their waxen thighs,
  And light them at the fiery glow-worm's eyes,
  To have my love to bed and to arise;
  And pluck the wings from painted butterflies,
  To fan the moonbeams from his sleeping eyes:
  Nod to him, elves, and do him courtesies.

FIRST FAIRY. Hail, mortal!

SECOND FAIRY. Hail!

THIRD FAIRY. Hail!

FOURTH FAIRY. Hail!

BOTTOM. I cry your worships mercy, heartily: I beseech your
  worship's name.

COBWEB. Cobweb.

BOTTOM. I shall desire you of more acquaintance, good Master
   Cobweb: if I cut my finger, I shall make bold with you.
   Your name, honest gentleman?

PEASEBLOSSOM. Peaseblossom.

BOTTOM. I pray you, commend me to Mistress Squash, your
   mother, and to Master Peascod, your father. Good Master
   Peaseblossom, I shall desire you of more acquaintance too.
   Your name, I beseech you, Sir?

MUSTARDSEED. Mustardseed.

BOTTOM. Good Master Mustardseed, I know your patience
   well: that same cowardly, giant-like ox-beef hath devoured
   many a gentleman of your house: I promise you your kindred hath made my eyes water ere now. I desire your more
   acquaintance, good Master Mustardseed.

TITANIA. Come, wait upon him; lead him to my bower.
      The moon methinks looks with a watery eye;
   And when she weeps, weeps every little flower,
      Lamenting some enforced chastity.
   Tie up my love's tongue, bring him silently.   [*Exeunt.*

SCENE II — *Another part of the wood.*

Enter OBERON.]

OBERON. I wonder if Titania be awaked;
   Then, what it was that next came in her eye,
   Which she must dote on in extremity.

Enter PUCK.]

   Here comes my messenger.
                                    How now, mad spirit!
   What night-rule now about this haunted grove?

PUCK. My mistress with a monster is in love.
   Near to her close and consecrated bower,
   While she was in her dull and sleeping hour,
   A crew of patches, rude mechanicals,
   That work for bread upon Athenian stalls,
   Were met together to rehearse a play,
   Intended for great Theseus' nuptial-day.
   The shallowest thick-skin of that barren sort,

Who Pyramus presented, in their sport
Forsook his scene, and enter'd in a brake:
When I did him at this advantage take,
An ass's nowl I fixed on his head:
Anon his Thisbe must be answered,
And forth my mimic comes. When they him spy,
As wild geese that the creeping fowler eye,
Or russet-pated choughs, many in sort,
Rising and cawing at the gun's report,
Sever themselves and madly sweep the sky,
So, at his sight, away his fellows fly;
And, at our stamp, here o'er and o'er one falls;
He murder cries, and help from Athens calls.
Their sense thus weak, lost with their fears thus strong,
Made senseless things begin to do them wrong;
For briers and thorns at their apparel snatch;
Some sleeves, some hats, from yielders all things catch.
I led them on in this distracted fear,
And left sweet Pyramus translated there:
When in that moment, so it came to pass,
Titania waked, and straightway loved an ass.

OBERON. This falls out better than I could devise.
But hast thou yet latch'd the Athenian's eyes
With a love-juice, as I did bid thee do?

PUCK. I took him sleeping,—that is finish'd too,—
And the Athenian woman by his side;
That, when he waked, of force she must be eyed.

Enter HERMIA *and* DEMETRIUS.]

OBERON. Stand close: this is the same Athenian.

PUCK. This is the woman, but not this the man.

DEMETRIUS. O, why rebuke you him that loves you so?
Lay breath so bitter on your bitter foe.

HERMIA. Now I but chide; but I should use thee worse,
For thou, I fear, hast given me cause to curse.
If thou hast slain Lysander in his sleep,
Being o'er shoes in blood, plunge in the deep,
And kill me too.
The sun was not so true unto the day

As he to me: would he have stolen away
From sleeping Hermia? I'll believe as soon
This whole earth may be bored, and that the moon
May through the center creep, and so displease
Her brother's noontide with the Antipodes.
It cannot be but thou hast murder'd him;
So should a murderer look, so dead, so grim.

DEMETRIUS. So should the murder'd look; and so should I,
Pierced through the heart with your stern cruelty:
Yet you, the murderer, look as bright, as clear,
As yonder Venus in her glimmering sphere.

HERMIA. What's this to my Lysander? where is he?
Ah, good Demetrius, wilt thou give him me?

DEMETRIUS. I had rather give his carcass to my hounds.

HERMIA. Out, dog! out, cur! thou drivest me past the bounds
Of maiden's patience. Hast thou slain him, then?
Henceforth be never number'd among men!
O, once tell true, tell true, even for my sake!
Durst thou have look'd upon him being awake,
And hast thou kill'd him sleeping? O brave touch!
Could not a worm, an adder, do so much?
An adder did it; for with doubler tongue
Than thine, thou serpent, never adder stung.

DEMETRIUS. You spend your passion on a misprised mood:
I am not guilty of Lysander's blood;
Nor is he dead, for aught that I can tell.

HERMIA. I pray thee, tell me then that he is well.

DEMETRIUS. An if I could, what should I get therefore?

HERMIA. A privilege, never to see me more.
And from thy hated presence part I so:
See me no more, whether he be dead or no.   [Exit.

DEMETRIUS. There is no following her in this fierce vein:
Here therefore for a while I will remain.
So sorrow's heaviness doth heavier grow
For debt that bankrupt sleep doth sorrow owe;
Which now in some slight measure it will pay,
If for his tender here I make some stay.
                                        [Lies down and sleeps.

OBERON. What hast thou done? thou hast mistaken quite,
    And laid the love-juice on some true-love's sight:
    Of thy misprision must perforce ensue
    Some true love turn'd, and not a false turn'd true.

PUCK. Then fate o'er-rules, that, one man holding troth,
    A million fail, confounding oath on oath.

OBERON. About the wood go swifter than the wind,
    And Helena of Athens look thou find:
    All fancy-sick she is and pale of cheer,
    With sighs of love, that costs the fresh blood dear:
    By some illusion see thou bring her here:
    I 'll charm his eyes against she do appear.

PUCK. I go, I go; look how I go,
    Swifter than arrow from the Tartar's bow.   [*Exit.*

OBERON.   Flower of this purple dye,
          Hit with Cupid's archery,
          Sink in apple of his eye.
          When his love he doth espy,
          Let her shine as gloriously
          As the Venus of the sky.
          When thou wakest, if she be by,
          Beg of her for remedy.

Re-enter PUCK.]

PUCK.   Captain of our fairy band,
          Helena is here at hand;
          And the youth, mistook by me,
          Pleading for a lover's fee.
          Shall we their fond pageant see?
          Lord, what fools these mortals be!

OBERON.   Stand aside: the noise they make
          Will cause Demetrius to awake.

PUCK.   Then will two at once woo one;
          That must needs be sport alone;
          And those things do best please me
          That befall preposterously.

Enter LYSANDER *and* HELENA.]

LYSANDER. Why should you think that I should woo in scorn?

    Scorn and derision never come in tears:
Look, when I vow, I weep; and vows so born,
    In their nativity all truth appears.
How can these things in me seem scorn to you,
Bearing the badge of faith, to prove them true?

HELENA. You do advance your cunning more and more.
    When truth kills truth, O devilish-holy fray!
These vows are Hermia's: will you give her o'er?
    Weigh oath with oath, and you will nothing weigh:
Your vows to her and me, put in two scales,
Will even weigh; and both as light as tales.

LYSANDER. I had no judgment when to her I swore.

HELENA. Nor none, in my mind, now you give her o'er.

LYSANDER. Demetrius loves her, and he loves not you.

DEMETRIUS. [Awaking] O Helen, goddess, nymph, perfect,
divine!
To what, my love, shall I compare thine eyne?
Crystal is muddy. O, how ripe in show
Thy lips, those kissing cherries, tempting grow!
That pure congealed white, high Taurus' snow,
Fann'd with the eastern wind, turns to a crow
When thou hold'st up thy hand: O, let me kiss
This princess of pure white, this seal of bliss!

HELENA. O spite! O hell! I see you all are bent
To set against me for your merriment:
If you were civil and knew courtesy,
You would not do me thus much injury.
Can you not hate me, as I know you do,
But you must join in souls to mock me too?
If you were men, as men you are in show,
You would not use a gentle lady so;
To vow, and swear, and superpraise my parts,
When I am sure you hate me with your hearts.
You both are rivals, and love Hermia;
And now both rivals, to mock Helena:
A trim exploit, a manly enterprise,
To conjure tears up in a poor maid's eyes
With your derision! none of noble sort

Would so offend a virgin, and extort
A poor soul's patience, all to make you sport.

LYSANDER. You are unkind, Demetrius; be not so;
For you love Hermia; this you know I know:
And here, with all good will, with all my heart,
In Hermia's love I yield you up my part;
And yours of Helena to me bequeath,
Whom I do love, and will do till my death.

HELENA. Never did mockers waste more idle breath.

DEMETRIUS. Lysander, keep thy Hermia; I will none:
If e'er I loved her, all that love is gone.
My heart to her but as guest-wise sojourn'd,
And now to Helen is it home return'd,
There to remain.

LYSANDER. Helen, it is not so.

DEMETRIUS. Disparage not the faith thou dost not know,
Lest, to thy peril, thou aby it dear.
Look, where thy love comes; yonder is thy dear.

Re-enter HERMIA.]

HERMIA. Dark night, that from the eye his function takes,
The ear more quick of apprehension makes;
Wherein it doth impair the seeing sense,
It pays the hearing double recompense.
Thou are not by mine eye, Lysander, found;
Mine ear, I thank it, brought me to thy sound.
But why unkindly didst thou leave me so?

LYSANDER. Why should he stay, whom love doth press to go?

HERMIA. What love could press Lysander from my side?

LYSANDER. Lysander's love, that would not let him bide,
Fair Helena, who more engilds the night
Than all yon fiery oes and eyes of light.
Why seek'st thou me? could not this make thee know,
The hate I bare thee made me leave thee so?

HERMIA. You speak not as you think: it cannot be.

HELENA. Lo, she is one of this confederacy!
Now I perceive they have conjoin'd all three
To fashion this false sport, in spite of me.
Injurious Hermia! most ungrateful maid!

Have you conspired, have you with these contrived
To bait me with this foul derision?
Is all the counsel that we two have shared,
The sisters' vows, the hours that we have spent,
When we have chid the hasty-footed time
For parting us,—O, is all forgot?
All school-days' friendship, childhood innocence?
We, Hermia, like two artificial gods,
Have with our needles created both one flower,
Both on one sampler, sitting on one cushion,
Both warbling of one song, both in one key;
As if our hands, our sides, voices, and minds,
Had been incorporate. So we grew together,
Like to a double cherry, seeming parted,
But yet an union in partition;
Two lovely berries moulded on one stem;
So, with two seeming bodies, but one heart;
Two of the first, like coats in heraldry,
Due but to one, and crowned with one crest.
And will you rent our ancient love asunder,
To join with men in scorning your poor friend?
It is not friendly, 'tis not maidenly:
Our sex, as well as I, may chide you for it,
Though I alone do feel the injury.

HERMIA. I am amazed at your passionate words.
I scorn you not: it seems that you scorn me.

HELENA. Have you not set Lysander, as in scorn,
To follow me and praise my eyes and face?
And made your other love, Demetrius,
Who even but now did spurn me with his foot,
To call me goddess, nymph, divine and rare,
Precious, celestial? Wherefore speaks he this
To her he hates? and wherefore doth Lysander
Deny your love, so rich within his soul,
And tender me, forsooth, affection,
But by your setting on, by your consent?
What though I be not so in grace as you,
So hung upon with love, so fortunate,

But miserable most, to love unloved?
This you should pity rather than despise.

HERMIA. I understand not what you mean by this.

HELENA. Aye, do, persever, counterfeit sad looks,
Make mouths upon me when I turn my back;
Wink each at other; hold the sweet jest up:
This sport, well carried, shall be chronicled.
If you have any pity, grace, or manners,
You would not make me such an argument.
But fare ye well: 'tis partly my own fault;
Which death or absence soon shall remedy.

LYSANDER. Stay, gentle Helena; hear my excuse:
My love, my life, my soul, fair Helena!

HELENA. O excellent!

HERMIA.   Sweet, do not scorn her so.

DEMETRIUS. If she cannot entreat, I can compel.

LYSANDER. Thou canst compel no more than she entreat:
Thy threats have no more strength than her weak prayers.
Helen, I love thee; by my life, I do:
I swear by that which I will lose for thee,
To prove him false that says I love thee not.

DEMETRIUS. I say I love thee more than he can do.

LYSANDER. If thou say so, withdraw, and prove it too.

DEMETRIUS. Quick, come!

HERMIA.   Lysander, whereto tends all this?

LYSANDER. Away, you Ethiope!

DEMETRIUS.   No, no, sir; still
Seem to break loose; take on as you would follow,
But yet come not: you are a tame man, go!

LYSANDER. Hang off, thou cat, thou burr! vile thing, let loose,
Or I will shake thee from me like a serpent!

HERMIA. Why are you grown so rude? what change is this?
Sweet love,—

LYSANDER.   Thy love! out, tawny Tartar, out!
Out, loathed medicine! hated potion, hence!

HERMIA. Do you not jest?

HELENA.   Yes, sooth; and so do you.

LYSANDER. Demetrius, I will keep my word with thee.

DEMETRIUS. I would I had your bond, for I perceive
  A weak bond holds you: I 'll not trust your word.

LYSANDER. What, should I hurt her, strike her, kill her dead?
  Although I hate her, I 'll not harm her so.

HERMIA. What, can you do me greater harm than hate?
  Hate me! wherefore? O me! what news, my love!
  Am not I Hermia? are not you Lysander?
  I am as fair now as I was erewhile.
  Since night you loved me; yet since night you left me:
  Why, then you left me,—O, the gods forbid!—
  In earnest, shall I say?

LYSANDER.   Aye, by my life;
  And never did desire to see thee more.
  Therefore be out of hope, of question, of doubt;
  Be certain, nothing truer; 'tis no jest
  That I do hate thee, and love Helena.

HERMIA. O me! you juggler! you canker-blossom!
  You thief of love! what, have you come by night
  And stolen my love's heart from him?

HELENA.   Fine, i' faith!
  Have you no modesty, no maiden shame,
  No touch of bashfulness? What, will you tear
  Impatient answers from my gentle tongue?
  Fie, fie! you counterfeit, you puppet, you!

HERMIA. Puppet? why so? aye, that way goes the game.
  Now I perceive that she hath made compare
  Between our statures; she hath urged her height;
  And with her personage, her tall personage,
  Her height, forsooth, she hath prevail'd with him.
  And are you grown so high in his esteem,
  Because I am so dwarfish and so low?
  How low am I, thou painted maypole? speak;
  How low am I? I am not yet so low
  But that my nails can reach unto thine eyes.

HELENA. I pray you, though you mock me, gentlemen,
  Let her not hurt me: I was never curst;
  I have no gift at all in shrewishness;
  I am a right maid for my cowardice:

    Let her not strike me. You perhaps may think,
    Because she is something lower than myself,
    That I can match her.

HERMIA.   Lower! hark, again.

HELENA. Good Hermia, do not be so bitter with me,
    I evermore did love you, Hermia,
    Did ever keep your counsels, never wrong'd you;
    Save that, in love unto Demetrius,
    I told him of your stealth unto this wood.
    He follow'd you; for love I follow'd him;
    But he hath chid me hence, and threaten'd me
    To strike me, spurn me, nay, to kill me too:
    And now, so you will let me quiet go,
    To Athens will I bear my folly back,
    And follow you no further: let me go:
    You see how simple and how fond I am.

HERMIA. Why, get you gone: who is 't that hinders you?

HELENA. A foolish heart, that I leave here behind.

HERMIA. What, with Lysander?

HELENA.   With Demetrius.

LYSANDER. Be not afraid; she shall not harm thee, Helena.

DEMETRIUS. No, sir, she shall not, though you take her part.

HELENA. O, when she 's angry, she is keen and shrewd!
    She was a vixen when she went to school;
    And though she be but little, she is fierce.

HERMIA. Little again! nothing but low and little!
    Why will you suffer her to flout me thus?
    Let me come to her.

LYSANDER.   Get you gone, you dwarf;
    You minimus, of hindering knot-grass made;
    You bead, you acorn.

DEMETRIUS.   You are too officious
    In her behalf that scorns your services.
    Let her alone: speak not of Helena;
    Take not her part; for, if thou dost intend
    Never so little show of love to her,
    Thou shalt aby it.

LYSANDER.   Now she holds me not;

Now follow, if thou darest, to try whose right,
Of thine or mine, is most in Helena.

DEMETRIUS. Follow! nay, I 'll go with thee, cheek by jole.

[*Exeunt* LYSANDER *and* DEMETRIUS.

HERMIA. You, mistress, all this coil is 'long of you;
Nay, go not back.

HELENA.   I will not trust you, I
No longer stay in your curst company.
Your hands than mine are quicker for a fray.
My legs are longer though, to run away.   [*Exit.*

HERMIA. I am amazed, and know not what to say.   [*Exit.*

OBERON. This is thy negligence: still thou mistakest,
Or else committ'st thy knaveries willfully.

PUCK. Believe me, king of shadows, I mistook.
Did not you tell me I should know the man
By the Athenian garments he had on?
And so far blameless proves my enterprise,
That I have 'nointed an Athenian's eyes;
And so far am I glad it so did sort,
As this their jangling I esteem a sport.

OBERON. Thou see'st these lovers seek a place to fight:
Hie therefore, Robin, overcast the night;
The starry welkin cover thou anon
With drooping fog, as black as Acheron;
And lead these testy rivals so astray,
As one come not within another's way.
Like to Lysander sometime frame thy tongue,
Then stir Demetrius up with bitter wrong;
And sometime rail thou like Demetrius;
And from each other look thou lead them thus,
Till o'er their brows death-counterfeiting sleep
With leaden legs and batty wings doth creep:
Then crush this herb into Lysander's eye;
Whose liquor hath this virtuous property,
To take from thence all error with his might,
And make his eyeballs roll with wonted sight.
When they next wake, all this derision

Shall seem a dream and fruitless vision;
And back to Athens shall the lovers wend,
With league whose date till death shall never end.
Whiles I in this affair do thee employ,
I 'll to my queen and beg her Indian boy;
And then I will her charmed eye release
From monster's view, and all things shall be peace.

PUCK. My fairy lord, this must be done with haste,
For night's swift dragons cut the clouds full fast,
And yonder shines Aurora's harbinger;
At whose approach, ghosts, wandering here and there,
Troop home to churchyards: damned spirits all,
That in crossways and floods have burial,
Already to their wormy beds are gone;
For fear lest day should look their shames upon,
They willfully themselves exile from light,
And must for aye consort with black-brow'd night.

OBERON. But we are spirits of another sort:
I with the morning's love have oft made sport;
And, like a forester, the groves may tread,
Even till the eastern gate, all fiery-red,
Opening on Neptune with fair blessed beams,
Turns into yellow gold his salt green streams.
But, notwithstanding, haste; make no delay:
We may effect this business yet ere day.   [*Exit.*

PUCK.   Up and down, up and down,
          I will lead them up and down:
          I am fear'd in field and town:
          Goblin, lead them up and down.
Here comes one.

Re-enter LYSANDER.]

LYSANDER. Where art thou, proud Demetrius? speak thou now.
PUCK. Here, villain; drawn and ready. Where art thou?
LYSANDER. I will be with thee straight.
PUCK.   Follow me, then,
To plainer ground. [*Exit* LYSANDER, *as following the voice.*
Re-enter DEMETRIUS.]

DEMETRIUS.   Lysander! speak again:
  Thou runaway, thou coward, art thou fled?
  Speak! In some bush? Where dost thou hide thy head?

PUCK. Thou coward, art thou bragging to the stars,
  Telling the bushes that thou look'st for wars,
  And wilt not come? Come, recreant; come, thou child;
  I 'll whip thee with a rod: he is defiled
  That draws a sword on thee.

DEMETRIUS.   Yea, art thou there?

PUCK. Follow my voice: we 'll try no manhood here.   [Exeunt.
Re-enter LYSANDER.]

LYSANDER. He goes before me and still dares me on:
  When I come where he calls, then he is gone.
  The villain is much lighter-heel'd than I:
  I follow'd fast, but faster he did fly;
  That fallen am I in dark uneven way,
  And here will rest me. [Lies down.] Come, thou gentle day!
  For if but once thou show me thy gray light,
  I 'll find Demetrius, and revenge this spite.   [Sleeps.
Re-enter PUCK and DEMETRIUS.]

PUCK. Ho, ho, ho! Coward, why comest thou not?

DEMETRIUS. Abide me, if thou darest; for well I wot
  Thou runn'st before me, shifting every place,
  And darest not stand, nor look me in the face.
  Where art thou now?

PUCK.   Come hither: I am here.

DEMETRIUS. Nay, then, thou mock'st me. Thou shalt buy this
    dear,
  If ever I thy face by daylight see:
  Now, go thy way. Faintness constraineth me
  To measure out my length on this cold bed.
  By day's approach look to be visited. [Lies down and sleeps.
Re-enter HELENA.]

HELENA. O weary night, O long and tedious night,
  Abate thy hours! Shine comforts from the east,
  That I may back to Athens by daylight,
    From these that my poor company detest:

And sleep, that sometimes shuts up sorrow's eye,
Steal me awhile from mine own company.

                [Lies down and sleeps.

PUCK.   Yet but three? Come one more;
           Two of both kinds makes up four.
           Here she comes, curst and sad:
           Cupid is a knavish lad,
           Thus to make poor females mad.

Re-enter HERMIA.]

HERMIA. Never so weary, never so in woe;
    Bedabbled with the dew, and torn with briers;
    I can no further crawl, no further go;
       My legs can keep no pace with my desires.
    Here will I rest me till the break of day.
    Heavens shield Lysander, if they mean a fray!

                [Lies down and sleeps.

PUCK.   On the ground
             Sleep sound:
             I 'll apply
             To your eye,
    Gentle lover, remedy.

        [Squeezing the juice on LYSANDER'S *eye.*

             When thou wakest,
             Thou takest
             True delight
             In the sight
           Of thy former lady's eye:
          And the country proverb known,
          That every man should take his own,
          In your waking shall be shown:
             Jack shall have Jill;
             Nought shall go ill;
The man shall have his mare again, and all shall be well.

                       [Exit.

ACT IV

Scene I — *The same.*

Lysander, Demetrius, Helena, *and* Hermia, *lying asleep.*

Enter titania *and* bottom; peaseblossom, cobweb,
    moth, mustardseed, *and other* fairies *attend-
    ing;* oberon *behind unseen.*

titania. Come, sit thee down upon this flowery bed,
    While I thy amiable cheeks do coy,
And stick musk-roses in thy sleek smooth head,
    And kiss thy fair large ears, my gentle joy.

bottom. Where's Peaseblossom?

peaseblossom. Ready.

bottom. Scratch my head, Peaseblossom. Where's Mounsieur
    Cobweb?

cobweb. Ready.

bottom. Mounsieur Cobweb, good mounsieur, get you your
    weapons in your hand, and kill me a red-hipped humble-bee
    on the top of a thistle; and, good mounsieur, bring me the
    honey-bag. Do not fret yourself too much in the action,
    mounsieur; and, good mounsieur, have a care the honey-
    bag break not; I would be loth to have you overflown with
    a honey-bag, signior. Where's Mounsieur Mustardseed?

mustardseed. Ready.

bottom. Give me your neaf, Mounsieur Mustardseed.
    Pray you, leave your courtesy, good mounsieur.

mustardseed. What's your will?

bottom. Nothing, good mounsieur, but to help Cavalery Cob-
    web to scratch. I must to the barber's, mounsieur; for me-
    thinks I am marvelous hairy about the face; and I am such
    a tender ass, if my hair do but tickle me, I must scratch.

titania. What, wilt thou hear some music, my sweet love?

BOTTOM. I have a reasonable good ear in music. Let's have the
tongs and the bones.

TITANIA. Or say, sweet love, what thou desirest to eat.

BOTTOM. Truly, a peck of provender: I could munch your good
dry oats. Methinks I have a great desire to a bottle of hay;
good hay, sweet hay, hath no fellow.

TITANIA. I have a venturous fairy that shall seek the squirrel's
hoard, and fetch thee new nuts.

BOTTOM. I had rather have a handful or two of dried peas.
But, I pray you, let none of your people stir me: I have an
exposition of sleep come upon me.

TITANIA. Sleep thou, and I will wind thee in my arms.
Fairies, be gone, and be all ways away.   [*Exeunt* FAIRIES.
So doth the woodbine the sweet honeysuckle
Gently entwist; the female ivy so.
Enrings the barky fingers of the elm.
Oh, how I love thee! how I dote on thee!   [*They sleep.*
Enter PUCK.]

OBERON. [*Advancing*] Welcome, good Robin. See'st thou this
sweet sight?
Her dotage now I do begin to pity:
For, meeting her of late behind the wood,
Seeking sweet favors for this hateful fool,
I did upbraid her, and fall out with her;
For she his hairy temples then had rounded
With coronet of fresh and fragrant flowers;
And that same dew, which sometime on the buds
Was wont to swell, like round and orient pearls,
Stood now within the pretty flowerets' eyes,
Like tears, that did their own disgrace bewail.
When I had at my pleasure taunted her,
And she in mild terms begg'd my patience,
I then did ask of her her changeling child;
Which straight she gave me, and her fairy sent
To bear him to my bower in fairy land.
And now I have the boy, I will undo
This hateful imperfection of her eyes:

And, gentle Puck, take this transformed scalp
From off the head of this Athenian swain;
That, he awaking when the other do,
May all to Athens back again repair,
And think no more of this night's accidents,
But as the fierce vexation of a dream.
But first I will release the fairy queen.
    Be as thou wast wont to be;
    See as thou wast wont to see:
    Dian's bud o'er Cupid's flower
    Hath such force and blessed power.
Now, my Titania; wake you, my sweet queen.

TITANIA. My Oberon! what visions have I seen!
Methought I was enamor'd of an ass.

OBERON. There lies your love.

TITANIA.   How came these things to pass?
O, how mine eyes do loathe his visage now!

OBERON. Silence awhile. Robin, take off this head.
Titania, music call; and strike more dead
Than common sleep of all these five the sense.

TITANIA. Music, ho! music, such as charmeth sleep!
                         [Music, still.

PUCK. Now, when thou wakest, with thine own fool's eyes
   peep.

OBERON. Sound, music! Come, my queen take hands with me,
And rock the ground whereon these sleepers be.
Now thou and I are new in amity,
And will to-morrow midnight solemnly
Dance in Duke Theseus' house triumphantly,
And bless it to all fair prosperity:
There shall the pairs of faithful lovers be
Wedded, with Theseus, all in jollity.

PUCK.   Fairy king, attend, and mark:
      I do hear the morning lark.

OBERON.   Then, my queen, in silence sad,
      Trip we after night's shade:
      We the globe can compass soon,
      Swifter than the wandering moon.

TITANIA.   Come, my lord; and in our flight,
             Tell me how it came this night,
             That I sleeping here was found
             With these mortals on the ground.   [*Exeunt.*
                                        [*Horns winded within.*

Enter THESEUS, HIPPOLYTA, EGEUS, *and train.*]

THESEUS. Go, one of you, find out the forester;
  For now our observation is perform'd;
  And since we have the vaward of the day,
  My love shall hear the music of my hounds.
  Uncouple in the western valley; let them go:
  Dispatch, I say, and find the forester.   [*Exit an* ATTENDANT.
  We will, fair queen, up to the mountain's top,
  And mark the musical confusion
  Of hounds and echo in conjunction.

HIPPOLYTA. I was with Hercules and Cadmus once,
  When in a wood of Crete they bay'd the bear
  With hounds of Sparta: never did I hear
  Such gallant chiding; for, besides the groves,
  The skies, the fountains, every region near
  Seem'd all one mutual cry: I never heard
  So musical a discord, such sweet thunder.

THESEUS. My hounds are bred out of the Spartan kind,
  So flew'd, so sanded; and their heads are hung
  With ears that sweep away the morning dew;
  Crook-knee'd, and dew-lapp'd like Thessalian bulls;
  Slow in pursuit, but match'd in mouth like bells,
  Each under each. A cry more tuneable
  Was never holla'd to, nor cheer'd with horn,
  In Crete, in Sparta, nor in Thessaly:
  Judge when you hear. But, soft! what nymphs are these?

EGEUS. My lord, this is my daughter here asleep;
  And this, Lysander; this Demetrius is;
  This Helena, old Nedar's Helena:
  I wonder of their being here together.

THESEUS. No doubt they rose up early to observe
  The rite of May; and, hearing our intent,
  Came here in grace of our solemnity.

But speak, Egeus; is not this the day
That Hermia should give answer of her choice?

EGEUS. It is, my lord.

THESEUS. Go, bid the huntsmen awake them with their horns.
[*Horns and shout within.* LYSANDER, DEMETRIUS, HELENA,
and HERMIA, *wake and start up.*

Good morrow, friends. Saint Valentine is past:
Begin these wood-birds but to couple now?

LYSANDER. Pardon, my lord.

THESEUS.   I pray you all, stand up.
I know you two are rival enemies:
How comes this gentle concord in the world,
That hatred is so far from jealousy,
To sleep by hate, and fear no enmity?

LYSANDER. My lord, I shall reply amazedly,
Half sleep, half waking: but as yet, I swear,
I cannot truly say how I came here;
But, as I think,—for truly would I speak,
And now I do bethink me, so it is,—
I came with Hermia hither: our intent
Was to be gone from Athens, where we might,
Without the peril of the Athenian law.

EGEUS. Enough, enough, my lord; you have enough:
I beg the law, the law, upon his head.
They would have stolen away; they would, Demetrius,
Thereby to have defeated you and me,
You of your wife and me of my consent,
Of my consent that she should be your wife.

DEMETRIUS. My lord, fair Helen told me of their stealth,
Of this their purpose hither to this wood;
And I in fury hither follow'd them,
Fair Helena in fancy following me.
But, my good lord, I wot not by what power,—
But by some power it is,—my love to Hermia,
Melted as the snow, seems to me now
As the remembrance of an idle gaud,
Which in my childhood I did dote upon;

And all the faith, the virtue of my heart,
The object and the pleasure of mine eye,
Is only Helena. To her, my lord,
Was I betroth'd ere I saw Hermia:
But, like in sickness, did I loathe this food;
But, as in health, come to my natural taste,
Now I do wish it, love it, long for it,
And will for evermore be true to it.

THESEUS. Fair lovers, you are fortunately met:
Of this discourse we more will hear anon.
Egeus, I will overbear your will;
For in the temple, by and by, with us
These couples shall eternally be knit:
And, for the morning now is something worn,
Our purposed hunting shall be set aside.
Away with us to Athens! three and three,
We 'll hold a feast in great solemnity.
Come, Hippolyta. [*Exeunt* THESEUS, HIPPOLYTA, *and train.*

DEMETRIUS. These things seem small and undistinguishable,
Like far-off mountains turned into clouds.

HERMIA. Methinks I see these things with parted eye,
When every thing seems double.

HELENA.　　　　　　　　　　　　So methinks:
And I have found Demetrius like a jewel,
Mine own, and not mine own.

DEMETRIUS.　　　　　　　　　　　Are you sure
That we are awake? It seems to me
That yet we sleep, we dream. Do not you think
The Duke was here, and bid us follow him?

HERMIA. Yea; and my father.

HELENA.　　　　　　　　　　And Hippolyta.

LYSANDER. And he did bid us follow to the temple.

DEMETRIUS. Why, then, we are awake: let 's follow him;
And by the way let us recount our dreams.　　　[*Exeunt.*

BOTTOM. [*Awaking*] When my cue comes, call me, and I will
answer: my next is, 'Most fair Pyramus.' Higho-ho! Peter
Quince! Flute, the bellows-mender! Snout, the tinker!
Starveling! God's my life, stolen hence, and left me asleep!

I have had a most rare vision. I have had a dream, past the wit of a man to say what dream it was: man is but an ass, if he go about to expound this dream. Methought I was—there is no man can tell what. Methought I was,—and me-thought I had,—but man is but a patched fool, if he will offer to say what methought I had. The eye of man hath not heard, the ear of man hath not seen, man's hand is not able to taste, his tongue to conceive, nor his heart to report, what my dream was. I will get Peter Quince to write a bal-lad of this dream: it shall be called Bottom's Dream, be-cause it hath no bottom; and I will sing it in the latter end of a play, before the Duke: peradventure, to make it the more gracious, I shall sing it at her death.　　　　　*[Exit.*

SCENE II — *Athens.* QUINCE'S *house.*

Enter QUINCE, FLUTE, SNOUT, *and* STARVELING.]

QUINCE. Have you sent to Bottom's house? is he come home yet?

STARVELING. He cannot be heard of. Out of doubt he is trans-ported.

FLUTE. If he come not, then the play is marred: it goes not forward, doth it?

QUINCE. It is not possible: you have not a man in all Athens able to discharge Pyramus but he.

FLUTE. No, he hath simply the best wit of any handicraft man in Athens.

QUINCE. Yea, and the best person too; and he is a very para-mour for a sweet voice.

FLUTE. You must say 'paragon': a paramour is, God bless us, a thing of naught.

Enter SNUG.]

SNUG. Masters, the Duke is coming from the temple, and there is two or three lords and ladies more married: if our sport had gone forward, we had all been made men.

FLUTE. O sweet bully Bottom! Thus hath he lost sixpence a day during his life; he could not have 'scaped sixpence a day: an the Duke had not given him sixpence a day for

playing Pyramus, I 'll be hanged; he would have deserved
it: sixpence a day in Pyramus, or nothing.

Enter BOTTOM.]

BOTTOM. Where are these lads? where are these hearts?

QUINCE. Bottom! O most courageous day! O most happy hour!

BOTTOM. Masters, I am to discourse wonders: but ask me not
what; for if I tell you, I am no true Athenian. I will tell you
every thing, right as it fell out.

QUINCE. Let us hear, sweet Bottom.

BOTTOM. Not a word of me. All that I will tell you is, that the
Duke hath dined. Get your apparel together, good strings to
your beards, new ribbons to your pumps; meet presently at
the palace; every man look o'er his part; for the short and
the long is, our play is preferred. In any case, let Thisby
have clean linen; and let not him that plays the lion pare his
nails, for they shall hang out for the lion's claws. And, most
dear actors, eat no onions nor garlic, for we are to utter
sweet breath; and I do not doubt but to hear them say, it is
a sweet comedy. No more words: away! go, away!

[Exeunt.

ACT V

Scene I — *Athens. The palace of* Theseus.

Enter Theseus, Hippolyta, Philostrate, Lords,
 and Attendants.]

HIPPOLYTA. 'Tis strange, my Theseus, that these lovers speak
 of.

THESEUS. More strange than true: I never may believe
 These antique fables, nor these fairy toys.
 Lovers and madmen have such seething brains,
 Such shaping fantasies, that apprehend
 More than cool reason ever comprehends.
 The lunatic, the lover and the poet
 Are of imagination all compact:
 One sees more devils than vast hell can hold,
 That is, the madman: the lover, all as frantic,
 Sees Helen's beauty in a brow of Egypt:
 The poet's eye, in a fine frenzy rolling,
 Doth glance from heaven to earth, from earth to heaven;
 And as imagination bodies forth
 The forms of things unknown, the poet's pen
 Turns them to shapes, and gives to airy nothing
 A local habitation and a name.
 Such tricks hath strong imagination,
 That, if it would but apprehend some joy,
 It comprehends some bringer of that joy;
 Or in the night, imagining some fear,
 How easy is a bush supposed a bear!

HIPPOLYTA. But all the story of the night told over,
 And all their minds transfigured so together,
 More witnesseth than fancy's images,
 And grows to something of great constancy;
 But, howsoever, strange and admirable.

THESEUS. Here come the lovers, full of joy and mirth.

Enter LYSANDER, DEMETRIUS, HERMIA, *and* HELENA.]

    Joy, gentle friends! joy and fresh days of love
    Accompany your hearts!
LYSANDER.   More than to us
    Wait in your royal walks, your board, your bed!
THESEUS. Come now; what masques, what dances shall we
    have,
    To wear away this long age of three hours
    Between our after-supper and bed-time?
    Where is our usual manager of mirth?
    What revels are in hand? Is there no play,
    To ease the anguish of a torturing hour?
    Call Philostrate.
PHILOSTRATE.   Here, mighty Theseus.
THESEUS. Say, what abridgment have you for this evening?
    What masque? what music? How shall we beguile
    The lazy time, if not with some delight?
PHILOSTRATE. There is a brief how many sports are ripe:
    Make choice of which your highness will see first.
                              [Giving a paper.
THESEUS. [*Reads*] The battle with the Centaurs, to be sung
    By an Athenian eunuch to the harp.
    We 'll none of that: that have I told my love,
    In glory of my kinsman Hercules.
    [*Reads*] The riot of the tipsy Bacchanals,
    Tearing the Thracian singer in their rage.
    That is an old device; and it was play'd
    When I from Thebes came last a conqueror.
    [*Reads*] The thrice three Muses mourning for the death
    Of Learning, late deceased in beggary.
    That is some satire, keen and critical,
    Not sorting with a nuptial ceremony.
    [*Reads*] A tedious brief scene of young Pyramus
    And his love Thisbe; very tragical mirth.
    Merry and tragical! tedious and brief!
    That is, hot ice and wondrous strange snow.
    How shall we find the concord of this discord?
PHILOSTRATE. A play there is, my lord, some ten words long,

Which, is as brief as I have known a play;
But by ten words, my lord, it is too long,
Which makes it tedious; for in all the play
There is not one word apt, one player fitted:
And tragical, my noble lord, it is;
For Pyramus therein doth kill himself.
Which, when I saw rehearsed, I must confess,
Made mine eyes water; but more merry tears
The passion of loud laughter never shed.

THESEUS. What are they that do play it?

PHILOSTRATE. Hard-handed men, that work in Athens here,
Which never labor'd in their minds till now;
And now have toil'd their unbreathed memories
With this same play, against your nuptial.

THESEUS. And we will hear it.

PHILOSTRATE.   No, my noble lord;
It is not for you: I have heard it over,
And it is nothing, nothing in the world;
Unless you can find sport in their intents,
Extremely stretch'd and conn'd with cruel pain,
To do you service.

THESEUS.   I will hear that play;
For never any thing can be amiss,
When simpleness and duty tender it.
Go, bring them in: and take your places, ladies.

                              [*Exit* PHILOSTRATE.

HIPPOLYTA. I love not to see wretchedness o'ercharged,
And duty in his service perishing.

THESEUS. Why, gentle sweet, you shall see no such thing.

HIPPOLYTA. He says they can do nothing in this kind.

THESEUS. The kinder we, to give them thanks for nothing.
Our sport shall be to take what they mistake:
And what poor duty cannot do, noble respect
Takes it in might, not merit.
Where I have come, great clerks have purposed
To greet me with premeditated welcomes;
Where I have seen them shiver and look pale,

Make periods in the midst of sentences,
Throttle their practiced accent in their fears,
And, in conclusion, dumbly have broke off,
Not paying me a welcome. Trust me, sweet,
Out of this silence yet I picked a welcome;
And in the modesty of fearful duty
I read as much as from the rattling tongue
Of saucy and audacious eloquence.
Love, therefore, and tongue-tied simplicity
In least speak most, to my capacity.

Re-enter PHILOSTRATE.]

PHILOSTRATE. So please your grace, the Prologue is address'd.

THESEUS. Let him approach.   [*Flourish of trumpets.*

Enter QUINCE *for the Prologue.*]

PROLOGUE. If we offend, it is with our good will.
      That you should think, we come not to offend,
But with good will. To show our simple skill,
      That is the true beginning of our end.
Consider, then, we come but in despite.
      We do not come, as minding to content you,
Our true intent is. All for your delight,
      We are not here. That you should here repent you,
The actors are at hand; and, by their show,
You shall know all, that you are like to know.

THESEUS. This fellow doth not stand upon points.

LYSANDER. He hath rid his prologue like a rough colt; he knows
not the stop. A good moral, my lord: it is not enough to
speak, but to speak true.

HIPPOLYTA. Indeed he hath played on his prologue like a child
on a recorder; a sound, but not in government.

THESEUS. His speech was like a tangled chain; nothing im-
paired, but all disordered. Who is next?

Enter PYRAMUS *and* THISBE, WALL, MOONSHINE, *and* LION.]

PROLOGUE. Gentles, perchance you wonder at this show;
      But wonder on, till truth make all things plain.
This man is Pyramus, if you would know;
      This beauteous lady Thisby is certain.

This man, with lime and rough-cast, doth present
  Wall, that vile Wall which did these lovers sunder;
And through Wall's chink, poor souls, they are content
  To whisper. At the which let no man wonder.
This man, with lanthorn, dog, and bush of thorn,
  Presenteth Moonshine; for, if you will know,
By moonshine did these lovers think no scorn
  To meet at Ninus' tomb, there, there to woo.
This grisly beast, which Lion hight by name,
The trusty Thisby, coming first by night,
Did scare away, or rather did affright;
And, as she fled, her mantle she did fall,
  Which Lion vile with bloody mouth did stain.
Anon comes Pyramus, sweet youth and tall,
  And finds his trusty Thisby's mantle slain:
Whereat, with blade, with bloody blameful blade,
  He bravely broach'd his boiling bloody breast:
And Thisby, tarrying in mulberry shade,
  His dagger drew, and died. For all the rest,
Let Lion, Moonshine, Wall, and lovers twain
At large discourse, while here they do remain.

> [*Exeunt* PROLOGUE, PYRAMUS, THISBE, LION,
>   *and* MOONSHINE.

THESEUS. I wonder if the lion be to speak.

DEMETRIUS. No wonder, my lord: one lion may, when many
  asses do.

WALL. In this same interlude it doth befall
  That I, one Snout by name, present a wall;
  And such a wall, as I would have you think,
  That had in it a crannied hole or chink,
  Through which the lovers, Pyramus and Thisby,
  Did whisper often very secretly.
  This loam, this rough-cast, and this stone, doth show
  That I am that same wall; the truth is so:
  And this the cranny is, right and sinister,
  Through which the fearful lovers are to whisper.

THESEUS. Would you desire lime and hair to speak better?

DEMETRIUS. It is the wittiest partition that ever I heard discourse, my lord.

THESEUS. Pyramus draws near the wall: silence!

Re-enter PYRAMUS.]

PYRAMUS. O grim-look'd night! O night with hue so black!
    O night, which ever art when day is not!
O night, O night! alack, alack, alack,
    I fear my Thisby's promise is forgot!
And thou, O wall, O sweet, O lovely wall,
    That stand'st between her father's ground and mine!
Thou wall, O wall, O sweet and lovely wall,
    Show me thy chink, to blink through with mine eyne!
                            [WALL *holds up his fingers.*
Thanks, courteous wall: Jove shield thee well for this!
    But what see I? No Thisby do I see.
O wicked wall, through whom I see no bliss!
    Cursed be thy stones for thus deceiving me!

THESEUS. The wall, methinks, being sensible, should curse again.

PYRAMUS. No, in truth, sir, he should not. 'Deceiving me' is Thisby's cue: she is to enter now, and I am to spy her through the wall. You shall see, it will fall pat as I told you. Yonder she comes.

Re-enter THISBE.]

THISBE. O wall, full often hast thou heard my moans,
    For parting my fair Pyramus and me!
My cherry lips have often kiss'd thy stones,
    Thy stones with lime and hair knit up in thee.

PYRAMUS. I see a voice: now will I to the chink,
    To spy an I can hear my Thisby's face.
    Thisby!

THISBE. My love thou art, my love I think.

PYRAMUS. Think what thou wilt, I am thy lover's grace;
    And, like Limander, am I trusty still.

THISBE. And I like Helen, till the Fates me kill.

PYRAMUS. Not Shafalus to Procrus was so true.

THISBE. As Shafalus to Procrus, I to you.

PYRAMUS. O, kiss me through the hole of this vile wall!

THISBE. I kiss the wall's hole, not your lips at all.

PYRAMUS. Wilt thou at Ninny's tomb meet me straightway?

THISBE. 'Tide life, 'tide death, I come without delay.

[Exeunt PYRAMUS *and* THISBE.

WALL. Thus have I, wall, my part discharged so;

And, being done, thus wall away doth go.   [*Exit.*

THESEUS. Now is the mural down between the two neighbors.

DEMETRIUS. No remedy, my lord, when walls are so willful to
hear without warning.

HIPPOLYTA. This is the silliest stuff that ever I heard.

THESEUS. The best in this kind are but shadows; and the worst
are no worse, if imagination amend them.

HIPPOLYTA. It must be your imagination then, and not theirs.

THESEUS. If we imagine no worse of them than they of themselves, they may pass for excellent men. Here come two
noble beasts in, a man and a lion.

Re-enter LION *and* MOONSHINE.]

LION. You, ladies, you, whose gentle hearts do fear
The smallest monstrous mouse that creeps on floor,
May now perchance both quake and tremble here,
    When lion rough in wildest rage doth roar,
Then know that I, one Snug the joiner, am
A lion-fell, nor else no lion's dam;
For, if I should as lion come in strife
Into this place, 'twere pity on my life.

THESEUS. A very gentle beast, and of a good conscience.

DEMETRIUS. The very best at a beast, my lord, that e'er I saw.

LYSANDER. This lion is a very fox for his valor.

THESEUS. True; and a goose for his discretion.

DEMETRIUS. Not so, my lord; for his valor cannot carry his
discretion; and the fox carries the goose.

THESEUS. His discretion, I am sure, cannot carry his valor; for
the goose carries not the fox. It is well: leave it to his discretion, and let us listen to the moon.

MOON. This lanthorn doth the horned moon present;—

DEMETRIUS. He should have worn the horns on his head.

THESEUS. He is no crescent, and his horns are invisible within the circumference.

MOON. This lanthorn doth the horned moon present;
Myself the man i' the moon do seem to be.

THESEUS. This is the greatest error of all the rest: the man should be put into the lantern. How is it else the man i' the moon?

DEMETRIUS. He dares not come there for the candle; for, you see, it is already in snuff.

HIPPOLYTA. I am aweary of this moon: would he would change!

THESEUS. It appears, by his small light of discretion, that he is in the wane; but yet, in courtesy, in all reason, we must stay the time.

LYSANDER. Proceed, Moon.

MOON. All that I have to say, is, to tell you that the lanthorn is the moon; I, the man i' the moon; this thorn-bush, my thorn-bush; and this dog, my dog.

DEMETRIUS. Why, all these should be in the lantern; for all these are in the moon. But, silence! here comes Thisbe.

Re-enter THISBE.]

THISBE. This is old Ninny's tomb. Where is my love?

LION. [*Roaring*] Oh——   [THISBE *runs off*.

DEMETRIUS. Well roared, Lion.

THESEUS. Well run, Thisbe.

HIPPOLYTA. Well shone, Moon. Truly, the moon shines with a good grace.

                    [*The* LION *shakes* THISBE'S *mantle, and exit*.

THESEUS. Well moused, Lion.

DEMETRIUS. And then came Pyramus.

LYSANDER. And so the lion vanished.

Re-enter PYRAMUS.]

PYRAMUS. Sweet Moon, I thank thee for thy sunny beams;
    I thank thee, Moon, for shining now so bright;
  For, by thy gracious, golden, glittering gleams,
    I trust to take of truest Thisby sight.
            But stay, O spite!
            But mark, poor knight,

What dreadful dole is here!
    Eyes, do you see?
    How can it be?
O dainty duck! O dear!
    Thy mantle good,
    What, stain'd with blood!
Approach, ye Furies fell!
      O Fates, come, come,
      Cut thread and thrum;
Quail, crush, conclude, and quell!

THESEUS. This passion, and the death of a dear friend, would go near to make a man look sad.

HIPPOLYTA. Beshrew my heart, but I pity the man.

PYRAMUS. O wherefore, Nature, didst thou lions frame?
Since lion vile hath here deflower'd my dear;
Which is—no, no—which was the fairest dame
    That lived, that loved, that liked, that look'd with cheer.
      Come, tears, confound;
      Out, sword, and wound
The pap of Pyramus;
      Ay, that left pap,
      Where heart doth hop: [*Stabs himself.*
Thus die I, thus, thus, thus.
      Now am I dead,
      Now am I fled;
My soul is in the sky:
      Tongue, lose thy light;
      Moon, take thy flight: [*Exit* MOONSHINE.
Now die, die, die, die, die.   [*Dies.*

DEMETRIUS. No die, but an ace, for him; for he is but one.

LYSANDER. Less than an ace, man; for he is dead; he is nothing.

THESEUS. With the help of a surgeon he might yet recover, and prove an ass.

HIPPOLYTA. How chance Moonshine is gone before Thisbe comes back and finds her lover?

THESEUS. She will find him by starlight. Here she comes; and her passion ends the play.

Re-enter THISBE.]

HIPPOLYTA. Methinks she should not use a long one for such
  a Pyramus: I hope she will be brief.

DEMETRIUS. A mote will turn the balance, which Pyramus,
  which Thisbe, is the better; he for a man, God warrant us;
  she for a woman, God bless us.

LYSANDER. She hath spied him already with those sweet eyes.

DEMETRIUS. And thus she means, videlicet:—

THISBE.   Asleep, my love?
           What, dead, my dove?
  O Pyramus, arise!
           Speak, speak. Quite dumb?
           Dead, dead? A tomb
  Must cover thy sweet eyes.
           These lily lips,
           This cherry nose,
  These yellow cowslip cheeks,
           Are gone, are gone:
           Lovers, make moan:
  His eyes were green as leeks.
           O Sisters Three,
           Come, come to me,
  With hands as pale as milk:
           Lay them in gore,
           Since you have shore
  With shears his thread of silk.
           Tongue, not a word:
           Come, trusty sword;
  Come, blade, my breast imbrue: [*Stabs herself.*
           And, fare well, friends;
           Thus Thisbe ends:
  Adieu, adieu, adieu.   [*Dies.*

THESEUS. Moonshine and Lion are left to bury the dead.

DEMETRIUS. Ay, and Wall too.

BOTTOM. [*Starting up*] No, I assure you; the wall is down that
  parted their fathers. Will it please you to see the epilogue,
  or to hear a Bergomask dance between two of our company?

THESEUS. No epilogue, I pray you; for your play needs no ex-

cuse. Never excuse; for when the players are all dead, there
need none to be blamed. Marry, if he that writ it had played
Pyramus and hanged himself in Thisbe's garter, it would
have been a fine tragedy: and so it is, truly; and very no-
tably discharged. But, come, your Bergomask: let your epilogue alone.   [*A dance.*

The iron tongue of midnight hath told twelve:
Lovers, to bed; 'tis almost fairy time.
I fear we shall out-sleep the coming morn,
As much as we this night have overwatch'd.
This palpable-gross play hath well beguiled
The heavy gait of night. Sweet friends, to bed.
A fortnight hold we this solemnity,
In nightly revels and new jollity.   [*Exeunt.*

Enter PUCK.]

PUCK. Now the hungry lion roars,
    And the wolf behowls the moon;
Whilst the heavy ploughman snores,
    All with weary task fordone.
Now the wasted brands do glow,
    Whilst the screech-owl, screeching loud,
Puts the wretch that lies in woe
    In remembrance of a shroud.
Now it is the time of night,
    That the graves, all gaping wide,
Every one lets forth his sprite,
    In the church-way paths to glide:
And we fairies, that do run
    By the triple Hecate's team,
From the presence of the sun,
    Following darkness like a dream,
Now are frolic: not a mouse
Shall disturb this hallow'd house:
I am sent with broom before,
To sweep the dust behind the door.

Enter OBERON *and* TITANIA *with their train.*]

OBERON. Through the house give glimmering light,

By the dead and drowsy fire:
Every elf and fairy sprite
    Hop as light as bird from brier;
And this ditty, after me,
Sing, and dance it trippingly.
TITANIA. First, rehearse your song by rote,
To each word a warbling note:
Hand in hand, with fairy grace,
Will we sing, and bless this place.   [*Song and dance.*
OBERON. Now, until the break of day,
Through this house each fairy stray.
To the best bride-bed will we,
Which by us shall blessed be;
And the issue there create
Ever shall be fortunate.
So shall all the couples three
Ever true in loving be;
And the blots of Nature's hand
Shall not in their issue stand;
Never mole, hare lip, nor scar,
Nor mark prodigious, such as are
Despised in nativity,
Shall upon their children be.
With this field-dew consecrate,
Every fairy take his gait;
And each several chamber bless,
Through this palace, with sweet peace,
Ever shall in safety rest,
And the owner of it blest.
Trip away; make no stay;
Meet me all by break of day.
                    [*Exeunt* OBERON, TITANIA, *and train.*
PUCK. If we shadows have offended,
Think but this, and all is mended,
That you have but slumber'd here,
While these visions did appear.
And this weak and idle theme,

No more yielding but a dream,
Gentles, do not reprehend:
If you pardon, we will mend.
And, as I am an honest Puck,
If we have unearned luck
Now to 'scape the serpent's tongue,
We will make amends ere long;
Else the Puck a liar call:
So, good night unto you all.
Give me your hands, if we be friends,
And Robin shall restore amends.   [*Exit.*

As You Like It

INTRODUCTION TO

As You Like It

BY

MARK VAN DOREN

T HE airiness of *As You Like It* is as much the work of
thought as the reward of feeling. The comedy seems to
balance like a bubble on a point of thin space; yet space in its
neighborhood has not worn thin, and the bubble is as tough as
eternity, it does not break. This, doubtless, is because the sen-
timents of its author were at the moment in a state of rare
equilibrium, and because his nerves were happy in an unconscious health. Also, however, it is because his mind was
tuned to its task. *As You Like It* is so charming a comedy
that in order to enjoy it we need not think about it at all. But
if we do think about it we become aware of intellectual
operations noiselessly and expertly performed. We see an idea
anatomized until there is nothing left of it save its original
mystery. We watch an attitude as it is taken completely apart
and put completely together again. And all of this is done
without visible effort. Shakespeare's understanding of his subject increases until the subject is exhausted, until there is no
more to understand; and still there are no signs of labor or
fatigue. Shakespeare has been denied an intellect. But whatever it took to write *As You Like It* was among other things
mental, and the exact like of it, as well as the exact degree,
has never been seen in literature again.

As You Like It is a criticism of the pastoral sentiment, an
examination of certain familiar ideas concerning the simple
life and the golden age. It is not satire; its examination is
conducted without prejudice. For once in the world a propo-

sition is approached from all of its sides, and from top and bottom. The proposition is perhaps multiple: the country is more natural than the court, shepherds live lives of enviable innocence and simplicity, the vices that devour the heart of civilized man will drop from him as soon as he walks under a greenwood tree, perversion and malice cannot survive in the open air, the shade of beech trees is the only true Academy, one impulse from the vernal wood will teach us more than all the sages can. Yet it is single too, and pastoral literature has monotonously intoned it. Shakespeare relieves the monotony by statement which is also understanding, by criticism which is half laughter and half love—or, since his laughter is what it is, all love. The result is something very curious. When Rosalind has made her last curtsy and the comedy is done, the pastoral sentiment is without a leg to stand on, yet it stands; and not only stands but dances. The idea of the simple life has been smiled off the earth and yet here it still is, smiling back at us from every bough of Arden. The Forest of Arden has been demonstrated not to exist, yet none of its trees has fallen; rather the entire plantation waves forever, and the sun upon it will not cease. The doctrine of the golden age has been as much created as destroyed. We know there is nothing in it, and we know that everything is in it. We perceive how silly it is and why we shall never be able to do without it. We comprehend the long failure of cynicism to undo sentiment. Here there is neither sentiment nor cynicism; there is understanding. An idea is left hanging in free air, without contamination or support. That is the place for ideas, as Shakespeare the comic poet seems to have known without being told.

"Where will the old Duke live?" asks Orlando's villainous brother of the still more villainous wrestler Charles. The unscrupulous bruiser answers in terms that may surprise us by their prettiness:

They say he is already in the forest of Arden, and a many merry men with him; and there they live like the old Robin Hood of England. They say many young gentlemen flock to him every day, and fleet the time carelessly, as they did in the golden world.   [I, i]

That is the text to be annotated, the idea to be analyzed in the comedy to come. But analysis has already taken place, a cross-glance has already been shot by one whose mind will go on to draw lines in every direction athwart the theme. Shakespeare's first operation consists of putting such a speech into such a mouth, and letting it be ground between great molars there, unsympathetically. We get the doctrine, but we get it crooked, as comedy prefers: through the most unlikely medium, and the most unconscious. The first act is for the most part mechanically introductory to what follows; its business is to push everybody off to Arden, and Shakespeare writes it without much interest, since his sole interest is Arden. Rosalind is introduced, and of course it is important that we should find her from the first a gallant and witty girl, as we do. But she too is being saved for the forest. Charles's speech is the one memorable thing we have heard before we plunge into the depths of Arden at the beginning of the second act. But it is distinctly memorable, and it modifies the music which plays for us in the old Duke's mind.

> Now, my co-mates and brothers in exile,
> Hath not old custom made this life more sweet
> Than that of painted pomp? Are not these woods
> More free from peril than the envious court? . . .
> Sweet are the uses of adversity,
> Which, like the toad, ugly and venomous,
> Wears yet a precious jewel in his head;
> And this our life, exempt from public haunt,
> Finds tongues in trees, books in the running brooks,
> Sermons in stones, and good in every thing.   [II, i]

There is the text once more, translated into so quiet and so sweet a style that we may be tempted to believe it is the author speaking. But he was speaking as well in Charles; or rather he speaks in both—in their relation, which is only one of many relations the play will explore. The simple text will receive further statement through four pleasant acts. Good old Adam reminds Orlando of "the antique world" which was so much purer than "the fashion of these times" (II, iii). Shepherds appear named Corin and Silvius, and one of them goes sighing through the forest for love of his Phebe. A member of the Duke's retinue in exile knows how to be philosophical about everything; the humorous sadness of Jaques promises to ripen into wisdom now that ingratitude is forgotten and ambition can be shunned. We look to him for the sermons that so far have remained silent in their stones.

> Give me leave
> To speak my mind, and I will through and through
> Cleanse the foul body of the infected world,
> If they will patiently receive my medicine. [II, vii]

So radical a boast in such emancipated terms, delivered by one who sees through the mummery of manners and considers compliment to be but the encounter of two dog-apes (II, v), leads us to expect that in Jaques if in no one else the doctrine of the Duke will yield edifying fruit. Glimpses of a paradisal landscape are not withheld—boughs mossed with age, antique oaks whose roots peep out at brawling brooks, and purlieus of the forest where stand sheepcotes fenced about with olive trees. And Shakespeare by no means stops short of miraculous conversions under the influence of this place. It seems to work. Oliver's transformation tastes sweetly to him, making him the thing he is; he will live and die a shepherd. The base Duke Frederick scarcely sets foot in the forest before an old religious man, harmonious with the wild wood, turns him not only from his hatred for the old Duke but from the world. The text is given every opportunity to state itself, and nowhere does the comedy overtly contradict it.

All the while, however, it is being subtly undermined and sapped of its simplicity. Touchstone shreds it with the needle of his dialectic, with the razor of his parody. Silvius's cry of "Phebe, Phebe, Phebe" reminds him of his country love:

> I remember, when I was in love I broke my sword upon a stone, and bid him take that for coming a-night to Jane Smile; and I remember the kissing of her batlet and the cow's dugs that her pretty chopt hands had milk'd; and I remember the wooing of a peascod instead of her; from whom I took two cods and, giving her them again, said with weeping tears, "Wear these for my sake." [II, iv]

Encountering Corin in the forest and receiving from him the pastoral gospel—that courts are corrupt and manners unnatural—he juggles it till he has proved that courtiers are indistinguishable from shepherds, for tar on the hands of the one class is equivalent to civet on the hands of the other, and both substances are lowly born. When Corin takes refuge in the immemorial claim of the countryman that he lives and lets live, his only pride being to watch his ewes graze and his lambs suck, Touchstone trips him up by translating what he has said into the cynical language of cities:

That is another simple sin in you, to bring the ewes and the rams together, and to offer to get your living by the copulation of cattle; to be bawd to a bell-wether, and to betray a she-lamb of a twelvemonth to a crooked-pated, old, cuckoldy ram, out of all reasonable match. [III, ii]

Rosalind enters reading one of the poems Orlando has written for her on the bark of a tree. It is a bad poem, and she knows it; but Touchstone knows it well enough to have a parody ready (III, ii). He has no patience with country love, yet because he is where he is he cultivates the one wench available—ill-favored Audrey, whom the gods have not made poetical, and on whom literary puns are lost. He makes one nevertheless, on Ovid and the goats; and presses in at last among the country copulatives to be wedded with his poor virgin. He is without illusion; so much so that he will not claim he can do without it. His dryness touches the pastoral text throughout, and alters it; the detachment of his wit gives everything perspective, including himself. He is intellect afield; contemptuous of what he sees so far from home, but making the thin best of what is there. Not much is there when his withering, somewhat bored glance has circled the horizon.

Nor do we miss the sour look in Jaques's eyes as he roams this paradise. The exiled gentlemen are tyrants to the deer (II, i) even as their usurpers are to them.

> He pierceth through
> The body of the country, city, court,
> Yea, and of this our life. [II, i]

The songs which thread the play so prettily are little better than noise to him, and he parodies one of them without mercy

(II, v). Orlando does not impress him by the innocence and eagerness of his love; he is a young fool who mars trees with verses (III, ii). The huddle of marriages at the end is "another flood, and these couples are coming to the ark." He is not dry like Touchstone, for there is in him the juice of discontent; but he also takes down the temperature of romance, he sophisticates the pastoral text with grimaces of understanding.

But nothing is more characteristic of the comedy than the fact that its heroine is the most searching critic of its theme. Rosalind's laughter is neither dry nor wry; it is high and clear, it has a silver sound, and the sun dances among its fiery, impalpable particles. Her disguise as a man does not explain the quality of this laughter. There are as many kinds of men as of women, and a different girl would have become a different boy; one, for instance, who moped and sighed and languished in the purlieus of romance. Rosalind has no difficulty with the language of scoffing youth. To such a fellow the poems of Orlando are tedious homilies of love. "I was never so berhym'd since Pythagoras' time, that I was an Irish rat, which I can hardly remember" (III, ii). Her vocabulary is as tart and vernacular as that of Mercutio, Faulconbridge, or Hotspur. The skirts of the forest are for her the "fringe upon a petticoat," love is a madness deserving the dark house and the whip, if Orlando will accept her as his physician she will wash his liver "as clean as a sound sheep's heart," Phebe has no more beauty than without candle may go dark to bed, when lovers lack words they should kiss as orators in the same predicament spit, she will be as jealous over Orlando as a Barbary cock-pigeon over his hen, her affection hath an unknown bottom like the bay of Portugal, love hath made Silvius a tame snake. Language like this is not learned by putting on man's apparel, nor is there any sign that it goes against Rosalind's grain to jest about incontinence, your neighbor's bed, and the inevitable horns; there is a rank reality in her speech, as in the speech of Shakespeare's best women always. And she would appear to be without any understanding whatever of the rare states to which lovers can be reduced. Her account of Oliver and Celia is that they

> no sooner met but they look'd; no sooner look'd but they lov'd; no sooner lov'd but they sigh'd; no sooner sigh'd but they ask'd one another the reason; no sooner knew the reason but they sought the remedy; and in these degrees have they made a pair of stairs to marriage which they will climb incontinent, or else be incontinent before marriage. They are in the very wrath of love and they will together. Clubs cannot part them. [v, ii]

The tone is unsympathetic, logically enough for a young woman whose diatribe against the doctrine of the broken heart has become classic:

> The poor world is almost six thousand years old, and in all this time there was not any man died in his own person, videlicet, in a love-cause. Troilus had his brains dash'd out with a Grecian club; yet he did what he could to die before, and he is one of the patterns of love. Leander, he would have liv'd many a fair year though Hero had turn'd nun, if it had not been for a hot midsummer night; for, good youth, he went but forth to wash him in the Hellespont and being taken with the cramp was drown'd; and the foolish chroniclers of that age found it was—Hero of Sestos. But these are all lies. Men have died from time to time and worms have eaten them, but not for love. [iv, i]

The realism is uproarious, as the prose is artful and the wit is incessant. "You shall never take her without her answer," she warns Orlando of the true Rosalind, "unless you take her without her tongue." Her gaiety runs like quicksilver, and is as hard to head off. She is of great value for that reason to her author, who can so easily use her as a commentator on his play when it grows absurd—as, being a pastoral play, it must. He can use her, for instance, to silence Phebe, Silvius, Orlando, and even herself when the four of them have carried too far the liturgy of one another's names. "Pray you," she says, "no more of this; 't is like the howling of Irish wolves against the moon" (v, ii).

All this is true. Yet it is also true that Rosalind loves Orlando without limit, and that she is the happiest of many happy persons in Arden. Her criticism of love and cuckoo-land is unremitting, yet she has not annihilated them. Rather she has preserved them by removing the flaws of their softness. That is the duty of criticism—a simple duty for a girl with sound imagination and a healthy heart. As Arden emerges from the fires of *As You Like It* a perfected symbol of the golden age, so Rosalind steps forth not burned but brightened, a perfected symbol of the romantic heroine. Romance has been tested in her until we know it cannot shatter; laughter has made it sure of itself. There is only one thing sillier than being in love, and that is thinking it is silly to be in love. Rosalind skips through both errors to wisdom.

She, not Jaques, is the philosopher of the play. Hers is the only mind that never rests; his bogs down in the mire of melancholy, in the slough of self-love. He is too fond of believing he is wise to be as wise as he sounds, either in the set speech he makes about man's seven ages (II, vii) or in the insults he considers himself privileged at all times to deliver. His distrust of manners turns out to be the disaffection of a boor. His melancholy, like his wit, is an end in itself, a dyspeptic indulgence, an exercise of vanity that serves none of wisdom's purposes. "Motley's the only wear," he decides (II, vi), but when he is dressed in it he has no place to go. "I can suck melancholy out of a song as a weasel sucks eggs," he tells Amiens (II, v), and the figure is better than he knows. He slithers through Arden, in love with his own sad eyes. "Will you sit down with me?" he asks Orlando, "and we two will rail against our mistress the world, and all our misery." Orlando's answer is priggish, but it is nearer to the meaning of the play. "I will chide no breather in the world but myself, against whom I know most faults" (III, ii). Jaques is a fat and greasy citizen of the world of easy words. He is a fine poet at this stage of Shakespeare's career, but he will degenerate into Thersites and Apemantus. Rosalind it is who knows his weakness best.

JAQUES. I have neither the scholar's melancholy, which is emulation; nor the musician's, which is fantastical; nor the courtier's, which is proud; nor the soldier's, which is ambitious; nor the lawyer's, which is politic; nor the lady's, which is nice; nor the lover's, which is all these; but it is a melancholy of mine own, compounded of many simples, extracted from many objects; and indeed the sundry contemplation of my travels, in which my often rumination wraps me in a most humourous sadness—

ROSALIND. A traveller! By my faith, you have great reason to be sad. I fear you have sold your own lands to see other men's; then, to have seen much, and to have nothing, is to have rich eyes and poor hands.

JAQUES. Yes, I have gained my experience.

ROSALIND. And your experience makes you sad. I had rather have a fool to make me merry than experience to make me sad; and to travel for it too!   [IV, i]

Jaques has seen much and can say anything, but he has nothing. Experience has made him sad. The more experience Rosalind has the merrier she grows. She too is a traveler, but she has not sold her own lands. She has taken her integrity with her to Arden, tucked under her three-cornered cap. It is proper that the limitations of Jaques should be stated by her, for if in him we have the pastoral sentiment criticized we have in her the only intelligence capable of judging the criticism. She judges with more than intelligence—with, for instance, instinct and love—but that again is proper to the comedy of Shakespeare's prime.

The Story of the Play

ACT I

A DUKE OF FRANCE, being dispossessed of his dominions by his younger brother, Frederick, retires to the neighbouring Forest of Arden with a few of his faithful followers. His daughter Rosalind remains at her usurping uncle's court as companion for her beloved cousin, Celia. The two maidens witness a wrestling-match between the Duke's wrestler and Orlando, an unknown youth, in which the latter comes off victorious. Duke Frederick is pleased with the young man's prowess and is disposed to show him favour until he discovers Orlando to be the son of one of the banished Duke's friends. But Rosalind is delighted to hear of this connexion, since she has become favourably disposed towards Orlando.

The people are so fond of Rosalind because of her many accomplishments and for the sake of her father, that Duke Frederick in alarm banishes her also from the court. For love of her, Celia accompanies her cousin into exile.

ACT II

ROSALIND assumes male attire and takes Celia to the Forest of Arden, where they purchase a country-place and reside as brother and sister. To the same wood comes Orlando, who has been forced to flee from home to escape the evil designs of his elder brother, Oliver, and who joins the company of the banished Duke.

ACT III

ROSALIND is at first dismayed when she learns of the presence of Orlando in the forest, since she is dressed as a man. But presently her inventiveness leads her to make use of her disguise to test his affection for her, which had been aroused at the same time with her own for him on the day of the wrestling-match, and is now venting itself in sighs and in verses fastened at random on the trees. The lover is invited to visit the supposed youth and talk to him in the same manner that he would have talked to Rosalind. Orlando is glad to avail himself of this privilege, partly as an outlet to his pent-up sentiment, partly because Rosalind, even in man's garments, exerts a subtle fascination over him.

ACT IV

ORLANDO has the good fortune to rescue his brother Oliver from a serpent and a lioness, though becoming slightly wounded in an encounter with the beast. On finding him asleep, Orlando, remembering the wrongs at his hands, had been tempted to leave him to his fate, "but kindness, nobler ever than revenge," made him give aid. The two brothers are tenderly reconciled, and Oliver goes to acquaint Rosalind with Orlando's injury. Rosalind is not enough of a man to resist swooning at the tidings.

ACT V

OLIVER and Celia no sooner see each other than they fall desperately in love and resolve upon speedy marriage. Rosalind, who is satisfied with the strength of Orlando's devotion, promises him that the wedding ceremony shall include him also, and that she will find means to bring his lady-love hither. She seeks out the banished Duke, her father, and obtains his consent, and thereupon appears before them in her proper attire, to the great delight of Orlando and the Duke. The wedding, instead of being a double, is a quadruple event, since it includes besides these two couples, a shepherd and his lass (who had foolishly been attracted by Rosalind in her male attire), and Touchstone, the court clown, who had followed the two maidens to the forest and there become enamoured of a country wench. The wedding-party is made all the happier by the tidings that the usurping Duke Frederick, while on his way to the forest with a large army for the purpose of exterminating the exiles, had met an aged hermit who had converted him "both from his enterprise and from the world." Struck with remorse, he restores the dukedom to his banished brother and seeks the life of a recluse, leaving the rightful Duke and his followers free to resume their former rank.

J. WALKER MCSPADDEN

List of Characters

DUKE, *living in banishment*

FREDERICK, *his brother, and usurper of his dominions*

AMIENS, } *lords attending on*
JAQUES, } *the banished* DUKE

LE BEAU, *a courtier attending upon* FREDERICK

CHARLES, *wrestler to* FREDERICK

OLIVER, } *sons of* SIR ROW-
JAQUES, } LAND DE BOYS
ORLANDO, }

ADAM, } *servants to* OLIVER
DENNIS, }

TOUCHSTONE, *a clown*

SIR OLIVER MARTEXT, *a vicar*

CORIN, } *shepherds*
SYLVIUS, }

WILLIAM, *a country fellow, in love with* AUDREY

A person representing Hymen

ROSALIND, *daughter to the banished* DUKE

CELIA, *daughter to* FREDERICK

PHEBE, *a shepherdess*

AUDREY, *a country wench*

Lords, pages, and attendants, &c.

ORLANDO

ROSALIND

CELIA

TOUCHSTONE

JAQUES

Banbury

As You Like It

SCENE — OLIVER'S *house*; DUKE FREDERICK'S *court; and the Forest of Arden.*

ACT I

SCENE I — *Orchard of* OLIVER'S *house.*

Enter ORLANDO *and* ADAM.]

ORLANDO. As I remember, Adam, it was upon this fashion: bequeathed me by will but poor a thousand crowns, and, as thou sayest, charged my brother, on his blessing, to breed me well: and there begins my sadness. My brother Jaques he keeps at school, and report speaks goldenly of his profit: for my part, he keeps me rustically at home, or, to speak more properly, stays me here at home unkept; for call you that keeping for a gentleman of my birth, that differs not from the stalling of an ox? His horses are bred better; for, besides that they are fair with their feeding, they are taught their manage, and to that end riders dearly hired: but I, his brother, gain nothing under him but growth; for the which his animals on his dunghills are as much bound to him as I. Besides this nothing that he so plentifully gives me, the something that nature gave me his countenance seems to take from me: he lets me feed with his hinds, bars me the place of a brother, and, as much as in him lies, mines my gentility with my education. This is it, Adam, that grieves me; and the spirit of my father, which I think is within me, begins to mutiny against this servitude: I will no longer endure it, though yet I know no wise remedy how to avoid it.

ADAM. Yonder comes my master, your brother.

ORLANDO. Go apart, Adam, and thou shalt hear how he will shake me up.

Enter OLIVER.]

OLIVER. Now, sir! what make you here?

ORLANDO. Nothing: I am not taught to make any thing.

OLIVER. What mar you then, sir?

ORLANDO. Marry, sir, I am helping you to mar that which God made, a poor unworthy brother of yours, with idleness.

OLIVER. Marry, sir, be better employed, and be naught awhile.

ORLANDO. Shall I keep your hogs and eat husks with them? What prodigal portion have I spent, that I should come to such penury?

OLIVER. Know you where you are, sir?

ORLANDO. O, sir, very well, here in your orchard.

OLIVER. Know you before whom, sir?

ORLANDO. Aye, better than him I am before knows me. I know you are my eldest brother; and, in the gentle condition of blood, you should so know me. The courtesy of nations allows you my better, in that you are the first-born; but the same tradition takes not away my blood, were there twenty brothers betwixt us: I have as much of my father in me as you; albeit, I confess, your coming before me is nearer to his reverence.

OLIVER. What, boy!

ORLANDO. Come, come, elder brother, you are too young in this.

OLIVER. Wilt thou lay hands on me, villain?

ORLANDO. I am no villain; I am the youngest son of Sir Rowland de Boys; he was my father, and he is thrice a villain that says such a father begot villains. Wert thou not my brother, I would not take this hand from thy throat till this other had pulled out thy tongue for saying so; thou hast railed on thyself.

ADAM. Sweet masters, be patient: for your father's remembrance, be at accord.

OLIVER. Let me go, I say.

ORLANDO. I will not, till I please: you shall hear me. My father charged you in his will to give me good education: you have trained me like a peasant, obscuring and hiding from me all gentleman-like qualities. The spirit of my father grows strong in me, and I will no longer endure it: therefore allow me such exercises as may become a gentleman, or give me the poor allottery my father left me by testament; with that I will go buy my fortunes.

OLIVER. And what wilt thou do? beg, when that is spent? Well, sir, get you in: I will not long be troubled with you; you shall have some part of your will: I pray you, leave me.

ORLANDO. I will no further offend you than becomes me for my good.

OLIVER. Get you with him, you old dog.

ADAM. Is 'old dog' my reward? Most true, I have lost my teeth in your service. God be with my old master! he would not have spoke such a word.   [*Exeunt* ORLANDO *and* ADAM.

OLIVER. Is it even so? begin you to grow upon me? I will physic your rankness, and yet give no thousand crowns neither. Holla, Dennis!

Enter DENNIS.]

DENNIS. Calls your worship?

OLIVER. Was not Charles, the Duke's wrestler, here to speak with me?

DENNIS. So please you, he is here at the door and importunes access to you.

OLIVER. Call him in. [*Exit* DENNIS.] 'Twill be a good way; and to-morrow the wrestling is.

Enter CHARLES.]

CHARLES. Good morrow to your worship.

OLIVER. Good Monsieur Charles, what's the new news at the new court?

CHARLES. There's no news at the court, sir, but the old news: that is, the old Duke is banished by his younger brother the new Duke; and three or four loving lords have put themselves into voluntary exile with him, whose lands and revenues enrich the new Duke; therefore he gives them good leave to wander.

OLIVER. Can you tell if Rosalind, the Duke's daughter, be banished with her father?

CHARLES. O, no; for the Duke's daughter, her cousin, so loves her, being ever from their cradles bred together, that she would have followed her exile, or have died to stay behind her. She is at the court, and no less beloved of her uncle than his own daughter; and never two ladies loved as they do.

OLIVER. Where will the old Duke live?

CHARLES. They say he is already in the forest of Arden, and a many merry men with him; and there they live like the old Robin Hood of England: they say many young gentlemen flock to him every day, and fleet the time carelessly, as they did in the golden world.

OLIVER. What, you wrestle to-morrow before the new Duke?

CHARLES. Marry, do I, sir; and I came to acquaint you with a matter. I am given, sir, secretly to understand that your younger brother, Orlando, hath a disposition to come in disguised against me to try a fall. To-morrow, sir, I wrestle for my credit; and he that escapes me without some broken limb shall acquit him well. Your brother is but young and tender; and for your love, I would be loath to foil him, as I must, for my own honor, if he come in: therefore, out of my love to you, I came hither to acquaint you withal; that either you might stay him from his intendment, or brook such disgrace well as he shall run into; in that it is a thing of his own search and altogether against my will.

OLIVER. Charles, I thank thee for thy love to me, which thou shalt find I will most kindly requite. I had myself notice of my brother's purpose herein, and have by underhand means labored to dissuade him from it, but he is resolute. I'll tell thee, Charles:—it is the stubbornest young fellow of France; full of ambition, an envious emulator of every man's good parts, a secret and villainous contriver against me his natural brother: therefore use thy discretion; I had as lief thou didst break his neck as his finger. And thou wert best look to 't; for if thou dost him any slight disgrace, or if he do not mightily grace himself on thee, he will practise against thee by poison, entrap thee by some treacherous device, and never leave thee till he hath ta'en thy life by some indirect means or other; for, I assure thee, and almost with tears I speak it, there is not one so young and so villainous this day living. I speak but brotherly of him; but should I anatomize him to thee as he is, I must blush and weep, and thou must look pale and wonder.

CHARLES. I am heartily glad I came hither to you. If he come to-morrow, I 'll give him his payment: if ever he go alone again, I 'll never wrestle for prize more: and so, God keep your worship!

OLIVER. Farewell, good Charles. [*Exit* CHARLES.] Now will I stir this gamester: I hope I shall see an end of him; for my soul, yet I know not why, hates nothing more than he. Yet he's gentle; never schooled, and yet learned; full of noble device; of all sorts enchantingly beloved; and indeed so much in the heart of the world, and especially of my own people, who best know him, that I am altogether misprised: but it shall not be so long; this wrestler shall clear all: nothing remains but that I kindle the boy thither; which now I 'll go about.   [*Exit.*

SCENE II — *Lawn before the* DUKE'S *palace.*

Enter ROSALIND *and* CELIA.]

CELIA. I pray thee, Rosalind, sweet my coz, be merry.

ROSALIND. Dear Celia, I show more mirth than I am mistress of; and would you yet I were merrier? Unless you could teach me to forget a banished father, you must not learn me how to remember any extraordinary pleasure.

CELIA. Herein I see thou lovest me not with the full weight that I love thee. If my uncle, thy banished father, had banished thy uncle, the Duke my father, so thou hadst been still with me, I could have taught my love to take thy father for mine: so wouldst thou, if the truth of thy love to me were so righteously tempered as mine is to thee.

ROSALIND. Well, I will forget the condition of my estate, to rejoice in yours.

CELIA. You know my father hath no child but I, nor none is like to have: and, truly, when he dies, thou shalt be his heir; for what he hath taken away from thy father perforce, I will render thee again in affection; by mine honor,

I will; and when I break that oath, let me turn monster: therefore, my sweet Rose, my dear Rose, be merry.

ROSALIND. From henceforth I will, coz, and devise sports. Let me see; what think you of falling in love?

CELIA. Marry, I prithee, do, to make sport withal: but love no man in good earnest; nor no further in sport neither, than with safety of a pure blush thou mayst in honor come off again.

ROSALIND. What shall be our sport, then?

CELIA. Let us sit and mock the good housewife Fortune from her wheel, that her gifts may henceforth be bestowed equally.

ROSALIND. I would we could do so; for her benefits are mightily misplaced; and the bountiful blind woman doth most mistake in her gifts to women.

CELIA. 'Tis true; for those that she makes fair she scarce makes honest; and those that she makes honest she makes very ill-favoredly.

ROSALIND. Nay, now thou goest from Fortune's office to Nature's: Fortune reigns in gifts of the world, not in the lineaments of nature.

Enter TOUCHSTONE.]

CELIA. No? when Nature hath made a fair creature may she not by Fortune fall into the fire? Though Nature hath given us wit to flout at Fortune, hath not Fortune sent in this fool to cut off the argument?

ROSALIND. Indeed, there is Fortune too hard for Nature when Fortune makes Nature's natural the cutter-off of Nature's wit.

CELIA. Peradventure this is not Fortune's work neither, but Nature's; who perceiveth our natural wits too dull to reason of such goddesses, and hath sent this natural for our whetstone; for always the dullness of the fool is the whetstone of the wits. How now, wit! whither wander you?

TOUCHSTONE. Mistress, you must come away to your father.

CELIA. Were you made the messenger?

TOUCHSTONE. No, by mine honor, but I was bid to come for you.

ROSALIND. Where learned you that oath, fool?

TOUCHSTONE. Of a certain knight that swore by his honor they were good pancakes, and swore by his honor the mustard was naught; now I'll stand to it, the pancakes were naught and the mustard was good, and yet was not the knight forsworn.

CELIA. How prove you that, in the great heap of your knowledge?

ROSALIND. Aye, marry, now unmuzzle your wisdom.

TOUCHSTONE. Stand you both forth now: stroke your chins, and swear by your beards that I am a knave.

CELIA. By our beards, if we had them, thou art.

TOUCHSTONE. By my knavery, if I had it, then I were; but if you swear by that that is not, you are not forsworn: no more was this knight, swearing by his honor, for he never had any; or if he had, he had sworn it away before ever he saw those pancakes or that mustard.

CELIA. Prithee, who is't that thou meanest?

TOUCHSTONE. One that old Frederick, your father, loves.

CELIA. My father's love is enough to honor him: enough! speak no more of him; you'll be whipped for taxation one of these days.

TOUCHSTONE. The more pity, that fools may not speak wisely what wise men do foolishly.

CELIA. By my troth, thou sayest true; for since the little wit that fools have was silenced, the little foolery that wise men have makes a great show. Here comes Monsieur Le Beau.

ROSALIND. With his mouth full of news.

CELIA. Which he will put on us, as pigeons feed their young.

ROSALIND. Then shall we be news-crammed.

CELIA. All the better; we shall be the more marketable.
Enter LE BEAU.]
    Bon jour, Monsieur Le Beau; what's the news?

LE BEAU. Fair princess, you have lost much good sport.

CELIA. Sport! of what color?

LE BEAU. What color madam! how shall I answer you?

ROSALIND. As wit and fortune will.

TOUCHSTONE. Or as the Destinies decree.

CELIA. Well said: that was laid on with a trowel.

TOUCHSTONE. Nay, if I keep not my rank,—

ROSALIND. Thou losest thy old smell.

LE BEAU. You amaze me, ladies: I would have told you of good wrestling, which you have lost the sight of.

ROSALIND. Yet tell us the manner of the wrestling.

LE BEAU. I will tell you the beginning; and, if it please your ladyships, you may see the end; for the best is yet to do; and here, where you are, they are coming to perform it.

CELIA. Well, the beginning, that is dead and buried.

LE BEAU. There comes an old man and his three sons,—

CELIA. I could match this beginning with an old tale.

LE BEAU. Three proper young men, of excellent growth and presence.

ROSALIND. With bills on their necks, 'Be it known unto all men by these presents.'

LE BEAU. The eldest of the three wrestled with Charles, the Duke's wrestler; which Charles in a moment threw him, and broke three of his ribs, that there is little hope of life in him: so he served the second, and so the third. Yonder they lie; the poor old man, their father, making such pitiful dole over them that all the beholders take his part with weeping.

ROSALIND. Alas!

TOUCHSTONE. But what is the sport, monsieur, that the ladies have lost?

LE BEAU. Why, this that I speak of.

TOUCHSTONE. Thus men may grow wiser every day: it is the first time that ever I heard breaking of ribs was sport for ladies.

CELIA. Or I, I promise thee.

ROSALIND. But is there any else longs to see this broken music in his sides? is there yet another dotes upon rib-breaking? Shall we see this wrestling, cousin?

LE BEAU. You must, if you stay here; for here is the place appointed for the wrestling, and they are ready to perform it.

CELIA. Yonder, sure, they are coming: let us now stay and see it.

Flourish. Enter DUKE FREDERICK, LORDS, ORLANDO,
            CHARLES, *and* ATTENDANTS.]

DUKE FREDERICK. Come on: since the youth will not be entreated, his own peril on his forwardness.

ROSALIND. Is yonder the man?

LE BEAU. Even he, madam.

CELIA. Alas, he is too young! yet he looks successfully.

DUKE FREDERICK. How now, daughter and cousin! are you
crept hither to see the wrestling?

ROSALIND. Aye, my liege, so please you give us leave.

DUKE FREDERICK. You will take little delight in it, I can tell
you, there is such odds in the man. In pity of the challenger's youth I would fain dissuade him, but he will not
be entreated. Speak to him, ladies; see if you can move him.

CELIA. Call him hither, good Monsieur Le Beau.

DUKE FREDERICK. Do so: I 'll not be by.

LE BEAU. Monsieur the challenger, the princess calls for you.

ORLANDO. I attend them with all respect and duty.

ROSALIND. Young man, have you challenged Charles the
wrestler?

ORLANDO. No, fair princess; he is the general challenger: I
come but in, as others do, to try with him the strength of
my youth.

CELIA. Young gentleman, your spirits are too bold for your
years. You have seen cruel proof of this man's strength: if
you saw yourself with your eyes, or knew yourself with
your judgment, the fear of your adventure would counsel
you to a more equal enterprise. We pray you, for your
own sake, to embrace your own safety, and give over this
attempt.

ROSALIND. Do, young sir; your reputation shall not therefore
be misprised: we will make it our suit to the Duke that the
wrestling might not go forward.

ORLANDO. I beseech you, punish me not with your hard
thoughts; wherein I confess me much guilty, to deny so
fair and excellent ladies any thing. But let your fair eyes
and gentle wishes go with me to my trial: wherein if I be
foiled, there is but one shamed that was never gracious;

if killed, but one dead that is willing to be so: I shall do my friends no wrong, for I have none to lament me; the world no injury, for in it I have nothing: only in the world I fill up a place, which may be better supplied when I have made it empty.

ROSALIND. The little strength that I have, I would it were with you.

CELIA. And mine, to eke out hers.

ROSALIND. Fare you well: pray heaven I be deceived in you!

CELIA. Your heart's desires be with you!

CHARLES. Come, where is this young gallant that is so desirous to lie with his mother earth?

ORLANDO. Ready, sir; but his will hath in it a more modest working.

DUKE FREDERICK. You shall try but one fall.

CHARLES. No, I warrant your Grace, you shall not entreat him to a second, that have so mightily persuaded him from a first.

ORLANDO. You mean to mock me after; you should not have mocked me before: but come your ways.

ROSALIND. Now Hercules be thy speed, young man!

CELIA. I would I were invisible, to catch the strong fellow by the leg.   [*They wrestle.*

ROSALIND. O excellent young man!

CELIA. If I had a thunderbolt in mine eye, I can tell who should down.   [*Shout.* CHARLES *is thrown.*

DUKE FREDERICK. No more, no more.

ORLANDO. Yes, I beseech your Grace: I am not yet well breathed.

DUKE FREDERICK. How dost thou, Charles?

LE BEAU. He cannot speak, my lord.

DUKE FREDERICK. Bear him away. What is thy name, young man?

ORLANDO. Orlando, my liege; the youngest son of Sir Rowland de Boys.

DUKE FREDERICK. I would thou hadst been son to some man else:

The world esteem'd thy father honorable,

But I did find him still mine enemy:
Thou shouldst have better pleased me with this deed,
Hadst thou descended from another house.
But fare thee well; thou art a gallant youth:
I would thou hadst told me of another father.

[Exeunt DUKE FREDERICK, *train, and* LE BEAU.

CELIA. Were I my father, coz, would I do this?

ORLANDO. I am more proud to be Sir Rowland's son,
His youngest son; and would not change that calling,
To be adopted heir to Frederick.

ROSALIND. My father loved Sir Rowland as his soul,
And all the world was of my father's mind:
Had I before known this young man his son,
I should have given him tears unto entreaties,
Ere he should thus have ventured.

CELIA.   Gentle cousin,
Let us go thank him and encourage him:
My father's rough and envious disposition
Sticks me at heart. Sir, you have well deserved:
If you do keep your promises in love
But justly, as you have exceeded all promise,
Your mistress shall be happy.

ROSALIND.   Gentleman,

[Giving him a chain from her neck.

Wear this for me, one out of suits with fortune,
That could give more, but that her hand lacks means.
Shall we go, coz?

CELIA.   Aye. Fare you well, fair gentleman.

ORLANDO. Can I not say, I thank you? My better parts
Are all thrown down, and that which here stands up
Is but a quintain, a mere lifeless block.

ROSALIND. He calls us back: my pride fell with my fortunes;
I'll ask him what he would. Did you call, sir?
Sir, you have wrestled well and overthrown
More than your enemies.

CELIA.   Will you go, coz?

ROSALIND. Have with you. Fare you well.

[Exeunt ROSALIND *and* CELIA.

ORLANDO. What passion hangs these weights upon my tongue?
    I cannot speak to her, yet she urged conference.
    O poor Orlando, thou art overthrown!
    Or Charles or something weaker masters thee.

Re-enter LE BEAU.]

LE BEAU. Good sir, I do in friendship counsel you
    To leave this place. Albeit you have deserved
    High commendation, true applause, and love,
    Yet such is now the Duke's condition,
    That he misconstrues all that you have done.
    The Duke is humorous: what he is, indeed,
    More suits you to conceive than I to speak of.

ORLANDO. I thank you, sir: and, pray you, tell me this;
    Which of the two was daughter of the Duke,
    That here was at the wrestling?

LE BEAU. Neither his daughter, if we judge by manners;
    But yet, indeed, the lesser is his daughter:
    The other is daughter to the banish'd Duke,
    And here detain'd by her usurping uncle,
    To keep his daughter company; whose loves
    Are dearer than the natural bond of sisters.
    But I can tell you that of late this Duke
    Hath ta'en displeasure 'gainst his gentle niece,
    Grounded upon no other argument
    But that the people praise her for her virtues,
    And pity her for her good father's sake;
    And, on my life, his malice 'gainst the lady
    Will suddenly break forth. Sir, fare you well:
    Hereafter, in a better world than this,
    I shall desire more love and knowledge of you.

ORLANDO. I rest much bounden to you: fare you well.

                                          [*Exit* LE BEAU.

    Thus must I from the smoke into the smother;
    From tyrant Duke unto a tyrant brother:
    But heavenly Rosalind!   [*Exit.*

SCENE III — *A room in the palace.*

Enter CELIA *and* ROSALIND.]

CELIA. Why, cousin! why, Rosalind! Cupid have mercy! not a word?

ROSALIND. Not one to throw at a dog.

CELIA. No, thy words are too precious to be cast away upon curs; throw some of them at me; come, lame me with reasons.

ROSALIND. Then there were two cousins laid up; when the one should be lamed with reasons and the other mad without any.

CELIA. But is all this for your father?

ROSALIND. No, some of it is for my child's father. O, how full of briers is this working-day world!

CELIA. They are but burs, cousin, thrown upon thee in holiday foolery: if we walk not in the trodden paths, our very petticoats will catch them.

ROSALIND. I could shake them off my coat: these burs are in my heart.

CELIA. Hem them away.

ROSALIND. I would try, if I could cry hem and have him.

CELIA. Come, come, wrestle with thy affections.

ROSALIND. O, they take the part of a better wrestler than myself!

CELIA. O, a good wish upon you! you will try in time, in despite of a fall. But, turning these jests out of service, let us talk in good earnest: is it possible, on such a sudden, you should fall into so strong a liking with old Sir Rowland's youngest son?

ROSALIND. The Duke my father loved his father dearly.

CELIA. Doth it therefore ensue that you should love his son dearly? By this kind of chase, I should hate him, for my father hated his father dearly; yet I hate not Orlando.

ROSALIND. No, faith, hate him not, for my sake.

CELIA. Why should I not? doth he not deserve well?

ROSALIND. Let me love him for that, and do you love him be-
　cause I do. Look, here comes the Duke.

CELIA. With his eyes full of anger.

Enter DUKE FREDERICK, *with* LORDS.]

DUKE FREDERICK. Mistress, dispatch you with your safest haste
　And get you from our court.

ROSALIND.　　　　　　　　Me, uncle?

DUKE FREDERICK.　　　　　　　　You, cousin:
　Within these ten days if that thou be'st found
　So near our public court as twenty miles,
　Thou diest for it.

ROSALIND.　　　　I do beseech your Grace,
　Let me the knowledge of my fault bear with me:
　If with myself I hold intelligence,
　Or have acquaintance with mine own desires;
　If that I do not dream, or be not frantic,—
　As I do trust I am not,—then, dear uncle,
　Never so much as in a thought unborn
　Did I offend your Highness.

DUKE FREDERICK.　　　　　　Thus do all traitors:
　If their purgation did consist in words,
　They are as innocent as grace itself:
　Let it suffice thee that I trust thee not.

ROSALIND. Yet your mistrust cannot make me a traitor:
　Tell me whereon the likelihood depends.

DUKE FREDERICK. Thou art thy father's daughter; there's
　enough.

ROSALIND. So was I when your Highness took his dukedom;
　So was I when your Highness banish'd him:
　Treason is not inherited, my lord;
　Or, if we did derive it from our friends,
　What's that to me? my father was no traitor:
　Then, good my liege, mistake me not so much
　To think my poverty is treacherous.

CELIA. Dear sovereign, hear me speak.

DUKE FREDERICK. Aye, Celia; we stay'd her for your sake,
　Else had she with her father ranged along.

CELIA. I did not then entreat to have her stay;
    It was your pleasure and your own remorse:
    I was too young that time to value her;
    But now I know her: if she be a traitor,
    Why so am I; we still have slept together,
    Rose at an instant, learn'd, play'd, eat together,
    And wheresoe'er we went, like Juno's swans,
    Still we went coupled and inseparable.
DUKE FREDERICK. She is too subtle for thee; and her smooth-
        ness,
    Her very silence and her patience
    Speak to the people, and they pity her.
    Thou art a fool: she robs thee of thy name;
    And thou wilt show more bright and seem more virtuous
    When she is gone. Then open not thy lips:
    Firm and irrevocable is my doom
    Which I have pass'd upon her; she is banish'd.
CELIA. Pronounce that sentence then on me, my liege:
    I cannot live out of her company.
DUKE FREDERICK. You are a fool. You, niece, provide yourself:
    If you outstay the time, upon mine honor,
    And in the greatness of my word, you die.
                        [Exeunt DUKE FREDERICK and LORDS.
CELIA. O my poor Rosalind, whither wilt thou go?
    Wilt thou change fathers? I will give thee mine.
    I charge thee, be not thou more grieved than I am.
ROSALIND. I have more cause.
CELIA.   Thou hast not, cousin;
    Prithee, be cheerful: know'st thou not, the Duke
    Hath banish'd me, his daughter?
ROSALIND.   That he hath not.
CELIA. No, hath not? Rosalind lacks then the love
    Which teacheth thee that thou and I am one:
    Shall we be sunder'd? shall we part, sweet girl?
    No: let my father seek another heir.
    Therefore devise with me how we may fly,
    Whither to go and what to bear with us;
    And do not seek to take your change upon you,

To bear your griefs yourself and leave me out;
For, by this heaven, now at our sorrows pale,
Say what thou canst, I 'll go along with thee.

ROSALIND. Why, whither shall we go?

CELIA. To seek my uncle in the forest of Arden.

ROSALIND. Alas, what danger will it be to us,
Maids as we are, to travel forth so far!
Beauty provoketh thieves sooner than gold.

CELIA. I'll put myself in poor and mean attire
And with a kind of umber smirch my face;
The like do you: so shall we pass along
And never stir assailants.

ROSALIND.   Were it not better,
Because that I am more than common tall,
That I did suit me all points like a man?
A gallant curtle-axe upon my thigh,
A boar-spear in my hand; and—in my heart
Lie there what hidden woman's fear there will—
We'll have a swashing and a martial outside,
As many other mannish cowards have
That do outface it with their semblances.

CELIA. What shall I call thee when thou art a man?

ROSALIND. I 'll have no worse a name than Jove's own page;
And therefore look you call me Ganymede.
But what will you be call'd?

CELIA. Something that hath a reference to my state:
No longer Celia, but Aliena.

ROSALIND. But, cousin, what if we assay'd to steal
The clownish fool out of your father's court?
Would he not be a comfort to our travel?

CELIA. He 'll go along o'er the wide world with me;
Leave me alone to woo him. Let's away,
And get our jewels and our wealth together;
Devise the fittest time and safest way
To hide us from pursuit that will be made
After my flight. Now go we in content
To liberty and not to banishment.   [*Exeunt.*

ACT II

Scene I — *The Forest of Arden.*

Enter Duke Senior, Amiens, *and two or three* Lords,
    like foresters.]

DUKE SENIOR. Now, my co-mates and brothers in exile,
    Hath not old custom made this life more sweet
    Than that of painted pomp? Are not these woods
    More free from peril than the envious court?
    Here feel we but the penalty of Adam,
    The season's difference; as the icy fang
    And churlish chiding of the winter's wind,
    Which, when it bites and blows upon my body,
    Even till I shrink with cold, I smile and say
    'This is no flattery: these are counsellors
    That feelingly persuade me what I am.'
    Sweet are the uses of adversity;
    Which, like the toad, ugly and venomous,
    Wears yet a precious jewel in his head:
    And this our life exempt from public haunt
    Finds tongues in trees, books in the running brooks,
    Sermons in stones and good in every thing.
    I would not change it.
AMIENS.   Happy is your Grace,
    That can translate the stubbornness of fortune
    Into so quiet and so sweet a style.
DUKE SENIOR. Come, shall we go and kill us venison?
    And yet it irks me the poor dappled fools,
    Being native burghers of this desert city,
    Should in their own confines with forked heads
    Have their round haunches gored.
FIRST LORD.   Indeed, my Lord,
    The melancholy Jaques grieves at that,
    And, in that kind, swears you do more usurp

Than doth your brother that hath banish'd you.
To-day my Lord of Amiens and myself
Did steal behind him as he lay along
Under an oak whose antique root peeps out
Upon the brook that brawls along this wood:
To the which place a poor sequester'd stag,
That from the hunter's aim had ta'en a hurt,
Did come to languish, and indeed, my lord,
The wretched animal heaved forth such groans,
That their discharge did stretch his leathern coat
Almost to bursting, and the big round tears
Coursed one another down his innocent nose
In piteous chase; and thus the hairy fool,
Much marked of the melancholy Jaques,
Stood on the extremest verge of the swift brook,
Augmenting it with tears.

DUKE SENIOR.　　　　　　　But what said Jaques?
Did he not moralize this spectacle?

FIRST LORD. O, yes, into a thousand similes.
First, for his weeping into the needless stream;
'Poor deer,' quoth he, 'thou makest a testament
As worldlings do, giving thy sum of more
To that which had too much:' then, being there alone,
Left and abandon'd of his velvet friends;
' 'Tis right,' quoth he; 'thus misery doth part
The flux of company:' anon a careless herd,
Full of the pasture, jumps along by him
And never stays to greet him; 'Aye,' quoth Jaques,
'Sweep on, you fat and greasy citizens;
'Tis just the fashion: wherefore do you look
Upon that poor and broken bankrupt there?'
Thus most invectively he pierceth through
The body of the country, city, court,
Yea, and of this our life; swearing that we
Are mere usurpers, tyrants and what's worse,
To fright the animals and to kill them up
In their assign'd and native dwelling-place.

DUKE SENIOR. And did you leave him in this contemplation?

SECOND LORD. We did, my lord, weeping and commenting
   Upon the sobbing deer.
DUKE SENIOR.   Show me the place!
   I love to cope him in these sullen fits,
   For then he's full of matter.
FIRST LORD. I 'll bring you to him straight.   [Exeunt.

SCENE II — *A room in the palace.*

Enter DUKE FREDERICK, *with* LORDS.]
DUKE FREDERICK. Can it be possible that no man saw them?
   It cannot be: some villains of my court
   Are of consent and sufferance in this.
FIRST LORD. I cannot hear of any that did see her.
   The ladies, her attendants of her chamber,
   Saw her a-bed, and in the morning early
   They found the bed untreasured of their mistress.
SECOND LORD. My lord, the roynish clown, at whom so oft
   Your Grace was wont to laugh, is also missing.
   Hisperia, the princess' gentlewoman,
   Confesses that she secretly o'erheard
   Your daughter and her cousin much commend
   The parts and graces of the wrestler
   That did but lately foil the sinewy Charles;
   And she believes, wherever they are gone,
   That youth is surely in their company.
DUKE FREDERICK. Send to his brother; fetch that gallant hither;
   If he be absent, bring his brother to me;
   I'll make him find him: do this suddenly,
   And let not search and inquisition quail
   To bring again these foolish runaways.   [Exeunt.

SCENE III — *Before* OLIVER'S *house.*

Enter ORLANDO *and* ADAM, *meeting.*]
ORLANDO. Who's there?
ADAM. What, my young master? O my gentle master!
   O my sweet master! O you memory

Of old Sir Rowland! why, what make you here?
Why are you virtuous? why do people love you?
And wherefore are you gentle, strong and valiant?
Why would you be so fond to overcome
The bonny priser of the humorous Duke?
Your praise is come too swiftly home before you.
Know you not, master, to some kind of men
Their graces serve them but as enemies?
No more do yours: your virtues, gentle master,
Are sanctified and holy traitors to you.
O, what a world is this, when what is comely
Envenoms him that bears it!

ORLANDO. Why, what's the matter?

ADAM.   O unhappy youth!
Come not within these doors; within this roof
The enemy of all your graces lives:
Your brother—no, no brother; yet the son—
Yet not the son, I will not call him son,
Of him I was about to call his father,—
Hath heard your praises, and this night he means
To burn the lodging where you use to lie
And you within it: if he fail of that,
He will have other means to cut you off.
I overheard him and his practices.
This is no place; this house is but a butchery:
Abhor it, fear it, do not enter it.

ORLANDO. Why, whither, Adam, wouldst thou have me go?

ADAM. No matter whither, so you come not here.

ORLANDO. What, wouldst thou have me go and beg my food?
Or with a base and boisterous sword enforce
A thievish living on the common road?
This I must do, or know not what to do:
Yet this I will not do, do how I can;
I rather will subject me to the malice
Of a diverted blood and bloody brother.

ADAM. But do not so. I have five hundred crowns,
The thrifty hire I saved under your father,
Which I did store to be my foster-nurse

When service should in my old limbs lie lame,
And unregarded age in corners thrown:
Take that, and He that doth the ravens feed,
Yea, providently caters for the sparrow,
Be comfort to my age! Here is the gold;
All this I give you. Let me be your servant:
Though I look old, yet I am strong and lusty;
For in my youth I never did apply
Hot and rebellious liquors in my blood,
Nor did not with unbashful forehead woo
The means of weakness and debility;
Therefore my age is as a lusty winter,
Frosty, but kindly: let me go with you;
I 'll do the service of a younger man
In all your business and necessities.

ORLANDO. O good old man, how well in thee appears
The constant service of the antique world,
When service sweat for duty, not for meed!
Thou art not for the fashion of these times,
Where none will sweat but for promotion,
And having that do choke their service up
Even with the having: it is not so with thee.
But, poor old man, thou prunest a rotten tree,
That cannot so much as a blossom yield
In lieu of all thy pains and husbandry.
But come thy ways; we 'll go along together,
And ere we have thy youthful wages spent,
We 'll light upon some settled low content.

ADAM. Master, go on, and I will follow thee,
To the last gasp, with truth and loyalty.
From seventeen years till now almost fourscore
Here lived I, but now live here no more.
At seventeen years many their fortunes seek;
But at fourscore it is too late a week:
Yet fortune cannot recompense me better
Than to die well and not my master's debtor.　　　[*Exeunt.*

SCENE IV — *The Forest of Arden.*

Enter ROSALIND *for Ganymede,* CELIA *for Aliena,*
        and TOUCHSTONE.]

ROSALIND. O Jupiter, how weary are my spirits!

TOUCHSTONE. I care not for my spirits, if my legs were not weary.

ROSALIND. I could find in my heart to disgrace my man's apparel and to cry like a woman; but I must comfort the weaker vessel, as doublet and hose ought to show itself courageous to petticoat: therefore, courage, good Aliena.

CELIA. I pray you, bear with me; I cannot go no further.

TOUCHSTONE. For my part, I had rather bear with you than bear you: yet I should bear no cross, if I did bear you; for I think you have no money in your purse.

ROSALIND. Well, this is the forest of Arden.

TOUCHSTONE. Aye, now am I in Arden; the more fool I; when I was at home, I was in a better place: but travelers must be content.

ROSALIND. Aye, be so, good Touchstone.

Enter CORIN *and* SILVIUS.]

Look you, who comes here; a young man and an old in solemn talk.

CORIN. That is the way to make her scorn you still.

SILVIUS. O Corin, that thou knew'st how I do love her!

CORIN. I partly guess; for I have loved ere now.

SILVIUS. No, Corin, being old, thou canst not guess,
Though in thy youth thou wast as true a lover
As ever sigh'd upon a midnight pillow:
But if thy love were ever like to mine,—
As sure I think did never man love so,
How many actions most ridiculous
Hast thou been drawn to by thy fantasy?

CORIN. Into a thousand that I have forgotten.

SILVIUS. O, thou didst then ne'er love so heartily!
If thou remember'st not the slightest folly
That ever love did make thee run into,

Thou hast not loved:
Or if thou hast not sat as I do now,
Wearing thy hearer in thy mistress' praise,
Thou hast not loved:
Or if thou hast not broke from company
Abruptly, as my passion now makes me,
Thou hast not loved.
O Phebe, Phebe, Phebe!   [*Exit.*

ROSALIND. Alas, poor shepherd! searching of thy wound, I
have by hard adventure found mine own.

TOUCHSTONE. And I mine. I remember, when I was in love
I broke my sword upon a stone and bid him take that for
coming a-night to Jane Smile: and I remember the kissing
of her batler and the cow's dugs that her pretty chopt hands
had milked: and I remember the wooing of a peascod instead of her; from whom I took two cods and, giving her
them again, said with weeping tears 'Wear these for my
sake.' We that are true lovers run into strange capers; but as
all is mortal in nature, so is all nature in love mortal in folly.

ROSALIND. Thou speakest wiser than thou art ware of.

TOUCHSTONE. Nay, I shall ne'er be ware of mine own wit till
I break my shins against it.

ROSALIND. Jove, Jove! this shepherd's passion
Is much upon my fashion.

TOUCHSTONE. And mine; but it grows something stale with me.

CELIA. I pray you, one of you question yond man
If he for gold will give us any food:
I faint almost to death.

TOUCHSTONE.   Holla, you clown!

ROSALIND. Peace, fool: he's not thy kinsman.

CORIN.   Who calls?

TOUCHSTONE. Your betters, sir.

CORIN.   Else are they very wretched.

ROSALIND. Peace, I say. Good even to you, friend.

CORIN. And to you, gentle sir, and to you all.

ROSALIND. I prithee, shepherd, if that love or gold
Can in this desert place buy entertainment,
Bring us where we may rest ourselves and feed:

Here's a young maid with travel much oppress'd
And faints for succor.

CORIN.   Fair sir, I pity her
And wish, for her sake more than for mine own,
My fortunes were more able to relieve her;
But I am shepherd to another man
And do not shear the fleeces that I graze:
My master is of churlish disposition
And little recks to find the way to heaven
By doing deeds of hospitality:
Besides, his cote, his flocks and bounds of feed
Are now on sale, and at our sheepcote now,
By reason of his absence, there is nothing
That you will feed on; but what is, come see,
And in my voice most welcome shall you be.

ROSALIND. What is he that shall buy his flock and pasture?

CORIN. That young swain that you saw here but erewhile,
That little cares for buying any thing.

ROSALIND. I pray thee, if it stand with honesty,
Buy thou the cottage, pasture and the flock,
And thou shalt have to pay for it of us.

CELIA. And we will mend thy wages. I like this place,
And willingly could waste my time in it.

CORIN. Assuredly the thing is to be sold:
Go with me: if you like upon report
The soil, the profit and this kind of life,
I will your very faithful feeder be
And buy it with your gold right suddenly.   [*Exeunt.*

SCENE V — *The forest.*

Enter AMIENS, JAQUES, *and others.*]

SONG.

AMIENS. Under the greenwood tree
          Who loves to lie with me,
          And turn his merry note
          Unto the sweet bird's throat,

    Come hither, come hither, come hither:
       Here shall he see
       No enemy
    But winter and rough weather.

JAQUES. More, more, I prithee, more.

AMIENS. It will make you melancholy, Monsieur Jaques.

JAQUES. I thank it. More, I prithee, more. I can suck melancholy out of a song, as a weasel sucks eggs. More, I prithee, more.

AMIENS. My voice is ragged: I know I cannot please you.

JAQUES. I do not desire you to please me; I do desire you to sing. Come, more; another stanzo: call you 'em stanzos?

AMIENS. What you will, Monsieur Jaques.

JAQUES. Nay, I care not for their names; they owe me nothing. Will you sing?

AMIENS. More at your request than to please myself.

JAQUES. Well then, if ever I thank any man, I 'll thank you; but that they call compliment is like the encounter of two dog-apes, and when a man thanks me heartily, methinks I have given him a penny and he renders me the beggarly thanks. Come, sing; and you that will not, hold your tongues.

AMIENS. Well, I 'll end the song. Sirs, cover the while; the Duke will drink under this tree. He hath been all this day to look you.

JAQUES. And I have been all this day to avoid him. He is too disputable for my company: I think of as many matters as he; but I give heaven thanks, and make no boast of them. Come, warble, come.

SONG.

    Who doth ambition shun, [*All together here.*
       And loves to live i' the sun,
       Seeking the food he eats,
       And pleased with what he gets,
    Come hither, come hither, come hither:
       Here shall he see
       No enemy
    But winter and rough weather.

JAQUES. I 'll give you a verse to this note, that I made yesterday in despite of my invention.

AMIENS. And I 'll sing it.

JAQUES. Thus it goes:—

> If it do come to pass
>   That any man turn ass,
>   Leaving his wealth and ease
>   A stubborn will to please,
> Ducdame, ducdame, ducdame:
>   Here shall he see
>   Gross fools as he,
> And if he will come to me.

AMIENS. What's that 'ducdame'?

JAQUES. 'Tis a Greek invocation, to call fools into a circle. I 'll
go sleep, if I can; if I cannot, I 'll rail against all the first-
born of Egypt.

AMIENS. And I 'll go seek the Duke: his banquet is prepared.
                                                    [*Exeunt severally.*

SCENE VI — *The forest.*

Enter ORLANDO *and* ADAM.]

ADAM. Dear master, I can go no further; O, I die for food!
Here lie I down, and measure out my grave. Farewell, kind
master.

ORLANDO. Why, how now, Adam! no greater heart in thee?
Live a little; comfort a little; cheer thyself a little. If this
uncouth forest yield anything savage, I will either be food
for it or bring it for food to thee. Thy conceit is nearer death
than thy powers. For my sake be comfortable; hold death
awhile at the arm's end: I will here be with thee presently;
and if I bring thee not something to eat, I will give thee
leave to die: but if thou diest before I come, thou art a
mocker of my labor. Well said! thou lookest cheerly, and
I 'll be with thee quickly. Yet thou liest in the bleak air:
come, I will bear thee to some shelter; and thou shalt not
die for lack of a dinner, if there live any thing in this desert.
Cheerly, good Adam!   [*Exeunt.*

SCENE VII — *The forest.*

A table set out. Enter DUKE SENIOR, AMIENS, *and*
    LORDS *like outlaws.*]

DUKE SENIOR. I think he be transform'd into a beast;
    For I can no where find him like a man.

FIRST LORD. My lord, he is but even now gone hence:
    Here was he merry, hearing of a song.

DUKE SENIOR. If he, compact of jars, grow musical,
    We shall have shortly discord in the spheres.
    Go, seek him: tell him I would speak with him.

Enter JAQUES.]

FIRST LORD. He saves my labor by his own approach.

DUKE SENIOR. Why, how now, monsieur! what a life is this,
    That your poor friends must woo your company?
    What, you look merrily!

JAQUES. A fool, a fool! I met a fool i' the forest,
    A motley fool; a miserable world!
    As I do live by food, I met a fool;
    Who laid him down and bask'd him in the sun
    And rail'd on Lady Fortune in good terms,
    In good set terms, and yet a motley fool.
    'Good morrow, fool,' quoth I. 'No sir,' quoth he,
    'Call me not fool till heaven hath sent me fortune:'
    And then he drew a dial from his poke,
    And, looking on it with lack-luster eye,
    Says very wisely, 'It is ten o'clock:
    Thus we may see,' quoth he, 'how the world wags:
    'Tis but an hour ago since it was nine;
    And after one hour more 'twill be eleven;
    And so, from hour to hour, we ripe and ripe,
    And then, from hour to hour, we rot and rot;
    And thereby hangs a tale.' When I did hear
    The motley fool thus moral on the time,
    My lungs began to crow like chanticleer,
    That fools should be so deep-contemplative;
    And I did laugh sans intermission

An hour by his dial. O noble fool!
A worthy fool! Motley's the only wear.

DUKE SENIOR. What fool is this?

JAQUES. O worthy fool! One that hath been a courtier,
And says, if ladies be but young and fair,
They have the gift to know it: and in his brain,
Which is as dry as the remainder biscuit
After a voyage, he hath strange places cramm'd
With observation, the which he vents
In mangled forms. O that I were a fool!
I am ambitious for a motley coat.

DUKE SENIOR. Thou shalt have one.

JAQUES.　　　　　　　　　　It is my only suit;
Provided that you weed your better judgments
Of all opinion that grows rank in them
That I am wise. I must have liberty
Withal, as large a charter as the wind,
To blow on whom I please; for so fools have;
And they that are most galled with my folly,
They most must laugh. And why, sir, must they so?
The 'why' is plain as way to parish church:
He that a fool doth very wisely hit
Doth very foolishly, although he smart,
Not to seem senseless of the bob; if not,
The wise man's folly is anatomized
Even by the squandering glances of the fool.
Invest me in my motley; give me leave
To speak my mind, and I will through and through
Cleanse the foul body of the infected world,
If they will patiently receive my medicine.

DUKE SENIOR. Fie on thee! I can tell what thou wouldst do.

JAQUES. What, for a counter, would I do but good?

DUKE SENIOR. Most mischievous foul sin, in chiding sin:
For thou thyself hast been a libertine,
As sensual as the brutish sting itself;
And all the embossed sores and headed evils,
That thou with license of free foot has caught,
Wouldst thou disgorge into the general world.

JAQUES. Why, who cries out on pride,
    That can therein tax any private party?
    Doth it not flow as hugely as the sea,
    Till that the weary very means do ebb?
    What woman in the city do I name,
    When that I say the city-woman bears
    The cost of princes on unworthy shoulders?
    Who can come in and say that I mean her,
    When such a one as she such is her neighbor?
    Or what is he of basest function,
    That says his bravery is not on my cost,
    Thinking that I mean him, but therein suits
    His folly to the mettle of my speech?
    There then; how then? what then? Let me see wherein
    My tongue hath wrong'd him: if it do him right,
    Then he hath wrong'd himself: if he be free,
    Why then my taxing like a wild-goose flies,
    Unclaim'd of any man. But who comes here?

Enter ORLANDO, with his sword drawn.]

ORLANDO. Forbear, and eat no more.

JAQUES.   Why, I have eat none yet.

ORLANDO. Nor shalt not, till necessity be served.

JAQUES. Of what kind should this cock come of?

DUKE SENIOR. Art thou thus bolden'd, man, by thy distress?
    Or else a rude despiser of good manners,
    That in civility thou seem'st so empty?

ORLANDO. You touch'd my vein at first; the thorny point
    Of bare distress hath ta'en from me the show
    Of smooth civility: yet am I inland bred
    And know some nurture. But forbear; I say:
    He dies that touches any of this fruit
    Till I and my affairs are answered.

JAQUES. An you will not be answered with reason, I must die.

DUKE SENIOR. What would you have? Your gentleness shall
        force,
    More than your force move us to gentleness.

ORLANDO. I almost die for food; and let me have it.

DUKE SENIOR. Sit down and feed, and welcome to our table.

ORLANDO. Speak you so gently? Pardon me, I pray you:
  I thought that all things had been savage here;
  And therefore put I on the countenance
  Of stern commandment. But whate'er you are
  That in this desert inaccessible,
  Under the shade of melancholy boughs,
  Lose and neglect the creeping hours of time;
  If ever you have look'd on better days,
  If ever been where bells have knoll'd to church,
  If ever sat at any good man's feast,
  If ever from your eyelids wiped a tear
  And know what 'tis to pity and be pitied,
  Let gentleness my strong enforcement be:
  In the which hope I blush, and hide my sword.

DUKE SENIOR. True is it that we have seen better days,
  And have with holy bell been knoll'd to church,
  And sat at good men's feasts, and wiped our eyes
  Of drops that sacred pity hath engender'd:
  And therefore sit you down in gentleness
  And take upon command what help we have
  That to your wanting may be minister'd.

ORLANDO. Then but forbear your food a little while,
  Whiles, like a doe, I go to find my fawn
  And give it food. There is an old poor man,
  Who after me hath many a weary step
  Limp'd in pure love: till he be first suffic'd,
  Oppress'd with two weak evils, age and hunger,
  I will not touch a bit.

DUKE SENIOR.   Go find him out,
  And we will nothing waste till you return.

ORLANDO. I thank ye; and be blest for your good comfort!
                                              [*Exit.*

DUKE SENIOR. Thou seest we are not all alone unhappy:
  This wide and universal theater
  Presents more woeful pageants than the scene
  Wherein we play in.

JAQUES. All the world's a stage
And all the men and women merely players:
They have their exits and their entrances;
And one man in his time plays many parts,
His acts being seven ages. At first the infant,
Mewling and puking in the nurse's arms.
Then the whining school-boy, with his satchel
And shining morning face, creeping like snail
Unwillingly to school. And then the lover,
Sighing like furnace, with a woeful ballad
Made to his mistress' eyebrow. Then a soldier,
Full of strange oaths, and bearded like the pard,
Jealous in honor, sudden and quick in quarrel,
Seeking the bubble reputation
Even in the cannon's mouth. And then the justice,
In fair round belly with good capon lined,
With eyes severe and beard of formal cut,
Full of wise saws and modern instances;
And so he plays his part. The sixth age shifts
Into the lean and slipper'd pantaloon,
With spectacles on nose and pouch on side,
His youthful hose, well saved, a world too wide
For his shrunk shank; and his big manly voice,
Turning again toward childish treble, pipes
And whistles in his sound. Last scene of all,
That ends this strange eventful history,
Is second childishness and mere oblivion,
Sans teeth, sans eyes, sans taste, sans every thing.

Re-enter ORLANDO *with* ADAM.]

DUKE SENIOR. Welcome. Set down your venerable burthen,
And let him feed.

ORLANDO. I thank you most for him.

ADAM. So had you need:
I scarce can speak to thank you for myself.

DUKE SENIOR. Welcome; fall to: I will not trouble you
As yet, to question you about your fortunes.
Give us some music; and, good cousin, sing.

Song.

AMIENS. Blow, blow, thou winter wind,
  Thou art not so unkind
   As man's ingratitude;
  Thy tooth is not so keen,
  Because thou art not seen,
   Although thy breath be rude
 Heigh-ho! sing, heigh-ho! unto the green holly:
 Most friendship is feigning, most loving mere folly:
  Then heigh-ho, the holly!
   This life is most jolly.

  Freeze, freeze, thou bitter sky,
  That dost not bite so nigh
   As benefits forgot:
  Though thou the waters warp,
  Thy sting is not so sharp
   As friend remember'd not.
 Heigh-ho! sing, &c.

DUKE SENIOR. If that you were the good Sir Rowland's son,
As you have whisper'd faithfully you were,
And as mine eye doth his effigies witness
Most truly limn'd and living in your face,
Be truly welcome hither: I am the Duke
That loved your father: the residue of your fortune,
Go to my cave and tell me. Good old man,
Thou art right welcome as thy master is.
Support him by the arm. Give me your hand,
And let me all your fortunes understand.   *[Exeunt.*

ACT III

SCENE I — *A room in the palace.*

Enter DUKE FREDERICK, LORDS, *and* OLIVER.]

DUKE FREDERICK. Not see him since? Sir, sir, that cannot be:
　But were I not the better part made mercy,
　I should not seek an absent argument
　Of my revenge, thou present. But look to it:
　Find out thy brother, wheresoe'er he is;
　Seek him with candle; bring him dead or living
　Within this twelvemonth, or turn thou no more
　To seek a living in our territory.
　Thy lands and all things that thou dost call thine
　Worth seizure do we seize into our hands,
　Till thou canst quit thee by thy brother's mouth
　Of what we think against thee.

OLIVER. O that your Highness knew my heart in this!
　I never loved my brother in my life.

DUKE FREDERICK. More villain thou. Well, push him out of
　doors;
　And let my officers of such a nature
　Make an extent upon his house and lands:
　Do this expediently and turn him going.   [*Exeunt.*

SCENE II — *The forest.*

Enter ORLANDO, *with a paper.*]

ORLANDO. Hang there, my verse, in witness of my love:
　　And thou, thrice-crowned queen of night, survey
　With thy chaste eye, from thy pale sphere above,
　　Thy huntress' name that my full life doth sway.
　O Rosalind! these trees shall be my books
　　And in their barks my thoughts I 'll character;
　That every eye which in this forest looks

Shall see thy virtue witness'd every where.
Run, run, Orlando; carve on every tree
The fair, the chaste and unexpressive she.   [*Exit.*
Enter CORIN *and* TOUCHSTONE.]

CORIN. And how like you this shepherd's life,
  Master Touchstone?

TOUCHSTONE. Truly, shepherd, in respect of itself, it is a good
  life; but in respect that it is a shepherd's life, it is naught.
  In respect that it is solitary, I like it very well; but in respect that it is private, it is a very vile life. Now, in respect
  it is in the fields, it pleaseth me well; but in respect it is not
  in the court, it is tedious. As it is a spare life, look you, it
  fits my humor well; but as there is no more plenty in it, it
  goes much against my stomach. Hast any philosophy in
  thee, shepherd?

CORIN. No more but that I know the more one sickens the
  worse at ease he is; and that he that wants money, means
  and content is without their good friends; that the property
  of rain is to wet and fire to burn; that good pasture makes
  fat sheep, and that a great cause of the night is lack of the
  sun; that he that hath learned no wit by nature nor art may
  complain of good breeding or comes of a very dull kindred.

TOUCHSTONE. Such a one is a natural philosopher.
  Wast ever in court, shepherd?

CORIN. No, truly.

TOUCHSTONE. Then thou art damned.

CORIN. Nay, I hope.

TOUCHSTONE. Truly, thou art damned, like an ill-roasted egg
  on one side.

CORIN. For not being at court? Your reason.

TOUCHSTONE. Why, if thou never wast at court, thou never
  sawest good manners; if thou never sawest good manners,
  then thy manners must be wicked; and wickedness is sin,
  and sin is damnation. Thou art in a parlous state, shepherd.

CORIN. Not a whit, Touchstone: those that are good manners
  at the court are as ridiculous in the country as the behavior
  of the country is most mockable at the court. You told me
  you salute not at the court, but you kiss your hands: that

courtesy would be uncleanly, if courtiers were shepherds.

TOUCHSTONE. Instance, briefly; come, instance.

CORIN. Why, we are still handling our ewes, and their fells, you know, are greasy.

TOUCHSTONE. Why, do not your courtier's hands sweat? and is not the grease of a mutton as wholesome as the sweat of a man? Shallow, shallow. A better instance, I say; come.

CORIN. Besides, our hands are hard.

TOUCHSTONE. Your lips will feel them the sooner. Shallow again. A more sounder instance, come.

CORIN. And they are often tarred over with the surgery of our sheep; and would you have us kiss tar? The courtier's hands are perfumed with civet.

TOUCHSTONE. Most shallow man! thou worm's-meat, in respect of a good piece of flesh indeed! Learn of the wise, and perpend: civet is of a baser birth than tar, the very uncleanly flux of a cat. Mend the instance, shepherd.

CORIN. You have too courtly a wit for me: I 'll rest.

TOUCHSTONE. Wilt thou rest damned? God help thee, shallow man! God make incision in thee! thou art raw.

CORIN. Sir, I am a true laborer: I earn that I eat, get that I wear, owe no man hate, envy no man's happiness, glad of other men's good, content with my harm and the greatest of my pride is to see my ewes graze and my lambs suck.

TOUCHSTONE. That is another simple sin in you, to bring the ewes and the rams together and to offer to get your living by the copulation of cattle; to be bawd to a bell-wether, and to betray a she-lamb of a twelvemonth to a crooked-pated, old, cuckoldly ram, out of all reasonable match. If thou beest not damned for this, the devil himself will have no shepherds; I cannot see else how thou shouldst 'scape.

CORIN. Here comes young Master Ganymede, my new mistress's brother.

Enter ROSALIND, *with a paper, reading.*]

ROSALIND. From the east to western Ind,
No jewel is like Rosalind.
Her worth, being mounted on the wind,
Through all the world bears Rosalind.

> All the pictures fairest lined
> Are but black to Rosalind.
> Let no face be kept in mind
> But the fair of Rosalind.

TOUCHSTONE. I'll rhyme you so eight years together, dinners
and suppers and sleeping-hours excepted: it is the right
butter-women's rank to market.

ROSALIND. Out, fool!

TOUCHSTONE. For a taste:

> If a hart do lack a hind,
> Let him seek out Rosalind.
> If the cat will after kind,
> So be sure will Rosalind.
> Winter garments must be lined,
> So must slender Rosalind.
> They that reap must sheaf and bind;
> Then to cart with Rosalind.
> Sweetest nut hath sourest rind,
> Such a nut is Rosalind.
> He that sweetest rose will find,
> Must find love's prick and Rosalind.

This is the very false gallop of verses: why do you infect
yourself with them?

ROSALIND. Peace! you dull fool: I found them on a tree.

TOUCHSTONE. Truly, the tree yields bad fruit.

ROSALIND. I'll graff it with you, and then I shall graff it with
a medlar: then it will be the earliest fruit i' the country; for
you'll be rotten ere you be half ripe, and that's the right
virtue of the medlar.

TOUCHSTONE. You have said; but whether wisely or no, let the
forest judge.

Enter CELIA, with a writing.]

ROSALIND. Peace!
Here comes my sister, reading: stand aside.

CELIA. [*Reads*]

> Why should this a desert be?
> For it is unpeopled? No;

Tongues I 'll hang on every tree,
  That shall civil sayings show:
Some, how brief the life of man
  Runs his erring pilgrimage,
That the stretching of a span
  Buckles in his sum of age;
Some of violated vows
  'Twixt the souls of friend and friend:
But upon the fairest boughs,
  Or at every sentence end,
Will I Rosalinda write,
  Teaching all that read to know
The quintessence of every sprite
  Heaven would in little show.
Therefore Heaven Nature charged
  That one body should be fill'd
With all graces wide-enlarged:
  Nature presently distill'd
Helen's cheek, but not her heart,
  Cleopatra's majesty,
Atalanta's better part,
  Sad Lucretia's modesty.
Thus Rosalind of many parts
  By heavenly synod was devised;
Of many faces, eyes and hearts,
  To have the touches dearest prized.
Heaven would that she these gifts should have,
And I to live and die her slave.

ROSALIND. O most gentle pulpiter! what tedious homily of love
  have you wearied your parishioners withal, and never cried
  'Have patience, good people!'
CELIA. How now! back, friends! Shepherd, go off a little. Go
  with him, sirrah.
TOUCHSTONE. Come, shepherd, let us make an honorable re-
  treat; though not with bag and baggage, yet with script
  and scrippage.   [Exeunt CORIN and TOUCHSTONE.

CELIA. Didst thou hear these verses?

ROSALIND. O, yes, I heard them all, and more too; for some of them had in them more feet than the verses would bear.

CELIA. That's no matter: the feet might bear the verses.

ROSALIND. Aye, but the feet were lame and could not bear themselves without the verse and therefore stood lamely in the verse.

CELIA. But didst thou hear without wondering how thy name should be hanged and carved upon these trees?

ROSALIND. I was seven of the nine days out of the wonder before you came; for look here what I found on a palm tree. I was never so berhymed since Pythagoras' time, that I was an Irish rat, which I can hardly remember.

CELIA. Trow you who hath done this?

ROSALIND. Is it a man?

CELIA. And a chain, that you once wore, about his neck. Change you color?

ROSALIND. I prithee, who?

CELIA. O Lord, Lord! it is a hard matter for friends to meet; but mountains may be removed with earthquakes and so encounter.

ROSALIND. Nay, but who is it?

CELIA. Is it possible?

ROSALIND. Nay, I prithee now with most petitionary vehemence, tell me who it is.

CELIA. O wonderful, wonderful, and most wonderful wonderful! and yet again wonderful, and after that, out of all whooping!

ROSALIND. Good my complexion! dost thou think, though I am caparisoned like a man, I have a doublet and hose in my disposition? One inch of delay more is a South-sea of discovery; I prithee, tell me who is it quickly, and speak apace. I would thou couldst stammer, that thou might'st pour this concealed man out of thy mouth, as wine comes out of a narrow-mouthed bottle, either too much at once, or none at all. I prithee, take the cork out of thy mouth that I may drink thy tidings.

CELIA. So you may put a man in your belly.

ROSALIND. Is he of God's making? What manner of man? Is his head worth a hat? Or his chin worth a beard?

CELIA. Nay, he hath but a little beard.

ROSALIND. Why, God will send more, if the man will be thankful: let me stay the growth of his beard, if thou delay me not the knowledge of his chin.

CELIA. It is young Orlando, that tripped up the wrestler's heels and your heart both in an instant.

ROSALIND. Nay, but the devil take mocking: speak sad brow and true maid.

CELIA. I' faith, coz, 'tis he.

ROSALIND. Orlando?

CELIA. Orlando.

ROSALIND. Alas the day! what shall I do with my doublet and hose? What did he when thou sawest him? What said he? How looked he? Wherein went he? What makes he here? Did he ask for me? Where remains he? How parted he with thee? and when shalt thou see him again? Answer me in one word.

CELIA. You must borrow me Gargantua's mouth first: 'tis a word too great for any mouth of this age's size. To say aye and no to these particulars is more than to answer in a catechism.

ROSALIND. But doth he know that I am in this forest and in man's apparel? Looks he as freshly as he did the day he wrestled?

CELIA. It is as easy to count atomies as to resolve the propositions of a lover; but take a taste of my finding him, and relish it with good observance. I found him under a tree, like a dropped acorn.

ROSALIND. It may well be called Jove's tree, when it drops forth such fruit.

CELIA. Give me audience, good madam.

ROSALIND. Proceed.

CELIA. There lay he, stretched along, like a wounded knight.

ROSALIND. Though it be pity to see such a sight, it well becomes the ground.

CELIA. Cry 'holla' to thy tongue, I prithee; it curvets unseasonably. He was furnished like a hunter.

ROSALIND. O, ominous! he comes to kill my heart.

CELIA. I would sing my song without a burden: thou bringest me out of tune.

ROSALIND. Do you not know I am a woman? when I think, I must speak. Sweet, say on.

CELIA. You bring me out. Soft! comes he not here?

Enter ORLANDO *and* JAQUES.]

ROSALIND. 'Tis he: slink by, and note him.

JAQUES. I thank you for your company; but, good faith, I had as lief have been myself alone.

ORLANDO. And so had I; but yet, for fashion' sake, I thank you too for your society.

JAQUES. God buy you: let's meet as little as we can.

ORLANDO. I do desire we may be better strangers.

JAQUES. I pray you, mar no more trees with writing love-songs in their barks.

ORLANDO. I pray you, mar no more of my verses with reading them ill-favoredly.

JAQUES. Rosalind is your love's name?

ORLANDO. Yes, just.

JAQUES. I do not like her name.

ORLANDO. There was no thought of pleasing you when she was christened.

JAQUES. What stature is she of?

ORLANDO. Just as high as my heart.

JAQUES. You are full of pretty answers. Have you not been acquainted with goldsmiths' wives, and conned them out of rings?

ORLANDO. Not so; but I answer you right, painted cloth, from whence you have studied your questions?

JAQUES. You have a nimble wit: I think 'twas made of Atalanta's heels. Will you sit down with me, and we two will rail against our mistress the world, and all our misery?

ORLANDO. I will chide no breather in the world but myself, against whom I know most faults.

JAQUES. The worst fault you have is to be in love.

ORLANDO. 'Tis a fault I will not change for your best virtue. I am weary of you.

JAQUES. By my troth. I was seeking for a fool when I found you.

ORLANDO. He is drowned in the brook: look but in, and you shall see him.

JAQUES. There I shall see mine own figure.

ORLANDO. Which I take to be either a fool or a cipher.

JAQUES. I'll tarry no longer with you: farewell, good Signior Love.

ORLANDO. I am glad of your departure: adieu, good Monsieur Melancholy. [*Exit* JAQUES.

ROSALIND. [*Aside to Celia*] I will speak to him like a saucy lackey, and under that habit play the knave with him. Do you hear, forester?

ORLANDO. Very well: what would you?

ROSALIND. I pray you, what is 't o'clock?

ORLANDO. You should ask me what time o' day: there's no clock in the forest.

ROSALIND. Then there is no true lover in the forest; else sighing every minute and groaning every hour would detect the lazy foot of Time as well as a clock.

ORLANDO. And why not the swift foot of Time? had not that been as proper?

ROSALIND. By no means, sir: Time travels in divers paces with divers persons. I'll tell you who Time ambles withal, who Time trots withal, who Time gallops withal and who he stands still withal.

ORLANDO. I prithee, who doth he trot withal?

ROSALIND. Marry, he trots hard with a young maid between the contract of her marriage and the day it is solemnized: if the interim be but a se'nnight, Time's pace is so hard that it seems the length of seven year.

ORLANDO. Who ambles Time withal?

ROSALIND. With a priest that lacks Latin, and a rich man that hath not the gout; for the one sleeps easily because he cannot study, and the other lives merrily because he feels no pain; the one lacking the burden of lean and wasteful learning, the other knowing no burden of heavy tedious penury: these Time ambles withal.

ORLANDO. Who doth he gallop withal?

ROSALIND. With a thief to the gallows; for though he go as softly as foot can fall, he thinks himself too soon there.

ORLANDO. Who stays it still withal?

ROSALIND. With lawyers in the vacation; for they sleep between term and term and then they perceive not how Time moves.

ORLANDO. Where dwell you, pretty youth?

ROSALIND. With this shepherdess, my sister: here in the skirts of the forest, like fringe upon a petticoat.

ORLANDO. Are you native of this place?

ROSALIND. As the cony that you see dwell where she is kindled.

ORLANDO. Your accent is something finer than you could purchase in so removed a dwelling.

ROSALIND. I have been told so of many: but indeed an old religious uncle of mine taught me to speak, who was in his youth an inland man; one that knew courtship too well, for there he fell in love. I have heard him read many lectures against it, and I thank God I am not a woman, to be touched with so many giddy offenses as he hath generally taxed their whole sex withal.

ORLANDO. Can you remember any of the principal evils that he laid to the charge of women?

ROSALIND. There were none principal; they were all like one another as half-pence are, every one fault seeming monstrous till his fellow-fault came to match it.

ORLANDO. I prithee, recount some of them.

ROSALIND. No, I will not cast away my physic but on those that are sick. There is a man haunts the forest, that abuses our young plants with carving Rosalind on their barks; hangs odes upon hawthorns and elegies on brambles; all, forsooth, deifying the name of Rosalind: if I could meet that fancy-monger, I would give him some good counsel, for he seems to have the quotidian of love upon him.

ORLANDO. I am he that is so love-shaked: I pray you, tell me your remedy.

ROSALIND. There is none of my uncle's marks upon you: he taught me how to know a man in love; in which cage of rushes I am sure you are not prisoner.

ORLANDO. What were his marks?

ROSALIND. A lean cheek, which you have not; a blue eye and sunken, which you have not; an unquestionable spirit, which you have not; a beard neglected, which you have not; but I pardon you for that, for simply your having in beard is a younger brother's revenue: then your hose should be ungartered, your bonnet unbanded, your sleeve unbuttoned, your shoe untied and every thing about you demonstrating a careless desolation; but you are no such man; you are rather point-device in your accouterments, as loving yourself than seeming the lover of any other.

ORLANDO. Fair youth, I would I could make thee believe I love.

ROSALIND. Me believe it! you may as soon make her that you love believe it; which, I warrant, she is apter to do than to confess she does: that is one of the points in the which women still give the lie to their consciences. But, in good sooth, are you he that hangs the verses on the trees, wherein Rosalind is so admired?

ORLANDO. I swear to thee, youth, by the white hand of Rosalind, I am that he, that unfortunate he.

ROSALIND. But are you so much in love as your rhymes speak?

ORLANDO. Neither rhyme nor reason can express how much.

ROSALIND. Love is merely a madness; and, I tell you, deserves as well a dark house and a whip as madmen do: and the reason why they are not so punished and cured is, that the lunacy is so ordinary that the whippers are in love too. Yet I profess curing it by counsel.

ORLANDO. Did you ever cure any so?

ROSALIND. Yes, one, and in this manner. He was to imagine me his love, his mistress; and I set him every day to woo me: at which time would I, being but a moonish youth, grieve, be effeminate, changeable, longing and liking; proud, fantastical, apish, shallow, inconstant, full of tears, full of smiles; for every passion something and for no passion truly any thing, as boys and women are for the most part cattle of this color: would now like him, now loathe him; then entertain him, then forswear him; now weep for him, then spit at him; that I drave my suitor from his mad humor of love to a living humor of madness; which was, to forswear the full stream of the world and to live in a nook merely monastic. And thus I cured him; and this way will I take upon me to wash your liver as clean as a sound sheep's heart, that there shall not be one spot of love in 't.

ORLANDO. I would not be cured, youth.

ROSALIND. I would cure you, if you would but call me Rosalind and come every day to my cote and woo me.

ORLANDO. Now, by the faith of my love, I will: tell me where it is.

ROSALIND. Go with me to it and I 'll show it you: and by the way you shall tell me where in the forest you live. Will you go?

ORLANDO. With all my heart, good youth.

ROSALIND. Nay, you must call me Rosalind. Come, sister, will you go? [*Exeunt.*

SCENE III — *The forest.*

Enter TOUCHSTONE *and* AUDREY; JAQUES *behind.*]

TOUCHSTONE. Come apace, good Audrey: I will fetch up your goats, Audrey. And how, Audrey? am I the man yet? doth my simple feature content you?

AUDREY. Your features! Lord warrant us! what features?

TOUCHSTONE. I am here with thee and thy goats, as the most capricious poet, honest Ovid, was among the Goths.

JAQUES. [*Aside*] O knowledge ill-inhabited, worse than Jove in a thatched house!

TOUCHSTONE. When a man's verses cannot be understood, nor a man's good wit seconded with the forward child, understanding, it strikes a man more dead than a great reckoning in a little room. Truly, I would the gods had made thee poetical.

AUDREY. I do not know what 'poetical' is: is it honest in deed and word? is it a true thing?

TOUCHSTONE. No, truly; for the truest poetry is the most feigning; and lovers are given to poetry, and what they swear in poetry may be said as lovers they do feign.

AUDREY. Do you wish then that the gods had made me poetical?

TOUCHSTONE. I do, truly; for thou swearest to me thou art honest; now, if thou wert a poet, I might have some hope thou didst feign.

AUDREY. Would you not have me honest?

TOUCHSTONE. No, truly, unless thou wert hard-favored; for honesty coupled to beauty is to have honey a sauce to sugar.

JAQUES. [*Aside*] A material fool!

AUDREY. Well, I am not fair; and therefore I pray the gods make me honest.

TOUCHSTONE. Truly, and to cast away honesty upon a foul slut were to put good meat into an unclean dish.

AUDREY. I am not a slut, though I thank the gods I am foul.

TOUCHSTONE. Well, praised be the gods for thy foulness! sluttishness may come hereafter. But be it as it may be, I will marry thee, and to that end I have been with Sir Oliver Martext the vicar of the next village, who hath promised to meet me in this place of the forest and to couple us.

JAQUES. [*Aside*] I would fain see this meeting.

AUDREY. Well, the gods give us joy!

TOUCHSTONE. Amen. A man may, if he were of a fearful heart, stagger in this attempt; for here we have no temple but the wood, no assembly but horn-beasts. But what though? Courage! As horns are odious, they are necessary. It is said, 'many a man knows no end of his goods:' right; many a man has good horns, and knows no end of them. Well, that is the dowry of his wife; 'tis none of his own getting. Horns?—

even so:—poor men alone? No, no; the noblest deer hath
them as huge as the rascal. Is the single man therefore
blessed? No: as a walled town is more worthier than a village, so is the forehead of a married man more honorable
than the bare brow of a bachelor; and by how much defense is better than no skill, by so much is a horn more precious than to want. Here comes Sir Oliver.

Enter SIR OLIVER MARTEXT.]

Sir Oliver Martext, you are well met: will you dispatch us
here under this tree, or shall we go with you to your chapel?

SIR OLIVER. Is there none here to give the woman?

TOUCHSTONE. I will not take her on gift of any man.

SIR OLIVER. Truly, she must be given, or the marriage is not
lawful.

JAQUES. Proceed, proceed: I 'll give her.

TOUCHSTONE. Good even, good Master What-ye-call't: how do
you, sir? You are very well met: God 'ild you for your last
company: I am very glad to see you: even a toy in hand
here, sir: nay, pray be covered.

JAQUES. Will you be married, motley?

TOUCHSTONE. As the ox hath his bow, sir, the horse his curb
and the falcon her bells, so man hath his desires; and as
pigeons bill, so wedlock would be nibbling.

JAQUES. And will you, being a man of your breeding, be married under a bush like a beggar? Get you to church, and
have a good priest that can tell you what marriage is: this
fellow will but join you together as they join wainscot; then
one of you prove a shrunk panel, and like green timber
warp, warp.

TOUCHSTONE. [*Aside*] I am not in the mind but I were better
to be married of him than of another: for he is not like to
marry me well; and not being well married, it will be a
good excuse for me hereafter to leave my wife.

JAQUES. Go thou with me, and let me counsel thee.

TOUCHSTONE. Come, sweet Audrey:
We must be married, or we must live in bawdry.
Farewell, good Master Oliver: not,—

> O sweet Oliver,
> O brave Oliver,
>   Leave me not behind thee:
> but,—
>   Wind away,
>   Begone, I say,
> I will not to wedding with thee.

>   [*Exeunt* JAQUES, TOUCHSTONE, *and* AUDREY.

SIR OLIVER. 'Tis no matter: ne'er a fantastical knave of them all shall flout me out of my calling.   [*Exit.*

SCENE IV — *The forest.*

Enter ROSALIND *and* CELIA.]

ROSALIND. Never talk to me; I will weep.

CELIA. Do, I prithee; but yet have the grace to consider that tears do not become a man.

ROSALIND. But have I not cause to weep?

CELIA. As good cause as one would desire; therefore weep.

ROSALIND. His very hair is of the dissembling color.

CELIA. Something browner than Judas's: marry, his kisses are Judas's own children.

ROSALIND. I' faith, his hair is of a good color.

CELIA. An excellent color: your chestnut was ever the only color.

ROSALIND. And his kissing is as full of sanctity as the touch of holy bread.

CELIA. He hath bought a pair of cast lips of Diana: a nun of winter's sisterhood kisses not more religiously; the very ice of chastity is in them.

ROSALIND. But why did he swear he would come this morning, and comes not?

CELIA. Nay, certainly, there is no truth in him.

ROSALIND. Do you think so?

CELIA. Yes; I think he is not a pick-purse nor a horse-stealer; but for his verity in love, I do think him as concave as a covered goblet or a worm-eaten nut.

ROSALIND. Not true in love?

CELIA. Yes, when he is in; but I think he is not in.

ROSALIND. You have heard him swear downright he was.

CELIA. 'Was' is not 'is': besides, the oath of a lover is no stronger than the word of a tapster; they are both the confirmer of false reckonings. He attends here in the forest on the Duke your father.

ROSALIND. I met the Duke yesterday and had much question with him: he asked me of what parentage I was; I told him, of as good as he; so he laughed and let me go. But what talk we of fathers, when there is such a man as Orlando?

CELIA. O, that's a brave man! he writes brave verses, speaks brave words, swears brave oaths and breaks them bravely, quite traverse, athwart the heart of his lover; as a puisny tilter, that spurs his horse but on one side, breaks his staff like a noble goose: but all's brave that youth mounts and folly guides. Who comes here?

Enter CORIN.]

CORIN. Mistress and master, you have oft inquired
After the shepherd that complain'd of love,
Who you saw sitting by me on the turf,
Praising the proud disdainful shepherdess
That was his mistress.

CELIA.   Well, and what of him?

CORIN. If you will see a pageant truly play'd,
Between the pale complexion of true love
And the red glow of scorn and proud disdain,
Go hence a little and I shall conduct you,
If you will mark it.

ROSALIND.   O, come, let us remove:
The sight of lovers feedeth those in love.
Bring us to this sight, and you shall say
I'll prove a busy actor in their play.   [*Exeunt.*

SCENE V — *Another part of the forest.*

Enter SILVIUS *and* PHEBE.]

SILVIUS. Sweet Phebe, do not scorn me; do not, Phebe;
Say that you love me not, but say not so

In bitterness. The common executioner,
Whose heart the accustom'd sight of death makes hard,
Falls not the axe upon the humbled neck
But first begs pardon: will you sterner be
Than he that dies and lives by bloody drops?
Enter ROSALIND, CELIA, *and* CORIN, *behind.*]

PHEBE. I would not be thy executioner:
I fly thee, for I would not injure thee.
Thou tell'st me there is murder in mine eye:
'Tis pretty, sure, and very probable,
That eyes, that are the frail'st and softest things,
Who shut their coward gates on atomies,
Should be call'd tyrants, butchers, murderers!
Now I do frown on thee with all my heart;
And if mine eyes can wound, now let them kill thee:
Now counterfeit to swoon; why now fall down;
Or if thou canst not, O, for shame, for shame,
Lie not, to say mine eyes are murderers!
Now show the wound mine eye hath made in thee:
Scratch thee but with a pin and there remains
Some scar of it; lean but upon a rush,
The cicatrice and capable impressure
Thy palm some moment keeps; but now mine eyes,
Which I have darted at thee, hurt thee not,
Nor, I am sure, there is no force in eyes
That can do hurt.

SILVIUS.   O dear Phebe,
If ever,—as that ever may be near,—
You meet in some fresh cheek the power of fancy,
Then shall you know the wounds invisible
That love's keen arrows make.

PHEBE.   But till that time
Come not thou near me: and when that time comes,
Afflict me with thy mocks, pity me not;
As till that time I shall not pity thee.

ROSALIND. And why, I pray you? Who might be your mother,
That you insult, exult, and all at once,
Over the wretched? What though you have no beauty,—

As, by my faith, I see no more in you
Than without candle may go dark to bed,—
Must you be therefore proud and pitiless?
Why, what means this? Why do you look on me?
I see no more in you than in the ordinary
Of nature's sale-work. 'Od's my little life,
I think she means to tangle my eyes too!
No, faith, proud mistress, hope not after it:
'Tis not your inky brows, your black silk hair,
Your bugle eyeballs, nor your cheek of cream,
That can entame my spirits to your worship.
You foolish shepherd, wherefore do you follow her,
Like foggy south, puffing with wind and rain?
You are a thousand times a properer man
Than she a woman; 'tis such fools as you
That makes the world full of ill-favor'd children:
'Tis not her glass, but you, that flatters her;
And out of you she sees herself more proper
Than any of her lineaments can show her.
But, mistress, know yourself: down on your knees,
And thank heaven, fasting, for a good man's love:
For I must tell you friendly in your ear,
Sell when you can: you are not for all markets.
Cry the man mercy; love him; take his offer:
Foul is most foul, being foul to be a scoffer.
So take her to thee, shepherd: fare you well.

PHEBE. Sweet youth, I pray you, chide a year together:
I had rather hear you chide than this man woo.

ROSALIND. He 's fallen in love with your foulness and she 'll
fall in love with my anger. If it be so, as fast as she answers
thee with frowning looks, I 'll sauce her with bitter words.
Why look you so upon me?

PHEBE. For no ill will I bear you.

ROSALIND. I pray you, do not fall in love with me,
For I am falser than vows made in wine:
Besides, I like you not. If you will know my house,
'Tis at the tuft of olives here hard by.
Will you go, sister? Shepherd, ply her hard.

Come, sister. Shepherdess, look on him better,
And be not proud: though all the world could see,
None could be so abused in sight as he.
Come, to our flock.   [*Exeunt* ROSALIND, CELIA *and* CORIN.

PHEBE. Dead shepherd, now I find thy saw of might,
'Who ever loved that loved not at first sight?'

SILVIUS. Sweet Phebe,—

PHEBE.   Ha, what say'st thou, Silvius?

SILVIUS. Sweet Phebe, pity me.

PHEBE. Why, I am sorry for thee, gentle Silvius.

SILVIUS. Wherever sorrow is, relief would be:
If you do sorrow at my grief in love,
By giving love your sorrow and my grief
Were both extermined.

PHEBE. Thou hast my love: is not that neighborly?

SILVIUS. I would have you.

PHEBE.   Why, that were covetousness,
Silvius, the time was that I hated thee,
And yet it is not that I bear thee love;
But since that thou canst talk of love so well,
Thy company, which erst was irksome to me,
I will endure, and I 'll employ thee too:
But do not look for further recompense
Than thine own gladness that thou art employ'd.

SILVIUS. So holy and so perfect is my love,
And I in such a poverty of grace,
That I shall think it a most plenteous crop
To glean the broken ears after the man
That the main harvest reaps: loose now and then
A scatter'd smile, and that I 'll live upon.

PHEBE. Know'st thou the youth that spoke to me erewhile?

SILVIUS. Not very well, but I have met him oft;
And he hath bought the cottage and the bounds
That the old carlot once was master of.

PHEBE. Think not I love him, though I ask for him;
'Tis but a peevish boy; yet he talks well;
But what care I for words? yet words do well
When he that speaks them pleases those that hear.

It is a pretty youth: not very pretty:
But, sure he's proud, and yet his pride becomes him:
He'll make a proper man: the best thing in him
Is his complexion; and faster than his tongue
Did make offense his eye did heal it up.
He is not very tall; yet for his years he's tall:
His leg is but so so; and yet 'tis well:
There was a pretty redness in his lip,
A little riper and more lusty red
Than that mix'd in his cheek; 'twas just the difference
Betwixt the constant red and mingled damask.
There be some women, Silvius, had they mark'd him
In parcels as I did, would have gone near
To fall in love with him: but, for my part,
I love him not nor hate him not; and yet
I have more cause to hate him than to love him:
For what had he to do to chide at me?
He said mine eyes were black and my hair black;
And, now I am remember'd, scorn'd at me:
I marvel why i answer'd not again:
But that's all one; omittance is no quittance.
I'll write to him a very taunting letter,
And thou shalt bear it: wilt thou, Silvius?

SILVIUS. Phebe, with all my heart.

PHEBE.   I'll write it straight;
The matter's in my head and in my heart:
I will be bitter with him and passing short.
Go with me, Silvius.   [Exeunt.

ACT IV

Scene I — *The forest.*

Enter ROSALIND, CELIA, *and* JAQUES.]

JAQUES. I prithee, pretty youth, let me be better acquainted with thee.

ROSALIND. They say you are a melancholy fellow.

JAQUES. I am so; I do love it better than laughing.

ROSALIND. Those that are in extremity of either are abominable fellows, and betray themselves to every modern censure worse than drunkards.

JAQUES. Why, 'tis good to be sad and say nothing.

ROSALIND. Why then, 'tis good to be a post.

JAQUES. I have neither the scholar's melancholy, which is emulation; nor the musician's, which is fantastical; nor the courtier's, which is proud; nor the soldier's, which is ambitious; nor the lawyer's, which is politic; nor the lady's, which is nice; nor the lover's, which is all these: but it is a melancholy of mine own, compounded of many simples, extracted from many objects; and indeed the sundry contemplation of my travels, in which my often rumination wraps me in a most humorous sadness.

ROSALIND. A traveler! By my faith, you have great reason to be sad: I fear you have sold your own lands to see other men's; then, to have seen much, and to have nothing, is to have rich eyes and poor hands.

JAQUES. Yes, I have gained my experience.

ROSALIND. And your experience makes you sad: I had rather have a fool to make me merry than experience to make me sad; and to travel for it too!

Enter ORLANDO.]

ORLANDO. Good-day and happiness, dear Rosalind!

JAQUES. Nay, then, God buy you, an you talk in blank verse.
[*Exit.*

ROSALIND. Farewell, Monsieur Traveler: look you lisp and

wear strange suits; disable all the benefits of your own country; be out of love with your nativity and almost chide God for making you that countenance you are; or I will scarce think you have swam in a gondola. Why, how now, Orlando! where have you been all this while? You a lover! And you serve me such another trick, never come in my sight more.

ORLANDO. My fair Rosalind, I come within an hour of my promise.

ROSALIND. Break an hour's promise in love! He that will divide a minute into a thousand parts, and break but a part of the thousandth part of a minute in the affairs of love, it may be said of him that Cupid hath clapped him o' the shoulder, but I 'll warrant him heart-whole.

ORLANDO. Pardon me, dear Rosalind.

ROSALIND. Nay, an you be so tardy, come no more in my sight: I had as lief be wooed of a snail.

ORLANDO. Of a snail?

ROSALIND. Aye, of a snail; for though he comes slowly, he carries his house on his head; a better jointure, I think, than you make a woman: besides, he brings his destiny with him.

ORLANDO. What's that?

ROSALIND. Why, horns, which such as you are fain to be beholding to your wives for: but he comes armed in his fortunes and prevents the slander of his wife.

ORLANDO. Virtue is no horn-maker; and my Rosalind is virtuous.

ROSALIND. And I am your Rosalind.

CELIA. It pleases him to call you so; but he hath a Rosalind of a better leer than you.

ROSALIND. Come, woo me, woo me; for now I am in a holiday humor and like enough to consent. What would you say to me now, an I were your very very Rosalind?

ORLANDO. I would kiss before I spoke.

ROSALIND. Nay, you were better speak first; and when you were graveled for lack of matter, you might take occasion to kiss. Very good orators, when they are out, they will spit;

and for lovers lacking—God warn us!—matter, the cleanliest shift is to kiss.

ORLANDO. How if the kiss be denied?

ROSALIND. Then she puts you to entreaty and there begins new matter.

ORLANDO. Who could be out, being before his beloved mistress?

ROSALIND. Marry, that should you, if I were your mistress, or I should think my honesty ranker than my wit.

ORLANDO. What, of my suit?

ROSALIND. Not out of your apparel, and yet out of your suit. Am not I your Rosalind?

ORLANDO. I take some joy to say you are, because I would be talking of her.

ROSALIND. Well, in her person, I say I will not have you.

ORLANDO. Then in mine own person I die.

ROSALIND. No, faith, die by attorney. The poor world is almost six thousand years old, and in all this time there was not any man died in his own person, videlicet, in a love-cause. Troilus had his brains dashed out with a Grecian club; yet he did what he could to die before, and he is one of the patterns of love. Leander, he would have lived many a fair year, though Hero had turned nun, if it had not been for a hot midsummer night; for, good youth, he went but forth to wash him in the Hellespont and being taken with the cramp was drowned: and the foolish chroniclers of that age found it was 'Hero of Sestos.' But these are all lies: men have died from time to time and worms have eaten them, but not for love.

ORLANDO. I would not have my right Rosalind of this mind; for, I protest, her frown might kill me.

ROSALIND. By this hand, it will not kill a fly. But come, now I will be your Rosalind in a more coming-on disposition, and ask me what you will, I will grant it.

ORLANDO. Then love me, Rosalind.

ROSALIND. Yes, faith, will I, Fridays and Saturdays and all.

ORLANDO. And wilt thou have me?

ROSALIND. Aye, and twenty such.

ORLANDO. What sayest thou?

ROSALIND. Are you not good?

ORLANDO. I hope so.

ROSALIND. Why then, can one desire too much of a good thing? Come, sister, you shall be the priest and marry us. Give me your hand, Orlando. What do you say, sister?

ORLANDO. Pray thee, marry us.

CELIA. I cannot say the words.

ROSALIND. You must begin, 'Will you, Orlando—'

CELIA. Go to. Will you, Orlando, have to wife this Rosalind?

ORLANDO. I will.

ROSALIND. Aye, but when?

ORLANDO. Why now; as fast as she can marry us.

ROSALIND. Then you must say 'I take thee, Rosalind, for wife.'

ORLANDO. I take thee, Rosalind, for wife.

ROSALIND. I might ask you for your commission; but I do take thee, Orlando, for my husband: there's a girl goes before the priest; and certainly a woman's thought runs before her actions.

ORLANDO. So do all thoughts; they are winged.

ROSALIND. Now tell me how long you would have her after you have possessed her.

ORLANDO. For ever and a day.

ROSALIND. Say 'a day,' without the 'ever.' No, no, Orlando; men are April when they woo, December when they wed: maids are May when they are maids, but the sky changes when they are wives. I will be more jealous of thee than a Barbary cock-pigeon over his hen, more clamorous than a parrot against rain, more new-fangled than an ape, more giddy in my desires than a monkey: I will weep for nothing, like Diana in the fountain, and I will do that when you are disposed to be merry; I will laugh like a hyen, and that when thou art inclined to sleep.

ORLANDO. But will my Rosalind do so?

ROSALIND. By my life, she will do as I do.

ORLANDO. O, but she is wise.

ROSALIND. Or else she could not have the wit to do this: the wiser, the waywarder: make the doors upon a woman's wit and it will out at the casement; shut that and 'twill out at the key-hole; stop that, 'twill fly with the smoke out at the chimney.

ORLANDO. A man that had a wife with such a wit, he might say 'Wit, whither wilt?'

ROSALIND. Nay, you might keep that check for it till you met your wife's wit going to your neighbor's bed.

ORLANDO. And what wit could wit have to excuse that?

ROSALIND. Marry, to say she came to seek you there. You shall never take her without her answer, unless you take her without her tongue. O, that woman that cannot make her fault her husband's occasion, let her never nurse her child herself, for she will breed it like a fool!

ORLANDO. For these two hours, Rosalind, I will leave thee.

ROSALIND. Alas, dear love, I cannot lack thee two hours!

ORLANDO. I must attend the Duke at dinner: by two o'clock I will be with thee again.

ROSALIND. Aye, go your ways, go your ways; I knew what you would prove: my friends told me as much, and I thought no less: that flattering tongue of yours won me: 'tis but one cast away, and so, come, death! Two o'clock is your hour?

ORLANDO. Aye, sweet Rosalind.

ROSALIND. By my troth, and in good earnest, and so God mend me, and by all pretty oaths that are not dangerous, if you break one jot of your promise or come one minute behind your hour, I will think you the most pathetical break-promise, and the most hollow lover, and the most unworthy of her you call Rosalind, that may be chosen out of the gross band of the unfaithful: therefore beware my censure and keep your promise.

ORLANDO. With no less religion than if thou wert indeed my Rosalind: so adieu.

ROSALIND. Well, Time is the old justice that examines all such offenders, and let Time try: adieu.   [Exit ORLANDO.

CELIA. You have simply misused our sex in your love-prate: we must have your doublet and hose plucked over your head, and show the world what the bird hath done to her own nest.

ROSALIND. O coz, coz, coz, my pretty little coz, that thou didst know how many fathom deep I am in love! But it cannot be sounded: my affection hath an unknown bottom, like the bay of Portugal.

CELIA. Or rather, bottomless; that as fast as you pour affection in, it runs out.

ROSALIND. No, that same wicked bastard of Venus that was begot of thought, conceived of spleen, and born of madness, that blind rascally boy that abuses every one's eyes because his own are out, let him be judge how deep I am in love. I'll tell thee, Aliena, I cannot be out of the sight of Orlando: I'll go find a shadow and sigh till he come.

CELIA. And I 'll sleep.　　　　　　　　　　　　　　*[Exeunt.*

SCENE II — *The forest.*

Enter JAQUES, LORDS, *and* FORESTERS.]

JAQUES. Which is he that killed the deer?

A LORD. Sir, it was I.

JAQUES. Let's present him to the Duke, like a Roman conqueror; and it would do well to set the deer's horns upon his head, for a branch of victory. Have you no song, forester, for this purpose?

FORESTER. Yes, sir.

JAQUES. Sing it: 'tis no matter how it be in tune, so it make noise enough.

SONG.

FORESTER. What shall he have that kill'd the deer?
　　　　His leather skin and horns to wear.
　　　　　　Then sing him home:
　　　　　　　　[The rest shall bear this burden.
　　　Take thou no scorn to wear the horn;
　　　It was a crest ere thou wast born:
　　　　　Thy father's father wore it,
　　　　　And thy father bore it:
　　　The horn, the horn, the lusty horn
　　　Is not a thing to laugh to scorn.　　　*[Exeunt.*

SCENE III — *The forest.*

Enter ROSALIND *and* CELIA.]

ROSALIND. How say you now? Is it not past two o'clock? and
  here much Orlando!

CELIA. I warrant you, with pure love and troubled brain, he
  hath ta'en his bow and arrows and is gone forth to sleep.
  Look, who comes here.

Enter SILVIUS.]

SILVIUS. My errand is to you, fair youth;
  My gentle Phebe bid me give you this:
  I know not the contents; but, as I guess
  By the stern brow and waspish action
  Which she did use as she was writing of it,
  It bears an angry tenor: pardon me;
  I am but as a guiltless messenger.

ROSALIND. Patience herself would startle at this letter
  And play the swaggerer; bear this, bear all:
  She says I am not fair, that I lack manners;
  She calls me proud, and that she could not love me,
  Were man as rare as phœnix. 'Od's my will!
  Her love is not the hare that I do hunt:
  Why writes she so to me? Well, shepherd, well,
  This is a letter of your own device.

SILVIUS. No, I protest, I know not the contents.
  Phebe did write it.

ROSALIND.   Come, come, you are a fool,
  And turn'd into the extremity of love.
  I saw her hand: she has a leathern hand,
  A freestone-color'd hand; I verily did think
  That her old gloves were on, but 'twas her hands:
  She has a housewife's hand; but that 's no matter:
  I say she never did invent this letter;
  This is a man's invention and his hand.

SILVIUS. Sure, it is hers.

ROSALIND. Why, 'tis a boisterous and a cruel style,
  A style for challengers; why, she defies me,

    Like Turk to Christian: women's gentle brain
    Could not drop forth such giant-rude invention,
    Such Ethiope words, blacker in their effect
    Than in their countenance. Will you hear the letter?

SILVIUS. So please you, for I never heard it yet;
    Yet heard too much of Phebe's cruelty.

ROSALIND. She Phebes me: mark how the tyrant writes.
    [*Reads*] Art thou god to shepherd turn'd,
          That a maiden's heart hath burn'd?
    Can a woman rail thus?

SILVIUS. Call you this railing?

ROSALIND. [*Reads*]
        Why, thy godhead laid apart,
        Warr'st thou with a woman's heart?
    Did you ever hear such railing?
        Whiles the eye of man did woo me,
        That could do no vengeance to me.
    Meaning me a beast.
        If the scorn of your bright eyne
        Have power to raise such love in mine,
        Alack, in me what strange effect
        Would they work in mild aspect!
        Whiles you chide me, I did love;
        How then might your prayers move!
        He that brings this love to thee
        Little knows this love in me:
        And by him seal up thy mind;
        Whether that thy youth and kind
        Will the faithful offer take
        Of me and all that I can make;
        Or else by him my love deny,
        And then I'll study how to die.

SILVIUS. Call you this chiding?

CELIA. Alas, poor shepherd!

ROSALIND. Do you pity him? no, he deserves no pity. Wilt
    thou love such a woman? What, to make thee an instru-
    ment and play false strains upon thee! not to be endured!

Well, go your way to her, for I see love hath made thee
a tame snake, and say this to her: that if she love me, I
charge her to love thee; if she will not, I will never have
her unless thou entreat for her. If you be a true lover, hence,
and not a word; for here comes more company.

[Exit SILVIUS.

Enter OLIVER.]

OLIVER. Good morrow, fair ones: pray you, if you know,
    Where in the purlieus of this forest stands
    A sheep-cote fenced about with olive-trees?
CELIA. West of this place, down in the neighbor bottom:
    The rank of osiers by the murmuring stream
    Left on your right hand brings you to the place.
    But at this hour the house doth keep itself;
    There's none within.
OLIVER. If that an eye may profit by a tongue,
    Then should I know you by description;
    Such garments and such years: 'The boy is fair,
    Of female favor, and bestows himself
    Like a ripe sister: the woman low,
    And browner than her brother.' Are not you
    The owner of the house I did enquire for?
CELIA. It is no boast, being ask'd, to say we are.
OLIVER. Orlando doth commend him to you both,
    And to that youth he calls his Rosalind
    He sends this bloody napkin. Are you he?
ROSALIND. I am: what must we understand by this?
OLIVER. Some of my shame; if you will know of me
    What man I am, and how, and why, and where
    This handkercher was stain'd.
CELIA.   I pray you, tell it.
OLIVER. When last the young Orlando parted from you
    He left a promise to return again
    Within an hour, and pacing through the forest,
    Chewing the food of sweet and bitter fancy,
    Lo, what befell! he threw his eye aside,
    And mark what object did present itself:

Under an oak, whose boughs were moss'd with age
And high top bald with dry antiquity,
A wretched ragged man, o'ergrown with hair,
Lay sleeping on his back: about his neck
A green and gilded snake had wreathed itself,
Who with her head nimble in threats approach'd
The opening of his mouth; but suddenly,
Seeing Orlando, it unlink'd itself,
And with indented glides did slip away
Into a bush: under which bush's shade
A lioness, with udders all drawn dry,
Lay couching, head on ground, with catlike watch,
When that the sleeping man should stir; for 'tis
The royal disposition of that beast
To prey on nothing that doth seem as dead:
This seen, Orlando did approach the man
And found it was his brother, his elder brother.

CELIA. O, I have heard him speak of that same brother;
And he did render him the most unnatural
That lived amongst men.

OLIVER.   And well he might so do,
For well I know he was unnatural.

ROSALIND. But, to Orlando: did he leave him there,
Food to the suck'd and hungry lioness?

OLIVER. Twice did he turn his back and purposed so;
But kindness, nobler ever than revenge,
And nature, stronger than his just occasion,
Made him give battle to the lioness,
Who quickly fell before him: in which hurtling
From miserable slumber I awaked.

CELIA. Are you his brother?

ROSALIND.   Was't you he rescued?

CELIA. Was't you that did so oft contrive to kill him?

OLIVER. 'Twas I; but 'tis not I: I do not shame
To tell you what I was, since my conversion
So sweetly tastes, being the thing I am.

ROSALIND. But, for the bloody napkin?

OLIVER.   By and by.
When from the first to last betwixt us two
Tears our recountments had most kindly bathed,
As how I came into that desert place;
In brief, he led me to the gentle Duke,
Who gave me fresh array and entertainment,
Committing me unto my brother's love;
Who led me instantly unto his cave,
There stripp'd himself, and here upon his arm
The lioness had torn some flesh away,
Which all this while had bled; and now he fainted
And cried, in faintings, upon Rosalind.
Brief, I recover'd him, bound up his wound;
And, after some small space, being strong at heart,
He sent me hither, stranger as I am,
To tell this story, that you might excuse
His broken promise, and to give this napkin,
Dyed in his blood unto the shepherd youth
That he in sport doth call his Rosalind.   [ROSALIND *swoons.*

CELIA. Why, how now, Ganymede! sweet Ganymede!

OLIVER. Many will swoon when they do look on blood.

CELIA. There is more in it. Cousin Ganymede!

OLIVER. Look, he recovers.

ROSALIND. I would I were at home.

CELIA.   We 'll lead you thither.
I pray you, will you take him by the arm?

OLIVER. Be of good cheer, youth: you a man! you lack a man's
heart.

ROSALIND. I do so, I confess it. Ah, sirrah, a body would think
this was well counterfeited! I pray you, tell your brother
how well I counterfeited. Heigh-ho!

OLIVER. This was not counterfeit: there is too great testimony
in your complexion that it was a passion of earnest.

ROSALIND. Counterfeit, I assure you.

OLIVER. Well then, take a good heart and counterfeit to be
a man.

ROSALIND. So I do: but, i' faith, I should have been a woman
by right.

CELIA. Come, you look paler and paler: pray you, draw home-
wards. Good sir, go with us.

OLIVER. That will I, for I must bear answer back
How you excuse my brother, Rosalind.

ROSALIND. I shall devise something: but, I pray you, commend
my counterfeiting to him. Will you go? [*Exeunt.*

ACT V

SCENE I — *The forest.*

Enter TOUCHSTONE *and* AUDREY.]

TOUCHSTONE. We shall find a time, Audrey; patience, gentle Audrey.

AUDREY. Faith, the priest was good enough, for all the old gentleman's saying.

TOUCHSTONE. A most wicked Sir Oliver, Audrey, a most vile Martext. But, Audrey, there is a youth here in the forest lays claim to you.

AUDREY. Aye, I know who 'tis: he hath no interest in me in the world: here comes the man you mean.

TOUCHSTONE. It is meat and drink to me to see a clown: by my troth, we that have good wits have much to answer for; we shall be flouting; we cannot hold.

Enter WILLIAM.]

WILLIAM. Good even, Audrey.

AUDREY. God ye good even, William.

WILLIAM. And good even to you, sir.

TOUCHSTONE. Good even, gentle friend. Cover thy head, cover thy head; nay, prithee, be covered. How old are you, friend?

WILLIAM. Five and twenty, sir.

TOUCHSTONE. A ripe age. Is thy name William?

WILLIAM. William, sir.

TOUCHSTONE. A fair name. Wast born i' the forest here?

WILLIAM. Aye, sir, I thank God.

TOUCHSTONE. 'Thank God'; a good answer. Art rich?

WILLIAM. Faith, sir, so so.

TOUCHSTONE. 'So so' is good, very good, very excellent good; and yet it is not; it is but so so. Art thou wise?

WILLIAM. Aye, sir, I have a pretty wit.

TOUCHSTONE. Why, thou sayest well. I do now remember a saying, 'The fool doth think he is wise, but the wise man knows himself to be a fool.' The heathen philosopher, when he had a desire to eat a grape, would open his lips when he put it into his mouth; meaning thereby that grapes were made to eat and lips to open. You do love this maid?

WILLIAM. I do, sir.

TOUCHSTONE. Give me your hand. Art thou learned?

WILLIAM. No, sir.

TOUCHSTONE. Then learn this of me: to have, is to have; for it is a figure in rhetoric that drink, being poured out of a cup into a glass, by filling the one doth empty the other; for all your writers do consent that *ipse* is he: now, you are not *ipse*, for I am he.

WILLIAM. Which he, sir?

TOUCHSTONE. He, sir, that must marry this woman. Therefore, you clown, abandon,—which is in the vulgar, leave,—the society,—which in the boorish is company,—of this female, —which in the common is woman; which together is, abandon the society of this female, or, clown, thou perishest; or, to thy better understanding, diest; or, to wit, I kill thee, make thee away, translate thy life into death, thy liberty into bondage: I will deal in poison with thee, or in bastinado, or in steel; I will bandy with thee in faction; I will o'er-run thee with policy; I will kill thee a hundred and fifty ways: therefore tremble, and depart.

AUDREY. Do, good William.

WILLIAM. God rest you merry, sir.   [*Exit.*
Enter CORIN.]

CORIN. Our master and mistress seek you; come, away, away!

TOUCHSTONE. Trip, Audrey! trip, Audrey! I attend, I attend.

SCENE II — *The forest.*

Enter ORLANDO *and* OLIVER.]

ORLANDO. Is't possible that on so little acquaintance you should like her? that but seeing you should love her? and loving woo? and, wooing, she should grant? and will you persever to enjoy her?

OLIVER. Neither call the giddiness of it in question, the poverty of her, the small acquaintance, my sudden wooing, nor her sudden consenting; but say with me, I love Aliena; say with her that she loves me; consent with both that we may enjoy each other: it shall be to your good; for my father's house and all the revenue that was old Sir Rowland's will I estate upon you, and here live and die a shepherd.

ORLANDO. You have my consent. Let your wedding be to-morrow: thither will I invite the Duke and all 's contented followers. Go you and prepare Aliena; for look you, here comes my Rosalind.

Enter ROSALIND.]

ROSALIND. God save you, brother.

OLIVER. And you, fair sister. [*Exit.*

ROSALIND. O, my dear Orlando, how it grieves me to see thee wear thy heart in a scarf!

ORLANDO. It is my arm.

ROSALIND. I thought thy heart had been wounded with the claws of a lion.

ORLANDO. Wounded it is, but with the eyes of a lady.

ROSALIND. Did your brother tell you how I counterfeited to swoon when he showed me your handkercher?

ORLANDO. Aye, and greater wonders than that.

ROSALIND. O, I know where you are: nay, 'tis true: there was never any thing so sudden but the fight of two rams, and Caesar's thrasonical brag of 'I came, saw, and overcame': for your brother and my sister no sooner met but they looked; no sooner looked but they loved; no sooner loved but they sighed; no sooner sighed but they asked one another the reason; no sooner knew the reason but they sought the remedy: and in these degrees have they made a pair of stairs to marriage which they will climb incontinent, or else be incontinent before marriage: they are in the very wrath of love and they will together; clubs cannot part them.

ORLANDO. They shall be married to-morrow, and I will bid the Duke to the nuptial. But, O, how bitter a thing it is to look into happiness, through another man's eyes! By so much the more shall I to-morrow be at the height of heart-heaviness,

by how much I shall think my brother happy in having
what he wishes for.

ROSALIND. Why, then, to-morrow I cannot serve your turn for
Rosalind?

ORLANDO. I can live no longer by thinking.

ROSALIND. I will weary you then no longer with idle talking.
Know of me then, for now I speak to some purpose, that I
know you are a gentleman of good conceit: I speak not this
that you should bear a good opinion of my knowledge, insomuch I say I know you are; neither do I labor for a greater
esteem than may in some little measure draw a belief from
you, to do yourself good and not to grace me. Believe then,
if you please, that I can do strange things. I have, since I
was three years old, conversed with a magician, most profound in his art and yet not damnable. If you do love Rosalind so near the heart as your gesture cries it out, when your
brother marries Aliena, shall you marry her: I know into
what straits of fortune she is driven; and it is not impossible
to me, if it appear not inconvenient to you, to set her before
your eyes to-morrow human as she is and without any danger.

ORLANDO. Speakest thou in sober meanings?

ROSALIND. By my life, I do; which I tender dearly, though I
say I am a magician. Therefore, put you in your best array;
bid your friends; for if you will be married to-morrow, you
shall; and to Rosalind, if you will.

Enter SILVIUS *and* PHEBE.]

Look, here comes a lover of mine and a lover of hers.

PHEBE. Youth, you have done me much ungentleness,
To show the letter that I writ to you.

ROSALIND. I care not if I have: it is my study
To seem despiteful and ungentle to you:
You are there followed by a faithful shepherd;
Look upon him, love him; he worships you.

PHEBE. Good shepherd, tell this youth what 'tis to love.

SILVIUS. It is to be all made of sighs and tears;
And so am I for Phebe.

PHEBE. And I for Ganymede.

ORLANDO. And I for Rosalind.

ROSALIND. And I for no woman.

SILVIUS. It is to be all made of faith and service;
And so am I for Phebe.

PHEBE. And I for Ganymede.

ORLANDO. And I for Rosalind.

ROSALIND. And I for no woman.

SILVIUS. It is to be all made of fantasy.
All made of passion, and all made of wishes;
All adoration, duty, and observance,
All humbleness, all patience, and impatience,
All purity, all trial, all observance;
And so am I for Phebe.

PHEBE. And so am I for Ganymede.

ORLANDO. And so am I for Rosalind.

ROSALIND. And so am I for no woman.

PHEBE. If this be so, why blame you me to love you?

SILVIUS. If this be so, why blame you me to love you?

ORLANDO. If this be so, why blame you me to love you?

ROSALIND. Who do you speak to, 'Why blame you me to love
you?'

ORLANDO. To her that is not here, nor doth not hear.

ROSALIND. Pray you, no more of this; 'tis like the howling of
Irish wolves against the moon. [*To* SILVIUS.] I will help you,
if I can: [*To* PHEBE.] I would love you, if I could. To-morrow meet me all together. [*To* PHEBE.] I will marry you, if
ever I marry woman, and I 'll be married to-morrow: [*To*
ORLANDO.] I will satisfy you, if ever I satisfied man, and you
shall be married to-morrow: [*To* SILVIUS.] I will content
you, if what pleases you contents you, and you shall be
married to-morrow. [*To* ORLANDO.] As you love Rosalind,
meet: [*To* SILVIUS.] As you love Phebe, meet: and as I love
no woman, I 'll meet. So, fare you well: I have left you
commands.

SILVIUS. I 'll not fail if I live.

PHEBE. Nor I.

ORLANDO. Nor I.

SCENE III — *The forest.*

Enter TOUCHSTONE *and* AUDREY.]

TOUCHSTONE. To-morrow is the joyful day, Audrey; to-morrow will we be married.

AUDREY. I do desire it with all my heart; and I hope it is no dishonest desire to desire to be a woman of the world. Here come two of the banished Duke's pages.

Enter two PAGES.]

FIRST PAGE. Well met, honest gentleman.

TOUCHSTONE. By my troth, well met. Come, sit, sit, and a song.

SECOND PAGE. We are for you: sit i' the middle.

FIRST PAGE. Shall we clap into 't roundly, without hawking or spitting or saying we are hoarse, which are the only prologues to a bad voice?

SECOND PAGE. I' faith, i' faith; and both in a tune, like two gipsies on a horse.

SONG

It was a lover and his lass,
    With a hey, and a ho, and a hey nonino,
That o'er the green corn-field did pass
    In the spring time, the only pretty ring time,
When birds do sing, hey ding a ding, ding:
Sweet lovers love the spring.

Between the acres of the rye.
    With a hey, and a ho, and a hey nonino,
These pretty country folks would lie,
    In the spring time, &c.

This carol they began that hour,
    With a hey, and a ho, and a hey nonino,
How that a life was but a flower
    In the spring time, &c.

And therefore take the present time,
    With a hey, and a ho, and a hey nonino;
For love is crowned with the prime
    In the spring time, &c.

TOUCHSTONE. Truly, young gentlemen, though there was no
    great matter in the ditty, yet the note was very untuneable.
FIRST PAGE. You are deceived, sir: we kept time, we lost not
    our time.
TOUCHSTONE. By my troth, yes; I count it but time lost to hear
    such a foolish song. God be wi' you; and God mend your
    voices! Come, Audrey.   [*Exeunt.*

SCENE IV — *The forest.*

Enter DUKE SENIOR, AMIENS, JAQUES, ORLANDO,
    OLIVER, *and* CELIA.]
DUKE SENIOR. Dost thou believe, Orlando, that the boy
    Can do all this that he hath promised?
ORLANDO. I sometimes do believe, and sometimes do not;
    As those that fear they hope, and know they fear.
Enter ROSALIND, SILVIUS, *and* PHEBE.]
ROSALIND. Patience once more, whiles our compact is urged:
    You say, if I bring in your Rosalind,
    You will bestow her on Orlando here?
DUKE SENIOR. That would I, had I kingdoms to give with her.
ROSALIND. And you say, you will have her, when I bring her.
ORLANDO. That would I, were I of all kingdoms king.
ROSALIND. You say, you'll marry me, if I be willing?
PHEBE. That will I, should I die the hour after.
ROSALIND. But if you do refuse to marry me,
    You'll give yourself to this most faithful shepherd?
PHEBE. So is the bargain.
ROSALIND. You say, that you'll have Phebe, if she will?
SILVIUS. Though to have her and death were both one thing.
ROSALIND. I have promised to make all this matter even.
    Keep you your word, O Duke, to give your daughter;
    You yours, Orlando, to receive his daughter:

Keep your word, Phebe, that you'll marry me,
Or else refusing me, to wed this shepherd:
Keep your word, Silvius, that you'll marry her,
If she refuse me: and from hence I go,
To make these doubts all even.

[*Exeunt* ROSALIND *and* CELIA.

DUKE SENIOR. I do remember in this shepherd boy
Some lively touches of my daughter's favor.

ORLANDO. My lord, the first time that I ever saw him
Methought he was a brother to your daughter;
But, my good lord, this boy is forest-born,
And hath been tutor'd in the rudiments
Of many desperate studies by his uncle,
Whom he reports to be a great magician,
Obscured in the circle of this forest.

Enter TOUCHSTONE *and* AUDREY.]

JAQUES. There is, sure, another flood toward, and these couples
are coming to the ark. Here comes a pair of very strange
beasts, which in all tongues are called fools.

TOUCHSTONE. Salutation and greeting to you all!

JAQUES. Good my lord, bid him welcome: this is the motley-
minded gentleman that I have so often met in the forest:
he hath been a courtier, he swears.

TOUCHSTONE. If any man doubt that, let him put me to my
purgation. I have trod a measure; I have flattered a lady;
I have been politic with my friend, smooth with mine
enemy; I have undone three tailors; I have had four quarrels, and like to have fought one.

JAQUES. And how was that ta'en up?

TOUCHSTONE. Faith, we met, and found the quarrel was upon
the seventh cause.

JAQUES. How seventh cause? Good my lord, like this fellow.

DUKE SENIOR. I like him very well.

TOUCHSTONE. God 'ild you, sir; I desire you of the like. I press
in here, sir, amongst the rest of the country copulatives, to
swear and to forswear; according as marriage binds and
blood breaks: a poor virgin, sir, an ill-favored thing, sir, but

mine own; a poor humor of mine, sir, to take that that no man else will: rich honesty dwells like a miser, sir, in a poor house; as your pearl in your foul oyster.

DUKE SENIOR. By my faith, he is very swift and sententious.

TOUCHSTONE. According to the fool's bolt, sir, and such dulcet diseases.

JAQUES. But, for the seventh cause; how did you find the quarrel on the seventh cause?

TOUCHSTONE. Upon a lie seven times removed:—bear your body more seeming, Audrey:—as thus, sir. I did dislike the cut of a certain courtier's beard: he sent me word, if I said his beard was not cut well, he was in the mind it was: this is called the Retort Courteous. If I sent him word again 'it was not well cut,' he would send me word, he cut it to please himself: this is called the Quip Modest. If again 'it was not well cut,' he disabled my judgment: this is called the Reply Churlish. If again 'it was not well cut,' he would answer, I spake not true: this is called the Reproof Valiant. If again 'it was not well cut,' he would say, I lie: this is called the Countercheck Quarrelsome: and so to the Lie Circumstantial and the Lie Direct.

JAQUES. And how oft did you say his beard was not well cut?

TOUCHSTONE. I durst go no further than the Lie Circumstantial, nor he durst not give me the Lie Direct; and so we measured swords and parted.

JAQUES. Can you nominate in order now the degrees of the lie?

TOUCHSTONE. O sir, we quarrel in print, by the book; as you have books for good manners: I will name you the degrees. The first, the Retort Courteous; the second, the Quip Modest; the third, the Reply Churlish; the fourth, the Reproof Valiant; the fifth, the Countercheck Quarrelsome; the sixth, the Lie with Circumstance; the seventh, the Lie Direct. All these you may avoid but the Lie Direct; and you may avoid that too, with an If. I knew when seven justices could not take up a quarrel, but when the parties were met themselves, one of them thought but of an If, as, 'If you said so, then I said so'; and they shook hands and swore brothers. Your If is the only peace-maker; much virtue in If.

JAQUES. Is not this a rare fellow, my lord? he's as good at any thing and yet a fool.

DUKE SENIOR. He uses his folly like a stalking-horse and under the presentation of that he shoots his wit.

Enter HYMEN, ROSALIND, *and* CELIA. *Still Music.*]

HYMEN. Then is there mirth in heaven,
    When earthly things made even
        Atone together.
    Good Duke, receive thy daughter:
    Hymen from heaven brought her,
        Yea, brought her hither,
    That thou mightst join her hand with his
    Whose heart within his bosom is.

ROSALIND. [*To* DUKE SENIOR.] To you I give myself, for I am yours.

[*To* ORLANDO.] To you I give myself, for I am yours.

DUKE SENIOR. If there be truth in sight, you are my daughter.

ORLANDO. If there be truth in sight, you are my Rosalind.

PHEBE.   If sight and shape be true,
        Why then, my love adieu!

ROSALIND. [*To* DUKE SENIOR.] I'll have no father, if you be not he:

[*To* ORLANDO.] I'll have no husband, if you be not he:

[*To* PHEBE.] Nor ne'er wed woman, if you be not she.

HYMEN. Peace, ho! I bar confusion:
    'Tis I must make conclusion
        Of these most strange events:
    Here's eight that must take hands
    To join in Hymen's bands,
        If truth holds true contents.
    You and you no cross shall part:
    You and you are heart in heart:
    You to his love must accord,
    Or have a woman to your lord:
    You and you are sure together,
    As the winter to foul weather.
    Whiles a wedlock-hymn we sing,
    Feed yourselves with questioning;

That reason wonder may diminish,
How thus we met, and these things finish.

Song

 Wedding is great Juno's crown:
  O blessed bond of board and bed!
 'Tis Hymen peoples every town;
  High wedlock then be honored:
 Honor, high honor and renown,
 To Hymen, god of every town!

DUKE SENIOR. O my dear niece, welcome thou art to me!
 Even daughter, welcome, in no less degree.
PHEBE. I will not eat my word, now thou art mine;
 Thy faith my fancy to thee doth combine.
Enter JAQUES DE BOYS.]
JAQUES DE BOYS. Let me have audience for a word or two;
 I am the second son of old Sir Rowland,
 That bring these tidings to this fair assembly.
 Duke Frederick, hearing how that every day
 Men of great worth resorted to this forest,
 Address'd a mighty power; which were on foot,
 In his own conduct, purposely to take
 His brother here and put him to the sword:
 And to the skirts of this wild wood he came;
 Where meeting with an old religious man,
 After some question with him, was converted
 Both from his enterprise and from the world;
 His crown bequeathing to his banish'd brother,
 And all their lands restored to them again
 That were with him exiled. This to be true,
 I do engage my life.
DUKE SENIOR.   Welcome, young man;
 Thou offer'st fairly to thy brothers' wedding:
 To one his lands withheld; and to the other
 A land itself at large, a potent dukedom.
 First, in this forest let us do those ends
 That here were well begun and well begot:

And after, every of this happy number,
That have endured shrewd days and nights with us,
Shall share the good of our returned fortune,
According to the measure of their states.
Meantime, forget this new-fallen dignity,
And fall into our rustic revelry.
Play, music! And you, brides and bridegrooms all
With measure heap'd in joy, to the measures fall.

JAQUES. Sir, by your patience. If I heard you rightly,
The Duke hath put on a religious life
And thrown into neglect the pompous court?

JAQUES DE BOYS. He hath.

JAQUES. To him will I: out of these convertites
There is much matter to be heard and learn'd.
[*To* DUKE SENIOR.] You to your former honor I bequeath;
Your patience and your virtue well deserve it:
[*To* ORLANDO.] You to a love, that your true faith doth merit:
[*To* OLIVER.] You to your land, and love, and great allies:
[*To* SILVIUS.] You to a long and well-deserved bed:
[*To* TOUCHSTONE.] And you to wrangling; for thy loving voy-
    age
Is but for two months victuall'd. So, to your pleasures:
I am for other than for dancing measures.

DUKE SENIOR. Stay, Jaques, stay.

JAQUES. To see no pastime I: what you would have
I 'll stay to know at your abandon'd cave.   [*Exit*.

DUKE SENIOR. Proceed, proceed: we will begin these rites,
As we do trust they 'll end, in true delights.   [*A dance*.

Epilogue

ROSALIND. It is not the fashion to see the lady the epilogue; but it is no more unhandsome than to see the lord the prologue. If it be true that good wine needs no bush, 'tis true that a good play needs no epilogue: yet to good wine they do use good bushes; and good plays prove the better by the help of good epilogues. What a case am I in then, that am neither a good epilogue, nor cannot insinuate with you in the behalf of a good play! I am not furnished like a beggar, therefore to beg will not become me: my way is to conjure you; and I'll begin with the women. I charge you, O women, for the love you bear to men, to like as much of this play as please you: and I charge you, O men, for the love you bear to women,—as I perceive by your simpering, none of you hates them,—that between you and the women the play may please. If I were a woman I would kiss as many of you as had beards that pleased me, complexions that liked me and breaths that I defied not: and, I am sure, as many as have good beards or good faces or sweet breaths will, for my kind offer, when I make curtsy, bid me farewell.

[*Exeunt.*

Twelfth Night

or

WHAT YOU WILL

Twelfth Night

MARK VAN DOREN

IF so absorbing a masterpiece as *Twelfth Night* permits the
reader to keep any other play in his mind while he reads,
that play is *The Merchant of Venice*. Once again Shakespeare
has built a world out of music and melancholy, and once
again this world is threatened by an alien voice. The opposi-
tion of Malvolio to Orsino and his class parallels the opposi-
tion of Shylock to Antonio and his friends. The parallel is not
precise, and the contrast is more subtly contrived; Shakespeare holds the balance in a more delicate hand, so that the
ejection of Malvolio is perhaps less painful to our sense of
justice than the punishments heaped upon Shylock until he is
crushed under their weight. But the parallel exists, and nothing provides a nicer opportunity for studying the way in
which Shakespeare, returning to a congenial theme, could
ripen and enrich it.

Orsino's opening speech is not merely accompanied by music; it discusses music, and it is music in itself. Furthermore,
a suggestion of surfeit or satiety occurs as early as the second
line: this suggestion, so consonant with Orsino's melancholy
tone, to be developed throughout a speech of considerable
complexity. For at more than one point *Twelfth Night* fore-
shadows the concentration and even the difficulty which will
be found in the poetry of the later plays.

> If music be the food of love, play on!
> Give me excess of it, that, surfeiting,
> The appetite may sicken, and so die.

> That strain again! It had a dying fall.
> O, it came o'er my ear like the sweet sound
> That breathes upon a bank of violets
> Stealing and giving odour. Enough! no more!
> 'T is not so sweet now as it was before.
> O spirit of love, how quick and fresh art thou,
> That, notwithstanding thy capacity
> Receiveth as the sea, nought enters there,
> Of what validity and pitch soe'er,
> But falls into abatement and low price
> Even in a minute! So full of shapes is fancy
> That it alone is high fantastical.

The music of *The Merchant of Venice* is freer than this, more
youthful and less tangled with ideas of sickness; and the bank
of violets has aged beyond the simple sweetness of Lorenzo's
bank whereon the moonlight slept. Orsino's love for Olivia
turns in upon him and torments him. He is as mannerly in his
sadness as Antonio was, but he knows, or thinks he knows, the
origin of his state. He may not wholly know; his melancholy
is in part a fine convention of his class, like the preference he
feels for olden days and the gentle idiom of an outmoded
music.

> Give me some music. Now,—good morrow, friends,—
> Now, good Cesario, but that piece of song,
> That old and antique song we heard last night.
> Methought it did relieve my passion much,
> More than light airs and recollected terms
> Of these most brisk and giddy-paced times. . . .
> O, fellow, come, the song we had last night.
> Mark it, Cesario, it is old and plain.
> The spinsters and the knitters in the sun
> And the free maids that weave their thread with bones
> Do use to chant it. It is silly sooth,
> And dallies with the innocence of love,
> Like the old age.   [II, iv]

Orsino is indeed an exquisitely finished portrait of his type.
His is the luxury of a "secret soul" (I, iv), and it is natural
that he should so easily understand the young gentleman who

is Viola in disguise, and who lets concealment, like a worm i'
the bud, feed on her damask cheek (II, iv). Viola's variety of
melancholy is green and yellow. Olivia's is "sad and civil"
(III, iv). But all of them are graced with sadness. It is the
mark of their citizenship in a world which knows a little less
than the world of *The Merchant of Venice* did what to do
with its treasure of wealth and beauty, and whose spoken
language has deepened its tone, complicated its syntax,
learned how to listen to itself. This is the way Orsino argues
himself into believing that Olivia will love him when she is
done mourning her dead brother:

> O, she that hath a heart of that fine frame
> To pay this debt of love but to a brother,
> How will she love when the rich golden shaft
> Hath kill'd the flock of all affections else
> That live in her; when liver, brain, and heart,
> These sovereign thrones, are all suppli'd, and fill'd
> Her sweet perfections with one self king!   [I, i]

And here is Olivia remembering how Cesario (Viola) had
spoken in her presence:

> "What is your parentage?"
> "Above my fortunes, yet my state is well.
> I am a gentleman." I'll be sworn thou art.
> Thy tongue, thy face, thy limbs, actions, and spirit
> Do give thee five-fold blazon. Not too fast! Soft, soft!
> Unless the master were the man. How now!
> Even so quickly may one catch the plague?
> Methinks I feel this youth's perfections
> With an invisible and subtle stealth
> To creep in at mine eyes. Well, let it be.   [I, v]

The involutions of such discourse are entirely natural to both
speakers. For their caste is the noblest in Illyria. One of them
is a lady and the other is a gentleman.

Sir Toby Belch is a gentleman too, or at any rate he belongs. He is an old relation and retainer in the somewhat clut-
tered household of Olivia. *The Merchant of Venice* never took

us so deep into domestic details. The household of Olivia is old-world, it is Merry England. At its center sits the lady Olivia, but there is room for every other kind of person here for whom a changing age has still not made existence impossible. There is the clown Feste and the clever servant Fabian; and there is the still cleverer servant Maria, whose extreme smallness is rendered clear to us, in the perverse language of a good-natured people, by such terms as "giant" and "Penthesilea," though she is also a "wren" and a "little villain." Chiefly, however, there is Sir Toby. He is gluttonous and drunken, and must be kept out of sight as much as possible; but Olivia would no more turn him away than she would refuse to hear an excellent old song sung to the lute. For one thing there is no place for Sir Toby to go. He is as old-fashioned as Falstaff, and as functionless in the modern world. "Am not I consanguineous? Am I not of her blood?" (II, iii). He even talks like Falstaff, puffingly and explosively, as he reminds Maria that he is Olivia's uncle. And for another thing he belongs. Old households harbor such old men. They are nuisances to be endured because they are symbols of enduringness, signs of the family's great age. Sir Toby has another parasite on him—Sir Andrew Aguecheek, whose foolish devotion to Olivia he makes use of to keep himself in money. For of course he has no money; and Sir Andrew has a little. It is a crowded household, swarming with gross life behind high walls of custom. When Sir Andrew says he is of the opinion that life consists of eating and drinking, Sir Toby applauds him roundly: "Thou'rt a scholar; let us therefore eat and drink" (II, iii). The fat old fellow's second appearance in the play (I, v) brings him on belching—"a plague o' these pickle-herring!" And he is ever as full of wine as he is loud with song. "How now, sot!" "Shall we make the welkin dance indeed? Shall we rouse the night-owl in a catch that will draw three souls out of one weaver? Shall we do that?" (II, iii).

It is to Sir Toby that Malvolio is most alien. "Dost thou think, because thou art virtuous, there shall be no more cakes and ale?" This most famous sentence in the play is more than Sir Toby disposing of his niece's steward; it is the old world resisting the new, it is the life of hiccups and melancholy trying to ignore latter-day puritanism and efficiency. On the occasion when it is spoken there is danger for Sir Toby in the fact that Olivia is moody with her new love for Cesario; she has lost patience with her kinsman's misdemeanors, and may send him off. But Malvolio is the last man on earth to come with the message. "Tell us something of him," says Sir Toby to Maria.

MARIA. Marry, sir, sometimes he is a kind of puritan.

SIR ANDREW. O, if I thought that, I'd beat him like a dog!

SIR TOBY. What, for being a puritan? Thy exquisite reason, dear knight?

SIR ANDREW. I have no exquisite reason for 't, but I have reason good enough. [II, iii]

So has Sir Toby, though neither of them is articulate enough to say what it is. Doubtless they have never thought it out. They only know that the sight of Malvolio, like the sound of his voice, threatens death to their existence. His own existence somehow challenges their right to be freely what they are. He is of a new order—ambitious, self-contained, cold and intelligent, and dreadfully likely to prevail. That is why Sir Toby and his retinue hate him. Feste at the end provides too simple an explanation. The humiliation of Malvolio, he says, was his personal revenge upon one who had discounted him to his mistress as "a barren rascal," a jester unworthy of his hire. But the others had been as active as Feste, and they had had no such motive. "The devil a puritan that he is," Maria insists, "or anything constantly, but a time-pleaser; an affection'd ass" (II, iii). Puritan or not, Malvolio has offended them as a class. They could have forgiven his being a climber, his having affection for himself, if he had been any other kind of man than the cool kind he is.

The earliest protest against his disposition is made in fact by Olivia herself, on the occasion when Feste has been amus-

ing her with samples of his wit and Malvolio, asked for his
opinion of the stuff, cuts in with this commentary:

> I marvel your ladyship takes delight in such a barren rascal. I
> saw him put down the other day with an ordinary fool that has no
> more brain than a stone. Look you now, he's out of his guard al-
> ready. Unless you laugh and minister occasion to him, he is gagg'd.
> I protest, I take these wise men, that crow so at these set kind of
> fools, no better than the fools' zanies.   [I, v]

He has appeared to be judging the kind of fool Feste is, and
his success within that kind; but Olivia sees through to the
root of the matter, which is that he does not like jesting at all.

> O, you are sick of self-love, Malvolio, and taste with a dis-
> temper'd appetite. To be generous, guiltless, and of free disposi-
> tion, is to take those things for bird-bolts that you deem cannon-
> bullets. There is no slander in an allow'd fool, though he do
> nothing but rail; nor no railing in a known discreet man, though
> he do nothing but reprove.

She gives him, in brief, a lesson in the manners of her breed.
If he supposes Feste's jibes at her to have been slanderous,
that is because he does not understand how little time her
people spend in thinking of themselves; if they are free and
generous, and know the code, they will laugh at things which
to an outsider must sound outrageous. Malvolio may have a
sense of humor, but it is not the kind that goes with her code.

Olivia does not bother with him again until he comes,
cross-gartered and smiling, to make her think him mad. Meanwhile the roysterers within her gates carry the criticism on.
And Malvolio is given a voice which perfectly explains the
criticism. The fatal difference between his nature and that of
the drunken singers in Olivia's cellar rings out as clearly as if
notes had been struck on a warning bell. To begin with there
is the fact that Malvolio hates music; as Shylock had de-
clared the harmonies of a carnival to be wrynecked and
squealing, so he denounces the strains of "O mistress mine,
where are you roaming?" as "the gabble of tinkers" (II, iii).
And then there is the icy, tight-lipped fashion of his speech, a

fashion that contrasts with the thoughtless, bawling, open-throated style of Sir Toby as frost contrasts with foam, and with the grave, rich style of Orsino or Olivia as steel contrasts with gold. In his niggard's nature he has developed a mannerism which he forces to do all the work of his thought. It is economical and efficient, and it attests his trained intelligence, but it cuts offensively into the hearing of his foes.

> Do ye make an alehouse of my lady's house, that ye squeak out your coziers' catches *without any mitigation or remorse of voice?*
>
> [II, iii]

> And then *to have the humour of state;* and *after a demure travel of regard,* . . . to ask for my kinsman Toby. . . . Seven of my people, *with an obedient start,* make out for him. . . . I extend my hand to him thus, *quenching my familiar smile with an austere regard of control.*
>
> [II, v]

> I am no more mad than you are. Make the trial of it *in any constant question.*
>
> [IV, ii]

> And tell me, *in the modesty of honour.*
>
> [V, i]

> And, acting this *in an obedient hope.*
>
> [V, i]

The syntax is brilliantly condensed, but the tone is condescending; a man speaks who thinks of himself as master and frowns the while, tapping the floor till it tinkles like iron and winding up his watch as if it kept time for a universe of "lighter people" (V, i). No wonder his enemies loathe him. "O, for a stone-bow, to hit him in the eye!" (II, v). And no wonder, since their ears are clever, that they mimic his precious manner when they compose the note he is to read as a love-letter from Olivia:

> Let thy tongue tang *arguments of state;* put thyself *into the trick of singularity.*
>
> [II, v]

They have not failed to notice his lordly way with the little word "of," or the practice of his hand as he plucks the string of any other preposition, or the miracle by which he can give an effect of terseness to polysyllables. And they have studied his vocabulary as though it were an index of terms never to be used again. "I might say 'element,'" Feste observes, "but the word is overworn" (III, i). The word is Malvolio's, though we are not aware of this till later. "You are idle shallow things; I am not of your element" (III, iv), he draws himself straighter and higher than ever and announces as gables announce icicles.

"He hath been most notoriously abus'd" (v, i). Olivia's line rights Malvolio's wrong, but her household will never grant him the last justice of love. Where there is such difference there cannot be love. That is what *Twelfth Night* is most interested in saying, and saying with an impartiality which precludes sentiment. The balance between Malvolio and his enemies is delicate; they are attractive, as all loose livers are, yet there is an integrity in his tightness, a loftiness other than the misguided one, which we cannot but respect. Modern audiences have bestowed more sympathy upon Malvolio than Shakespeare perhaps intended, so that the balance is now not what it was. It can scarcely be overthrown, however, whatever changes the whirligig of time brings in. The foundation for comedy here is too firm for that, the counterpoint of effects is too sanely arranged. This world of music and mannerly sadness is not sentimentally conceived. Even within its gates the violin voice of Orsino is corrected by the bawling bass of Sir Toby, and the elegant neuroses of the nobility are parodied on servants' tongues. "Now, the melancholy god protect thee," calls Feste after Orsino, mocking him. And Fabian, told of the plot against Malvolio, can rub his hands and say: "If I lose a scruple of this sport, let me be boil'd to death with melancholy" (II, v). A balance of tones is maintained, indeed, everywhere in *Twelfth Night*. Nature and artifice, sanity and sentiment, are so equally at home here that they can with the greatest difficulty be distinguished from one another; nor in our delight are we disposed to try.

All the while, of course, a story of twins is being told, and three cases of love at first sight (Viola and Orsino, Olivia and Viola, Sebastian and Olivia) are being dove-tailed into a pattern of romance. Shakespeare's interest in Viola cannot be doubted.

> My father had a daughter lov'd a man,
> As it might be, perhaps, were I a woman,
> I should your lordship.   [II, iv]

Nor can that of the audience, for she is Julia grown to greatness. But other portions of the pattern deserve and are given only such attention as is necessary. The confusion of the twins and the farce of the fencing-match are not what the comedy is essentially about, any more than the marriage of Olivia and Sebastian is—and the perfunctoriness of Shakespeare's feeling with respect to that marriage is clearly confessed in the kind of verse he gives the priest to speak (v, i). Even Viola, much as we like her, stands a little to one side of the center. The center is Malvolio. The drama is between his mind and the music of old manners.

The Story of the Play

ACT I

SEBASTIAN and Viola, twins, are separated by shipwreck and each believes the other lost. Viola is cast ashore on the coast of Illyria. She thereupon dons male attire and obtains service as page with the Duke Orsino, who has been vainly suing for the hand of Olivia, a native lady. The Duke is pleased with the appearance of his new page and sends Viola to pay court for him to Olivia, which she does with so much gracefulness and eloquence that the lady becomes enamoured of the supposed youth instead of the master.

ACT II

OLIVIA sends favours and messages to Viola in which, naturally, the latter takes no interest. Viola, in turn, has conceived a passion for the Duke, which she is compelled to hide.

Olivia's steward, Malvolio, is so priggish and conceited that others of her household contrive a practical joke against him, sending him an anonymous love-letter which he is given to believe is from Olivia herself.

ACT III

MALVOLIO follows instructions contained in the letter, and behaves so ridiculously that his mistress believes him demented.

Meanwhile Olivia's love for Viola becomes so intense that she sues openly to the fictitious page, much to the latter's distress. Sir Andrew Aguecheek, a foolish suitor of Olivia's, is displeased at the favours shown the page, and in a spirit of bravado challenges Viola. Though both are eager to avoid the conflict, it is only averted by the arrival of officers.

ACT IV

SEBASTIAN, Viola's brother, who was also cast up by the sea, comes to Illyria. He looks so much like his sister—especially since she is in men's garments—that Sir Andrew mistakes him for the page and renews the fight. This time he does not encounter a woman's shrinking spirit or weak arm, and he is soundly belaboured. Soon after, Olivia also meets Sebastian, supposes him to be Viola and reiterates her devotion. The delighted Sebastian returns love for love and they are secretly espoused before a priest.

ACT V

OLIVIA encounters Viola in company with the Duke and greets her by the title of husband. The bewildered page disavows the title, but the priest who performed the ceremony vouches for it. The Duke is much disgruntled that his favourite page should so abuse his confidence. Viola is meeting with general disfavour, when her brother Sebastian arrives on the scene, and the two who had thought each other dead are reunited. Olivia discovers that she has espoused the brother, after having wooed the sister, while the Duke finds that his attachment for his page becomes love when Viola resumes her feminine attire.

The secret of Malvolio's dementia is revealed, and he is released from the confinement in which he has been held.

J. WALKER McSPADDEN

List of Characters

ORSINO,
　　　　Duke of Illyria

SEBASTIAN,
　　　　brother to VIOLA

ANTONIO,
　　　　a sea captain,
　　friend to SEBASTIAN

A Sea Captain,
　　　　friend to VIOLA

VALENTINE, }
CURIO,　　 }
　　gentlemen attending
　　　　on the DUKE

SIR TOBY BELCH,
　　　　uncle to OLIVIA

SIR ANDREW AGUECHEEK

MALVOLIO,
　　　　steward to OLIVIA

FABIAN,　　　　 }
FESTE, a clown, }
　　servants to OLIVIA

OLIVIA

VIOLA

MARIA,
　　OLIVIA's woman

Lords, Priests, Sailors,
Officers, Musicians,
　　　　and
other Attendants

OLIVIA

VIOLA

MALVOLIO

MARIA

SIR TOBY BELCH

Twelfth Night; or, What You Will

SCENE — *A city in* ILLYRIA, *and the sea-coast near it.*

ACT I

SCENE I — *An apartment in the* DUKE'S *palace.*

Enter DUKE, CURIO, *and other* LORDS; MUSICIANS
attending.]

DUKE. If music be the food of love, play on;
Give me excess of it, that, surfeiting,
The appetite may sicken, and so die.
That strain again! it had a dying fall:
O, it came o'er my ear like the sweet sound,
That breathes upon a bank of violets,
Stealing and giving odor! Enough; no more:
'Tis not so sweet now as it was before.
O spirit of love, how quick and fresh art thou!
That, notwithstanding thy capacity
Receiveth as the sea, nought enters there,
Of what validity and pitch soe'er,
But falls into abatement and low price,
Even in a minute! so full of shapes is fancy,
That it alone is high fantastical.

CURIO. Will you go hunt, my lord?

DUKE.   What, Curio?

CURIO. The hart.

DUKE. Why, so I do, the noblest that I have:
O, when mine eyes did see Olivia first,
Methought she purged the air of pestilence!
That instant was I turn'd into a hart;
And my desires, like fell and cruel hounds,
E'er since pursue me.

186

Enter VALENTINE.]
                       How now! what news from her?
VALENTINE. So please my lord, I might not be admitted;
  But from her handmaid do return this answer:
  The element itself, till seven years' heat,
  Shall not behold her face at ample view;
  But, like a cloistress, she will veiled walk
  And water once a day her chamber round
  With eye-offending brine: all this to season
  A brother's dead love, which she would keep fresh
  And lasting in her sad remembrance.
DUKE. O, she that hath a heart of that fine frame
  To pay this debt of love but to a brother,
  How will she love, when the rich golden shaft
  Hath kill'd the flock of all affections else
  That live in her; when liver, brain and heart,
  These sovereign thrones, are all supplied, and fill'd
  Her sweet perfections with one self king!
  Away before me to sweet beds of flowers:
  Love-thoughts lie rich when canopied with bowers.
                            [*Exeunt.*

SCENE II — *The sea-coast.*

Enter VIOLA, *a* CAPTAIN, *and* SAILORS.]
VIOLA. What country, friends, is this?
CAPTAIN. This is Illyria, lady.
VIOLA. And what should I do in Illyria?
  My brother he is in Elysium.
  Perchance he is not drown'd: what think you, sailors?
CAPTAIN. It is perchance that you yourself were saved.
VIOLA. O my poor brother! and so perchance may he be.
CAPTAIN. True, madam: and, to comfort you with chance,
  Assure yourself, after our ship did split,
  When you and those poor number saved with you
  Hung on our driving boat, I saw your brother,
  Most provident in peril, bind himself,
  Courage and hope both teaching him the practice,

To a strong mast that lived upon the sea;
Where, like Arion on the dolphin's back,
I saw him hold acquaintance with the waves
So long as I could see.

VIOLA. For saying so, there 's gold:
Mine own escape unfoldeth to my hope,
Whereto thy speech serves for authority,
The like of him. Know'st thou this country?

CAPTAIN. Aye, madam, well; for I was bred and born
Not three hours' travel from this very place.

VIOLA. Who governs here?

CAPTAIN. A noble Duke, in nature as in name.

VIOLA. What is his name?

CAPTAIN. Orsino.

VIOLA. Orsino! I have heard my father name him:
He was a bachelor then.

CAPTAIN. And so is now, or was so very late;
For but a month ago I went from hence,
And then 'twas fresh in murmur,—as, you know,
What great ones do the less will prattle of,—
That he did seek the love of fair Olivia.

VIOLA. What 's she?

CAPTAIN. A virtuous maid, the daughter of a count
That died some twelvemonth since; then leaving her
In the protection of his son, her brother,
Who shortly also died: for whose dear love,
They say, she hath abjured the company
And sight of men.

VIOLA.   O that I served that lady,
And might not be delivered to the world,
Till I had made mine own occasion mellow,
What my estate is!

CAPTAIN.   That were hard to compass;
Because she will admit no kind of suit,
No, not the Duke's.

VIOLA. There is a fair behavior in thee, captain;
And though that nature with a beauteous wall
Doth oft close in pollution, yet of thee

I will believe thou hast a mind that suits
With this thy fair and outward character.
I prithee, and I 'll pay thee bounteously,
Conceal me what I am, and be my aid
For such disguise as haply shall become
The form of my intent. I 'll serve this Duke:
Thou shalt present me as an eunuch to him:
It may be worth thy pains; for I can sing,
And speak to him in many sorts of music,
That will allow me very worth his service.
What else may hap to time I will commit;
Only shape thou thy silence to my wit.

CAPTAIN. Be you his eunuch, and your mute I 'll be:
When my tongue blabs, then let mine eyes not see.

VIOLA. I thank thee: lead me on.　　　　　　　*[Exeunt.*

SCENE III — OLIVIA's *house.*

Enter SIR TOBY BELCH *and* MARIA.]

SIR TOBY. What a plague means my niece, to take the death of
her brother thus? I am sure care 's an enemy to life.

MARIA. By my troth, Sir Toby, you must come in earlier o'
nights: your cousin, my lady, takes great exceptions to your
ill hours.

SIR TOBY. Why, let her except, before excepted.

MARIA. Aye, but you must confine yourself within the modest
limits of order.

SIR TOBY. Confine! I 'll confine myself no finer than I am: these
clothes are good enough to drink in; and so be these boots
too: an they be not, let them hang themselves in their own
straps.

MARIA. That quaffing and drinking will undo you: I heard my
lady talk of it yesterday; and of a foolish knight that you
brought in one night here to be her wooer.

SIR TOBY. Who, Sir Andrew Aguecheek?

MARIA. Aye, he.

SIR TOBY. He 's as tall a man as any 's in Illyria.

MARIA. What 's that to the purpose?

SIR TOBY. Why, he has three thousand ducats a year.

MARIA. Aye, but he 'll have but a year in all these ducats; he 's a very fool and a prodigal.

SIR TOBY. Fie, that you'll say so! he plays o' the viol-de-gamboys, and speaks three or four languages word for word without book, and hath all the good gifts of nature.

MARIA. He hath indeed, almost natural: for besides that he 's a fool, he 's a great quarreler: and but that he hath the gift of a coward to allay the gust he hath in quarreling, 'tis thought among the prudent he would quickly have the gift of a grave.

SIR TOBY. By this hand, they are scoundrels and subtractors that say so of him. Who are they?

MARIA. They that add, moreover, he 's drunk nightly in your company.

SIR TOBY. With drinking healths to my niece: I 'll drink to her as long as there is a passage in my throat and drink in Illyria: he 's a coward and a coystrill that will not drink to my niece till his brains turn o' the toe like a parish-top. What, wench! Castiliano vulgo; for here comes Sir Andrew Agueface.

Enter SIR ANDREW AGUECHEEK.]

SIR ANDREW. Sir Toby Belch! how now, Sir Toby Belch!

SIR TOBY. Sweet Sir Andrew!

SIR ANDREW. Bless you, fair shrew.

MARIA. And you too, sir.

SIR TOBY. Accost, Sir Andrew, accost.

SIR ANDREW. What 's that?

SIR TOBY. My niece's chambermaid.

SIR ANDREW. Good Mistress Accost, I desire better acquaintance.

MARIA. My name is Mary, sir.

SIR ANDREW. Good Mistress Mary Accost,—

SIR TOBY. You mistake, knight: 'accost' is front her, board her, woo her, assail her.

SIR ANDREW. By my troth, I would not undertake her in this company. Is that the meaning of 'accost'?

MARIA. Fare you well, gentlemen.

SIR TOBY. An thou let part so, Sir Andrew, would thou mightst never draw sword again.

SIR ANDREW. An you part so, mistress, I would I might never draw sword again. Fair lady, do you think you have fools in hand?

MARIA. Sir, I have not you by the hand.

SIR ANDREW. Marry, but you shall have; and here 's my hand.

MARIA. Now, sir, 'thought is free': I pray you, bring your hand to the buttery-bar and let it drink.

SIR ANDREW. Wherefore, sweetheart? what 's your metaphor?

MARIA. It 's dry, sir.

SIR ANDREW. Why, I think so: I am not such an ass but I can keep my hand dry. But what 's your jest?

MARIA. A dry jest, sir.

SIR ANDREW. Are you full of them?

MARIA. Aye, sir, I have them at my fingers' ends: marry, now I let go your hand, I am barren.   [*Exit.*

SIR TOBY. O knight, thou lackest a cup of canary: when did I see thee so put down?

SIR ANDREW. Never in your life, I think; unless you see canary put me down. Methinks sometimes I have no more wit than a Christian or an ordinary man has: but I am a great eater of beef and I believe that does harm to my wit.

SIR TOBY. No question.

SIR ANDREW. An I thought that, I 'ld forswear it. I 'll ride home to-morrow, Sir Toby.

SIR TOBY. Pourquoi, my dear knight?

SIR ANDREW. What is 'pourquoi'? do or not do? I would I had bestowed that time in the tongues that I have in fencing, dancing and bear-baiting: O, had I but followed the arts!

SIR TOBY. Then hadst thou had an excellent head of hair.

SIR ANDREW. Why, would that have mended my hair?

SIR TOBY. Past question; for thou seest it will not curl by nature.

SIR ANDREW. But it becomes me well enough, does 't not?

SIR TOBY. Excellent; it hangs like flax on a distaff; and I hope to see a housewife take thee between her legs and spin it off.

SIR ANDREW. Faith, I 'll home to-morrow, Sir Toby: your niece will not be seen; or if she be, it 's four to one she 'll none of me: the count himself here hard by woos her.

SIR TOBY. She 'll none o' the count: she 'll not match above her degree, neither in estate, years, nor wit; I have heard her swear 't. Tut, there 's life in 't, man.

SIR ANDREW. I 'll stay a month longer. I am a fellow o' the strangest mind i' the world; I delight in masques and revels sometimes altogether.

SIR TOBY. Art thou good at these kickshawses, knight?

SIR ANDREW. As any man in Illyria, whatsoever he be, under the degree of my betters; and yet I will not compare with an old man.

SIR TOBY. What is thy excellence in a galliard, knight?

SIR ANDREW. Faith, I can cut a caper.

SIR TOBY. And I can cut the mutton to 't.

SIR ANDREW. And I think I have the back-trick simply as strong as any man in Illyria.

SIR TOBY. Wherefore are these things hid? wherefore have these gifts a curtain before 'em? are they like to take dust, like Mistress Mall's picture? why dost thou not go to church in a galliard and come home in a coranto? My very walk should be a jig; I would not so much as make water but in a sink-a-pace. What dost thou mean? Is it a world to hide virtues in? I did think, by the excellent constitution of thy leg, it was formed under the star of a galliard.

SIR ANDREW. Aye, 'tis strong, and it does indifferent well in a flame-colored stock. Shall we set about some revels?

SIR TOBY. What shall we do else? were we not born under Taurus?

SIR ANDREW. Taurus! That 's sides and heart.

SIR TOBY. No, sir; it is legs and thighs. Let me see thee caper: ha! higher: ha, ha! excellent!   [*Exeunt.*

SCENE IV — *The* DUKE'S *palace.*

Enter VALENTINE, *and* VIOLA *in man's attire.*]

VALENTINE. If the Duke continue these favors towards you,
 Cesario, you are like to be much advanced: he hath known
 you but three days, and already you are no stranger.

VIOLA. You either fear his humor or my negligence, that you
 call in question the continuance of his love: is he inconstant, sir, in his favors?

VALENTINE. No, believe me.

VIOLA. I thank you. Here comes the count.

Enter DUKE, CURIO, *and* ATTENDANTS.]

DUKE. Who saw Cesario, ho?

VIOLA. On your attendance, my lord; here.

DUKE. Stand you a while aloof. Cesario,
 Thou know'st no less but all; I have unclasp'd
 To thee the book even of my secret soul:
 Therefore, good youth, address thy gait unto her;
 Be not denied access, stand at her doors,
 And tell them, there thy fixed foot shall grow
 Till thou have audience.

VIOLA.   Sure, my noble lord,
 If she be so abandon'd to her sorrow
 As it is spoke, she never will admit me.

DUKE. Be clamorous and leap all civil bounds
 Rather than make unprofited return.

VIOLA. Say I do speak with her, my lord, what then?

DUKE. O, then unfold the passion of my love,
 Surprise her with discourse of my dear faith:
 It shall become thee well to act my woes;
 She will attend it better in thy youth
 Than in a nuncio's of more grave aspect.

VIOLA. I think not so, my lord.

DUKE.   Dear lad, believe it;
 For they shall yet belie thy happy years,
 That say thou art a man; Diana's lip

Is not more smooth and rubious; thy small pipe
Is as the maiden's organ, shrill and sound;
And all is semblative a woman's part.
I know thy constellation is right apt
For this affair. Some four or five attend him;
All, if you will; for I myself am best
When least in company. Prosper well in this,
And thou shalt live as freely as thy lord,
To call his fortunes thine.

VIOLA.   I 'll do my best
To woo your lady: [*Aside*] yet, a barful strife!
Whoe'er I woo, myself would be his wife.   [*Exeunt.*

Scene V — Olivia's *house.*

Enter MARIA *and* CLOWN.]

MARIA. Nay, either tell me where thou hast been, or I will not
open my lips so wide as a bristle may enter in way of thy
excuse: my lady will hang thee for thy absence.

CLOWN. Let her hang me: he that is well hanged in this world
needs to fear no colors.

MARIA. Make that good.

CLOWN. He shall see none to fear.

MARIA. A good lenten answer: I can tell thee where that saying was born, of 'I fear no colors.'

CLOWN. Where, good Mistress Mary?

MARIA. In the wars; and that may you be bold to say in your
foolery.

CLOWN. Well, God give them wisdom that have it; and those
that are fools, let them use their talents.

MARIA. Yet you will be hanged for being so long absent; or, to
be turned away, is not that as good as a hanging to you?

CLOWN. Many a good hanging prevents a bad marriage; and,
for turning away, let summer bear it out.

MARIA. You are resolute, then?

CLOWN. Not so, neither; but I am resolved on two points.

MARIA. That if one break, the other will hold; or, if both
break, your gaskins fall.

CLOWN. Apt, in good faith; very apt. Well, go thy way; if Sir
Toby would leave drinking, thou wert as witty a piece of
Eve's flesh as any in Illyria.

MARIA. Peace, you rogue, no more o' that. Here comes my
lady: make your excuse wisely, you were best. [*Exit.*

CLOWN. Wit, an 't be thy will, put me into good fooling! Those
wits, that think they have thee, do very oft prove fools; and
I, that am sure I lack thee, may pass for a wise man: for
what says Quinapalus? 'Better a witty fool than a foolish
wit.'

Enter LADY OLIVIA *with* MALVOLIO.]

God bless thee, lady.

OLIVIA. Take the fool away.

CLOWN. Do you not hear, fellows? Take away the lady.

OLIVIA. Go to, you 're a dry fool; I 'll no more of you: besides,
you grow dishonest.

CLOWN. Two faults, madonna, that drink and good counsel
will amend: for give the dry fool drink, then is the fool not
dry: bid the dishonest man mend himself; if he mend, he is
no longer dishonest; if he cannot, let the botcher mend him.
Any thing that 's mended is but patched: virtue that trans-
gresses is but patched with sin; and sin that amends is but
patched with virtue. If that this simple syllogism will serve,
so; if it will not, what remedy? As there is no true cuckold
but calamity, so beauty 's a flower. The lady bade take away
the fool; therefore I say again, take her away.

OLIVIA. Sir, I bade them take away you.

CLOWN. Misprision in the highest degree! Lady, *cucullus non
facit monachum*; that 's as much to say as I wear not motley in my brain. Good madonna, give me leave to prove you
a fool.

OLIVIA. Can you do it?

CLOWN. Dexteriously, good madonna.

OLIVIA. Make your proof.

CLOWN. I must catechize you for it, madonna: good my mouse
of virtue, answer me.

OLIVIA. Well, sir, for want of other idleness, I 'll bide your
proof.

CLOWN. Good madonna, why mournest thou?

OLIVIA. Good fool, for my brother's death.

CLOWN. I think his soul is in hell, madonna.

OLIVIA. I know his soul is in heaven, fool.

CLOWN. The more fool, madonna, to mourn for your brother's soul being in heaven. Take away the fool, gentlemen.

OLIVIA. What think you of this fool, Malvolio? doth he not mend?

MALVOLIO. Yes, and shall do till the pangs of death shake him: infirmity, that decays the wise, doth ever make the better fool.

CLOWN. God send you, sir, a speedy infirmity, for the better increasing your folly! Sir Toby will be sworn that I am no fox; but he will not pass his word for two pence that you are no fool.

OLIVIA. How say you to that, Malvolio?

MALVOLIO. I marvel your ladyship takes delight in such a barren rascal: I saw him put down the other day with an ordinary fool that has no more brain than a stone. Look you now, he 's out of his guard already; unless you laugh and minister occasion to him, he is gagged. I protest, I take these wise men, that crow so at these set kind of fools, no better than fools' zanies.

OLIVIA. O, you are sick of self-love, Malvolio, and taste with a distempered appetite. To be generous, guiltless and of free disposition, is to take those things for bird-bolts that you deem cannon-bullets: there is no slander in an allowed fool, though he do nothing but rail; nor no railing in a known discreet man, though he do nothing but reprove.

CLOWN. Now Mercury endue thee with leasing, for thou speakest well of fools!

Re-enter MARIA.]

MARIA. Madam, there is at the gate a young gentleman much desires to speak with you.

OLIVIA. From the Count Orsino, is it?

MARIA. I know not, madam: 'tis a fair young man, and well attended.

OLIVIA. Who of my people hold him in delay?

MARIA. Sir Toby, madam, your kinsman.

OLIVIA. Fetch him off, I pray you; he speaks nothing but madman: fie on him! [*Exit* MARIA.] Go you, Malvolio: if it be a suit from the count, I am sick, or not at home; what you will, to dismiss it. [*Exit* MALVOLIO.] Now you see, sir, how your fooling grows old, and people dislike it.

CLOWN. Thou hast spoke for us, madonna, as if thy eldest son should be a fool; whose skull Jove cram with brains! for,— here he comes,—one of thy kin has a most weak pia mater.

Enter SIR TOBY.]

OLIVIA. By mine honor, half drunk. What is he at the gate, cousin?

SIR TOBY. A gentleman.

OLIVIA. A gentleman! what gentleman?

SIR TOBY. 'Tis a gentleman here—a plague o' these pickle-herring! How now, sot!

CLOWN. Good Sir Toby!

OLIVIA. Cousin, cousin, how have you come so early by this lethargy?

SIR TOBY. Lechery! I defy lechery. There's one at the gate.

OLIVIA. Aye, marry, what is he?

SIR TOBY. Let him be the devil, an he will, I care not: give me faith, say I. Well, it's all one.   [*Exit.*

OLIVIA. What's a drunken man like, fool?

CLOWN. Like a drowned man, a fool and a mad man: one draught above heat makes him a fool; the second mads him; and a third drowns him.

OLIVIA. Go thou and seek the crowner, and let him sit o' my coz; for he's in the third degree of drink, he's drowned: go look after him.

CLOWN. He is but mad yet, madonna; and the fool shall look to the madman.   [*Exit.*

Re-enter MALVOLIO.]

MALVOLIO. Madam, yond young fellow swears he will speak with you. I told him you were sick; he takes on him to understand so much, and therefore comes to speak with you. I told him you were asleep; he seems to have a foreknowledge of that too, and therefore comes to speak with you.

What is to be said to him, lady? he 's fortified against any denial.

OLIVIA. Tell him he shall not speak with me.

MALVOLIO. Has been told so; and he says, he 'll stand at your door like a sheriff's post, and be the supporter to a bench, but he 'll speak with you.

OLIVIA. What kind o' man is he?

MALVOLIO. Why, of mankind.

OLIVIA. What manner of man?

MALVOLIO. Of very ill manner: he 'll speak with you, will you or no.

OLIVIA. Of what personage and years is he?

MALVOLIO. Not yet old enough for a man, nor young enough for a boy; as a squash is before 'tis a peascod, or a codling when 'tis almost an apple: 'tis with him in standing water, between boy and man. He is very well-favored and he speaks very shrewishly; one would think his mother's milk were scarce out of him.

OLIVIA. Let him approach: call in my gentlewoman.

MALVOLIO. Gentlewoman, my lady calls.   [*Exit.*
Re-enter MARIA.]

OLIVIA. Give me my veil: come, throw it o'er my face.
We 'll once more hear Orsino's embassy.

Enter VIOLA, *and* ATTENDANTS.]

VIOLA. The honorable lady of the house, which is she?

OLIVIA. Speak to me; I shall answer for her. Your will?

VIOLA. Most radiant, exquisite and unmatchable beauty,—I pray you, tell me if this be the lady of the house, for I never saw her: I would be loath to cast away my speech, for besides that it is excellently well penned, I have taken great pains to con it. Good beauties, let me sustain no scorn; I am very comptible, even to the least sinister usage.

OLIVIA. Whence came you, sir?

VIOLA. I can say little more than I have studied, and that question 's out of my part. Good gentle one, give me modest assurance if you be the lady of the house, that I may proceed in my speech.

OLIVIA. Are you a comedian?

VIOLA. No, my profound heart: and yet, by the very fangs of malice I swear, I am not that I play. Are you the lady of the house?

OLIVIA. If I do not usurp myself, I am.

VIOLA. Most certain, if you are she, you do usurp yourself; for what is yours to bestow is not yours to reserve. But this is from my commission: I will on with my speech in your praise, and then show you the heart of my message.

OLIVIA. Come to what is important in 't: I forgive you the praise.

VIOLA. Alas, I took great pains to study it, and 'tis poetical.

OLIVIA. It is the more like to be feigned. I pray you, keep it in. I heard you were saucy at my gates, and allowed your approach rather to wonder at you than to hear you. If you be not mad, be gone; if you have reason, be brief; 'tis not that time of moon with me to make one in so skipping a dialogue.

MARIA. Will you hoist sail, sir? here lies your way.

VIOLA. No, good swabber; I am to hull here a little longer. Some mollification for your giant, sweet lady. Tell me your mind: I am a messenger.

OLIVIA. Sure, you have some hideous matter to deliver, when the courtesy of it is so fearful. Speak your office.

VIOLA. It alone concerns your ear. I bring no overture of war, no taxation of homage: I hold the olive in my hand; my words are as full of peace as matter.

OLIVIA. Yet you began rudely. What are you? what would you?

VIOLA. The rudeness that hath appeared in me have I learned from my entertainment. What I am, and what I would, are as secret as maiden-head; to your ears, divinity, to any other's, profanation.

OLIVIA. Give us the place alone: we will hear this divinity. [*Exeunt* MARIA *and* ATTENDANTS.] Now, sir, what is your text?

VIOLA. Most sweet lady,—

OLIVIA. A comfortable doctrine, and much may be said of it. Where lies your text?

VIOLA. In Orsino's bosom.

OLIVIA. In his bosom! In what chapter of his bosom?

VIOLA. To answer by the method, in the first of his heart.

OLIVIA. O, I have read it: it is heresy. Have you no more to say?

VIOLA. Good madam, let me see your face.

OLIVIA. Have you any commission from your lord to negotiate with my face? You are now out of your text: but we will draw the curtain and show you the picture. Look you, sir, such a one I was this present: is 't not well done?

                                                          [*Unveiling.*

VIOLA. Excellently done, if God did all.

OLIVIA. 'Tis in grain, sir; 'twill endure wind and weather.

VIOLA. 'Tis beauty truly blent, whose red and white
Nature's own sweet and cunning hand laid on:
Lady, you are the cruel'st she alive,
If you will lead these graces to the grave
And leave the world no copy.

OLIVIA. O, sir, I will not be so hard-hearted; I will give out divers schedules of my beauty: it shall be inventoried, and every particle and utensil labeled to my will: as, item, two lips indifferent red; item, two gray eyes, with lids to them; item, one neck, one chin, and so forth. Were you sent hither to praise me?

VIOLA. I see you what you are, you are too proud;
But, if you were the devil, you are fair.
My lord and master loves you: O, such love
Could be but recompensed, though you were crown'd
The nonpareil of beauty!

OLIVIA.   How does he love me?

VIOLA. With adorations, fertile tears,
With groans that thunder love, with sighs of fire.

OLIVIA. Your lord does know my mind; I cannot love him:
Yet I suppose him virtuous, know him noble,
Of great estate, of fresh and stainless youth;
In voices well divulged, free, learn'd and valiant;
And in dimension and the shape of nature
A gracious person: but yet I cannot love him;
He might have took his answer long ago.

VIOLA. If I did love you in my master's flame,
　　With such a suffering, such a deadly life,
　　In your denial I would find no sense;
　　I would not understand it.

OLIVIA. 　　　　　　Why, what would you?

VIOLA. Make me a willow cabin at your gate,
　　And call upon my soul within the house;
　　Write loyal cantons of contemned love
　　And sing them loud even in the dead of night;
　　Halloo your name to the reverberate hills,
　　And make the babbling gossip of the air
　　Cry out 'Olivia!' O, you should not rest
　　Between the elements of air and earth,
　　But you should pity me!

OLIVIA. 　　　　　　You might do much.
　　What is your parentage?

VIOLA. Above my fortunes, yet my state is well:
　　I am a gentleman.

OLIVIA. 　　　　　Get you to your lord;
　　I cannot love him: let him send no more;
　　Unless, perchance, you come to me again,
　　To tell me how he takes it. Fare you well:
　　I thank you for your pains: spend this for me.

VIOLA. I am no fee'd post, lady; keep your purse:
　　My master, not myself, lacks recompense.
　　Love make his heart of flint that you shall love;
　　And let your fervor, like my master's, be
　　Placed in contempt! Farewell, fair cruelty. 　　　[*Exit.*

OLIVIA. 'What is your parentage?'
　　'Above my fortunes, yet my state is well:
　　I am a gentleman.' I 'll be sworn thou art;
　　Thy tongue, thy face, thy limbs, actions, and spirit,
　　Do give thee five-fold blazon: not too fast: soft, soft!
　　Unless the master were the man. How now!
　　Even so quickly may one catch the plague?
　　Methinks I feel this youth's perfections
　　With an invisible and subtle stealth

To creep in at mine eyes. Well, let it be.
What ho, Malvolio!

Re-enter MALVOLIO.]

MALVOLIO.   Here, madam, at your service.

OLIVIA. Run after that same peevish messenger,
The county's man: he left this ring behind him,
Would I or not: tell him I 'll none of it.
Desire him not to flatter with his lord,
Nor hold him up with hopes; I am not for him:
If that the youth will come this way to-morrow,
I 'll give him reasons for 't; hie thee, Malvolio.

MALVOLIO. Madam, I will.   [*Exit.*

OLIVIA. I do I know not what, and fear to find
Mine eye too great a flatterer for my mind.
Fate, show thy force: ourselves we do not owe;
What is decreed must be, and be this so.   [*Exit.*

ACT II

Scene I — *The sea-coast.*

Enter ANTONIO *and* SEBASTIAN.]

ANTONIO. Will you stay no longer? nor will you not that I go with you?

SEBASTIAN. By your patience, no. My stars shine darkly over me: the malignancy of my fate might perhaps distemper yours; therefore I shall crave of you your leave that I may bear my evils alone: it were a bad recompense for your love, to lay any of them on you.

ANTONIO. Let me yet know of you whither you are bound.

SEBASTIAN. No, sooth, sir: my determinate voyage is mere extravagancy. But I perceive in you so excellent a touch of modesty, that you will not extort from me what I am willing to keep in; therefore it charges me in manners the rather to express myself. You must know of me then, Antonio, my name is Sebastian, which I called Roderigo. My father was that Sebastian of Messaline, whom I know you have heard of. He left behind him myself and a sister, both born in an hour: if the heavens had been pleased, would we had so ended! but you, sir, altered that; for some hour before you took me from the breach of the sea was my sister drowned.

ANTONIO. Alas the day.

SEBASTIAN. A lady, sir, though it was said she much resembled me, was yet of many accounted beautiful: but, though I could not with such estimable wonder overfar believe that, yet thus far I will boldly publish her; she bore a mind that envy could not but call fair. She is drowned already, sir, with salt water, though I seem to drown her remembrance again with more.

ANTONIO. Pardon me, sir, your bad entertainment.

SEBASTIAN. O good Antonio, forgive me your trouble.

ANTONIO. If you will not murder me for my love, let me be your servant.

SEBASTIAN. If you will not undo what you have done, that is,
kill him whom you have recovered, desire it not. Fare ye
well at once: my bosom is full of kindness, and I am yet so
near the manners of my mother, that upon the least occasion more mine eyes will tell tales of me. I am bound to the
Count Orsino's court: farewell.   [*Exit.*

ANTONIO. The gentleness of all the gods go with thee!
I have many enemies in Orsino's court,
Else would I very shortly see thee there.
But, come what may, I do adore thee so,
That danger shall seem sport, and I will go.   [*Exit.*

SCENE II — *A street.*

Enter VIOLA, MALVOLIO *following.*]

MALVOLIO. Were not you even now with the Countess Olivia?

VIOLA. Even now, sir; on a moderate pace I have since arrived
but hither.

MALVOLIO. She returns this ring to you, sir: you might have
saved me my pains, to have taken it away yourself. She
adds, moreover, that you should put your lord into a desperate assurance she will none of him: and one thing more,
that you be never so hardy to come again in his affairs, unless it be to report your lord's taking of this. Receive it so.

VIOLA. She took the ring of me: I'll none of it.

MALVOLIO. Come, sir, you peevishly threw it to her; and her
will is, it should be so returned: if it be worth stooping for,
there it lies in your eye; if not, be it his that finds it.   [*Exit.*

VIOLA. I left no ring with her: what means this lady?
Fortune forbid my outside have not charm'd her!
She made good view of me; indeed, so much,
That methought her eyes had lost her tongue,
For she did speak in starts distractedly.
She loves me, sure; the cunning of her passion
Invites me in this churlish messenger.
None of my lord's ring! why, he sent her none.
I am the man: if it be so, as 'tis,
Poor lady, she were better love a dream.
Disguise, I see, thou art a wickedness,

Wherein the pregnant enemy does much.
How easy is it for the proper-false
In women's waxen hearts to set their forms!
Alas, our frailty is the cause, not we!
For such as we are made of, such we be.
How will this fadge? my master loves her dearly;
And I, poor monster, fond as much on him;
And she, mistaken, seems to dote on me.
What will become of this? As I am man,
My state is desperate for my master's love;
As I am woman,—now alas the day!—
What thriftless sighs shall poor Olivia breathe!
O time! thou must untangle this, not I;
It is too hard a knot for me to untie!　　　　　　*[Exit.*

Scene III — Olivia's *house.*

Enter Sir Toby *and* Sir Andrew.]

Sir Toby. Approach, Sir Andrew: not to be abed after midnight is to be up betimes; and 'diluculo surgere,' thou know'st,—

Sir Andrew. Nay, by my troth, I know not: but I know, to be up late is to be up late.

Sir Toby. A false conclusion: I hate it as an unfilled can. To be up after midnight and to go to bed then, is early: so that to go to bed after midnight is to go to bed betimes. Does not our life consist of the four elements?

Sir Andrew. Faith, so they say; but I think it rather consists of eating and drinking.

Sir Toby. Thou 'rt a scholar; let us therefore eat and drink. Marian, I say! a stoup of wine!

Enter Clown.]

Sir Andrew. Here comes the fool, i' faith.

Clown. How now, my hearts! did you never see the picture of 'we three'?

Sir Toby. Welcome, ass. Now let 's have a catch.

Sir Andrew. By my troth, the fool has an excellent breast. I had rather than forty shillings I had such a leg, and so sweet a breath to sing, as the fool has. In sooth, thou wast

in very gracious fooling last night, when thou spokest of
Pigrogromitus, of the Vapians passing the equinoctial of
Queubus: 'twas very good, i' faith. I sent thee sixpence for
thy leman: hadst it?

CLOWN. I did impeticos thy gratillity; for Malvolio's nose is no
whipstock: my lady has a white hand, and the Myrmidons
are no bottle-ale houses.

SIR ANDREW. Excellent! why, this is the best fooling, when all
is done. Now, a song.

SIR TOBY. Come on; there is sixpence for you: let 's have a
song.

SIR ANDREW. There 's a testril of me, too: if one knight give a—

CLOWN. Would you have a love-song, or a song of good life?

SIR TOBY. A love-song, a love-song.

SIR ANDREW. Aye, aye: I care not for good life.

CLOWN. [Sings]

> O mistress mine, where are you roaming?
> O, stay and hear; your true love's coming,
>   That can sing both high and low:
> Trip no further, pretty sweeting;
> Journeys end in lovers meeting,
>   Every wise man's son doth know.

SIR ANDREW. Excellent good, i' faith.

SIR TOBY. Good, good.

CLOWN. [Sings]

> What is love? 'tis not hereafter;
> Present mirth hath present laughter;
>   What 's to come is still unsure:
> In delay there lies no plenty;
> Then come kiss me, sweet and twenty,
>   Youth 's a stuff will not endure.

SIR ANDREW. A mellifluous voice, as I am true knight.

SIR TOBY. A contagious breath.

SIR ANDREW. Very sweet and contagious, i' faith.

SIR TOBY. To hear by the nose, it is dulcet in contagion. But
shall we make the welkin dance indeed? shall we rouse the
night-owl in a catch that will draw three souls out of one
weaver? shall we do that?

SIR ANDREW. An you love me, let's do 't. I am dog at a catch.

CLOWN. By 'r lady, sir, and some dogs will catch well.

SIR ANDREW. Most certain. Let our catch be, 'Thou knave.'

CLOWN. 'Hold thy peace, thou knave,' knight? I shall be constrained in 't to call thee knave, knight.

SIR ANDREW. 'Tis not the first time I have constrained one to call me knave. Begin, fool: it begins 'Hold thy peace.'

CLOWN. I shall never begin if I hold my peace.

SIR ANDREW. Good, i' faith. Come, begin.   [*Catch sung.*
Enter MARIA.]

MARIA. What a caterwauling do you keep here! If my lady have not called up her steward Malvolio and bid him turn you out of doors, never trust me.

SIR TOBY. My lady's a Cataian, we are politicians, Malvolio 's a Peg-a-Ramsey, and 'Three merry men be we.' Am not I consanguineous? am I not of her blood? Tillyvally. Lady! [*Sings*] 'There dwelt a man in Babylon, lady, lady!'

CLOWN. Beshrew me, the knight 's in admirable fooling.

SIR ANDREW. Aye, he does well enough if he be disposed, and so do I too: he does it with a better grace, but I do it more natural.

SIR TOBY. [*Sings*] 'O, the twelfth day of December,'—

MARIA. For the love o' God, peace!
Enter MALVOLIO.]

MALVOLIO. My masters, are you mad? or what are you? Have you no wit, manners, nor honesty, but to gabble like tinkers at this time of night? Do ye make an alehouse of my lady's house, that ye squeak out your coziers' catches without any mitigation or remorse of voice? Is there no respect of place, persons, nor time in you?

SIR TOBY. We did keep time, sir, in our catches. Sneck up!

MALVOLIO. Sir Toby, I must be round with you. My lady bade me tell you, that, though she harbors you as her kinsman, she 's nothing allied to your disorders. If you can separate yourself and your misdemeanors, you are welcome to the house; if not, an it would please you to take leave of her, she is very willing to bid you farewell.

SIR TOBY. 'Farewell, dear heart, since I must needs be gone.'

MARIA. Nay, good Sir Toby.

CLOWN. 'His eyes do show his days are almost done.'

MALVOLIO. Is 't even so?

SIR TOBY. 'But I will never die.'

CLOWN. Sir Toby, there you lie.

MALVOLIO. This is much credit to you.

SIR TOBY. 'Shall I bid him go?'

CLOWN. 'What an if you do?'

SIR TOBY. 'Shall I bid him go, and spare not?'

CLOWN. 'O no, no, no, no, you dare not.'

SIR TOBY. Out o' tune, sir: ye lie. Art any more than a steward? Dost thou think, because thou art virtuous, there shall be no more cakes and ale?

CLOWN. Yes, by Saint Anne, and ginger shall be hot i' the mouth too.

SIR TOBY. Thou 'rt i' the right. Go, sir, rub your chain with crums. A stoup of wine, Maria!

MALVOLIO. Mistress Mary, if you prized my lady's favor at any thing more than contempt, you would not give means for this uncivil rule: she shall know of it, by this hand. [*Exit.*

MARIA. Go shake your ears.

SIR ANDREW. 'Twere as good a deed as to drink when a man 's a-hungry, to challenge him the field, and then to break promise with him and make a fool of him.

SIR TOBY. Do 't, knight: I 'll write thee a challenge; or I 'll deliver thy indignation to him by word of mouth.

MARIA. Sweet Sir Toby, be patient for to-night: since the youth of the count's was to-day with my lady, she is much out of quiet. For Monsieur Malvolio, let me alone with him: if I do not gull him into a nayword, and make him a common recreation, do not think I have wit enough to lie straight in my bed; I know I can do it.

SIR TOBY. Possess us, possess us; tell us something of him.

MARIA. Marry, sir, sometimes he is a kind of puritan.

SIR ANDREW. O, if I thought that, I 'ld beat him like a dog!

SIR TOBY. What, for being a puritan? thy exquisite reason, dear knight?

SIR ANDREW. I have no exquisite reason for 't, but I have reason good enough.

MARIA. The devil a puritan that he is, or any thing constantly, but a time-pleaser; an affectioned ass, that cons state without book and utters it by great swarths: the best persuaded of himself, so crammed, as he thinks, with excellencies, that it is his grounds of faith that all that look on him love him; and on that vice in him will my revenge find notable cause to work.

SIR TOBY. What wilt thou do?

MARIA. I will drop in his way some obscure epistles of love; wherein, by the color of his beard, the shape of his leg, the manner of his gait, the expressure of his eye, forehead, and complexion, he shall find himself most feelingly personated. I can write very like my lady your niece: on a forgotten matter we can hardly make distinction of our hands.

SIR TOBY. Excellent! I smell a device.

SIR ANDREW. I have 't in my nose too.

SIR TOBY. He shall think, by the letters that thou wilt drop, that they come from my niece, and that she 's in love with him.

MARIA. My purpose is, indeed, a horse of that color.

SIR ANDREW. And your horse now would make him an ass.

MARIA. Ass, I doubt not.

SIR ANDREW. O, 'twill be admirable!

MARIA. Sport royal, I warrant you: I know my physic will work with him. I will plant you two, and let the fool make a third, where he shall find the letter: observe his construction of it. For this night, to bed, and dream on the event. Farewell. [*Exit.*

SIR TOBY. Good night, Penthesilea.

SIR ANDREW. Before me, she 's a good wench.

SIR TOBY. She 's a beagle, true-bred, and one that adores me: what o' that?

SIR ANDREW. I was adored once too.

SIR TOBY. Let 's to bed, knight. Thou hadst need send for more money.

SIR ANDREW. If I cannot recover your niece, I am a foul way out.

SIR TOBY. Send for money, knight; if thou hast her not i' the
  end, call me cut.

SIR ANDREW. If I do not, never trust me, take it how you will.

SIR TOBY. Come, come, I 'll go burn some sack; 'tis too late to
  go to bed now: come, knight; come, knight.   [*Exeunt.*

SCENE IV — *The* DUKE'S *palace.*

Enter DUKE, VIOLA, CURIO, *and others.*]

DUKE. Give me some music. Now, good morrow, friends,
  Now, good Cesario, but that piece of song,
  That old and antique song we heard last night:
  Methought it did relieve my passion much,
  More than light airs and recollected terms
  Of these most brisk and giddy-paced times:
  Come, but one verse.

CURIO. He is not here, so please your lordship, that should
  sing it.

DUKE. Who was it?

CURIO. Feste, the jester, my lord; a fool that the lady Olivia's
  father took much delight in.
  He is about the house.

DUKE. Seek him out, and play the tune the while.

                    [*Exit* CURIO. *Music plays.*

  Come hither, boy: if ever thou shalt love,
  In the sweet pangs of it remember me;
  For such as I am all true lovers are,
  Unstaid and skittish in all motions else,
  Save in the constant image of the creature
  That is beloved. How dost thou like this tune?

VIOLA. It gives a very echo to the seat
  Where love is throned.

DUKE.   Thou dost speak masterly:
  My life upon 't, young though thou art, thine eye
  Hath stay'd upon some favor that it loves:
  Hath it not, boy?

VIOLA.   A little, by your favor.

DUKE. What kind of woman is 't?

VIOLA.   Of your complexion.

DUKE. She is not worth thee, then. What years, i' faith?

VIOLA. About your years, my lord.

DUKE. Too old, by heaven: let still the woman take
 An elder than herself; so wears she to him,
 So sways she level in her husband's heart:
 For, boy, however we do praise ourselves,
 Our fancies are more giddy and unfirm,
 More longing, wavering, sooner lost and worn,
 Than women's are.

VIOLA.   I think it well, my lord.

DUKE. Then let thy love be younger than thyself,
 Or thy affection cannot hold the bent;
 For women are as roses, whose fair flower
 Being once display'd, doth fall that very hour.

VIOLA. And so they are: alas, that they are so;
 To die, even when they to perfection grow!

Re-enter CURIO *and* CLOWN.]

DUKE. O, fellow, come, the song we had last night.
 Mark it, Cesario, it is old and plain;
 The spinsters and the knitters in the sun
 And the free maids that weave their thread with bones
 Do use to chant it: it is silly sooth,
 And dallies with the innocence of love,
 Like the old age.

CLOWN. Are you ready, sir?

DUKE. Aye; prithee, sing.   [*Music.*

SONG.

CLOWN. Come away, come away, death,
  And in sad cypress let me be laid;
 Fly away, fly away, breath;
  I am slain by a fair cruel maid.
 My shroud of white, stuck all with yew,
   O, prepare it!
 My part of death, no one so true
   Did share it.

 Not a flower, not a flower sweet,
  On my black coffin let there be strown;

  Not a friend, not a friend greet
   My poor corpse, where my bones shall be
    thrown:
  A thousand thousand sighs to save,
    Lay me, O, where
  Sad true lover never find my grave,
    To weep there!

DUKE. There 's for thy pains.

CLOWN. No pains, sir; I take pleasure in singing, sir.

DUKE. I 'll pay thy pleasure then.

CLOWN. Truly, sir, and pleasure will be paid, one time or another.

DUKE. Give me now leave to leave thee.

CLOWN. Now, the melancholy god protect thee; and the tailor make thy doublet of changeable taffeta, for thy mind is a very opal. I would have men of such constancy put to sea, that their business might be every thing and their intent every where; for that 's it that always makes a good voyage of nothing. Farewell.   [*Exit.*

DUKE. Let all the rest give place.

      [CURIO *and* ATTENDANTS *retire.*
      Once more, Cesario,
Get thee to yond same sovereign cruelty:
Tell her, my love, more noble than the world,
Prizes not quantity of dirty lands;
The parts that fortune hath bestow'd upon her,
Tell her, I hold as giddily as fortune;
But 'tis that miracle and queen of gems
That nature pranks her in attracts my soul.

VIOLA. But if she cannot love you, sir?

DUKE. I cannot be so answer'd.

VIOLA.   Sooth, but you must.
Say that some lady, as perhaps there is,
Hath for your love as great a pang of heart
As you have for Olivia: you cannot love her;
You tell her so; must she not then be answer'd?

DUKE. There is no woman's sides

Can bide the beating of so strong a passion
As love doth give my heart; no woman's heart
So big, to hold so much; they lack retention.
Alas, their love may be call'd appetite,—
No motion of the liver, but the palate,—
That suffer surfeit, cloyment and revolt;
But mine is all as hungry as the sea,
And can digest as much: make no compare
Between that love a woman can bear me
And that I owe Olivia.

VIOLA.   Aye, but I know,—

DUKE. What dost thou know?

VIOLA. Too well what love women to men may owe:
In faith, they are as true of heart as we.
My father had a daughter loved a man,
As it might be, perhaps, were I a woman,
I should your lordship.

DUKE.   And what 's her history?

VIOLA. A blank, my lord. She never told her love,
But let concealment, like a worm i' the bud,
Feed on her damask cheek; she pined in thought
And with a green and yellow melancholy
She sat like patience on a monument,
Smiling at grief. Was not this love indeed?
We men may say more, swear more: but indeed
Our shows are more than will; for still we prove
Much in our vows, but little in our love.

DUKE. But died thy sister of her love, my boy?

VIOLA. I am all the daughters of my father's house,
And all the brothers too: and yet I know not.
Sir, shall I to this lady?

DUKE.   Aye that 's the theme.
To her in haste; give her this jewel; say,
My love can give no place, bide no denay.   [*Exeunt.*

SCENE V — OLIVIA'S *garden.*

Enter SIR TOBY, SIR ANDREW, *and* FABIAN.]

SIR TOBY. Come thy ways, Signior Fabian.

FABIAN. Nay, I 'll come: if I lose a scruple of this sport, let me
be boiled to death with melancholy.

SIR TOBY. Wouldst thou not be glad to have the niggardly rascally sheep-biter come by some notable shame?

FABIAN. I would exult, man: you know, he brought me out o'
favor with my lady about a bear-baiting here.

SIR TOBY. To anger him we 'll have the bear again and we will
fool him black and blue: shall we not, Sir Andrew?

SIR ANDREW. An we do not, it is pity of our lives.

SIR TOBY. Here comes the little villain.

Enter MARIA.]

How now, my metal of India!

MARIA. Get ye all three into the box-tree: Malvolio's coming
down this walk: he has been yonder i' the sun practising
behavior to his own shadow this half hour: observe him, for
the love of mockery; for I know this letter will make a con-
templative idiot of him. Close, in the name of jesting! Lie
thou there [*throws down a letter*]; for here comes the trout
that must be caught with tickling.   [*Exit.*

Enter MALVOLIO.]

MALVOLIO. 'Tis but fortune; all is fortune. Maria once told me
she did affect me: and I have heard herself come thus near,
that, should she fancy, it should be one of my complexion.
Besides, she uses me with a more exalted respect than any
one else that follows her. What should I think on 't?

SIR TOBY. Here 's an overweening rogue!

FABIAN. O, peace! Contemplation makes a rare turkey-cock of
him: how he jets under his advanced plumes!

SIR ANDREW. 'Slight, I could so beat the rogue!

SIR TOBY. Peace, I say.

MALVOLIO. To be Count Malvolio!

SIR TOBY. Ah, rogue!

SIR ANDREW. Pistol him, pistol him.

SIR TOBY. Peace, peace!

MALVOLIO. There is example for 't; the lady of the Strachy
married the yeoman of the wardrobe.

SIR ANDREW. Fie on him, Jezebel!

FABIAN. O, peace! now he 's deeply in: look how imagination blows him.

MALVOLIO. Having been three months married to her, sitting in my state,—

SIR TOBY. O, for a stone-bow, to hit him in the eye!

MALVOLIO. Calling my officers about me, in my branched velvet gown; having come from a day-bed, where I have left Olivia sleeping,—

SIR TOBY. Fire and brimstone!

FABIAN. O, peace, peace!

MALVOLIO. And then to have the humor of state; and after a demure travel of regard, telling them I know my place as I would they should do theirs, to ask for my kinsman Toby,—

SIR TOBY. Bolts and shackles!

FABIAN. O, peace, peace, peace! now, now.

MALVOLIO. Seven of my people, with an obedient start, make out for him: I frown the while; and perchance wind up my watch, or play with my—some rich jewel. Toby approaches; courtesies there to me,—

SIR TOBY. Shall this fellow live?

FABIAN. Though our silence be drawn from us with cars, yet peace.

MALVOLIO. I extend my hand to him thus, quenching my familiar smile with an austere regard of control,—

SIR TOBY. And does not Toby take you a blow o' the lips then.

MALVOLIO. Saying, 'Cousin Toby, my fortunes having cast me on your niece give me this prerogative of speech,'—

SIR TOBY. What, what?

MALVOLIO. 'You must amend your drunkenness.'

SIR TOBY. Out, scab!

FABIAN. Nay, patience, or we break the sinews of our plot.

MALVOLIO. 'Besides, you waste the treasure of your time with a foolish knight,'—

SIR ANDREW. That 's me, I warrant you.

MALVOLIO. 'One Sir Andrew,'—

SIR ANDREW. I knew 'twas I; for many do call me fool.

MALVOLIO. What employment have we here?

[Taking up the letter.

FABIAN. Now is the woodcock near the gin.

SIR TOBY. O, peace! and the spirit of humors intimate reading aloud to him.

MALVOLIO. By my life, this is my lady's hand: these be her very C's, her U's, and her T's; and thus makes she her great P's. It is, in contempt of question, her hand.

SIR ANDREW. Her C's, her U's and her T's: why that?

MALVOLIO. [Reads] To the unknown beloved, this, and my good wishes:—her very phrases! By your leave, wax. Soft! and the impressure her Lucrece, with which she uses to seal: 'tis my lady. To whom should this be?

FABIAN. This wins, him, liver and all.

MALVOLIO. [Reads] Jove knows I love:
        But who?
    Lips, do not move;
    No man must know.

'No man must know.' What follows? the numbers altered! 'No man must know:' if this should be thee, Malvolio?

SIR TOBY. Marry, hang thee, brock!

MALVOLIO. [Reads] I may command where I adore;
        But silence, like a Lucrece knife,
        With bloodless stroke my heart doth gore:
        M, O, A, I, doth sway my life.

FABIAN. A fustian riddle!

SIR TOBY. Excellent wench, say I.

MALVOLIO. 'M, O, A, I, doth sway my life.' Nay, but first, let me see, let me see, let me see.

FABIAN. What dish o' poison has she dressed him!

SIR TOBY. And with what wing the staniel checks at it!

MALVOLIO. 'I may command where I adore.' Why, she may command me: I serve her; she is my lady. Why, this is evident to any formal capacity; there is no obstruction in this: and the end,—what should that alphabetical position portend? If I could make that resemble something in me,—Softly! M, O, A, I,—

SIR TOBY. O, aye, make up that: he is now at a cold scant.

FABIAN. Sowter will cry upon 't for all this, though it be as rank as a fox.

MALVOLIO. M,—Malvolio; M,—why, that begins my name.

FABIAN. Did not I say he would work it out? the cur is excellent at faults.

MALVOLIO. M,—but then there is no consonancy in the sequel; that suffers under probation: A should follow, but O does.

FABIAN. And O shall end, I hope.

SIR TOBY. Aye, or I 'll cudgel him, and make him cry O!

MALVOLIO. And then I comes behind.

FABIAN. Aye, an you had any eye behind you, you might see more detraction at your heels than fortunes before you.

MALVOLIO. M, O, A, I; this simulation is not as the former: and yet, to crush this a little, it would bow to me, for every one of these letters are in my name. Soft! here follows prose. [*Reads*] If this fall into thy hand, revolve. In my stars I am above thee; but be not afraid of greatness: some are born great, some achieve greatness, and some have greatness thrust upon 'em. Thy Fates open their hands; let thy blood and spirit embrace them; and, to inure thyself to what thou art like to be, cast thy humble slough and appear fresh. Be opposite with a kinsman, surly with servants; let thy tongue tang arguments of state; put thyself into the trick of singularity: she thus advises thee that sighs for thee. Remember who commended thy yellow stockings, and wished to see thee ever crossed-gartered: I say, remember. Go to, thou art made, if thou desirest to be so; if not, let me see thee a steward still, the fellow of servants, and not worthy to touch Fortune's fingers. Farewell. She that would alter services with thee,

THE FORTUNATE-UNHAPPY.

Daylight and champain discovers not more; this is open. I will be proud, I will read politic authors, I will baffle Sir Toby, I will wash off gross acquaintance, I will be point-devise the very man. I do not now fool myself, to let imagination jade me; for every reason excites to this, that my lady loves me. She did commend my yellow stockings of late, she did praise my leg being cross-gartered; and in this she manifests herself to my love, and with a kind of injunction drives me to these habits of her liking. I thank my stars

I am happy. I will be strange, stout, in yellow stockings,
and cross-gartered, even with the swiftness of putting on.
Jove and my stars be praised! Here is yet a postscript.
[*Reads*] Thou canst not choose but know who I am. If thou
entertainest my love, let it appear in thy smiling; thy smiles
become thee well; therefore in my presence still smile, dear
my sweet, I prithee.

Jove, I thank thee: I will smile; I will do everything that
thou wilt have me.   [*Exit.*

FABIAN. I will not give my part of this sport for a pension of
thousands to be paid from the Sophy.

SIR TOBY. I could marry this wench for this device,—

SIR ANDREW. So could I too.

SIR TOBY. And ask no other dowry with her but such another
jest.

SIR ANDREW. Nor I neither.

FABIAN. Here comes my noble gull-catcher.

Re-enter MARIA.]

SIR TOBY. Wilt thou set thy foot o' my neck?

SIR ANDREW. Or o' mine either?

SIR TOBY. Shall I play my freedom at tray-trip, and become
thy bond-slave?

SIR ANDREW. I' faith, or I either?

SIR TOBY. Why, thou hast put him in such a dream, that when
the image of it leaves him he must run mad.

MARIA. Nay, but say true; does it work upon him?

SIR TOBY. Like aqua-vitæ with a midwife.

MARIA. If you will then see the fruits of the sport, mark his
first approach before my lady: he will come to her in yellow
stockings, and 'tis a color she abhors, and cross-gartered, a
fashion she detests; and he will smile upon her, which will
now be so unsuitable to her disposition, being addicted to a
melancholy as she is, that cannot but turn him into a notable contempt. If you will see it, follow me.

SIR TOBY. To the gates of Tartar, thou most excellent devil of
wit!

SIR ANDREW. I 'll make one too.   [*Exeunt.*

ACT III

Scene I — Olivia's *garden.*

Enter Viola, *and* Clown *with a tabor.*]

VIOLA. Save thee, friend, and thy music: dost thou live by thy tabor?

CLOWN. No, sir, I live by the church.

VIOLA. Art thou a churchman?

CLOWN. No such matter, sir: I do live by the church; for I do live at my house, and my house doth stand by the church.

VIOLA. So thou mayst say, the king lies by a beggar, if a beggar dwell near him; or, the church stands by thy tabor, if thy tabor stand by the church.

CLOWN. You have said, sir. To see this age! A sentence is but a cheveril glove to a good wit: how quickly the wrong side may be turned outward!

VIOLA. Nay, that 's certain; they that dally nicely with words may quickly make them wanton.

CLOWN. I would, therefore, my sister had had no name, sir.

VIOLA. Why, man?

CLOWN. Why, sir, her name 's a word; and to dally with that word might make my sister wanton. But indeed words are very rascals since bonds disgraced them.

VIOLA. Thy reason, man?

CLOWN. Troth, sir, I can yield you none without words; and words are grown so false, I am loath to prove reason with them.

VIOLA. I warrant thou art a merry fellow and carest for nothing.

CLOWN. Not so, sir, I do care for something; but in my conscience, sir, I do not care for you: if that be to care for nothing, sir, I would it would make you invisible.

VIOLA. Art not thou the Lady Olivia's fool?

CLOWN. No, indeed, sir! the Lady Olivia has no folly: she will keep no fool, sir, till she be married; and fools are as like husbands as pilchards are to herrings; the husband 's the bigger: I am indeed not her fool, but her corrupter of words.

VIOLA. I saw thee late at the Count Orsino's.

CLOWN. Foolery, sir, does walk about the orb like the sun, it shines every where. I would be sorry, sir, but the fool should be as oft with your master as with my mistress: I think I saw your wisdom there.

VIOLA. Nay, an thou pass upon me, I 'll no more with thee. Hold, there 's expenses for thee.

CLOWN. Now Jove, in his next commodity of hair, send thee a beard!

VIOLA. By my troth, I 'll tell thee, I am almost sick for one; [*Aside*] though I would not have it grow on my chin. Is thy lady within?

CLOWN. Would not a pair of these have bred, sir?

VIOLA. Yes, being kept together and put to use.

CLOWN. I would play Lord Pandarus of Phrygia, sir, to bring a Cressida to this Troilus.

VIOLA. I understand you, sir; 'tis well begged.

CLOWN. The matter, I hope, is not great, sir, begging but a beggar: Cressida was a beggar. My lady is within, sir. I will construe to them whence you come; who you are and what you would are out of my welkin, I might say 'element,' but the word is overworn.   [*Exit.*

VIOLA. This fellow is wise enough to play the fool;
   And to do that well craves a kind of wit:
   He must observe their mood on whom he jests,
   The quality of persons, and the time,
   And, like the haggard, check at every feather
   That comes before his eye. This is a practice
   As full of labor as a wise man's art:
   For folly that he wisely shows is fit;
   But wise men, folly-fall'n, quite taint their wit.

Enter SIR TOBY, *and* SIR ANDREW.]

SIR TOBY. Save you, gentleman.

VIOLA. And you, sir.

SIR ANDREW. Dieu vous garde, monsieur.

VIOLA. Et vous aussi; votre serviteur.

SIR ANDREW. I hope, sir, you are; and I am yours.

SIR TOBY. Will you encounter the house? my niece is desirous
you should enter, if your trade be to her.

VIOLA. I am bound to your niece, sir; I mean, she is the list of
my voyage.

SIR TOBY. Taste your legs, sir; put them to motion.

VIOLA. My legs do better understand me, sir, than I understand what you mean by bidding me taste my legs.

SIR TOBY. I mean, to go, sir, to enter.

VIOLA. I will answer you with gait and entrance.
But we are prevented.

Enter OLIVIA *and* MARIA.]
Most excellent accomplished lady, the heavens rain odors
on you!

SIR ANDREW. That youth 's a rare courtier: 'Rain odors;' well.

VIOLA. My matter hath no voice, lady, but to your own most
pregnant and vouchsafed ear.

SIR ANDREW. 'Odors,' 'pregnant,' and 'vouchsafed:'
I 'll get 'em all three all ready.

OLIVIA. Let the garden door be shut, and leave me to my hearing. [*Exeunt* SIR TOBY, SIR ANDREW, *and* MARIA.] Give me
your hand, sir.

VIOLA. My duty, madam, and most humble service.

OLIVIA. What is your name?

VIOLA. Cesario is your servant's name, fair princess.

OLIVIA. My servant, sir! 'Twas never merry world
Since lowly feigning was call'd compliment:
You 're servant to the Count Orsino, youth.

VIOLA. And he is yours, and his must needs be yours:
Your servant's servant is your servant, madam.

CLIVIA. For him, I think not on him: for his thoughts,
Would they were blanks, rather than fill'd with me!

VIOLA. Madam, I come to whet your gentle thoughts
On his behalf.

OLIVIA.   O, by your leave, I pray you;
I bade you never speak again of him:

But, would you undertake another suit,
I had rather hear you to solicit that
Than music from the spheres.

VIOLA. Dear lady,—

OLIVIA. Give me leave, beseech you. I did send,
After the last enchantment you did here,
A ring in chase of you: so did I abuse
Myself, my servant and, I fear me, you:
Under your hard construction must I sit,
To force that on you, in a shameful cunning,
Which you knew none of yours: what might you think?
Have you not set mine honor at the stake
And baited it with all the unmuzzled thoughts
That tyrannous heart can think? To one of your receiving
Enough is shown; a cypress, not a bosom,
Hides my heart. So, let me hear you speak.

VIOLA. I pity you.

OLIVIA. That 's a degree to love.

VIOLA. No, not a grize; for 'tis a vulgar proof,
That very oft we pity enemies.

OLIVIA. Why, then, methinks 'tis time to smile again.
O world, how apt the poor are to be proud!
If one should be a prey, how much the better
To fall before the lion than the wolf! [Clock strikes.
The clock upbraids me with the waste of time.
Be not afraid, good youth, I will not have you:
And yet, when wit and youth is come to harvest,
Your wife is like to reap a proper man;
There lies your way, due west.

VIOLA. Then westward-ho!
Grace and good disposition attend your ladyship!
You 'll nothing, madam, to my lord by me?

OLIVIA. Stay:
I prithee, tell me what thou think'st of me.

VIOLA. That you do think you are not what you are.

OLIVIA. If I think so, I think the same of you.

VIOLA. Then think you right: I am not what I am.

OLIVIA. I would you were as I would have you be!

VIOLA. Would it be better, madam, than I am?
  I wish it might, for now I am your fool.
OLIVIA. O, what a deal of scorn looks beautiful
  In the contempt and anger of his lip!
  A murderous guilt shows not itself more soon
  Than love that would seem hid: love's night is noon.
  Cesario, by the roses of the spring,
  By maidhood, honor, truth and every thing,
  I love thee so, that, mauger all thy pride,
  Nor wit nor reason can my passion hide.
  Do not extort thy reasons from this clause,
  For that I woo, thou therefore hast no cause;
  But rather reason thus with reason fetter,
  Love sought is good, but given unsought is better.
VIOLA. By innocence I swear, and by my youth,
  I have one heart, one bosom and one truth,
  And that no woman has; nor never none
  Shall mistress be of it, save I alone.
  And so adieu, good madam: never more
  Will I my master's tears to you deplore.
OLIVIA. Yet come again; for thou perhaps mayst move
  That heart, which now abhors, to like his love.   [Exeunt.

SCENE II — OLIVIA'S house.

Enter SIR TOBY, SIR ANDREW, and FABIAN.]
SIR ANDREW. No, faith, I 'll not stay a jot longer.
SIR TOBY. Thy reason, dear venom, give thy reason.
FABIAN. You must needs yield your reason, Sir Andrew.
SIR ANDREW. Marry, I saw your niece do more favors to the
  count's serving-man than ever she bestowed upon me; I saw
  't i' the orchard.
SIR TOBY. Did she see thee the while, old boy? tell me that.
SIR ANDREW. As plain as I see you now.
FABIAN. This was a great argument of love in her toward you.
SIR ANDREW. 'Slight, will you make an ass o' me?
FABIAN. I will prove it legitimate, sir, upon the oaths of judg-
  ment and reason.

SIR TOBY. And they have been grand-jurymen since before Noah was a sailor.

FABIAN. She did show favor to the youth in your sight only to exasperate you, to awake your dormouse valor, to put fire in your heart, and brimstone in your liver. You should then have accosted her; and with some excellent jests, fire-new from the mint, you should have banged the youth into dumbness. This was looked for at your hand, and this was balked: the double gilt of this opportunity you let time wash off, and you are now sailed into the north of my lady's opinion; where you will hang like an icicle on a Dutchman's beard, unless you do redeem it by some laudable attempt either of valor or policy.

SIR ANDREW. An 't be any way, it must be with valor; for policy I hate: I had as lief be a Brownist as a politician.

SIR TOBY. Why, then, build me thy fortunes upon the basis of valor. Challenge me the count's youth to fight with him; hurt him in eleven places: my niece shall take note of it; and assure thyself, there is no love-broker in the world can more prevail in man's commendation with woman than report of valor.

FABIAN. There is no way but this, Sir Andrew.

SIR ANDREW. Will either of you bear me a challenge to him?

SIR TOBY. Go, write it in a martial hand; be curst and brief; it is no matter how witty, so it be eloquent and full of invention: taunt him with the license of ink: if thou thou 'st him some thrice, it shall not be amiss; and as many lies as will lie in thy sheet of paper, although the sheet were big enough for the bed of Ware in England, set 'em down: go, about it. Let there be gall enough in thy ink, though thou write with a goose-pen, no matter: about it.

SIR ANDREW. Where shall I find you?

SIR TOBY. We 'll call thee at the cubiculo: go.

[*Exit* SIR ANDREW.

FABIAN. This is a dear manakin to you, Sir Toby.

SIR TOBY. I have been dear to him, lad, some two thousand strong, or so.

FABIAN. We shall have a rare letter from him: but you 'll not deliver 't?

SIR TOBY. Never trust me, then; and by all means stir on the youth to an answer. I think oxen and wainropes cannot hale them together. For Andrew, if he were opened, and you find so much blood in his liver as will clog the foot of a flea, I 'll eat the rest of the anatomy.

FABIAN. And his opposite, the youth, bears in his visage no great presage of cruelty.

Enter MARIA.]

SIR TOBY. Look, where the youngest wren of nine comes.

MARIA. If you desire the spleen, and will laugh yourselves into stitches, follow me. Yond gull Malvolio is turned heathen, a very renegado; for there is no Christian, that means to be saved by believing rightly, can ever believe such impossible passages of grossness. He 's in yellow stockings.

SIR TOBY. And cross-gartered?

MARIA. Most villanously; like a pedant that keeps a school i' the church. I have dogged him, like his murderer. He does obey every point of the letter that I dropped to betray him: he does smile his face into more lines than is in the new map with the augmentation of the Indies: you have not seen such thing as 'tis. I can hardly forbear hurling things at him. I know my lady will strike him: if she do, he 'll smile and take 't for a great favor.

SIR TOBY. Come, bring us, bring us where he is.   [*Exeunt.*

SCENE III — *A street.*

Enter SEBASTIAN *and* ANTONIO.]

SEBASTIAN. I would not by my will have troubled you;
   But, since you make your pleasure of your pains,
   I will no further chide you.

ANTONIO. I could not stay behind you; my desire,
   More sharp than filed steel, did spur me forth;
   And not all love to see you, though so much
   As might have drawn one to a longer voyage,

But jealousy what might befall your travel,
Being skilless in these parts; which to a stranger,
Unguided and unfriended, often prove
Rough and unhospitable: my willing love
The rather by these arguments of fear,
Set forth in your pursuit.

SEBASTIAN.   My kind Antonio,
I can no other answer make but thanks,
And thanks; and ever thanks; and oft good turns
Are shuffled off with such uncurrent pay:
But, were my worth as is my conscience firm,
You should find better dealing. What 's to do?
Shall we go see the reliques of this town?

ANTONIO. To-morrow, sir: best first go see your lodging.

SEBASTIAN. I am not weary, and 'tis long to night:
I pray you, let us satisfy our eyes
With the memorials and the things of fame
That do renown this city.

ANTONIO.   Would you 'ld pardon me;
I do not without danger walk these streets:
Once, in a sea-fight, 'gainst the count his galleys
I did some service; of such note indeed,
That were I ta'en here it would scarce be answer'd.

SEBASTIAN. Belike you slew great number of his people.

ANTONIO. The offense is not of such a bloody nature;
Albeit the quality of the time and quarrel
Might well have given us bloody argument.
It might have since been answer'd in repaying
What we took from them; which, for traffic's sake,
Most of our city did: only myself stood out;
For which, if I be lapsed in this place,
I shall pay dear.

SEBASTIAN.   Do not then walk too open.

ANTONIO. It doth not fit me. Hold, sir, here 's my purse.
In the south suburbs, at the Elephant,
Is best to lodge: I will bespeak our diet,
Whiles you beguile the time and feed your knowledge
With viewing of the town: there shall you have me.

SEBASTIAN. Why I your purse?

ANTONIO. Haply your eye shall light upon some toy
You have desire to purchase; and your store,
I think, is not for idle markets, sir.

SEBASTIAN. I 'll be your purse-bearer and leave you
For an hour.

ANTONIO.   To the Elephant.

SEBASTIAN.   I do remember.   [*Exeunt.*

SCENE IV — OLIVIA's *garden.*

Enter OLIVIA *and* MARIA.]

OLIVIA. I have sent after him: he says he 'll come;
How shall I feast him? what bestow of him?
For youth is bought more oft than begg'd or borrow'd.
I speak too loud.
Where is Malvolio? he is sad and civil,
And suits well for a servant with my fortunes:
Where is Malvolio?

MARIA. He 's coming, madam; but in very strange manner.
He is, sure, possessed, madam.

OLIVIA. Why, what 's the matter? does he rave?

MARIA. No, madam, he does nothing but smile: your ladyship
were best to have some guard about you, if he come; for,
sure, the man is tainted in 's wits.

OLIVIA. Go call him hither. [*Exit* MARIA.] I am as mad as he,
If sad and merry madness equal be.

Re-enter MARIA, *with* MALVOLIO.]
How now, Malvolio!

MALVOLIO. Sweet lady, ho, ho.

OLIVIA. Smilest thou?
I sent for thee upon a sad occasion.

MALVOLIO. Sad, lady? I could be sad: this does make some
obstruction in the blood, this cross-gartering; but what of
that? if it please the eye of one, it is with me as the very
true sonnet is, 'Please one, and please all.'

OLIVIA. Why, how dost thou, man? what is the matter with
thee?

MALVOLIO. Not black in my mind, though yellow in my legs. It did come to his hands, and commands shall be executed: I think we do know the sweet Roman hand.

OLIVIA. Wilt thou go to bed, Malvolio?

MALVOLIO. To bed! aye, sweet-heart, and I 'll come to thee.

OLIVIA. God comfort thee! Why dost thou smile so and kiss thy hand so oft?

MARIA. How do you, Malvolio?

MALVOLIO. At your request! yes; nightingales answer daws.

MARIA. Why appear you with this ridiculous boldness before my lady?

MALVOLIO. 'Be not afraid of greatness:' 'twas well writ.

OLIVIA. What meanest thou by that, Malvolio?

MALVOLIO. 'Some are born great,'—

OLIVIA. Ha!

MALVOLIO. 'Some achieve greatness,'—

OLIVIA. What sayest thou?

MALVOLIO. 'And some have greatness thrust upon them.'

OLIVIA. Heaven restore thee!

MALVOLIO. 'Remember who commended thy yellow stock-ings,'—

OLIVIA. Thy yellow stockings!

MALVOLIO. 'And wished to see thee cross-gartered.'

OLIVIA. Cross-gartered!

MALVOLIO. 'Go to, thou art made, if thou desirest to be so;'—

OLIVIA. Am I made?

MALVOLIO. 'If not, let me see thee a servant still.'

OLIVIA. Why, this is very midsummer madness.

Enter SERVANT.]

SERVANT. Madam, the young gentleman of the Count Orsino's is returned: I could hardly entreat him back: he attends your ladyship's pleasure.

OLIVIA. I 'll come to him [*Exit* SERVANT.] Good Maria, let this fellow be looked to. Where 's my cousin Toby? Let some of my people have a special care of him: I would not have him miscarry for the half of my dowry.

[*Exeunt* OLIVIA *and* MARIA.

MALVOLIO. O, ho! do you come near me now? no worse man
than Sir Toby to look to me! This concurs directly with the
letter: she sends him on purpose, that I may appear stubborn to him; for she incites me to that in the letter. 'Cast
thy humble slough,' says she; 'be opposite with a kinsman,
surly with servants; let thy tongue tang with arguments of
state; put thyself into the trick of singularity;' and consequently sets down the manner how; as, a sad face, a rever-
end carriage, a slow tongue, in the habit of some sir of note,
and so forth. I have limed her; but it is Jove's doing, and
Jove make me thankful! And when she went away now,
'Let this fellow be looked to:' fellow! not Malvolio, nor
after my degree, but fellow. Why, every thing adheres together, that no dram of a scruple, no scruple of a scruple,
no obstacle, no incredulous or unsafe circumstance—What
can be said? Nothing that can be can come between me and
the full prospect of my hopes. Well, Jove, not I, is the doer
of this, and he is to be thanked.

Re-enter MARIA, *with* SIR TOBY *and* FABIAN.]

SIR TOBY. Which way is he, in the name of sanctity? If all the
devils of hell be drawn in little, and Legion himself possessed him, yet I 'll speak to him.

FABIAN. Here he is, here he is. How is 't with you, sir? how
is 't with you, man?

MALVOLIO. Go off; I discard you: let me enjoy my private: go
off.

MARIA. Lo, how hollow the fiend speaks within him! did not
I tell you? Sir Toby, my lady prays you to have a care of
him.

MALVOLIO. Ah, ha! does she so?

SIR TOBY. Go to, go to; peace, peace; we must deal gently with
him; let me alone. How do you, Malvolio? how is 't with
you? What, man! defy the devil: consider, he 's an enemy
to mankind.

MALVOLIO. Do you know what you say?

MARIA. La you, an you speak ill of the devil, how he takes it
at heart! Pray God, he be not bewitched!

FABIAN. Carry his water to the wise woman.

MARIA. Marry, and it shall be done to-morrow morning, if I live. My lady would not lose him for more than I'll say.

MALVOLIO. How now, mistress!

MARIA. O Lord!

SIR TOBY. Prithee, hold thy peace; this is not the way: do you not see you move him? let me alone with him.

FABIAN. No way but gentleness; gently, gently: the fiend is rough, and will not be roughly used.

SIR TOBY. Why, how now, my bawcock! how dost thou, chuck?

MALVOLIO. Sir!

SIR TOBY. Aye, Biddy, come with me. What, man! 'tis not for gravity to play at cherrypit with Satan: hang him, foul collier!

MARIA. Get him to say his prayers, good Sir Toby, get him to pray.

MALVOLIO. My prayers, minx!

MARIA. No, I warrant you, he will not hear of godliness.

MALVOLIO. Go, hang yourselves all! you are idle shallow things: I am not of your element: you shall know more hereafter.   [Exit.

SIR TOBY. Is 't possible?

FABIAN. If this were played upon a stage now, I could condemn it as an improbable fiction.

SIR TOBY. His very genius hath taken the infection of the device, man.

MARIA. Nay, pursue him now, lest the device take air and taint.

FABIAN. Why, we shall make him mad indeed.

MARIA. The house will be the quieter.

SIR TOBY. Come, we'll have him in a dark room and bound. My niece is already in the belief that he's mad: we may carry it thus, for our pleasure and his penance, till our very pastime, tired out of breath, prompt us to have mercy on him: at which time we will bring the device to the bar and crown thee for a finder of madmen. But see, but see.

Enter SIR ANDREW.]

FABIAN. More matter for a May morning.

SIR ANDREW. Here 's the challenge, read it: I warrant there 's vinegar and pepper in 't.

FABIAN. Is 't so saucy?

SIR ANDREW. Aye, is 't, I warrant him: do but read.

SIR TOBY. Give me. [*Reads*] Youth, whatsoever thou art, thou art but a scurvy fellow.

FABIAN. Good, and valiant.

SIR TOBY. [*Reads*] Wonder not, nor admire not in thy mind, why I do call thee so, for I will show thee no reason for 't.

FABIAN. A good note; that keeps you from the blow of the law.

SIR TOBY. [*Reads*] Thou comest to the lady Olivia, and in my sight she uses thee kindly: but thou liest in thy throat; that is not the matter I challenge thee for.

FABIAN. Very brief, and to exceeding good sense—less.

SIR TOBY. [*Reads*] I will waylay thee going home; where if it be thy chance to kill me,—

FABIAN. Good.

SIR TOBY [*Reads*] Thou killest me like a rogue and a villain.

FABIAN. Still you keep o' the windy side of the law: good.

SIR TOBY [*Reads*] Fare thee well; and God have mercy upon one of our souls! He may have mercy upon mine; but my hope is better, and so look to thyself. Thy friend, as thou usest him, and thy sworn enemy, ANDREW AGUECHEEK. If this letter move him not, his legs cannot: I 'll give 't him.

MARIA. You may have very fit occasion for 't: he is now in some commerce with my lady, and will by and by depart.

SIR TOBY. Go, Sir Andrew; scout me for him at the corner of the orchard like a bum-baily: so soon as ever thou seest him, draw; and, as thou drawest, swear horrible; for it comes to pass oft that a terrible oath, with a swaggering accent sharply twanged off, gives manhood more approbation than ever proof itself would have earned him. Away!

SIR ANDREW. Nay, let me alone for swearing. [*Exit.*

SIR TOBY. Now will not I deliver his letter: for the behavior of the young gentleman gives him out to be of good capacity and breeding; his employment between his lord and my niece confirms no less: therefore this letter, being so excellently ignorant, will breed no terror in the youth: he will

find it comes from a clodpole. But, sir, I will deliver his challenge by word of mouth; set upon Aguecheek a notable report of valor; and drive the gentleman, as I know his youth
will aptly receive it, into a most hideous opinion of his rage,
skill, fury and impetuosity. This will so fright them both,
that they will kill one another by the look, like cockatrices.

Re-enter OLIVIA, *with* VIOLA.]

FABIAN. Here he comes with your niece: give them way till he
take leave, and presently after him.

SIR TOBY. I will meditate the while upon some horrid message
for a challenge.   [*Exeunt* SIR TOBY, FABIAN, *and* MARIA.

OLIVIA. I have said too much unto a heart of stone,
And laid mine honor too unchary out:
There 's something in me that reproves my fault;
But such a headstrong potent fault it is,
That it but mocks reproof.

VIOLA. With the same 'havior that your passion bears
Goes on my master's grief.

OLIVIA. Here, wear this jewel for me, 'tis my picture;
Refuse it not; it hath no tongue to vex you;
And I beseech you come again to-morrow.
What shall you ask of me that I 'll deny,
That honor saved may upon asking give?

VIOLA. Nothing but this;—your true love for my master.

OLIVIA. How with mine honor may I give him that
Which I have given to you?

VIOLA.   I will acquit you.

OLIVIA. Well, come again to-morrow: fare thee well:
A fiend like thee might bear my soul to hell.   [*Exit.*

Re-enter SIR TOBY *and* FABIAN.]

SIR TOBY. Gentleman, God save thee.

VIOLA. And you, sir.

SIR TOBY. That defense thou hast, betake thee to 't: of what
nature the wrongs are thou hast done him, I know not; but
thy intercepter, full of despite, bloody as the hunter, attends
thee at the orchard-end: dismount thy tuck, be yare in thy
preparation, for thy assailant is quick, skillful and deadly.

VIOLA. You mistake, sir; I am sure no man hath any quarrel to me: my remembrance is very free and clear from any image of offense done to any man.

SIR TOBY. You 'll find it otherwise, I assure you: therefore, if you hold your life at any price, betake you to your guard; for your opposite hath in him what youth, strength, skill and wrath can furnish man withal.

VIOLA. I pray you, sir, what is he?

SIR TOBY. He is knight, dubbed with unhatched rapier and on carpet consideration; but he is a devil in private brawl: souls and bodies hath he divorced three; and his incensement at this moment is so implacable, that satisfaction can be none but by pangs of deaths and sepulcher. Hob, nob, is his word; give 't or take 't.

VIOLA. I will return again into the house and desire some conduct of the lady. I am no fighter. I have heard of some kind of men that put quarrels purposely on others, to taste their valor: belike this is a man of that quirk.

SIR TOBY. Sir, no; his indignation derives itself out of a very competent injury: therefore, get you on and give him his desire. Back you shall not to the house, unless you undertake that with me which with as much safety you might answer him: therefore, on, or strip your sword stark naked; for meddle you must, that 's certain, or forswear to wear iron about you.

VIOLA. This is as uncivil as strange. I beseech you, do me this courteous office, as to know of the knight what my offense to him is: it is something of my negligence, nothing of my purpose.

SIR TOBY. I will do so. Signior Fabian, stay you by this gentleman till my return.   [*Exit.*

VIOLA. Pray you, sir, do you know of this matter?

FABIAN. I know the knight is incensed against you, even to a mortal arbitrement; but nothing of the circumstance more.

VIOLA. I beseech you, what manner of man is he?

FABIAN. Nothing of that wonderful promise, to read him by his form, as you are like to find him in the proof of his valor.

He is, indeed, sir, the most skillful, bloody and fatal opposite that you could possibly have found in any part of Illyria.
Will you walk towards him? I will make your peace with
him if I can.

VIOLA. I shall be much bound to you for 't: I am one that had
rather go with sir priest than sir knight: I care not who
knows so much of my mettle.   [*Exeunt.*

Re-enter SIR TOBY, *with* SIR ANDREW.]

SIR TOBY. Why, man, he 's a very devil; I have not seen such
a firago. I had a pass with him, rapier, scabbard and all,
and he gives me the stuck in with such a mortal motion,
that it is inevitable; and on the answer, he pays you as
surely as your feet hit the ground they step on. They say
he has been fencer to the Sophy.

SIR ANDREW. Pox on 't, I 'll not meddle with him.

SIR TOBY. Aye, but he will not now be pacified: Fabian can
scarce hold him yonder.

SIR ANDREW. Plague on 't, an I thought he had been valiant
and so cunning in fence I 'ld have seen him damned ere
I 'ld have challenged him. Let him let the matter slip, and
I 'll give him my horse, gray Capilet.

SIR TOBY. I 'll make the motion: stand here, make a good show
on 't: this shall end without the perdition of souls. [*Aside*]
Marry, I 'll ride your horse as well as I ride you.

Re-enter FABIAN *and* VIOLA.]

[*To* FABIAN.] I have his horse to take up the quarrel: I have
persuaded him the youth 's a devil.

FABIAN. He is as horribly conceited of him; and pants and
looks pale, as if a bear were at his heels.

SIR TOBY. [*To* VIOLA.] There 's no remedy, sir; he will fight
with you for 's oath sake: marry, he hath better bethought
him of his quarrel, and he finds that now scarce to be worth
talking of: therefore draw, for the supportance of his vow;
he protests he will not hurt you.

VIOLA. [*Aside*] Pray God defend me! A little thing would
make me tell them how much I lack of a man.

FABIAN. Give ground, if you see him furious.

SIR TOBY. Come, Sir Andrew, there 's no remedy; the gentle-

man will, for his honor's sake, have one bout with you; he
cannot by the duello avoid it: but he has promised me, as
he is a gentleman and a soldier, he will not hurt you. Come
on; to 't.

SIR ANDREW. Pray God, he keep his oath!

VIOLA. I do assure you, 'tis against my will. 　　　[*They draw.*
Enter ANTONIO.]

ANTONIO. Put up your sword. If this young gentleman
　Have done offense, I take the fault on me:
　If you offend him, I for him defy you.

SIR TOBY. You, sir! why, what are you?

ANTONIO. One, sir, that for his love dares yet do more
　Than you have heard him brag to you he will.

SIR TOBY. Nay, if you be an undertaker, I am for you.
　　　　　　　　　　　　　　　　　　　　　　[*They draw.*

Enter OFFICERS.]

FABIAN. O good Sir Toby, hold! here come the officers.

SIR TOBY. I 'll be with you anon.

VIOLA. Pray, sir, put your sword up, if you please.

SIR ANDREW. Marry, will I, sir; and, for that I promised you,
　I 'll be as good as my word: he will bear you easily and
　reins well.

FIRST OFFICER. This is the man; do thy office.

SECOND OFFICER. Antonio, I arrest thee at the suit of Count
　Orsino.

ANTONIO. You do mistake me, sir.

FIRST OFFICER. No, sir, no jot; I know your favor well,
　Though now you have no sea-cap on your head.
　Take him away: he knows I know him well.

ANTONIO. I must obey. [*To* VIOLA.] This comes with seeking
　you:
　But there 's no remedy; I shall answer it.
　What will you do, now my necessity
　Makes me to ask you for my purse? It grieves me
　Much more for what I cannot do for you
　Than what befalls myself. You stand amazed;
　But be of comfort.

SECOND OFFICER. Come, sir, away.

ANTONIO. I must entreat of you some of that money.

VIOLA. What money, sir?
　For the fair kindness you have show'd me here,
　And, part, being prompted by your present trouble,
　Out of my lean and low ability
　I 'll lend you something: my having is not much;
　I 'll make division of my present with you:
　Hold, there 's half my coffer.

ANTONIO.　　　　　　　　　Will you deny me now?
　Is 't possible that my deserts to you
　Can lack persuasion? Do not tempt my misery,
　Lest that it make me so unsound a man
　As to upbraid you with those kindnesses
　That I have done for you.

VIOLA.　　　　　　　　　I know of none;
　Nor know I you by voice or any feature:
　I hate ingratitude more in a man
　Than lying vainness, babbling drunkenness,
　Or any taint of vice whose strong corruption
　Inhabits our frail blood.

ANTONIO.　　　　　　　　O heavens themselves!

SECOND OFFICER. Come, sir, I pray you, go.

ANTONIO. Let me speak a little. This youth that you see here
　I snatch'd one half out of the jaws of death;
　Relieved him with such sanctity of love;
　And to his image, which methought did promise
　Most venerable worth, did I devotion.

FIRST OFFICER. What 's that to us? The time goes by: away!

ANTONIO. But O how vile an idol proves this god!
　Thou hast, Sebastian, done good feature shame.
　In nature there 's no blemish but the mind;
　None can be call'd deform'd but the unkind:
　Virtue is beauty; but the beauteous evil
　Are empty trunks, o'erflourish'd by the devil.

FIRST OFFICER. The man grows mad: away with him!
　Come, come, sir.

ANTONIO.　　　　　　Lead me on.　　　[Exit with OFFICERS.

VIOLA. Methinks his words do from such passion fly,
That he believes himself: so do not I.
Prove true, imagination, O prove true,
That I, dear brother, be now ta'en for you!

SIR TOBY. Come hither, knight; come hither, Fabian: we 'll
whisper o'er a couplet or two of most sage saws.

VIOLA. He named Sebastian: I my brother know
Yet living in my glass; even such and so
In favor was my brother, and he went
Still in this fashion, color, ornament,
For him I imitate: O, if it prove,
Tempests are kind and salt waves fresh in love! [*Exit.*

SIR TOBY. A very dishonest paltry boy, and more a coward
than a hare: his dishonesty appears in leaving his friend
here in necessity and denying him; and for his cowardship,
ask Fabian.

FABIAN. A coward, a most devout coward, religious in it.

SIR ANDREW. 'Slid, I 'll after him again and beat him.

SIR TOBY. Do; cuff him soundly, but never draw thy sword.

SIR ANDREW. An I do not,— [*Exit.*

FABIAN. Come, let 's see the event.

SIR TOBY. I dare lay any money 'twill be nothing yet.

[*Exeunt.*

ACT IV

SCENE I — *Before* OLIVIA'S *house.*

Enter SEBASTIAN *and* CLOWN.]

CLOWN. Will you make me believe that I am not sent for you?

SEBASTIAN. Go to, go to, thou art a foolish fellow:
Let me be clear of thee.

CLOWN. Well held out, i' faith! No, I do not know you; nor I
am not sent to you by my lady, to bid you come speak with
her; nor your name is not Master Cesario; nor this is not
my nose neither. Nothing that is so is so.

SEBASTIAN. I prithee, vent thy folly somewhere else:
Thou know'st not me.

CLOWN. Vent my folly! he has heard that word of some great
man and now applies it to a fool. Vent my folly! I am afraid
this great lubber, the world, will prove a cockney. I prithee
now, ungird thy strangeness and tell me what I shall vent
to my lady: shall I vent to her that thou art coming?

SEBASTIAN. I prithee, foolish Greek, depart from me:
There 's money for thee: if you tarry longer,
I shall give worse payment.

CLOWN. By my troth, thou hast an open hand. These wise men
that give fools money get themselves a good report—after
fourteen years' purchase.

Enter SIR ANDREW, SIR TOBY, *and* FABIAN.]

SIR ANDREW. Now, sir, have I met you again? there 's for you.

SEBASTIAN. Why, there 's for thee, and there, and there. Are
all the people mad?

SIR TOBY. Hold, sir, or I 'll throw your dagger o'er the house.

CLOWN. This will I tell my lady straight: I would not be in
some of your coats for two pence.   [*Exit.*

SIR TOBY. Come on, sir; hold.

SIR ANDREW. Nay, let him alone: I 'll go another way to work
with him; I 'll have an action of battery against him, if there

be any law in Illyria: though I struck him first, yet it 's no
matter for that.

SEBASTIAN. Let go thy hand.

SIR TOBY. Come, sir, I will not let you go. Come, my young
soldier, put up your iron: you are well fleshed; come on.

SEBASTIAN. I will be free from thee. What wouldst thou now?
If thou darest tempt me further, draw thy sword.

SIR TOBY. What, what? Nay, then I must have an ounce or two
of this malapert blood from you.

Enter OLIVIA.]

OLIVIA. Hold, Toby; on thy life, I charge thee, hold!

SIR TOBY. Madam!

OLIVIA. Will it be ever thus? Ungracious wretch,
Fit for the mountains and the barbarous caves,
Where manners ne'er were preach'd! out of my sight!
Be not offended, dear Cesario.
Rudesby, be gone!
        [*Exeunt* SIR TOBY, SIR ANDREW, *and* FABIAN.
              I prithee, gentle friend,
Let thy fair wisdom, not thy passion, sway
In this uncivil and unjust extent
Against thy peace. Go with me to my house;
And hear thou there how many fruitless pranks
This ruffian hath botch'd up, that thou thereby
Mayst smile at this: thou shalt not choose but go:
Do not deny. Beshrew his soul for me,
He started one poor heart of mine in thee.

SEBASTIAN. What relish is in this? how runs the stream?
Or I am mad, or else this is a dream:
Let fancy still my sense in Lethe steep;
If it be thus to dream, still let me sleep!

OLIVIA. Nay, come, I prithee: would thou 'ldst be ruled by me!

SEBASTIAN. Madam, I will.

OLIVIA.   O, say so, and so be!   [*Exeunt.*

Scene II — Olivia's *house.*

Enter MARIA *and* CLOWN.]

MARIA. Nay, I prithee, put on this gown and this beard; make
  him believe thou art Sir Topas the curate: do it quickly;
  I 'll call Sir Toby the whilst.   [*Exit.*

CLOWN. Well, I 'll put it on, and I will dissemble myself in 't;
  and I would I were the first that ever dissembled in such a
  gown. I am not tall enough to become the function well,
  nor lean enough to be thought a good student; but to be
  said an honest man and a good housekeeper goes as fairly
  as to say a careful man and a great scholar. The competitors
  enter.

Enter SIR TOBY *and* MARIA.]

SIR TOBY. Jove bless thee, master Parson.

CLOWN. Bonos dies, Sir Toby; for, as the old hermit of Prague,
  that never saw pen and ink, very wittily said to a niece of
  King Gorboduc, 'That that is is;' so I, being master Parson,
  am master Parson; for, what is 'that' but 'that,' and 'is' but
  'is'?

SIR TOBY. To him, Sir Topas.

CLOWN. What, ho, I say! peace in this prison!

SIR TOBY. The knave counterfeits well; a good knave.

MALVOLIO. [*Within*] Who calls there?

CLOWN. Sir Topas the curate, who comes to visit Malvolio the
  lunatic.

MALVOLIO. Sir Topas, Sir Topas, good Sir Topas, go to my
  lady.

CLOWN. Out, hyperbolical fiend! how vexest thou this man!
  talkest thou nothing but of ladies?

SIR TOBY. Well said, master Parson.

MALVOLIO. Sir Topas, never was man thus wronged: good Sir
  Topas, do not think I am mad: they have laid me here in
  hideous darkness.

CLOWN. Fie, thou dishonest Satan! I call thee by the most
  modest terms; for I am one of those gentle ones that will use

the devil himself with courtesy: sayest thou that house is dark?

MALVOLIO. As hell, Sir Topas.

CLOWN. Why, it hath bay windows transparent as barricadoes, and the clearstories toward the south north are as lustrous as ebony; and yet complainest thou of obstruction?

MALVOLIO. I am not mad, Sir Topas: I say to you, this house is dark.

CLOWN. Madman, thou errest: I say, there is no darkness but ignorance; in which thou art more puzzled than the Egyptians in their fog.

MALVOLIO. I say, this house is as dark as ignorance, though ignorance were as dark as hell; and I say, there was never man thus abused. I am no more mad than you are: make the trial of it in any constant question.

CLOWN. What is the opinion of Pythagoras concerning wild fowl?

MALVOLIO. That the soul of our grandam might haply inhabit a bird.

CLOWN. What thinkest thou of his opinion?

MALVOLIO. I think nobly of the soul, and no way approve his opinion.

CLOWN. Fare thee well. Remain thou still in darkness: thou shalt hold the opinion of Pythagoras ere I will allow of thy wits; and fear to kill a woodcock, lest thou dispossess the soul of thy grandam. Fare thee well.

MALVOLIO. Sir Topas, Sir Topas!

SIR TOBY. My most exquisite Sir Topas!

CLOWN. Nay, I am for all waters.

MARIA. Thou mightst have done this without thy beard and gown: he sees thee not.

SIR TOBY. To him in thine own voice, and bring me word how thou findest him: I would we were well rid of this knavery. If he may be conveniently delivered, I would he were; for I am now so far in offense with my niece, that I cannot pursue with any safety this sport to the upshot. Come by and by to my chamber.   [*Exeunt* SIR TOBY *and* MARIA.

CLOWN. [*Singing*] Hey, Robin, jolly Robin,
          Tell me how thy lady does.

MALVOLIO. Fool,—

CLOWN. My lady is unkind, perdy.

MALVOLIO. Fool,—

CLOWN. Alas, why is she so?

MALVOLIO. Fool, I say,—

CLOWN. She loves another—Who calls, ha?

MALVOLIO. Good fool, as ever thou wilt deserve well at my hand, help me to a candle, and pen, ink and paper: as I am a gentleman, I will live to be thankful to thee for 't.

CLOWN. Master Malvolio!

MALVOLIO. Aye, good fool.

CLOWN. Alas, sir, how fell you besides your five wits?

MALVOLIO. Fool, there was never man so notoriously abused: I am as well in my wits, fool, as thou art.

CLOWN. But as well? then you are mad indeed, if you be no better in your wits than a fool.

MALVOLIO. They have here propertied me; keep me in darkness, send ministers to me, asses, and do all they can to face me out of my wits.

CLOWN. Advise you what you say; the minister is here. Malvolio, Malvolio, thy wits the heavens restore! endeavor thyself to sleep, and leave thy vain bibble babble.

MALVOLIO. Sir Topas,—

CLOWN. Maintain no words with him, good fellow. Who, I, sir? not I, sir. God be wi' you, good Sir Topas. Marry, amen. I will, sir, I will.

MALVOLIO. Fool, fool, fool, I say,—

CLOWN. Alas, sir, be patient. What say you, sir? I am shent for speaking to you.

MALVOLIO. Good fool, help me to some light and some paper: I tell thee, I am as well in my wits as any man in Illyria.

CLOWN. Well-a-day that you were, sir!

MALVOLIO. By this hand, I am. Good fool, some ink, paper and light; and convey what I will set down to my lady: it shall advantage thee more than ever the bearing of letter did.

CLOWN. I will help you to 't. But tell me true, are you not mad
   indeed? or do you but counterfeit?

MALVOLIO. Believe me, I am not; I tell thee true.

CLOWN. Nay, I 'll ne'er believe a madman till I see his brains.
   I will fetch you light and paper and ink.

MALVOLIO. Fool, I 'll requite it in the highest degree: I prithee,
   be gone.

CLOWN. [*Singing*] I am gone, sir.
> And anon, sir,
> I 'll be with you again,
> In a trice,
> Like to the old vice,
> Your need to sustain;
> Who, with dagger of lath,
> In his rage and his wrath,
> Cries, ah, ha! to the devil:
> Like a mad lad,
> Pare thy nails, dad;
> Adieu, goodman devil.

SCENE III — OLIVIA's *garden.*

Enter SEBASTIAN.]

SEBASTIAN. This is the air; that is the glorious sun;
   This pearl she gave me, I do feel 't and see 't;
   And though 'tis wonder that enwraps me thus,
   Yet 'tis not madness. Where 's Antonio, then?
   I could not find him at the Elephant:
   Yet there he was; and there I found this credit,
   That he did range the town to seek me out.
   His counsel now might do me golden service;
   For though my soul disputes well with my sense,
   That this may be some error, but no madness,
   Yet doth this accident and flood of fortune
   So far exceed all instance, all discourse,
   That I am ready to distrust mine eyes
   And wrangle with my reason, that persuades me
   To any other trust but that I am mad,

Or else the lady's mad; yet, if 'twere so,
She could not sway her house, command her followers,
Take and give back affairs and their dispatch
With such a smooth, discreet, and stable bearing
As I perceive she does: there 's something in 't
That is deceivable. But here the lady comes.

Enter OLIVIA *and* PRIEST.]

OLIVIA. Blame not this haste of mine. If you mean well,
Now go with me and with this holy man
Into the chantry by: there, before him,
And underneath that consecrated roof,
Plight me the full assurance of your faith;
That my most jealous and too doubtful soul
May live at peace. He shall conceal it
Whiles you are willing it shall come to note,
What time we will our celebration keep
According to my birth. What do you say?

SEBASTIAN. I 'll follow this good man, and go with you;
And having sworn truth, ever will be true.

OLIVIA. Then lead the way, good father; and heavens so shine,
That they may fairly note this act of mine! [*Exeunt.*

ACT V

Scene I — *Before* Olivia's *house.*

Enter Clown *and* Fabian.]

FABIAN. Now, as thou lovest me, let me see his letter.

CLOWN. Good Master Fabian, grant me another request.

FABIAN. Any thing.

CLOWN. Do not desire to see this letter.

FABIAN. This is, to give a dog, and in recompense desire my
dog again.

Enter DUKE, VIOLA, CURIO, *and* LORDS.]

DUKE. Belong you to the Lady Olivia, friends?

CLOWN. Aye, sir; we are some of her trappings.

DUKE. I know thee well: how dost thou, my good fellow?

CLOWN. Truly, sir, the better for my foes and the worse for
my friends.

DUKE. Just the contrary; the better for thy friends.

CLOWN. No, sir, the worse.

DUKE. How can that be?

CLOWN. Marry, sir, they praise me and make an ass of me; now
my foes tell me plainly I am an ass: so that by my foes, sir,
I profit in the knowledge of myself; and by my friends I am
abused: so that, conclusions to be as kisses, if your four
negatives make your two affirmatives, why then, the worse
for my friends, and the better for my foes.

DUKE. Why, this is excellent.

CLOWN. By my troth, sir, no; though it please you to be one
of my friends.

DUKE. Thou shalt not be the worse for me: there 's gold.

CLOWN. But that it would be double-dealing, sir, I would you
could make it another.

DUKE. O, you give me ill counsel.

CLOWN. Put your grace in your pocket, sir, for this once, and
let your flesh and blood obey it.

DUKE. Well, I will be so much a sinner, to be a double-dealer: there 's another.

CLOWN. Primo, secundo, tertio, is a good play; and the old saying is, the third pays for all: the triplex, sir, is a good tripping measure; or the bells of Saint Bennet, sir, may put you in mind; one, two, three.

DUKE. You can fool no more money out of me at this throw: if you will let your lady know I am here to speak with her, and bring her along with you, it may awake my bounty further.

CLOWN. Marry, sir, lullaby to your bounty till I come again. I go, sir; but I would not have you to think that my desire of having is the sin of covetousness: but, as you say, sir, let your bounty take a nap, I will awake it anon.   [*Exit.*

VIOLA. Here comes the man, sir, that did rescue me.
Enter ANTONIO *and* OFFICERS.]

DUKE. That face of his I do remember well;
Yet, when I saw it last, it was besmear'd
As black as Vulcan in the smoke of war:
A bawbling vessel was he captain of,
For shallow draught and bulk unprizable;
With which such scathful grapple did he make
With the most noble bottom of our fleet,
That very envy and the tongue of loss
Cried fame and honor on him. What 's the matter?

FIRST OFFICER. Orsino, this is that Antonio
That took the Phœnix and her fraught from Candy;
And this is he that did the Tiger board,
When your young nephew Titus lost his leg:
Here in the streets, desperate of shame and state,
In private brabble did we apprehend him.

VIOLA. He did me kindness, sir, drew on my side;
But in conclusion put strange speech upon me:
I know not what 'twas but distraction.

DUKE. Notable pirate! thou salt-water thief!
What foolish boldness brought thee to their mercies,
Whom thou, in terms so bloody and so dear,
Hast made thine enemies?

ANTONIO.   Orsino, noble sir,
Be pleased that I shake off these names you give me:
Antonio never yet was thief or pirate,
Though I confess, on base and ground enough,
Orsino's enemy. A witchcraft drew me hither:
That most ingrateful boy there by your side,
From the rude sea's enraged and foamy mouth
Did I redeem; a wreck past hope he was:
His life I gave him and did thereto add
My love, without retention or restraint,
All his in dedication; for his sake
Did I expose myself, pure for his love,
Into the danger of this adverse town;
Drew to defend him when he was beset:
Where being apprehended, his false cunning,
Not meaning to partake with me in danger,
Taught him to face me out of his acquaintance,
And grew a twenty years removed thing
While one would wink; denied me mine own purse,
Which I had recommended to his use
Not half an hour before.

VIOLA.   How can this be?

DUKE. When came he to this town?

ANTONIO. To-day, my lord; and for three months before,
No interim, not a minute's vacancy,
Both day and night did we keep company.

Enter OLIVIA *and* ATTENDANTS.]

DUKE. Here comes the countess: now heaven walks on earth.
But for thee, fellow; fellow, thy words are madness:
Three months this youth hath tended upon me;
But more of that anon. Take him aside.

OLIVIA. What would my lord, but that he may not have,
Wherein Olivia may seem serviceable?
Cesario, you do not keep promise with me.

VIOLA. Madam!

DUKE. Gracious Olivia,—

OLIVIA. What do you say, Cesario? Good my lord,—

VIOLA. My lord would speak; my duty hushes me.

OLIVIA. If it be aught to the old tune, my lord,
It is as fat and fulsome to mine ear
As howling after music.

DUKE. Still so cruel?

OLIVIA. Still so constant, lord.

DUKE. What, to perverseness? you uncivil lady,
To whose ingrate and unauspicious altars
My soul the faithfull'st offerings hath breathed out
That e'er devotion tender'd! What shall I do?

OLIVIA. Even what it please my lord, that shall become him.

DUKE. Why should I not, had I the heart to do it,
Like to the Egyptian thief at point of death,
Kill what I love?—a savage jealousy
That sometimes savors nobly. But hear me this:
Since you to non-regardance cast my faith,
And that I partly know the instrument
That screws me from my true place in your favor,
Live you the marble-breasted tyrant still;
But this your minion, whom I know you love,
And whom, by heaven I swear, I tender dearly,
Him will I tear out of that cruel eye,
Where he sits crowned in his master's spite.
Come, boy, with me; my thoughts are ripe in mischief:
I 'll sacrifice the lamb that I do love,
To spite a raven's heart within a dove.

VIOLA. And I, most jocund, apt and willingly,
To do you rest, a thousand deaths would die.

OLIVIA. Where goes Cesario?

VIOLA. After him I love
More than I love these eyes, more than my life,
More, by all mores, than e'er I shall love wife.
If I do feign, you witnesses above
Punish my life for tainting of my love!

OLIVIA. Aye me, detested! how am I beguiled!

VIOLA. Who does beguile you? who does do you wrong?

OLIVIA. Hast thou forgot thyself? is it so long?
Call forth the holy father.

DUKE. Come, away!

OLIVIA. Whither, my lord? Cesario, husband, stay.

DUKE. Husband!

OLIVIA.   Aye, husband: can he that deny?

DUKE. Her husband, sirrah!

VIOLA.   No, my lord, not I.

OLIVIA. Alas, it is the baseness of thy fear
    That makes thee strangle thy propriety:
    Fear not, Cesario; take thy fortunes up;
    Be that thou know'st thou art, and then thou art
    As great as that thou fear'st.

Enter PRIEST.]

                       O, welcome, father!
    Father, I charge thee, by thy reverence,
    Here to unfold, though lately we intended
    To keep in darkness what occasion now
    Reveals before 'tis ripe, what thou dost know
    Hath newly pass'd between this youth and me.

PRIEST. A contract of eternal bond of love,
    Confirm'd by mutual joinder of your hands,
    Attested by the holy close of lips,
    Strengthen'd by interchangement of your rings;
    And all the ceremony of this compact
    Seal'd in my function, by my testimony:
    Since when, my watch hath told me, toward my grave
    I have travel'd but two hours.

DUKE. O thou dissembling cub! what wilt thou be
    When time hath sow'd a grizzle on thy case?
    Or will not else thy craft so quickly grow,
    That thine own trip shall be thine overthrow?
    Farewell, and take her; but direct thy feet
    Where thou and I henceforth may never meet.

VIOLA. My lord, I do protest—

OLIVIA.   O, do not swear!
    Hold little faith, though thou hast too much fear.

Enter SIR ANDREW.]

SIR ANDREW. For the love of God, a surgeon! Send one pres-
    ently to Sir Toby.

OLIVIA. What's the matter?

SIR ANDREW. He has broke my head across and has given Sir
    Toby a bloody coxcomb too: for the love of God, your help!
    I had rather than forty pound I were at home.

OLIVIA. Who has done this, Sir Andrew?

SIR ANDREW. The count's gentleman, one Cesario: we took him
    for a coward, but he's the very devil incardinate.

DUKE. My gentleman, Cesario?

SIR ANDREW. 'Od's lifelings, here he is! You broke my head for
    nothing; and that that I did, I was set on to do 't by Sir
    Toby.

VIOLA. Why do you speak to me? I never hurt you:
    You drew your sword upon me without cause;
    But I bespake you fair, and hurt you not.

SIR ANDREW. If a bloody coxcomb be a hurt, you have hurt
    me: I think you set nothing by a bloody coxcomb.

Enter SIR TOBY *and* CLOWN.]
    Here comes Sir Toby halting; you shall hear more: but if he
    had not been in drink, he would have tickled you other
    gates than he did.

DUKE. How now, gentleman! how is 't with you?

SIR TOBY. That's all one: has hurt me, and there's the end on
    't. Sot, didst see Dick surgeon, sot?

CLOWN. O, he's drunk, Sir Toby, an hour agone; his eyes were
    set at eight i' the morning.

SIR TOBY. Then he's a rogue, and a passy measures pavin:
    I hate a drunken rogue.

OLIVIA. Away with him! Who hath made this havoc with them?

SIR ANDREW. I'll help you, Sir Toby, because we'll be dressed
    together.

SIR TOBY. Will you help? an ass-head and a coxcomb and a
    knave, a thin-faced knave, a gull!

OLIVIA. Get him to bed, and let his hurt be look'd to.

            [*Exeunt* CLOWN, FABIAN, SIR TOBY *and* SIR ANDREW.
Enter SEBASTIAN.]

SEBASTIAN. I am sorry, madam, I have hurt your kinsman;
    But, had it been the brother of my blood,
    I must have done no less with wit and safety.
    You throw a strange regard upon me, and by that

I do perceive it hath offended you:
Pardon me, sweet one, even for the vows
We made each other but so late ago.

DUKE. One face, one voice, one habit, and two persons,
A natural perspective, that is and is not!

SEBASTIAN. Antonio, O my dear Antonio!
How have the hours rack'd and tortured me,
Since I have lost thee!

ANTONIO. Sebastian are you?

SEBASTIAN.　　　　　　　　Fear'st thou that, Antonio?

ANTONIO. How have you made division of yourself?
An apple, cleft in two, is not more twin
Than these two creatures. Which is Sebastian?

OLIVIA. Most wonderful!

SEBASTIAN. Do I stand there? I never had a brother;
Nor can there be that deity in my nature,
Of here and every where. I had a sister,
Whom the blind waves and surges have devour'd.
Of charity, what kin are you to me?
What countryman? what name? what parentage?

VIOLA. Of Messaline: Sebastian was my father;
Such a Sebastian was my brother too,
So went he suited to his watery tomb:
If spirits can assume both form and suit,
You come to fright us.

SEBASTIAN.　　　　　A spirit I am indeed;
But am in that dimension grossly clad
Which from the womb I did participate.
Were you a woman, as the rest goes even,
I should my tears let fall upon your cheek,
And say 'Thrice-welcome, drowned Viola!'

VIOLA. My father had a mole upon his brow.

SEBASTIAN. And so had mine.

VIOLA. And died that day when Viola from her birth
Had number'd thirteen years.

SEBASTIAN. O, that record is lively in my soul!
He finished indeed his mortal act
That day that made my sister thirteen years.

VIOLA. If nothing lets to make us happy both
But this my masculine usurp'd attire,
Do not embrace me till each circumstance
Of place, time, fortune, do cohere and jump
That I am Viola: which to confirm,
I 'll bring you to a captain in this town,
Where lie my maiden weeds; by whose gentle help
I was preserved to serve this noble count.
All the occurrence of my fortune since
Hath been between this lady and this lord.

SEBASTIAN. [*To* OLIVIA] So comes it, lady, you have been mis-
took:
But nature to her bias drew in that.
You would have been contracted to a maid;
Nor are you therein, by my life, deceived,
You are betroth'd both to a maid and man.

DUKE. Be not amazed; right noble is his blood.
If this be so, as yet the glass seems true,
I shall have share in this most happy wreck.
[*To* VIOLA] Boy, thou hast said to me a thousand times
Thou never shouldst love woman like to me.

VIOLA. And all those sayings will I over-swear;
And all those swearings keep as true in soul
As doth that orbed continent the fire
That severs day from night.

DUKE.   Give me thy hand;
And let me see thee in thy woman's weeds.

VIOLA. The captain that did bring me first on shore
Hath my maid's garments: he upon some action
Is now in durance, at Malvolio's suit,
A gentleman, and follower of my lady's.

OLIVIA. He shall enlarge him: fetch Malvolio hither:
And yet, alas, now I remember me,
They say, poor gentleman, he 's much distract.

Re-enter CLOWN *with a letter, and* FABIAN.]
A most extracting frenzy of mine own
From my remembrance clearly banish'd his.
How does he, sirrah?

CLOWN. Truly, madam, he holds Belzebub at the stave's end
   as well as a man in his case may do: has here writ a letter
   to you; I should have given 't you to-day morning, but as a
   madman's epistles are no gospels, so it skills not much when
   they are delivered.

OLIVIA. Open 't and read it.

CLOWN. Look then to be well edified when the fool delivers
   the madman. [*Reads*] By the Lord, madam,—

OLIVIA. How now! art thou mad?

CLOWN. No, madam, I do but read madness: an your ladyship
   will have it as it ought to be, you must allow Vox.

OLIVIA. Prithee, read i' thy right wits.

CLOWN. So I do, madonna; but to read his right wits is to read
   thus: therefore perpend, my princess, and give ear.

OLIVIA. Read it you, sirrah.   [*To* FABIAN.

FABIAN. By the Lord, madam, you wrong me and the world
   shall know it: though you have put me into darkness and
   given your drunken cousin rule over me, yet have I the
   benefit of my senses as well as your ladyship. I have your
   own letter that induced me to the semblance I put on; with
   the which I doubt not but to do myself much right, or you
   much shame. Think of me as you please. I leave my duty a
   little unthought of, and speak out of my injury.

                         THE MADLY-USED MALVOLIO.

OLIVIA. Did he write this?

CLOWN. Aye, madam.

DUKE. This savors not much of distraction.

OLIVIA. See him deliver'd, Fabian; bring him hither.

                                        [*Exit* FABIAN.

   My lord, so please you, these things further thought on,
   To think me as well a sister as a wife,
   One day shall crown the alliance on 't, so please you,
   Here at my house and at my proper cost.

DUKE. Madam, I am most apt to embrace your offer.

   [*To* VIOLA] Your master quits you; and for your service
      done him,
   So much against the mettle of your sex,
   So far beneath your soft and tender breeding,

And since you call'd me master for so long,
Here is my hand: you shall from this time be
Your master's mistress.

OLIVIA.   A sister! you are she.

Re-enter FABIAN, *with* MALVOLIO.]

DUKE. Is this the madman?

OLIVIA.   Aye, my lord, this same.
How now, Malvolio!

MALVOLIO.   Madam, you have done me wrong,
Notorious wrong.

OLIVIA.   Have I, Malvolio? no.

MALVOLIO. Lady, you have. Pray you, peruse that letter.
You must not now deny it is your hand:
Write from it, if you can, in hand or phrase;
Or say 'tis not your seal, not your invention:
You can say none of this: well, grant it then
And tell me, in the modesty of honor,
Why you have given me such clear lights of favor,
Bade me come smiling and cross-garter'd to you,
To put on yellow stockings and to frown
Upon Sir Toby and the lighter people;
And, acting this in an obedient hope,
Why have you suffer'd me to be imprison'd,
Kept in a dark house, visited by the priest,
And made the most notorious geck and gull
That e'er invention play'd on? tell me why.

OLIVIA. Alas, Malvolio, this is not my writing,
Though, I confess, much like the character:
But out of question 'tis Maria's hand.
And now I do bethink me, it was she
First told me thou wast mad; then camest in smiling,
And in such forms which here were presupposed
Upon thee in the letter. Prithee, be content:
This practice hath most shrewdly pass'd upon thee;
But when we know the grounds and authors of it,
Thou shalt be both the plaintiff and the judge
Of thine own cause.

FABIAN.   Good madam, hear me speak,

　　And let no quarrel nor no brawl to come
　　Taint the condition of this present hour,
　　Which I have wonder'd at. In hope it shall not,
　　Most freely I confess, myself and Toby
　　Set this device against Malvolio here,
　　Upon some stubborn and uncourteous parts
　　We had conceived against him: Maria writ
　　The letter at Sir Toby's great importance;
　　In recompense whereof he hath married her.
　　How with a sportful malice it was follow'd
　　May rather pluck on laughter than revenge;
　　If that the injuries be justly weigh'd
　　That have on both sides pass'd.

OLIVIA. Alas, poor fool, how have they baffled thee!

CLOWN. Why, 'some are born great, some achieve greatness,
　　and some have greatness thrown upon them.' I was one, sir,
　　in this interlude; one Sir Topas, sir; but that 's all one. 'By
　　the Lord, fool, I am not mad.' But do you remember?
　　'Madam, why laugh you at such a barren rascal? an you
　　smile not, he 's gagged:' and thus the whirligig of time
　　brings in his revenges.

MALVOLIO. I 'll be revenged on the whole pack of you.　[*Exit.*

OLIVIA. He hath been most notoriously abused.

DUKE. Pursue him, and entreat him to a peace:
　　He hath not told us of the captain yet:
　　When that is known, and golden time convents,
　　A solemn combination shall be made
　　Of our dear souls. Meantime, sweet sister,
　　We will not part from hence. Cesario, come;
　　For so you shall be, while you are a man;
　　But when in other habits you are seen,
　　Orsino's mistress and his fancy's queen.
　　　　　　　　　　　　　[*Exeunt all, except* CLOWN.

CLOWN. [*Sings*]
　　When that I was and a little tiny boy,
　　　　With hey, ho, the wind and the rain,
　　A foolish thing was but a toy,
　　　　For the rain it raineth every day.

But when I came to man's estate,
   With hey, ho, &c.
'Gainst knaves and thieves men shut their gate,
   For the rain, &c.

But when I came, alas! to wive,
   With hey, ho, &c.
By swaggering could I never thrive,
   For the rain, &c.

But when I came unto my beds,
   With hey, ho, &c.
With toss-pots still had drunken heads,
   For the rain, &c.

A great while ago the world begun,
   With hey, ho, &c.
But that 's all one, our play is done,
   And we 'll strive to please you every day.   [*Exit.*

The Tempest

INTRODUCTION TO

The Tempest

BY

MARK VAN DOREN

IF Shakespeare thought of *The Tempest* as the last play he
would write he may have said to himself—silently, we
must assume—that he could afford to let action come in it
to a kind of rest; that its task was not so much to tell a story
as to fix a vision; that the symbols he hitherto had defined his
art by concealing might now confess themselves, even ob-
trude themselves, in measured dance and significant song;
and that while he was at it he would recapitulate his poetic
career. It is interesting to conjecture thus, but it is perilous.
The Tempest does bind up in final form a host of themes with
which its author has been concerned. It is a mirror in which,
if we hold it very still, we can gaze backward at all of the
recent plays; and behind them will be glimpses of a past as
old as the tragedies, the middle comedies, and even *A Midsummer Night's Dream.* Or it is a thicket of resonant trees,
in an odd angle of the Shakespearean wood, which hums with
echoes of every distant aisle. And certainly its symbols expose
themselves as their ancestors in Shakespeare seldom or never
did. The play seems to order itself in terms of its meanings;
things in it stand for other things, so that we are tempted to
search its dark backward for a single meaning, quite final for
Shakespeare and quite abstract. The trouble is that the meanings are not self-evident. One interpretation of *The Tempest*
does not agree with another. And there is deeper trouble in
the truth that any interpretation, even the wildest, is more or
less plausible. This deep trouble, and this deep truth, should

warn us that *The Tempest* is a composition about which we had better not be too knowing. If it is one of Shakespeare's successes, and obviously it is, it will not yield its secret easily; or it has no secret to yield. Notwithstanding its visionary grace, its tendency toward lyric abstraction, it keeps that life-like surface and that humor with which Shakespeare has always protected his meaning if he had one: that impenetrable shield off which the spears of interpretation invariably glance —or return, bent in the shaft and dulled at the point, to the hand of the thrower. It may well be that Shakespeare in *The Tempest* is telling us for the last time, and consciously for the last time, about the world. But what he is telling us cannot be simple, or we could agree that it is this or that. Perhaps it is this: that the world is not simple. Or, mysteriously enough, that it is what we all take it to be, just as *The Tempest* is whatever we would take it to be. Any set of symbols, moved close to this play, lights up as in an electric field. Its meaning, in other words, is precisely as rich as the human mind, and it says that the world is what it is. But what the world is cannot be said in a sentence. Or even in a poem as complete and beautiful as *The Tempest*.

Separations and reconciliations are woven here within the circle of a remote and musical island where an enchanter, controlling the black magic of native witchcraft with the white magic of his liberal art, controls also a tempest until it brings to pass all things he has desired. The ship it founders on the shore, or seems to founder, carries his two chief enemies: his brother Antonio, whose treason has put the sea between them, and Alonso king of Naples, confederate to this treason. Prospero as duke of Milan had honored his brother with "confidence sans bound." But Antonio had abused his trust, and that is the first separation. The second has occurred likewise before the play begins, and nothing in the play can cure it. Alonso has lost his fair daughter Claribel by marriage to the King of Tunis, and indeed it is from that "sweet marriage" that he is returning, bound sadly home for Naples, when he suffers shipwreck on Prospero's island. Alonso's loss of his remaining heir, his son Ferdinand, is temporary in so

far as Prospero merely keeps them apart on the island until
the separation has served its purpose, meanwhile entertaining
the prince with the unearthly music of Ariel and with the
charms of his own daughter Miranda; but it is permanent
when Ferdinand and Miranda give themselves away to each
other in love. And by the same blow, happy though it be,
Prospero loses Miranda. The plot of *The Tempest* is a com-
plex of separations—and, swiftly and harmoniously, of reconciliations, so that Gonzalo can say:

> In one voyage
> Did Claribel her husband find at Tunis,
> And Ferdinand, her brother, found a wife
> Where he himself was lost, Prospero his dukedom
> In a poor isle, and all of us ourselves
> When no man was his own.   [v, i]

But we have known from the beginning that Gonzalo would
have grounds for speaking so. Prospero's isle is not poor; it
is rich and strange and full of fair noises, and the magic with
which he controls it will maneuver all lives into peace. We
know this not merely from his assuring Miranda in the second
scene that the sea-storm has been "safely ordered," or from
Ariel's report that not a hair has perished, but from the sense
we always have here that danger is not real, that artifice is
disarmingly at work, and that woe is only waiting upon sea-
change. Tides of understanding must "shortly fill the reasonable shore" (v, i) when music like this music plays—constantly, and with such continuing sweetness that the one
unregenerate person on the island can speak of "sounds and
sweet airs that give delight and hurt not" (III, ii).

The hag-born Caliban is not deaf to the "thousand twangling instruments" that hum about his ears. He is, however,
the lowest inhabitant of the play; the human scale which
Shakespeare has built begins with him. The island as we
have it is among other things a microcosm of humanity, and
its meanest soul smells music rather than apprehends it; or
receives it at any rate in his grosser senses. We know Caliban
first of all by his style, which may not be the "special language" an old critical tradition says it is, but which gives us

a creature complete in beastliness. His characteristic speech
does not open the mouth to music; it closes it rather on harsh,
hissing, or guttural consonants that in the slowness with which
they must be uttered express the difficult progress of a mind
bemired in fact, an imagination beslimed with particulars.
Caliban has no capacity for abstraction, and consequently for
the rational harmonies of music and love.

> As wicked dew as e'er my mother brush'd
> With raven's feather from unwholesome fen
> Drop on you both! A south-west blow on ye
> And blister you all o'er! [I, ii]

The second of these sentences is scarcely articulated; it is a
mouthed curse which no tongue's skill can refine.

> This island's mine, by Sycorax my mother,
> Which thou tak'st from me. When thou cam'st first,
> Thou strok'dst me and made much of me, wouldst give me
> Water with berries in 't, and teach me how
> To name the bigger light, and how the less,
> That burn by day and night; and then I lov'd thee
> And show'd thee all the qualities o' the isle,
> The fresh springs, brine-pits, barren place and fertile.
> Curs'd be I that did so! All the charms
> Of Sycorax, toads, beetles, bats, light on you! [I, ii]

"Thou strok'dst me and made much of me"—the second word
is a thicket of vile sound, and the m's that follow are the mut-
terings of less than human lips.

> All the infections that the sun sucks up
> From bogs, fens, flats, on Prosper fall and make him
> By inch-meal a disease! His spirits hear me
> And yet I needs must curse. But they'll nor pinch,
> Fright me with urchin-shows, pitch me i' the mire,
> Nor lead me, like a firebrand, in the dark
> Out of my way, unless he bid 'em; but
> For every trifle are they set upon me,
> Sometime like apes that mow and chatter at me
> And after bite me, then like hedgehogs which
> Lie tumbling in my barefoot way and mount
> Their pricks at my footfall; sometime am I
> All wound with adders who with cloven tongues
> Do hiss me into madness. [II, ii]

"Like hedgehogs which lie tumbling"—the tongue of the speaker is thick in his throat, his palate is untrained.

> Pray you, tread softly, that the blind mole may not
> Hear a foot fall.   [IV, i]

Out of its context this has been thought pretty, but its context is an island among whose pits and thistles Caliban roots more like a hog than a man. He knows every detail of the place but he understands nothing.

> I'll show thee every fertile inch o' the island. . . .
> I'll show thee the best springs; I'll pluck thee berries;
> I'll fish for thee and get thee wood enough. . . .
> I prithee, let me bring thee where crabs grow;
> And I with my long nails will dig thee pig-nuts;
> Show thee a jay's nest and instruct thee how
> To snare the nimble marmoset. I'll bring thee
> To clust'ring filberts and sometimes I'll get thee
> Young scamels from the rock.   [II, ii]

"I'll dig thee pig-nuts," he promises the drunken Stephano, ignorant that Stephano is not a god. It may not matter what relation Caliban bears to Montaigne's cannibal—whether he is an answer to the doctrine of the noble savage, or whether he supports the doctrine by showing how nature is degraded upon contact with culture—so long as one sees that in Prospero's mind, which is the only mind where he counts, he is uneducable. He cannot take any print of goodness; he has that in him which good natures cannot abide to be with; he is a born devil on whose nature nurture can never stick. The phrases are Prospero's, for it is only Prospero who has taken pains with this thing of deformity, and it is only he who cares that failure has been his reward. He has failed with Caliban, either because Caliban was incapable of becoming man or because there is no art, Prospero's or Shakespeare's, by which the inhuman can be made human. Caliban represents the lower limit, as Prospero to his own confusion forgets for a moment when he loses himself in a certain "vanity" of his art and entertains Ferdinand with the pageant of Iris, Ceres, Juno, and the Naiads. Remembering Caliban's plot against his life, and remembering even more the intractable nature of the

beast, he starts suddenly and waves the pageant away—
explaining to Ferdinand that it has melted into air even as
the earth will dissolve into sleep when its dreamer ceases to
dream:

> You do look, my son, in a mov'd sort,
> As if you were dismay'd. Be cheerful, sir,
> Our revels now are ended. These our actors,
> As I foretold you, were all spirits, and
> Are melted into air, into thin air;
> And, like the baseless fabric of this vision,
> The cloud-capp'd towers, the gorgeous palaces,
> The solemn temples, the great globe itself,
> Yea, all which it inherit, shall dissolve
> And, like this insubstantial pageant faded,
> Leave not a rack behind. We are such stuff
> As dreams are made on, and our little life
> Is rounded with a sleep.　　　　　　　　　[IV, i]

Scarcely higher on the scale than Caliban stand Trinculo
and Stephano—or reel, for they are drunken rascals past re-
form, and there is no promise for them, as there is for Alonso
and Antonio, of "a clear life ensuing" (III, iii). Alonso and
Antonio will reach the reasonable shore and own themselves
again. When they do they will find Gonzalo there, for he has
never strayed away. The good old counselor who made it possible for Prospero to survive the voyage from Milan with his
daughter and his secret books, who amuses three cynical gentlemen with talk of the golden age (II, i), who seasons all of
his discourse with a wise wit, and who upon recognizing Prospero can weep, has always been possessed of an honor which
"cannot be measur'd or confin'd" (V, i). He sits near the top
of the scale, just beneath the honey-throated Ferdinand and
his admired Miranda. The top is reserved for these young
lovers who have yet to know the world, and who for that
reason alone are its best lovers. Ferdinand is all gallantry and
devotion, and the compliments he pays his island mistress are
worthy of one who when she first saw him could say: "Nothing natural I ever saw so noble" (I, ii). He had seemed to
her almost divine, as if the upper human limit were more than

reached in him. He continues to deserve her wonder, as she
his:

> You, O you,
> So perfect and so peerless, are created
> Of every creature's best. . . . I
> Beyond all limit of what else i' the world
> Do love, prize, honour you.   [III, i]

Miranda, as her name half tells, is all tears and wonder. Her
pity is had before it is asked, since she is without guile; and
she knows how to weep for joy when Ferdinand returns her
adoration. And if Shakespeare was thinking of *The Tempest*
as his last play he may have written a special meaning, not
to say a special irony, into these now famous words:

> O, wonder!
> How many goodly creatures are there here!
> How beauteous mankind is! O brave new world,
> That has such people in 't!   [v, i]

" 'T is new to thee," says Prospero quietly, noting that Miranda is more beautiful than any man she beholds, and more
virtuous. The carcass of the world that age hands on to youth
is suddenly not a carcass but a brave new goodly thing. There
is mystery in that, and an irony which works either way, for
both age and youth are as right as they are wrong.

Prospero is in one sense not measured on the scale, since
he himself is its measurer. Yet he has human traits, one of
which is his pride in his art and another of which is his stern-
ness as he employs it. For he belongs among the strict elders
of the later plays; his behavior not only toward Caliban but
toward the delightful Ariel is harsh with threats and curses,
and if his cruelty to Ferdinand is only feigned "lest too light
winning make the prize light" (I, ii), the feigner at least is
master of the mood.

> My father's of a better nature, sir,
> Than he appears by speech.   [I, ii]

But Miranda does not know her father perfectly. She perhaps
does not follow the turnings of his great speech on dreams.

She has never shared with him the secret knowledge to which
he bids farewell as he breaks his wand and takes breath for a
masterpiece of hymn new-harmonized from Arthur Golding's
Ovid:

> Ye elves of hills, brooks, standing lakes, and groves,
> And ye that on the sands with printless foot
> Do chase the ebbing Neptune, and do fly him
> When he comes back; you demi-puppets that
> By moonshine do the green sour ringlets make,
> Whereof the ewe not bites; and you whose pastime
> Is to make midnight mushrooms, that rejoice
> To hear the solemn curfew; by whose aid,
> Weak masters though ye be, I have bedimm'd
> The noontide sun, call'd forth the mutinous winds,
> And 'twixt the green sea and the azur'd vault
> Set roaring war; to the dread rattling thunder
> Have I given fire, and rifted Jove's stout oak
> With his own bolt; the strong-bas'd promontory
> Have I made shake, and by the spurs pluck'd up
> The pine and cedar; graves at my command
> Have wak'd their sleepers, op'd, and let 'em forth
> By my so potent art. But this rough magic
> I here abjure, and, when I have requir'd
> Some heavenly music, which even now I do,
> To work mine end upon their senses that
> This airy charm is for, I'll break my staff,
> Bury it certain fathoms in the earth,
> And deeper than did ever plummet sound
> I'll drown my book.   [v, i]

And if she is giving him any attention at the end she probably
does not guess what he means when he speaks of a retirement to Milan

> where
> Every third thought shall be my grave.   [v, i]

The meaning may be Shakespeare's no less than Prospero's.
If so, the ambiguity does admirably for an ending note.

Is Shakespeare Prospero, and is his magic the art with
which he has fabricated thirty-seven plays? Is he now bury-
ing his book—abandoning the theater—and retiring where
every third thought will be his grave? And does *The Tem-*

pest so signify? Answers are not too easy. Shakespeare has never dramatized himself before, and it may not have occurred to him to do so now. Also, *The Tempest* is not a cantata; it is still a play, and it is ballasted with much life. It has snarling beasts and belching drunkards to match its innocent angels and white magicians. It contains two of Shakespeare's finest songs—"Full fathom five thy father lies" and "Come unto these yellow sands"—and two of his coarsest—" 'Ban, 'Ban, Cacaliban" and "The master, the swabber, the boatswain, and I." And Ariel is more than an angelic musician; he is a mischief-maker, another Puck, unwilling at his work and restless under the burden of magic he bears. It can be doubted, in other words, that Shakespeare sat down solemnly to decorate his life's work with a secret signature. *The Tempest,* pressed a little, yields this meaning as it yields most of the meanings ingenuity can insist upon, and yields it with grace. But a better signature was the play itself, which, if its author had been given to such exercises, he might have recognized as one of the most beautiful literary objects ever made. He would scarcely, however, have been so conscious of what he had done. He is more likely to have let the moment go with four simple words: Now I will rest.

The Story of the Play

A TEMPEST-TOSSED vessel is wrecked upon the shores of an enchanted isle whereon dwell Prospero and his daughter, Miranda, alone save for the presence of Caliban, a deformed and brutish slave. During the storm Prospero tells his daughter of his past life: Formerly he had been Duke of Milan, but had been supplanted by his brother Antonio, with the aid of Alonso, King of Naples, who desired thereby to render Milan tributary to his kingdom. The conspirators had not dared to kill Prospero outright, but had contented themselves with setting him and his daughter, then three years old, adrift in a crazy boat upon the open sea. They would have perished miserably but for a humane Neapolitan named Gonzalo, who provisioned their craft, and thus enabled them to reach the island which they made their home. For twelve years they had quietly dwelt there—a period spent profitably by Prospero in the education of his daughter and in his own study of works on magic. Prospero ends his story by telling Miranda that a strange chance has sent all of his enemies to him in the ship which they have seen wrecked in the tempest raised by his art. Ariel, the chief of his spirits, now appears and reports that all the passengers have been brought safely to land. Ferdinand, the King's son, becomes separated from the rest, and they suppose him lost. Prospero leads him to his cell, where the prince and Miranda become mutually enamoured.

ACT II

ALONSO, Sebastian (his brother), Antonio, Gonzalo, and other victims of the shipwreck roam the island until all but Sebastian and Antonio are put to sleep by the invisible Ariel through the agency of gentle music. Sebastian and Antonio now plot to murder the King. Ariel frustrates their plans. In another part of the island two others of the company, Stephano and Trinculo, discover Caliban.

ACT III

THE three last named plot to despatch Caliban's master, Prospero, and seize upon the island for themselves. The King and his company meanwhile wander about oppressed by weariness, hunger, and mental aberration. Ariel tantalises them with the vision of a spectral banquet. At his cell Prospero sets Ferdinand to the task of carrying and piling logs, in order, as later develops, to test the prince's affection for Miranda, who, on her part, entreats Ferdinand to let her share in his arduous labours.

ACT IV

FERDINAND undergoes the trial worthily, and Prospero bestows his daughter's hand upon him, and entertains the lovers with a glimpse into the land of spirits. The entertainment is interrupted by Prospero, who, suddenly recollecting the conspiracy of Caliban and his confederates, calls Ariel, and prepares to frustrate them. The conspirators meet with severe punishment at the hands of Prospero and Ariel, who set upon them "divers spirits in the shape of dogs and hounds."

ACT V

THE KING and his company are brought by Ariel before Prospero, who is moved to be merciful because of their sufferings. He reveals his identity to them. The King begs of him pardon for the wrongs he has done him, and restores to him his dukedom. Prospero brings forward Ferdinand and Miranda, whose troth is ratified by Alonso. Prospero abjures the mystic art, and with the King and his train proceeds to Naples, by means of the magically preserved ship, to solemnize the nuptials of the lovers.

J. WALKER McSPADDEN

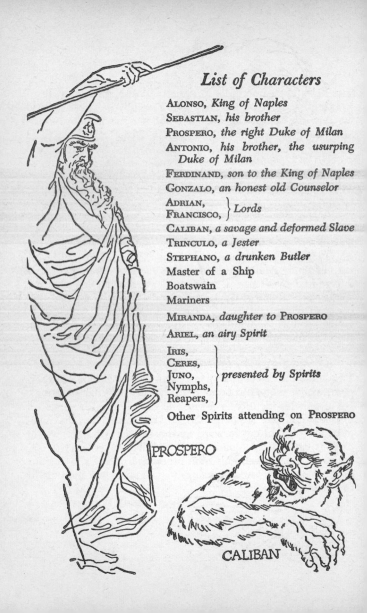

List of Characters

ALONSO, *King of Naples*

SEBASTIAN, *his brother*

PROSPERO, *the right Duke of Milan*

ANTONIO, *his brother, the usurping Duke of Milan*

FERDINAND, *son to the King of Naples*

GONZALO, *an honest old Counselor*

ADRIAN,
FRANCISCO, } *Lords*

CALIBAN, *a savage and deformed Slave*

TRINCULO, *a Jester*

STEPHANO, *a drunken Butler*

Master of a Ship

Boatswain

Mariners

MIRANDA, *daughter to* PROSPERO

ARIEL, *an airy Spirit*

IRIS,
CERES,
JUNO, } *presented by Spirits*
Nymphs,
Reapers,

Other Spirits attending on PROSPERO

PROSPERO

CALIBAN

FERDINAND

MIRANDA

ARIEL

The Tempest

ACT I

SCENE I — *On a ship at sea: a tempestuous noise
of thunder and lightning heard.*

Enter a SHIP-MASTER *and a* BOATSWAIN.]

MASTER. Boatswain!

BOATSWAIN. Here, master: what cheer?

MASTER. Good, speak to the mariners: fall to 't, yarely, or we
run ourselves aground: bestir, bestir.   [*Exit.*

Enter MARINERS.]

BOATSWAIN. Heigh, my hearts! cheerly, cheerly, my hearts!
yare, yare! Take in the topsail. Tend to the master's whistle.
Blow, till thou burst thy wind, if room enough!

Enter ALONSO, SEBASTIAN, ANTONIO, FERDINAND,
GONZALO, *and others.*]

ALONSO. Good boatswain, have care. Where 's the master?
Play the men.

BOATSWAIN. I pray now, keep below.

ANTONIO. Where is the master, boatswain?

BOATSWAIN. Do you not hear him? You mar our labor: keep
your cabins: you do assist the storm.

GONZALO. Nay, good, be patient.

BOATSWAIN. When the sea is. Hence! What cares these roarers
for the name of king? To cabin: silence! trouble us not.

GONZALO. Good, yet remember whom thou hast aboard.

BOATSWAIN. None that I more love than myself. You are a
counselor; if you can command these elements to silence,
and work the peace of the present, we will not hand a rope
more; use your authority: if you cannot, give thanks you
have lived so long, and make yourself ready in your cabin

for the mischance of the hour, if it so hap. Cheerly, good
hearts! Out of our way, I say.　　　　　　　　　[*Exit.*

GONZALO. I have great comfort from this fellow: methinks he
hath no drowning mark upon him; his complexion is perfect gallows. Stand fast, good Fate, to his hanging: make the
rope of his destiny our cable, for our own doth little advantage. If he be not born to be hanged, our case is miserable.
　　　　　　　　　　　　　　　　　　　　[*Exeunt.*

Re-enter BOATSWAIN.]

BOATSWAIN. Down with the topmast! yare! lower, lower! Bring
her to try with main-course. [*A cry within.*] A plague upon
this howling! they are louder than the weather or our office.

Re-enter SEBASTIAN, ANTONIO, *and* GONZALO.]
　　Yet again! what do you here? Shall we give o'er, and
drown? Have you a mind to sink?

SEBASTIAN. A pox o' your throat, you bawling, blasphemous,
incharitable dog!

BOATSWAIN. Work you, then.

ANTONIO. Hang, cur! hang, you whoreson, insolent noise-
maker. We are less afraid to be drowned than thou art.

GONZALO. I 'll warrant him for drowning; though the ship were
no stronger than a nutshell, and as leaky as an unstanched
wench.

BOATSWAIN. Lay her a-hold, a-hold! set her two courses; off to
sea again; lay her off.

Enter MARINERS *wet.*]

MARINERS. All lost! to prayers, to prayers! all lost!

BOATSWAIN. What, must our mouths be cold?

GONZALO. The king and prince at prayers! let 's assist them,
　　For our case is as theirs.

SEBASTIAN.　　　　　　　I 'm out of patience.

ANTONIO. We are merely cheated of our lives by drunkards:
　　This wide-chapp'd rascal,—would thou mightst lie drown-
　　　　ing
　　The washing of ten tides!

GONZALO.　　　　　　　He 'll be hang'd yet,
　　Though every drop of water swear against it,
　　And gape at widest to glut him.

[*A confused noise within:* 'Mercy on us!'—
'We split, we split!'—'Farewell, my wife and children!'—
'Farewell, brother!'—'We split, we split, we split!']

ANTONIO. Let 's all sink with the king.

SEBASTIAN. Let 's take leave of him.

                 [*Exeunt* ANTONIO *and* SEBASTIAN.

GONZALO. Now would I give a thousand furlongs of sea for an
acre of barren ground, long heath, brown furze, any thing.
The wills above be done! but I would fain die a dry death.

                         [*Exeunt.*

SCENE II — *The island. Before* PROSPERO'S *cell.*

Enter PROSPERO *and* MIRANDA.]

MIRANDA. If by your art, my dearest father, you have
Put the wild waters in this roar, allay them.
The sky, it seems, would pour down stinking pitch,
But that the sea, mounting to the welkin's cheek,
Dashes the fire out. O, I have suffer'd
With those that I saw suffer! a brave vessel,
Who had, no doubt, some noble creature in her,
Dash'd all to pieces. O, the cry did knock
Against my very heart! Poor souls, they perish'd!
Had I been any god of power, I would
Have sunk the sea within the earth, or ere
It should the good ship so have swallow'd and
The fraughting souls within her.

PROSPERO.   Be collected:
No more amazement: tell your piteous heart
There's no harm done.

MIRANDA.   O, woe the day!

PROSPERO.   No harm.
I have done nothing but in care of thee,
Of thee, my dear one, thee, my daughter, who
Art ignorant of what thou art, nought knowing
Of whence I am, nor that I am more better
Than Prospero, master of a full poor cell
And thy no greater father.

MIRANDA.　　　　　　　　More to know
　Did never meddle with my thoughts.
PROSPERO.　　　　　　　　　　'Tis time
　I should inform thee farther. Lend thy hand,
　And pluck my magic garment from me.—So:
　　　　　　　　　　　　[Lays down his mantle.
　Lie there, my art. Wipe thou thine eyes; have comfort.
　The direful spectacle of the wreck, which touch'd
　The very virtue of compassion in thee,
　I have with such provision in mine art
　So safely ordered, that there is no soul,
　No, not so much perdition as an hair
　Betid to any creature in the vessel
　Which thou heard'st cry, which thou saw'st sink. Sit down;
　For thou must now know farther.
MIRANDA.　　　　　　　　　You have often
　Begun to tell me what I am; but stopp'd,
　And left me to a bootless inquisition,
　Concluding 'Stay: not yet.'
PROSPERO.　　　　　　　The hour 's now come;
　The very minute bids thee ope thine ear;
　Obey, and be attentive. Canst thou remember
　A time before we came unto this cell?
　I do not think thou canst, for then thou wast not
　Out three years old.
MIRANDA.　　　　　　Certainly, sir, I can.
PROSPERO. By what? by any other house or person:
　Of any thing the image tell me, that
　Hath kept with thy remembrance.
MIRANDA.　　　　　　　　'Tis far off,
　And rather like a dream than an assurance
　That my remembrance warrants. Had I not
　Four or five women once that tended me?
PROSPERO. Thou hadst, and more, Miranda. But how is it
　That this lives in thy mind? What seest thou else
　In the dark backward and abysm of time?
　If thou remember'st aught ere thou camest here,
　How thou camest here thou mayst.

MIRANDA. But that I do not.

PROSPERO. Twelve year since, Miranda, twelve year since,
Thy father was the Duke of Milan, and
A prince of power.

MIRANDA. Sir, are not you my father?

PROSPERO. Thy mother was a piece of virtue, and
She said thou wast my daughter; and thy father
Was Duke of Milan; and his only heir
A princess, no worse issued.

MIRANDA. O the heavens!
What foul play had we, that we came from thence?
Or blessed was 't we did?

PROSPERO. Both, both, my girl:
By foul play, as thou say'st, were we heaved thence;
But blessedly holp thither.

MIRANDA. O, my heart bleeds
To think o' the teen that I have turn'd you to,
Which is from my remembrance! Please you, farther.

PROSPERO. My brother, and thy uncle, call'd Antonio,—
I pray thee, mark me,—that a brother should
Be so perfidious!—he whom, next thyself,
Of all the world I loved, and to him put
The manage of my state; as at that time
Through all the signories it was the first,
And Prospero the prime duke, being so reputed
In dignity, and for the liberal arts
Without a parallel; those being all my study,
The government I cast upon my brother,
And to my state grew stranger, being transported
And rapt in secret studies. Thy false uncle—
Dost thou attend me?

MIRANDA. Sir, most heedfully.

PROSPERO. Being once perfected how to grant suits,
How to deny them, who to advance, and who
To trash for over-topping, new created
The creatures that were mine, I say, or changed 'em,
Or else new form'd 'em; having both the key
Of officer and office, set all hearts i' the state

To what tune pleased his ear; that now he was
The ivy which had hid my princely trunk,
And suck'd my verdure out on 't. Thou attend'st not.

MIRANDA. O, good sir, I do.

PROSPERO.   I pray thee, mark me.
I, thus neglecting worldly ends, all dedicated
To closeness and the bettering of my mind
With that which, but my being so retired,
O'er-prized all popular rate, in my false brother
Awaked an evil nature; and my trust,
Like a good parent, did beget of him
A falsehood in its contrary, as great
As my trust was; which had indeed no limit,
A confidence sans bound. He being thus lorded,
Not only with what my revenue yielded,
But what my power might else exact, like one
Who having into truth, by telling of it,
Made such a sinner of his memory,
To credit his own lie, he did believe
He was indeed the duke; out o' the substitution,
And executing the outward face of royalty,
With all prerogative:—hence his ambition growing,—
Dost thou hear?

MIRANDA.   Your tale, sir, would cure deafness.

PROSPERO. To have no screen between this part he play'd
And him he play'd it for, he needs will be
Absolute Milan. Me, poor man, my library
Was dukedom large enough: of temporal royalties
He thinks me now incapable; confederates,
So dry he was for sway, wi' the King of Naples
To give him annual tribute, do him homage,
Subject his coronet to his crown, and bend
The dukedom, yet unbow'd,—alas, poor Milan!—
To most ignoble stooping.

MIRANDA.   O the heavens!

PROSPERO. Mark his condition, and the event; then tell me
If this might be a brother.

MIRANDA.   I should sin
To think but nobly of my grandmother:
Good wombs have borne bad sons.

PROSPERO.   Now the condition.
This King of Naples, being an enemy
To me inveterate, hearkens my brother's suit;
Which was, that he, in lieu o' the premises,
Of homage and I know not how much tribute,
Should presently extirpate me and mine
Out of the dukedom, and confer fair Milan,
With all the honors, on my brother: whereon,
A treacherous army levied, one midnight
Fated to the purpose, did Antonio open
The gates of Milan; and, i' the dead of darkness,
The ministers for the purpose hurried thence
Me and thy crying self.

MIRANDA.   Alack, for pity!
I, not remembering how I cried out then,
Will cry it o'er again: it is a hint
That wrings mine eyes to 't.

PROSPERO.   Hear a little further,
And then I 'll bring thee to the present business
Which now 's upon 's; without the which, this story
Were most impertinent.

MIRANDA.   Wherefore did they not
That hour destroy us?

PROSPERO.   Well demanded, wench:
My tale provokes that question. Dear, they durst not,
So dear the love my people bore me; nor set
A mark so bloody on the business; but
With colors fairer painted their foul ends.
In few, they hurried us aboard a bark,
Bore us some leagues to sea; where they prepared
A rotten carcass of a butt, not rigg'd,
Nor tackle, sail, nor mast; the very rats
Instinctively have quit it: there they hoist us,
To cry to the sea that roar'd to us; to sigh

    To the winds, whose pity, sighing back again,
    Did us but loving wrong.
MIRANDA.   Alack, what trouble
    Was I then to you!
PROSPERO.   O, a cherubin
    Thou wast that did preserve me. Thou didst smile,
    Infused with a fortitude from heaven,
    When I have deck'd the sea with drops full salt,
    Under my burthen groan'd; which raised in me
    An undergoing stomach, to bear up
    Against what should ensue.
MIRANDA.   How came we ashore?
PROSPERO. By Providence divine.
    Some food we had, and some fresh water, that
    A noble Neapolitan, Gonzalo,
    Out of his charity, who being then appointed
    Master of this design, did give us, with
    Rich garments, linens, stuffs and necessaries,
    Which since have steaded much; so, of his gentleness,
    Knowing I loved my books, he furnish'd me
    From mine own library with volumes that
    I prize above my dukedom.
MIRANDA.   Would I might
    But ever see that man!
PROSPERO.   Now I arise: [*Resumes his mantle.*
    Sit still, and hear the last of our sea-sorrow.
    Here in this island we arrived; and here
    Have I, thy schoolmaster, made thee more profit
    Than other princess' can, that have more time
    For vainer hours, and tutors not so careful.
MIRANDA. Heavens thank you for 't! And now, I pray you, sir,
    For still 'tis beating in my mind, your reason
    For raising this sea-storm?
PROSPERO.   Know thus far forth.
    By accident most strange, bountiful Fortune,
    Now my dear lady, hath mine enemies
    Brought to this shore; and by my prescience

I find my zenith doth depend upon
A most auspicious star, whose influence
If now I court not, but omit, my fortunes
Will ever after droop. Here cease more questions:
Thou art inclined to sleep; 'tis a good dullness,
And give it way: I know thou canst not choose.

          [MIRANDA *sleeps*.

Come away, servant, come. I am ready now.
Approach, my Ariel, come.

Enter ARIEL.]

ARIEL. All hail, great master! grave sir, hail! I come
To answer thy best pleasure; be 't to fly,
To swim, to dive into the fire, to ride
On the curl'd clouds, to thy strong bidding task
Ariel and all his quality.

PROSPERO.   Hast thou, spirit,
Perform'd to point the tempest that I bade thee?

ARIEL. To every article.
I boarded the king's ship; now on the beak,
Now in the waist, the deck, in every cabin,
I flamed amazement: sometime I 'ld divide,
And burn in many places; on the topmast,
The yards and bowsprit, would I flame distinctly,
Then meet and join. Jove's lightnings, the precursors
O' the dreadful thunder-claps, more momentary
And sight-outrunning were not: the fire and cracks
Of sulphurous roaring the most mighty Neptune
Seem to besiege, and make his bold waves tremble,
Yea, his dread trident shake.

PROSPERO.   My brave spirit!
Who was so firm, so constant, that this coil
Would not infect his reason?

ARIEL.   Not a soul
But felt a fever of the mad, and play'd
Some tricks of desperation. All but mariners
Plunged in the foaming brine, and quit the vessel,
Then all afire with me: the king's son, Ferdinand,
With hair up-staring,—then like reeds, not hair,—

Was the first man that leap'd; cried, 'Hell is empty,
And all the devils are here.'

PROSPERO. Why, that 's my spirit!
But was not this nigh shore?

ARIEL. Close by, my master.

PROSPERO. But are they, Ariel, safe?

ARIEL. Not a hair perish'd;
On their sustaining garments not a blemish,
But fresher than before: and, as thou badest me,
In troops I have dispersed them 'bout the isle.
The king's son have I landed by himself;
Whom I left cooling of the air with sighs
In an odd angle of the isle, and sitting,
His arms in this sad knot.

PROSPERO. Of the king's ship,
The mariners, say how thou hast disposed,
And all the rest o' the fleet.

ARIEL. Safely in harbor
Is the king's ship; in the deep nook, where once
Thou call'dst me up at midnight to fetch dew
From the still-vex'd Bermoothes, there she 's hid:
The mariners all under hatches stow'd;
Who, with a charm join'd to their suffer'd labor,
I have left asleep: and for the rest o' the fleet,
Which I dispersed, they all have met again,
And are upon the Mediterranean flote,
Bound sadly home for Naples;
Supposing that they saw the king's ship wreck'd,
And his great person perish.

PROSPERO. Ariel, thy charge
Exactly is perform'd: but there 's more work.
What is the time o' the day?

ARIEL. Past the mid season.

PROSPERO. At least two glasses. The time 'twixt six and now
Must by us both be spent most preciously.

ARIEL. Is there more toil? Since thou dost give me pains,
Let me remember thee what thou hast promised,
Which is not yet perform'd me.

PROSPERO.   How now? moody?
  What is 't thou canst demand?
ARIEL.   My liberty.
PROSPERO. Before the time be out? no more!
ARIEL.   I prithee,
  Remember I have done thee worthy service;
  Told thee no lies, made thee no mistakings, served
  Without or grudge or grumblings: thou didst promise
  To bate me a full year.
PROSPERO.   Dost thou forget
  From what a torment I did free thee?
ARIEL.   No.
PROSPERO. Thou dost, and think'st it much to tread the ooze
  Of the salt deep,
  To run upon the sharp wind of the north,
  To do me business in the veins o' the earth.
  When it is baked with frost.
ARIEL.   I do not, sir.
PROSPERO. Thou liest, malignant thing! hast thou forgot
  The foul witch Sycorax, who with age and envy
  Was grown into a hoop? hast thou forgot her?
ARIEL. No, sir.
PROSPERO.   Thou hast. Where was she born? speak; tell me.
ARIEL. Sir, in Argier.
PROSPERO.   O, was she so? I must
  Once in a month recount what thou hast been,
  Which thou forget'st. This damn'd witch Sycorax,
  For mischiefs manifold, and sorceries terrible
  To enter human hearing, from Argier,
  Thou know'st, was banish'd: for one thing she did
  They would not take her life. Is not this true?
ARIEL. Aye, sir.
PROSPERO. This blue-eyed hag was hither brought with child,
  And here was left by the sailors. Thou, my slave,
  As thou report'st thyself, wast then her servant;
  And, for thou wast a spirit too delicate
  To act her earthy and abhorr'd commands,
  Refusing her grand hests, she did confine thee,

By help of her more potent ministers,
And in her most unmitigable rage,
Into a cloven pine; within which rift
Imprison'd thou didst painfully remain
A dozen years; within which space she died,
And left thee there; where thou didst vent thy groans
As fast as mill-wheels strike. Then was this island—
Save for the son that she did litter here,
A freckled whelp hag-born—not honor'd with
A human shape.

ARIEL. 　　　　　Yes, Caliban her son.

PROSPERO. Dull thing, I say so; he, that Caliban,
Whom now I keep in service. Thou best know'st
What torment I did find thee in; thy groans
Did make wolves howl, and penetrate the breasts
Of ever-angry bears: it was a torment
To lay upon the damn'd, which Sycorax
Could not again undo: it was mine art,
When I arrived and heard thee, that made gape
The pine, and let thee out.

ARIEL. 　　　　　　I thank thee, master.

PROSPERO. If thou more murmur'st, I will rend an oak,
And peg thee in his knotty entrails, till
Thou hast howl'd away twelve winters.

ARIEL. 　　　　　　　　Pardon, master:
I will be correspondent to command,
And do my spiriting gently.

PROSPERO. 　　　　　Do so; and after two days
I will discharge thee.

ARIEL. 　　　　That 's my noble master!
What shall I do? say what; what shall I do?

PROSPERO. Go make thyself like a nymph o' the sea: be subject
To no sight but thine and mine; invisible
To every eyeball else. Go take this shape,
And hither come in 't; go hence with diligence!

　　　　　　　　　　　　　　　　　[*Exit* ARIEL.

Awake, dear heart, awake! thou hast slept well;
Awake!

MIRANDA. The strangeness of your story put
    Heaviness in me.

PROSPERO.   Shake it off. Come on;
    We 'll visit Caliban my slave, who never
    Yields us kind answer.

MIRANDA.   'Tis a villain, sir,
    I do not love to look on.

PROSPERO.   But, as 'tis,
    We cannot miss him: he does make our fire,
    Fetch in our wood, and serves in offices
    That profit us. What, ho! slave! Caliban!
    Thou earth, thou! speak.

CALIBAN.   [*Within*] There 's wood enough within.

PROSPERO. Come forth, I say! there 's other business for thee:
    Come, thou tortoise! when?

Re-enter ARIEL *like a water-nymph.*]
    Fine apparition! My quaint Ariel,
    Hark in thine ear.

ARIEL.   My lord, it shall be done.   [*Exit.*

PROSPERO. Thou poisonous slave, got by the devil himself
    Upon thy wicked dam, come forth!

Enter CALIBAN.]

CALIBAN. As wicked dew as e'er my mother brush'd
    With raven's feather from unwholesome fen
    Drop on you both! a south-west blow on ye
    And blister you all o'er!

PROSPERO. For this, be sure, to-night thou shalt have cramps,
    Side-stitches that shall pen thy breath up; urchins
    Shall, for that vast of night that they may work,
    All exercise on thee; thou shalt be pinch'd
    As thick as honeycomb, each pinch more stinging
    Than bees that made 'em.

CALIBAN.   I must eat my dinner.
    This island 's mine, by Sycorax my mother,
    Which thou takest from me. When thou camest first,
    Thou strokedst me, and madest much of me; wouldst give
       me
    Water with berries in 't; and teach me how

To name the bigger light, and how the less,
That burn by day and night: and then I loved thee,
And show'd thee all the qualities o' th' isle,
The fresh springs, brine-pits, barren place and fertile:
Cursed be I that I did so! All the charms
Of Sycorax, toads, beetles, bats, light on you!
For I am all the subjects that you have,
Which first was mine own king: and here you sty me
In this hard rock, whiles you do keep from me
The rest o' th' island.

PROSPERO.   Thou most lying slave,
Whom stripes may move, not kindness! I have used thee,
Filth as thou art, with human care; and lodged thee
In mine own cell, till thou didst seek to violate
The honor of my child.

CALIBAN. O ho, O ho! would 't had been done!
Thou didst prevent me; I had peopled else
This isle with Calibans.

PROSPERO.   Abhorred slave,
Which any print of goodness wilt not take,
Being capable of all ill! I pitied thee,
Took pains to make thee speak, taught thee each hour
One thing or other: when thou didst not, savage,
Know thine own meaning, but wouldst gabble like
A thing most brutish, I endow'd thy purposes
With words that made them known. But thy vile race,
Though thou didst learn, had that in 't which good natures
Could not abide to be with; therefore wast thou
Deservedly confined into this rock,
Who hadst deserved more than a prison.

CALIBAN. You taught me language; and my profit on 't
Is, I know how to curse. The red plague rid you
For learning me your language!

PROSPERO.   Hag-seed, hence!
Fetch us in fuel; and be quick, thou 'rt best,
To answer other business. Shrug'st thou, malice?
If thou neglect'st, or dost unwillingly
What I command, I 'll rack thee with old cramps,

Fill all thy bones with aches, make thee roar,
That beasts shall tremble at thy din.

CALIBAN. No, pray thee.

[*Aside*] I must obey: his art is of such power,
It would control my dam's god, Setebos,
And make a vassal of him.

PROSPERO. So, slave; hence! [*Exit* CALIBAN.

Re-enter ARIEL, *invisible, playing and singing;*
FERDINAND *following.*]

ARIEL'S *song.*

Come unto these yellow sands,
    And then take hands:
Courtsied when you have and kiss'd
    The wild waves whist:
Foot it featly here and there;
And, sweet sprites, the burthen bear.
        Hark, hark!
    BURTHEN [*dispersedly*]. Bow-wow.
ARIEL. The watch dogs bark:
    BURTHEN [*dispersedly*]. Bow-wow.
ARIEL. Hark, hark! I hear
    The strain of strutting chanticleer
    Cry, Cock-a-diddle-dow.

FERDINAND. Where should this music be? i' th' air or th' earth?
It sounds no more: and, sure, it waits upon
Some god o' th' island. Sitting on a bank,
Weeping again the king my father's wreck,
This music crept by me upon the waters,
Allaying both their fury and my passion
With its sweet air: thence I have follow'd it,
Or it hath drawn me rather. But 'tis gone.
No, it begins again.

ARIEL *sings.*

Full fathom five thy father lies;
    Of his bones are coral made;

> Those are pearls that were his eyes:
>> Nothing of him that doth fade,
> But doth suffer a sea-change
> Into something rich and strange.
> Sea-nymphs hourly ring his knell:
>> BURTHEN: Ding-dong

ARIEL. Hark! now I hear them,—Ding-dong, bell.

FERDINAND. The ditty does remember my drown'd father.
This is no mortal business, nor no sound
That the earth owes:—I hear it now above me.

PROSPERO. The fringed curtains of thine eye advance,
And say what thou seest yond.

MIRANDA.   What is 't? a spirit?
Lord, how it looks about! Believe me, sir,
It carries a brave form. But 'tis a spirit.

PROSPERO. No, wench; it eats and sleeps and hath such senses
As we have, such. This gallant which thou seest
Was in the wreck; and, but he 's something stain'd
With grief, that 's beauty's canker, thou mightst call him
A goodly person: he hath lost his fellows,
And strays about to find 'em.

MIRANDA.   I might call him
A thing divine; for nothing natural
I ever saw so noble.

PROSPERO.   [*Aside*] It goes on, I see,
As my soul prompts it. Spirit, fine spirit! I 'll free thee
Within two days for this.

FERDINAND.   Most sure, the goddess
On whom these airs attend! Vouchsafe my prayer
May know if you remain upon this island;
And that you will some good instruction give
How I may bear me here: my prime request,
Which I do last pronounce, is, O you wonder!
If you be maid or no?

MIRANDA.   No wonder, sir;
But certainly a maid.

FERDINAND. My language! heavens!
I am the best of them that speak this speech,
Were I but where 'tis spoken.

PROSPERO. How? the best?
What wert thou, if the King of Naples heard thee?

FERDINAND. A single thing, as I am now, that wonders
To hear thee speak of Naples. He does hear me;
And that he does I weep: myself am Naples,
Who with mine eyes, never since at ebb, beheld
The king my father wreck'd.

MIRANDA. Alack, for mercy!

FERDINAND. Yes, faith, and all his lords; the Duke of Milan
And his brave son being twain.

PROSPERO. [*Aside*] The Duke of Milan
And his more braver daughter could control thee,
If now 'twere fit to do 't. At the first sight
They have changed eyes. Delicate Ariel,
I 'll set thee free for this. [*To* FERDINAND.] A word, good sir;
I fear you have done yourself some wrong: a word.

MIRANDA. Why speaks my father so ungently? This
Is the third man that e'er I saw; the first
That e'er I sigh'd for: pity move my father
To be inclined my way!

FERDINAND. O, if a virgin,
And your affection not gone forth, I 'll make you
The queen of Naples.

PROSPERO. Soft, sir! one word more.
[*Aside*] They are both in either's powers: but this swift
business
I must uneasy make, lest too light winning
Make the prize light. [*To* FERDINAND.] One word more; I
charge thee
That thou attend me: thou dost here usurp
The name thou owest not; and hast put thyself
Upon this island as a spy, to win it
From me, the lord on 't.

FERDINAND. No, as I am a man.

MIRANDA. There 's nothing ill can dwell in such a temple:
   If the ill spirit have so fair a house,
   Good things will strive to dwell with 't.

PROSPERO.   Follow me.
   Speak not you for him; he 's a traitor. Come;
   I 'll manacle thy neck and feet together:
   Sea-water shalt thou drink; thy food shall be
   The fresh-brook muscles, wither'd roots, and husks
   Wherein the acorn cradled. Follow.

FERDINAND.   No;
   I will resist such entertainment till
   Mine enemy has more power.

             [*Draws, and is charmed from moving.*

MIRANDA.   O dear father,
   Make not too rash a trial of him, for
   He 's gentle, and not fearful.

PROSPERO.   What! I say,
   My foot my tutor? Put thy sword up, traitor;
   Who makest a show, but darest not strike, thy conscience
   Is so possess'd with guilt: come from thy ward;
   For I can here disarm thee with this stick
   And make thy weapon drop.

MIRANDA.   Beseech you, father.

PROSPERO. Hence! hang not on my garments.

MIRANDA.   Sir, have pity;
   I 'll be his surety.

PROSPERO.   Silence! one word more
   Shall make me chide thee, if not hate thee. What!
   An advocate for an impostor! hush!
   Thou think'st there is no more such shapes as he,
   Having seen but him and Caliban: foolish wench!
   To the most of men this is a Caliban,
   And they to him are angels.

MIRANDA.   My affections
   Are, then, most humble; I have no ambition
   To see a goodlier man.

PROSPERO.   Come on; obey:

Thy nerves are in their infancy again,
And have no vigor in them.

FERDINAND.   So they are:
My spirits, as in a dream, are all bound up.
My father's loss, the weakness which I feel,
The wreck of all my friends, nor this man's threats,
To whom I am subdued, are but light to me,
Might I but through my prison once a day
Behold this maid: all corners else o' th' earth
Let liberty make use of; space enough
Have I in such a prison.

PROSPERO.   [Aside] It works. [To FERDINAND.] Come
on.
Thou hast done well, fine Ariel! [To FERDINAND.] Follow
me.
[To ARIEL] Hark what thou else shalt do me.

MIRANDA.   Be of comfort;
My father 's of a better nature, sir,
Than he appears by speech: this is unwonted
Which now came from him.

PROSPERO.   Thou shalt be as free
As mountain winds: but then exactly do
All points of my command.

ARIEL.   To the syllable.

PROSPERO. Come, follow. Speak not for him.   [Exeunt.

ACT II

SCENE I — *Another part of the island.*

Enter ALONSO, SEBASTIAN, ANTONIO, GONZALO,
     ADRIAN, FRANCISCO, *and others.*]

GONZALO. Beseech you, sir, be merry; you have cause,
     So have we all, of joy; for our escape
     Is much beyond our loss. Our hint of woe
     Is common; every day, some sailor's wife,
     The masters of some merchant, and the merchant,
     Have just our theme of woe; but for the miracle,
     I mean our preservation, few in millions
     Can speak like us: then wisely, good sir, weigh
     Our sorrow with our comfort.

ALONSO.   Prithee, peace.

SEBASTIAN. He receives comfort like cold porridge.

ANTONIO. The visitor will not give him o'er so.

SEBASTIAN. Look, he 's winding up the watch of his wit; by
     and by it will strike.

GONZALO. Sir,—

SEBASTIAN. One: tell.

GONZALO. When every grief is entertain'd that 's offer'd,
     Comes to the entertainer—

SEBASTIAN. A dollar.

GONZALO. Dolor comes to him, indeed: you have spoken truer
     than you purposed.

SEBASTIAN. You have taken it wiselier than I meant you
     should.

GONZALO. Therefore, my lord,—

ANTONIO. Fie, what a spendthrift is he of his tongue!

ALONSO. I prithee, spare.

GONZALO. Well, I have done: but yet,—

SEBASTIAN. He will be talking.

ANTONIO. Which, of he or Adrian, for a good wager, first be-
     gins to crow?

SEBASTIAN. The old cock.

ANTONIO. The cockerel.

SEBASTIAN. Done. The wager?

ANTONIO. A laughter.

SEBASTIAN. A match!

ADRIAN. Though this island seem to be desert,—

SEBASTIAN. Ha, ha, ha!—So, you 're paid.

ADRIAN. Uninhabitable, and almost inaccessible,—

SEBASTIAN. Yet,—

ADRIAN. Yet, —

ANTONIO. He could not miss 't.

ADRIAN. It must needs be of subtle, tender and delicate temperance.

ANTONIO. Temperance was a delicate wench.

SEBASTIAN. Aye, and a subtle; as he most learnedly delivered.

ADRIAN. The air breathes upon us here most sweetly.

SEBASTIAN. As if it had lungs, and rotten ones.

ANTONIO. Or as 'twere perfumed by a fen.

GONZALO. Here is everything advantageous to life.

ANTONIO. True; save means to live.

SEBASTIAN. Of that there 's none, or little.

GONZALO. How lush and lusty the grass looks! how green!

ANTONIO. The ground, indeed, is tawny.

SEBASTIAN. With an eye of green in 't.

ANTONIO. He misses not much.

SEBASTIAN. No; he doth but mistake the truth totally.

GONZALO. But the rarity of it is,—which is indeed almost beyond credit,—

SEBASTIAN. As many vouched rarities are.

GONZALO. That our garments, being, as they were, drenched in the sea, hold, notwithstanding, their freshness and glosses, being rather new-dyed than stained with salt water.

ANTONIO. If but one of his pockets could speak, would it not say he lies?

SEBASTIAN. Aye, or very falsely pocket up his report.

GONZALO. Methinks our garments are now as fresh as when we put them on first in Afric, at the marriage of the king's fair daughter Claribel to the King of Tunis.

SEBASTIAN. 'Twas a sweet marriage, and we prosper well in our return.

ADRIAN. Tunis was never graced before with such a paragon to their queen.

GONZALO. Not since widow Dido's time.

ANTONIO. Widow! a pox o' that! How came that widow in? widow Dido!

SEBASTIAN. What if he had said 'widower Æneas' too? Good Lord, how you take it!

ADRIAN. 'Widow Dido' said you? you make me study of that: she was of Carthage, not of Tunis.

GONZALO. This Tunis, sir, was Carthage.

ADRIAN. Carthage?

GONZALO. I assure you, Carthage.

ANTONIO. His word is more than the miraculous harp.

SEBASTIAN. He hath raised the wall, and houses too.

ANTONIO. What impossible matter will he make easy next?

SEBASTIAN. I think he will carry this island home in his pocket, and give it his son for an apple.

ANTONIO. And, sowing the kernels of it in the sea, bring forth more islands.

GONZALO. Aye.

ANTONIO. Why, in good time.

GONZALO. Sir, we were talking that our garments seem now as fresh as when we were at Tunis at the marriage of your daughter, who is now queen.

ANTONIO. And the rarest that e'er came there.

SEBASTIAN. Bate, I beseech you, widow Dido.

ANTONIO. O, widow Dido! aye, widow Dido.

GONZALO. Is not, sir, my doublet as fresh as the first day I wore it? I mean, in a sort.

ANTONIO. That sort was well fished for.

GONZALO. When I wore it at your daughter's marriage?

ALONSO. You cram these words into mine ears against
The stomach of my sense. Would I had never
Married my daughter there! for, coming thence,
My son is lost, and, in my rate, she too,
Who is so far from Italy removed

I ne'er again shall see her. O thou mine heir
Of Naples and of Milan, what strange fish
Hath made his meal on thee?

FRANCISCO.   Sir, he may live:
I saw him beat the surges under him,
And ride upon their backs; he trod the water,
Whose enmity he flung aside, and breasted
The surge most swoln that met him; his bold head
'Bove the contentious waves he kept, and oar'd
Himself with his good arms in lusty stroke
To the shore, that o'er his wave-worn basis bow'd,
As stooping to relieve him: I not doubt
He came alive to land:

ALONSO.   No, no, he 's gone.

SEBASTIAN. Sir, you may thank yourself for this great loss,
That would not bless our Europe with your daughter,
But rather lose her to an African;
Where she, at least, is banish'd from your eye,
Who hath cause to wet the grief on 't.

ALONSO.   Prithee, peace.

SEBASTIAN. You were kneel'd to, and importuned otherwise,
By all of us; and the fair soul herself
Weigh'd between loathness and obedience, at
Which end o' the beam should bow. We have lost your son,
I fear, for ever: Milan and Naples have
Moe widows in them of this business' making
Than we bring men to comfort them:
The fault 's your own.

ALONSO.   So is the dear'st o' the loss.

GONZALO. My lord Sebastian,
The truth you speak doth lack some gentleness,
And time to speak it in: you rub the sore,
When you should bring the plaster.

SEBASTIAN. .   Very well.

ANTONIO. And most chirurgeonly.

GONZALO. It is foul weather in us all, good sir,
When you are cloudy.

SEBASTIAN.   Foul weather?

ANTONIO.   Very foul.

GONZALO. Had I plantation of this isle, my lord,—

ANTONIO. He 'ld sow 't with nettle-seed.

SEBASTIAN.   Or docks, or mallows.

GONZALO. And were the king on 't, what would I do?

SEBASTIAN. 'Scape being drunk for want of wine.

GONZALO. I' the commonwealth I would by contraries
　　Execute all things; for no kind of traffic
　　Would I admit; no name of magistrate;
　　Letters should not be known; riches, poverty,
　　And use of service, none; contract, succession,
　　Bourn, bound of land, tilth, vineyard, none;
　　No use of metal, corn, or wine, or oil;
　　No occupation; all men idle, all;
　　And women too, but innocent and pure;
　　No sovereignty;—

SEBASTIAN.   Yet he would be king on 't.

ANTONIO. The latter end of his commonwealth forgets the be-
　　ginning.

GONZALO. All things in common nature should produce
　　Without sweat or endeavor: treason, felony,
　　Sword, pike, knife, gun, or need of any engine,
　　Would I not have; but nature should bring forth,
　　Of it own kind, all foison, all abundance,
　　To feed my innocent people.

SEBASTIAN. No marrying 'mong his subjects?

ANTONIO. None, man; all idle; whores and knaves.

GONZALO. I would with such perfection govern, sir,
　　To excel the golden age.

SEBASTIAN.   'Save his majesty!

ANTONIO. Long live Gonzalo!

GONZALO.   And,—do you mark me, sir?

ALONSO. Prithee, no more: thou dost talk nothing to me.

GONZALO. I do well believe your highness; and did it to minis-
　　ter occasion to these gentlemen, who are of such sensible
　　and nimble lungs that they always use to laugh at nothing.

ANTONIO. 'Twas you we laughed at.

GONZALO. Who in this kind of merry fooling am nothing to
you: so you may continue, and laugh at nothing still.

ANTONIO. What a blow was there given!

SEBASTIAN. An it had not fallen flat-long.

GONZALO. You are gentlemen of brave mettle; you would lift
the moon out of her sphere, if she would continue in it five
weeks without changing.

Enter ARIEL *(invisible) playing solemn music.*]

SEBASTIAN. We would so, and then go a bat-fowling.

ANTONIO. Nay, good my lord, be not angry.

GONZALO. No, I warrant you; I will not adventure my discretion so weakly. Will you laugh me asleep, for I am very
heavy?

ANTONIO. Go sleep, and hear us.

[*All sleep except* ALONSO, SEBASTIAN, *and* ANTONIO.

ALONSO. What, all so soon asleep! I wish mine eyes
Would, with themselves, shut up my thoughts: I find
They are inclined to do so.

SEBASTIAN.   Please you, sir,
Do not omit the heavy offer of it:
It seldom visits sorrow; when it doth,
It is a comforter.

ANTONIO.   We two, my lord,
Will guard your person while you take your rest,
And watch your safety.

ALONSO.   Thank you.—Wondrous heavy.

[ALONSO *sleeps. Exit* ARIEL.

SEBASTIAN. What a strange drowsiness possesses them!

ANTONIO. It is the quality o' the climate.

SEBASTIAN.   Why
Doth it not then our eyelids sink? I find not
Myself disposed to sleep.

ANTONIO.   Nor I; my spirits are nimble.
They fell together all, as by consent;
They dropp'd, as by a thunder-stroke. What might,
Worthy Sebastian?—O, what might?—No more:—
And yet methinks I see it in thy face,

What thou shouldst be: the occasion speaks thee; and
My strong imagination sees a crown
Dropping upon thy head.

SEBASTIAN.　　　　　　　　　What, art thou waking?

ANTONIO. Do you not hear me speak?

SEBASTIAN.　　　　　　　　　I do; and surely
It is a sleepy language, and thou speak'st
Out of thy sleep. What is it thou didst say?
This is a strange repose, to be asleep
With eyes wide open; standing, speaking, moving,
And yet so fast asleep.

ANTONIO.　　　　　　　Noble Sebastian,
Thou let'st thy fortune sleep—die, rather; wink'st
Whiles thou art waking.

SEBASTIAN.　　　　　　　Thou dost snore distinctly;
There 's meaning in thy snores.

ANTONIO. I am more serious than my custom: you
Must be so too, if heed me; which to do
Trebles thee o'er.

SEBASTIAN.　　　　　Well, I am standing water.

ANTONIO. I 'll teach you how to flow.

SEBASTIAN.　　　　　　　　　Do so: to ebb
Hereditary sloth instructs me.

ANTONIO.　　　　　　　　　O,
If you but knew how you the purpose cherish
Whiles thus you mock it! how, in stripping it,
You more invest it! Ebbing men, indeed,
Most often do so near the bottom run
By their own fear or sloth.

SEBASTIAN.　　　　　　　Prithee, say on:
The setting of thine eye and cheek proclaim
A matter from thee; and a birth, indeed,
Which throes thee much to yield.

ANTONIO.　　　　　　　　Thus, sir:
Although this lord of weak remembrance, this,
Who shall be of as little memory
When he is earth'd, hath here almost persuaded,—

For he 's a spirit of persuasion, only
Professes to persuade,—the king his son 's alive,
'Tis as impossible that he 's undrown'd
As he that sleeps here swims.

SEBASTIAN.   I have no hope
That he 's undrown'd.

ANTONIO.   O, out of that 'no hope'
What great hope have you! no hope that way is
Another way so high a hope that even
Ambition cannot pierce a wink beyond,
But doubt discovery there. Will you grant with me
That Ferdinand is drown'd?

SEBASTIAN.   He 's gone.

ANTONIO.   Then, tell me.
Who 's the next heir of Naples?

SEBASTIAN.   Claribel.

ANTONIO. She that is queen of Tunis; she that dwells
Ten leagues beyond man's life; she that from Naples
Can have no note, unless the sun were post,—
The man i' the moon 's too slow,—till new-born chins
Be rough and razorable; she that from whom
We all were sea-swallow'd, though some cast again,
And by that destiny, to perform an act
Whereof what 's past is prologue; what to come,
Is yours and my discharge.

SEBASTIAN.   What stuff is this! how say you?
'Tis true, my brother's daughter 's queen of Tunis;
So is she heir of Naples; 'twixt which regions
There is some space.

ANTONIO.   A space whose every cubit
Seems to cry out, 'How shall that Claribel
Measure us back to Naples? Keep in Tunis,
And let Sebastian wake.' Say, this were death
That now hath seized them; why, they were no worse
Than now they are. There be that can rule Naples
As well as he that sleeps; lords that can prate
As amply and unnecessarily
As this Gonzalo; I myself could make

A chough of as deep chat. O, that you bore
The mind that I do! what a sleep were this
For your advancement! Do you understand me?

SEBASTIAN. Methinks I do.

ANTONIO.   And how does your content
Tender your own good fortune?

SEBASTIAN.   I remember
You did supplant your brother Prospero.

ANTONIO.   True:
And look how well my garments sit upon me;
Much feater than before: my brother's servants
Were then my fellows: now they are my men.

SEBASTIAN. But, for your conscience.

ANTONIO. Aye, sir; where lies that? if 'twere a kibe,
'Twould put me to my slipper: but I feel not
This deity in my bosom: twenty consciences,
That stand 'twixt me and Milan, candied be they,
And melt, ere they molest! Here lies your brother,
No better than the earth he lies upon,
If he were that which now he's like, that's dead;
Whom I, with this obedient steel, three inches of it,
Can lay to bed for ever; whiles you, doing thus,
To the perpetual wink for aye might put
This ancient morsel, this Sir Prudence, who
Should not upbraid our course. For all the rest,
They'll take suggestion as a cat laps milk;
They'll tell the clock to any business that
We say befits the hour.

SEBASTIAN.   Thy case, dear friend,
Shall be my precedent; as thou got'st Milan,
I'll come by Naples. Draw thy sword: one stroke
Shall free thee from the tribute which thou payest;
And I the king shall love thee.

ANTONIO.   Draw together;
And when I rear my hand, do you the like,
To fall in on Gonzalo.

SEBASTIAN.   O, but one word.   [*They talk apart.*
Re-enter ARIEL *invisible.*]

ARIEL. My master through his art foresees the danger
  That you, his friend, are in; and sends me forth,—
  For else his project dies,—to keep them living.

  [Sings in GONZALO'S *ear.*

  While you here do snoring lie,
  Open-eyed conspiracy
    His time doth take.
  If of life you keep a care,
  Shake off slumber, and beware:
    Awake, awake!

ANTONIO. Then let us both be sudden.

GONZALO.   Now, good angels
  Preserve the king!   *[They wake.*

ALONSO. Why, how now? ho, awake!—Why are you drawn?
  Wherefore this ghastly looking?

GONZALO.   What 's the matter?

SEBASTIAN. Whiles we stood here securing your repose,
  Even now, we heard a hollow burst of bellowing
  Like bulls, or rather lions: did 't not wake you?
  It struck mine ear most terribly.

ALONSO.   I heard nothing.

ANTONIO. O, 'twas a din to fright a monster's ear,
  To make an earthquake! sure, it was the roar
  Of a whole herd of lions.

ALONSO.   Heard you this, Gonzalo?

GONZALO. Upon mine honor, sir, I heard a humming,
  And that a strange one too, which did awake me:
  I shaked you, sir, and cried: as mine eyes open'd,
  I saw their weapons drawn:—there was a noise,
  That 's verily. 'Tis best we stand upon our guard,
  Or that we quit this place: let 's draw our weapons.

ALONSO. Lead off this ground; and let 's make further search
  For my poor son.

GONZALO.   Heavens keep him from these beasts!
  For he is, sure, i' th' island.

ALONSO.   Lead away.

ARIEL. Prospero my lord shall know what I have done
  So, king, go safely on to seek thy son.   *[Exeunt.*

SCENE II — *Another part of the island.*

Enter CALIBAN *with a burden of wood. A noise of thunder heard.*]

CALIBAN. All the infections that the sun sucks up
From bogs, fens, flats, on Prosper fall, and make him
By inch-meal a disease! his spirits hear me,
And yet I needs must curse. But they 'll nor pinch,
Fright me with urchin-shows, pitch me i' the mire,
Nor lead me, like a firebrand, in the dark
Out of my way, unless he bid 'em: but
For every trifle are they set upon me;
Sometime like apes, that mow and chatter at me,
And after bite me; then like hedgehogs, which
Lie tumbling in my barefoot way, and mount
Their pricks at my footfall; sometime am I
All wound with adders, who with cloven tongues
Do hiss me into madness.

Enter TRINCULO.]

Lo, now, lo!
Here comes a spirit of his, and to torment me
For bringing wood in slowly. I 'll fall flat;
Perchance he will not mind me.

TRINCULO. Here 's neither bush nor shrub, to bear off any
weather at all, and another storm brewing; I hear it sing
i' the wind: yond same black cloud, yond huge one, looks
like a foul bombard that would shed his liquor. If it should
thunder as it did before, I know not where to hide my head:
yond same cloud cannot choose but fall by pailfuls. What
have we here? a man or a fish? dead or alive? A fish: he
smells like a fish; a very ancient and fish-like smell; a kind
of not of the newest Poor-John. A strange fish! Were I in
England now, as once I was, and had but this fish painted,
not a holiday fool there but would give a piece of silver:
there would this monster make a man; any strange beast
there makes a man: when they will not give a doit to relieve
a lame beggar, they will lay out ten to see a dead Indian.

Legged like a man! and his fins like arms! Warm o' my
troth! I do now let loose my opinion; hold it no longer: this
is no fish, but an islander, that hath lately suffered by a
thunderbolt. [*Thunder.*] Alas, the storm is come again! my
best way is to creep under his gaberdine; there is no other
shelter hereabout: misery acquaints a man with strange
bed-fellows. I will here shroud till the dregs of the storm be
past.

Enter STEPHANO, *singing; a bottle in his hand.*]

STEPHANO.   I shall no more to sea, to sea,
                        Here shall I die a-shore,—

This is a very scurvy tune to sing at a man's funeral: well,
here's my comfort.   [*Drinks.*

[*Sings.*]
The master, the swabber, the boatswain, and I,
        The gunner, and his mate,
Loved Moll, Meg, and Marian, and Margery,
        But none of us cared for Kate;
        For she had a tongue with a tang,
        Would cry to a sailor, Go hang!
She loved not the savor of tar nor of pitch;
Yet a tailor might scratch her where'er she did itch.
        Then, to sea, boys, and let her go hang!

This is a scurvy tune too: but here's my comfort.   [*Drinks.*

CALIBAN. Do not torment me:—O!

STEPHANO. What's the matter? Have we devils here? Do you
put tricks upon 's with savages and men of Ind, ha? I have
not escaped drowning, to be afeard now of your four legs;
for it hath been said, As proper a man as ever went on four
legs cannot make him give ground; and it shall be said so
again, while Stephano breathes at nostrils.

CALIBAN. The spirit torments me:—O!

STEPHANO. This is some monster of the isle with four legs, who
hath got, as I take it, an ague. Where the devil should he
learn our language? I will give him some relief, if it be but
for that. If I can recover him, and keep him tame, and get
to Naples with him, he's a present for any emperor that
ever trod on neat's-leather.

CALIBAN. Do not torment me, prithee; I 'll bring my wood home faster.

STEPHANO. He 's in his fit now, and does not talk after the wisest. He shall taste of my bottle: if he have never drunk wine afore, it will go near to remove his fit. If I can recover him, and keep him tame, I will not take too much for him; he shall pay for him that hath him, and that soundly.

CALIBAN. Thou dost me yet but little hurt; thou wilt anon, I know it by thy trembling: now Prosper works upon thee.

STEPHANO. Come on your ways; open your mouth; here is that which will give language to you, cat: open your mouth; this will shake your shaking, I can tell you, and that soundly: you cannot tell who 's your friend: open your chaps again.

TRINCULO. I should know that voice: it should be—but he is drowned; and these are devils:—O defend me!

STEPHANO. Four legs and two voices,—a most delicate monster! His forward voice, now, is to speak well of his friend; his backward voice is to utter foul speeches and to detract. If all the wine in my bottle will recover him, I will help his ague. Come:—Amen! I will pour some in thy other mouth.

TRINCULO. Stephano!

STEPHANO. Doth thy other mouth call me? Mercy, mercy! This is a devil, and no monster: I will leave him; I have no long spoon.

TRINCULO. Stephano! If thou beest Stephano, touch me, and speak to me; for I am Trinculo,—be not afeard,—thy good friend Trinculo.

STEPHANO. If thou beest Trinculo, come forth: I 'll pull thee by the lesser legs: if any be Trinculo's legs, these are they. Thou art very Trinculo indeed! How camest thou to be the siege of this moon-calf? can he vent Trinculos?

TRINCULO. I took him to be killed with a thunderstroke. But art thou not drowned, Stephano? I hope, now, thou art not drowned. Is the storm over-blown? I hid me under the dead moon-calf's gaberdine for fear of the storm. And art thou living, Stephano? O Stephano, two Neapolitans 'scaped!

STEPHANO. Prithee, do not turn me about; my stomach is not constant.

CALIBAN. [*Aside*] These be fine things, an if they be not sprites.
That 's a brave god, and bears celestial liquor:
I will kneel to him.

STEPHANO. How didst thou 'scape? How camest thou hither? swear, by this bottle, how thou camest hither. I escaped upon a butt of sack, which the sailors heaved o'erboard, by this bottle! which I made of the bark of a tree with mine own hands, since I was cast ashore.

CALIBAN. I 'll swear, upon that bottle, to be thy true subject; for the liquor is not earthly.

STEPHANO. Here; swear, then, how thou escapedst.

TRINCULO. Swum ashore, man, like a duck: I can swim like a duck, I 'll be sworn.

STEPHANO. Here, kiss the book. Though thou canst swim like a duck, thou art made like a goose.

TRINCULO. O Stephano, hast any more of this?

STEPHANO. The whole butt, man: my cellar is in a rock by the sea-side, where my wine is hid. How now, moon-calf! how does thine ague?

CALIBAN. Hast thou not dropp'd from heaven?

STEPHANO. Out o' the moon, I do assure thee: I was the man i' the moon when time was.

CALIBAN. I have seen thee in her, and I do adore thee: my mistress show'd me thee, and thy dog, and thy bush.

STEPHANO. Come, swear to that; kiss the book: I will furnish it anon with new contents: swear.

TRINCULO. By this good light, this is a very shallow monster! I afeard of him! A very weak monster! The man i' the moon! A most poor credulous monster! Well drawn, monster, in good sooth!

CALIBAN. I 'll show thee every fertile inch o' th' island; and I will kiss thy foot: I prithee, be my god.

TRINCULO. By this light, a most perfidious and drunken monster! when 's god 's asleep, he 'll rob his bottle.

CALIBAN. I 'll kiss thy foot; I 'll swear myself thy subject.

STEPHANO. Come on, then; down, and swear.

TRINCULO. I shall laugh myself to death at this puppy-headed
   monster. A most scurvy monster! I could find in my heart
   to beat him,—

STEPHANO. Come, kiss.

TRINCULO. But that the poor monster's in drink.
   An abominable monster!

CALIBAN. I 'll show thee the best springs; I 'll pluck thee
   berries;
   I 'll fish for thee, and get thee wood enough.
   A plague upon the tyrant that I serve!
   I 'll bear him no more sticks, but follow thee,
   Thou wondrous man.

TRINCULO. A most ridiculous monster, to make a wonder of
   a poor drunkard!

CALIBAN. I prithee, let me bring thee where crabs grow;
   And I with my long nails will dig thee pignuts;
   Show thee a jay's nest, and instruct thee how
   To snare the nimble marmoset; I 'll bring thee
   To clustering filberts, and sometimes I 'll get thee
   Young scamels from the rock. Wilt thou go with me?

STEPHANO. I prithee now, lead the way, without any more
   talking. Trinculo, the king and all our company else being
   drowned, we will inherit here: here; bear my bottle: fellow
   Trinculo, we 'll find him by and by again.

CALIBAN. [*Sings drunkenly*]
      Farewell, master; farewell, farewell!

TRINCULO. A howling monster; a drunken monster!

CALIBAN.   No more dams I 'll make for fish;
               Nor fetch in firing
               At requiring;
            Nor scrape trencher, nor wash dish:
               'Ban, 'Ban, Cacaliban
            Has a new master:—get a new man.
   Freedom, hey-day! hey-day, freedom! freedom, hey-day,
   freedom!

STEPHANO. O brave monster! Lead the way.   [*Exeunt.*

ACT III

Scene I — *Before* Prospero's *cell.*

Enter Ferdinand, *bearing a log.*]

FERDINAND. There be some sports are painful, and their labor
　　Delight in them sets off: some kinds of baseness
　　Are nobly undergone, and most poor matters
　　Point to rich ends. This my mean task
　　Would be as heavy to me as odious, but
　　The mistress which I serve quickens what 's dead,
　　And makes my labors pleasures: O, she is
　　Ten times more gentle than her father 's crabbed,
　　And he 's composed of harshness. I must remove
　　Some thousands of these logs, and pile them up,
　　Upon a sore injunction: my sweet mistress
　　Weeps when she sees me work, and says, such baseness
　　Had never like executor. I forget:
　　But these sweet thoughts do even refresh my labors,
　　Most busy lest, when I do it.

Enter MIRANDA; *and* PROSPERO *at a distance, unseen.*]

MIRANDA.　　　　　　　　Alas, now, pray you,
　　Work not so hard: I would the lightning had
　　Burnt up those logs that you are enjoin'd to pile!
　　Pray, set it down, and rest you: when this burns,
　　'Twill weep for having wearied you. My father
　　Is hard at study; pray, now, rest yourself;
　　He 's safe for these three hours.

FERDINAND.　　　　　　　　O most dear mistress,
　　The sun will set before I shall discharge
　　What I must strive to do.

MIRANDA.　　　　　　　If you 'll sit down,
　　I 'll bear your logs the while: pray, give me that;
　　I 'll carry it to the pile.

FERDINAND.   No, precious creature;
  I had rather crack my sinews, break my back,
  Than you should such dishonor undergo,
  While I sit lazy by.

MIRANDA.   It would become me
  As well as it does you: and I should do it
  With much more ease; for my good will is to it,
  And yours it is against.

PROSPERO.   Poor worm, thou art infected!
  This visitation shows it.

MIRANDA.   You look wearily.

FERDINAND. No, noble mistress; 'tis fresh morning with me
  When you are by at night. I do beseech you,—
  Chiefly that I might set it in my prayers,—
  What is your name?

MIRANDA.   Miranda.—O my father,
  I have broke your hest to say so!

FERDINAND.   Admired Miranda!
  Indeed the top of admiration! worth
  What's dearest to the world! Full many a lady
  I have eyed with best regard, and many a time
  The harmony of their tongues hath into bondage
  Brought my too diligent ear: for several virtues
  Have I liked several women; never any
  With so full soul, but some defect in her
  Did quarrel with the noblest grace she owed,
  And put it to the foil: but you, O you,
  So perfect and so peerless, are created
  Of every creature's best!

MIRANDA.   I do not know
  One of my sex; no woman's face remember,
  Save, from my glass, mine own; nor have I seen
  More that I may call men than you, good friend,
  And my dear father: how features are abroad,
  I am skilless of; but, by my modesty,
  The jewel in my dower, I would not wish
  Any companion in the world but you;
  Nor can imagination form a shape,

Besides yourself, to like of. But I prattle
Something too wildly, and my father's precepts
I therein do forget.

FERDINAND.   I am, in my condition,
A prince, Miranda; I do think, a king;
I would, not so!—and would no more endure
This wooden slavery than to suffer
The flesh-fly blow my mouth. Hear my soul speak:
The very instant that I saw you, did
My heart fly to your service; there resides,
To make me slave to it; and for your sake
Am I this patient log-man.

MIRANDA.   Do you love me?

FERDINAND. O heaven, O earth, bear witness to this sound,
And crown what I profess with kind event,
If I speak true! if hollowly, invert
What best is boded me to mischief! I,
Beyond all limit of what else i' the world,
Do love, prize, honor you.

MIRANDA.   I am a fool
To weep at what I am glad of.

PROSPERO.   Fair encounter
Of two most rare affections! Heavens rain grace
On that which breeds between 'em!

FERDINAND.   Wherefore weep you?

MIRANDA. At mine unworthiness, that dare not offer
What I desire to give; and much less take
What I shall die to want. But this is trifling;
And all the more it seeks to hide itself,
The bigger bulk it shows. Hence, bashful cunning!
And prompt me, plain and holy innocence!
I am your wife, if you will marry me;
If not, I 'll die your maid: to be your fellow
You may deny me; but I 'll be your servant,
Whether you will or no.

FERDINAND.   My mistress, dearest;
And I thus humble ever.

MIRANDA.   My husband, then?

FERDINAND. Aye, with a heart as willing
As bondage e'er of freedom: here 's my hand.

MIRANDA. And mine, with my heart in 't: and now farewell
Till half an hour hence.

FERDINAND.   A thousand thousand!

               [*Exeunt* FERDINAND *and* MIRANDA *severally.*

PROSPERO. So glad of this as they I cannot be,
Who are surprised withal; but my rejoicing
At nothing, can be more. I 'll to my book;
For yet, ere supper-time, must I perform
Much business appertaining.   [*Exit.*

SCENE II — *Another part of the island.*

Enter CALIBAN, STEPHANO, *and* TRINCULO.]

STEPHANO. Tell not me;—when the butt is out, we will drink
water; not a drop before: therefore bear up, and board 'em.
Servant-monster, drink to me.

TRINCULO. Servant-monster! the folly of this island!
They say there 's but five upon this isle: we are three of
them; if th' other two be brained like us, the state totters.

STEPHANO. Drink, servant-monster, when I bid thee: thy eyes
are almost set in thy head.

TRINCULO. Where should they be set else? he were a brave
monster indeed, if they were set in his tail.

STEPHANO. My man-monster hath drowned his tongue in sack:
for my part, the sea cannot drown me; I swam, ere I could
recover the shore, five-and-thirty leagues off and on. By this
light, thou shalt be my lieutenant, monster, or my standard.

TRINCULO. Your lieutenant, if you list; he 's no standard.

STEPHANO. We 'll not run, Monsieur Monster.

TRINCULO. Nor go neither; but you 'll lie, like dogs, and yet say
nothing neither.

STEPHANO. Moon-calf, speak once in thy life, if thou beest a
good moon-calf.

CALIBAN. How does thy honor? Let me lick thy shoe. I 'll not
serve him, he is not valiant.

TRINCULO. Thou liest, most ignorant monster: I am in case to
justle a constable. Why, thou deboshed fish, thou, was there
ever man a coward that hath drunk so much sack as I to-
day? Wilt thou tell a monstrous lie, being but half a fish
and half a monster?

CALIBAN. Lo, how he mocks me! wilt thou let him, my lord?

TRINCULO. 'Lord,' quoth he! That a monster should be such a
natural!

CALIBAN. Lo, lo, again! bite him to death, I prithee.

STEPHANO. Trinculo, keep a good tongue in your head: if you
prove a mutineer,—the next tree! The poor monster 's my
subject, and he shall not suffer indignity.

CALIBAN. I thank my noble lord. Wilt thou be pleased to
hearken once again to the suit I made to thee?

STEPHANO. Marry, will I: kneel and repeat it; I will stand, and
so shall Trinculo.

Enter ARIEL, *invisible.*]

CALIBAN. As I told thee before, I am subject to a tyrant, a sor-
cerer, that by his cunning hath cheated me of the island.

ARIEL. Thou liest.

CALIBAN. Thou liest, thou jesting monkey, thou:
I would my valiant master would destroy thee!
I do not lie.

STEPHANO. Trinculo, if you trouble him any more in 's tale,
by this hand, I will supplant some of your teeth.

TRINCULO. Why, I said nothing.

STEPHANO. Mum, then, and no more. Proceed.

CALIBAN. I say, by sorcery he got this isle;
From me he got it. If thy greatness will
Revenge it on him,—for I know thou darest,
But this thing dare not,—

STEPHANO. That 's most certain.

CALIBAN. Thou shalt be lord of it, and I 'll serve thee.

STEPHANO. How now shall this be compassed? Canst thou
bring me to the party?

CALIBAN. Yea, yea, my lord: I 'll yield him thee asleep,
Where thou mayst knock a nail into his head.

ARIEL. Thou liest; thou canst not.

CALIBAN. What a pied ninny 's this! Thou scurvy patch!
　I do beseech thy greatness, give him blows,
　And take his bottle from him: when that 's gone,
　He shall drink nought but brine; for I 'll not show him
　Where the quick freshes are.

STEPHANO. Trinculo, run into no further danger: interrupt the
　monster one word further, and, by this hand, I 'll turn my
　mercy out o' doors, and make a stock-fish of thee.

TRINCULO. Why, what did I? I did nothing. I 'll go farther off.

STEPHANO. Didst thou not say he lied?

ARIEL. Thou liest.

STEPHANO. Do I so? take thou that.　　　　　　　　*[Beats him.*
　As you like this, give me the lie another time.

TRINCULO. I did not give the lie. Out o' your wits, and hearing
　too? A pox o' your bottle! this can sack and drinking do. A
　murrain on your monster, and the devil take your fingers!

CALIBAN. Ha, ha, ha!

STEPHANO. Now, forward with your tale.—Prithee, stand far-
　ther off.

CALIBAN. Beat him enough: after a little time,
　I 'll beat him too.

STEPHANO.　　　　　Stand farther.—Come, proceed.

CALIBAN. Why, as I told thee, 'tis a custom with him
　I' th' afternoon to sleep: there thou mayst brain him,
　Having first seized his books; or with a log
　Batter his skull, or paunch him with a stake,
　Or cut his wezand with thy knife. Remember
　First to possess his books; for without them
　He 's but a sot, as I am, nor hath not
　One spirit to command: they all do hate him
　As rootedly as I. Burn but his books.
　He has brave utensils,—for so he calls them,—
　Which, when he has a house, he 'll deck withal.
　And that most deeply to consider is
　The beauty of his daughter; he himself
　Calls her a nonpareil: I never saw a woman,
　But only Sycorax my dam and she;
　But she as far surpasseth Sycorax

As great'st does least.

STEPHANO. Is it so brave a lass?

CALIBAN. Aye, lord; she will become thy bed, I warrant,
And bring thee forth brave brood.

STEPHANO. Monster, I will kill this man: his daughter and I
will be king and queen,—save our graces!—and Trinculo
and thyself shall be viceroys. Dost thou like the plot, Trinculo?

TRINCULO. Excellent.

STEPHANO. Give me thy hand: I am sorry I beat thee; but,
while thou livest, keep a good tongue in thy head.

CALIBAN. Within this half hour will he be asleep:
Wilt thou destroy him then?

STEPHANO. Aye, on mine honor.

ARIEL. This will I tell my master.

CALIBAN. Thou makest me merry; I am full of pleasure:
Let us be jocund: will you troll the catch
You taught me but while-ere?

STEPHANO. At thy request, monster, I will do reason, any reason.—Come on, Trinculo, let us sing.   [*Sings.*
        Flout 'em and scout 'em,
            And scout 'em and flout 'em;
                Thought is free.

CALIBAN. That 's not the tune.
                        [ARIEL *plays the tune on a tabor and pipe.*

STEPHANO. What is this same?

TRINCULO. This is the tune of our catch, played by the picture
of Nobody.

STEPHANO. If thou beest a man, show thyself in thy likeness:
if thou beest a devil, take 't as thou list.

TRINCULO. O, forgive me my sins!

STEPHANO. He that dies pays all debts: I defy thee.
Mercy upon us!

CALIBAN. Art thou afeard?

STEPHANO. No, monster, not I.

CALIBAN. Be not afeard; the isle is full of noises,
Sounds and sweet airs, that give delight, and hurt not.
Sometimes a thousand twangling instruments

Will hum about mine ears; and sometime voices,
That, if I then had waked after long sleep,
Will make me sleep again: and then, in dreaming,
The clouds methought would open, and show riches
Ready to drop upon me; that, when I waked,
I cried to dream again.

STEPHANO. This will prove a brave kingdom to me, where I
shall have my music for nothing.

CALIBAN. When Prospero is destroyed.

STEPHANO. That shall be by and by: I remember the story.

TRINCULO. The sound is going away; let 's follow it, and after
do our work.

STEPHANO. Lead, monster; we 'll follow. I would I could see
this taborer; he lays it on.

TRINCULO. Wilt come? I 'll follow, Stephano.   [*Exeunt.*

SCENE III — *Another part of the island.*

Enter ALONSO, SEBASTIAN, ANTONIO, GONZALO, ADRIAN,
     FRANCISCO, *and others.*]

GONZALO. By 'r lakin, I can go no further, sir;
My old bones ache: here 's a maze trod, indeed,
Through forth-rights and meanders! By your patience,
I needs must rest me.

ALONSO.   Old lord, I cannot blame thee,
Who am myself attach'd with weariness,
To the dulling of my spirits: sit down, and rest.
Even here I will put off my hope, and keep it
No longer for my flatterer: he is drown'd
Whom thus we stray to find; and the sea mocks
Our frustrate search on land. Well, let him go.

ANTONIO. [*Aside to* SEBASTIAN.] I am right glad that he 's so
out of hope.
Do not, for one repulse, forego the purpose
That you resolved to effect.

SEBASTIAN.   [*Aside to* ANTONIO.] The next advantage
Will we take thoroughly.

ANTONIO.   [*Aside to* SEBASTIAN.] Let it be to-night;
For, now they are oppress'd with travel, they
Will not, nor cannot, use such vigilance
As when they are fresh.

SEBASTIAN.   [*Aside to* ANTONIO.] I say, to-night:
  no more.   [*Solemn and strange music.*

ALONSO. What harmony is this?—My good friends, hark!

GONZALO. Marvelous sweet music!

Enter PROSPERO *above, invisible. Enter several strange
      Shapes, bringing in a banquet: they dance
      about it with gentle actions of salutation; and,
      inviting King, &c. to eat, they depart.*]

ALONSO. Give us kind keepers, heavens!—What were these?

SEBASTIAN. A living drollery. Now I will believe
That there are unicorns; that in Arabia
There is one tree, the phœnix' throne; one phœnix
At this hour reigning there.

ANTONIO.   I 'll believe both;
And what does else want credit, come to me,
And I 'll be sworn 'tis true: travelers ne'er did lie,
Though fools at home condemn 'em.

GONZALO.   If in Naples
I should report this now, would they believe me?
If I should say, I saw such islanders,—
For, certes, these are people of the island,—
Who, though they are of monstrous shape, yet, note,
Their manners are more gentle-kind than of
Our human generation you shall find
Many, nay, almost any.

PROSPERO.   [*Aside*] Honest lord,
Thou has said well; for some of you there present
Are worse than devils.

ALONSO.   I cannot too much muse
Such shapes, such gesture, and such sound, expressing—
Although they want the use of tongue—a kind
Of excellent dumb discourse.

PROSPERO.   [*Aside*] Praise in departing.

FRANCISCO. They vanish'd strangely.

SEBASTIAN.   No matter, since
　　They have left their viands behind; for we have stomachs.—
　　Will 't please you taste of what is here?

ALONSO.   Not I.

GONZALO. Faith, sir, you need not fear. When we were boys,
　　Who would believe that there were mountaineers
　　Dew-lapp'd like bulls, whose throats had hanging at 'em
　　Wallets of flesh? or that there were such men
　　Whose heads stood in their breasts? which now we find
　　Each putter-out of five for one will bring us
　　Good warrant of.

ALONSO.   I will stand to, and feed,
　　Although my last: no matter, since I feel
　　The best is past. Brother, my lord the duke,
　　Stand to, and do as we.

Thunder and lightning. Enter ARIEL, *like a harpy; claps*
　　his wings upon the table; and, with a quaint
　　device, the banquet vanishes.]

ARIEL.. You are three men of sin, whom Destiny,—
　　That hath to instrument this lower world
　　And what is in 't,—the never-surfeited sea
　　Hath caused to belch up you; and on this island,
　　Where man doth not inhabit,—you 'mongst men
　　Being most unfit to live. I have made you mad;
　　And even with such-like valor men hang and drown
　　Their proper selves.

　　　　　　　　　[ALONSO, SEBASTIAN &c. *draw their swords.*
　　　　　　　　You fools! I and my fellows
　　Are ministers of Fate: the elements,
　　Of whom your swords are temper'd, may as well
　　Wound the loud winds, or with bemock'd-at stabs
　　Kill the still-closing waters, as diminish
　　One dowle that 's in my plume: my fellow-ministers
　　Are like invulnerable. If you could hurt,
　　Your swords are now too massy for your strengths,
　　And will not be uplifted. But remember,—

For that 's my business to you,—that you three
From Milan did supplant good Prospero;
Exposed unto the sea, which hath requit it,
Him and his innocent child: for which foul deed
The powers, delaying, not forgetting, have
Incensed the seas and shores, yea, all the creatures,
Against your peace. Thee of thy son, Alonso,
They have bereft; and do pronounce by me:
Lingering perdition—worse than any death
Can be at once—shall step by step attend
You and your ways; whose wraths to guard you from,—
Which here, in this most desolate isle, else falls
Upon your heads,—is nothing but heart-sorrow
And a clear life ensuing.

*He vanishes in thunder; then, to soft music, enter the
        Shapes again, and dance, with mocks and
        mows, and carrying out the table.*]

PROSPERO. Bravely the figure of this harpy has thou
Perform'd, my Ariel; a grace it had, devouring:
Of my instruction hast thou nothing bated
In what thou hadst to say: so, with good life
And observation strange, my meaner ministers
Their several kinds have done. My high charms work,
And these mine enemies are all knit up
In their distractions: they now are in my power;
And in these fits I leave them, while I visit
Young Ferdinand,—whom they suppose is drown'd,—
And his and mine loved darling.   [*Exit above.*

GONZALO. I' the name of something holy, sir, why stand you
In this strange stare?

ALONSO.   O, it is monstrous, monstrous!
Methought the billows spoke, and told me of it;
The winds did sing it to me; and the thunder,
That deep and dreadful organ-pipe, pronounced
The name of Prosper: it did bass my trespass.
Therefore my son i' th' ooze is bedded; and
I 'll seek him deeper than e'er plummet sounded,
And with him there lie mudded.   [*Exit.*

SEBASTIAN.　　　　　　　　　　　But one fiend at a time,
　　I 'll fight their legions o'er.
ANTONIO.　　　　　　　　　　I 'll be thy second.
　　　　　　　　　　　　[*Exeunt* SEBASTIAN *and* ANTONIO.
GONZALO. All three of them are desperate: their great guilt,
　　Like poison given to work a great time after,
　　Now 'gins to bite the spirits. I do beseech you,
　　That are of suppler joints, follow them swiftly,
　　And hinder them from what this ecstasy
　　May now provoke them to.
ADRIAN.　　　　　　　　　Follow, I pray you.　　[*Exeunt.*

ACT IV

SCENE I — *Before* PROSPERO's *cell.*

Enter PROSPERO, FERDINAND, *and* MIRANDA.]

PROSPERO. If I have too austerely punish'd you,
  Your compensation makes amends; for I
  Have given you here a third of mine own life,
  Or that for which I live; who once again
  I tender to thy hand: all thy vexations
  Were but my trials of thy love, and thou
  Hast strangely stood the test: here, afore Heaven,
  I ratify this my rich gift. O Ferdinand,
  Do not smile at me that I boast her off,
  For thou shalt find she will outstrip all praise,
  And make it halt behind her.

FERDINAND.   I do believe it
  Against an oracle.

PROSPERO. Then, as my gift, and thine own acquisition
  Worthily purchased, take my daughter: but
  If thou dost break her virgin-knot before
  All sanctimonious ceremonies may
  With full and holy rite be minister'd,
  No sweet aspersion shall the heavens let fall
  To make this contract grow; but barren hate,
  Sour-eyed disdain and discord shall bestrew
  The union of your bed with weeds so loathly
  That you shall hate it both: therefore take heed,
  As Hymen's lamps shall light you.

FERDINAND.   As I hope
  For quiet days, fair issue and long life,
  With such love as 'tis now, the murkiest den,
  The most opportune place, the strong'st suggestion
  Our worser genius can, shall never melt
  Mine honor into lust, to take away

    The edge of that day's celebration
    When I shall think, or Phœbus' steeds are founder'd,
    Or Night kept chain'd below.

PROSPERO.   Fairly spoke.
    Sit, then, and talk with her; she is thine own.
    What, Ariel! my industrious servant, Ariel!

Enter ARIEL.]

ARIEL. What would my potent master? here I am.

PROSPERO. Thou and thy meaner fellows your last service
    Did worthily perform; and I must use you
    In such another trick. Go bring the rabble,
    O'er whom I give thee power, here to this place:
    Incite them to quick motion; for I must
    Bestow upon the eyes of this young couple
    Some vanity of mine art: it is my promise,
    And they expect it from me.

ARIEL.   Presently?

PROSPERO. Aye, with a twink.

ARIEL. Before you can say, 'come,' and 'go,'
       And breathe twice, and cry, 'so, so,'
       Each one, tripping on his toe,
       Will be here with mop and mow,
       Do you love me, master? no?

PROSPERO. Dearly, my delicate Ariel. Do not approach
    Till thou dost hear me call.

ARIEL.   Well, I conceive.   [*Exit.*

PROSPERO. Look thou be true; do not give dalliance
    Too much the rein: the strongest oaths are straw
    To the fire i' the blood: be more abstemious,
    Or else, good night your vow!

FERDINAND.   I warrant you, sir;
    The white cold virgin snow upon my heart
    Abates the ardor of my liver.

PROSPERO.   Well.
    Now come, my Ariel! bring a corollary,
    Rather than want a spirit: appear, and pertly!
    No tongue! all eyes! be silent.   [*Soft music.*

Enter IRIS.]

IRIS. Ceres, most bounteous lady, thy rich leas
    Of wheat, rye, barley, vetches, oats, and pease;
    Thy turfy mountains, where live nibbling sheep,
    And flat meads thatch'd with stover, them to keep;
    Thy banks with pioned and twilled brims,
    Which spongy April at thy hest betrims,
    To make cold nymphs chaste crowns; and thy broom-groves,
    Whose shadow the dismissed bachelor loves,
    Being lass-lorn; thy pole-clipt vineyard;
    And thy sea-marge, sterile and rocky-hard,
    Where thou thyself dost air;—the queen o' the sky,
    Whose watery arch and messenger am I,
    Bids thee leave these; and with her sovereign grace,
    Here, on this grass-plot, in this very place,
    To come and sport:—her peacocks fly amain:
    Approach, rich Ceres, her to entertain.

Enter CERES.]

CERES. Hail, many-color'd messenger, that ne'er
    Dost disobey the wife of Jupiter;
    Who, with thy saffron wings, upon my flowers
    Diffusest honey-drops, refreshing showers;
    And with each end of thy blue bow dost crown
    My bosky acres and my unshrubb'd down,
    Rich scarf to my proud earth;—why hath thy queen
    Summon'd me hither, to this short-grass'd green?

IRIS. A contract of true love to celebrate;
    And some donation freely to estate
    On the blest lovers.

CERES.   Tell me, heavenly bow,
    If Venus or her son, as thou dost know,
    Do now attend the queen? Since they did plot
    The means that dusky Dis my daughter got,
    Her and her blind boy's scandal'd company
    I have forsworn.

IRIS.   Of her society
    Be not afraid: I met her deity
    Cutting the clouds towards Paphos, and her son
    Dove-drawn with her. Here thought they to have done

Some wanton charm upon this man and maid,
Whose vows are, that no bed-right shall be paid
Till Hymen's torch be lighted: but in vain;
Mars's hot minion is return'd again;
Her waspish-headed son has broke his arrows,
Swears he will shoot no more, but play with sparrows,
And be a boy right out.

CERES.   High'st queen of state,
Great Juno, comes; I know her by her gait.

Enter JUNO.]

JUNO. How does my bounteous sister? Go with me
To bless this twain, that they may prosperous be,
And honor'd in their issue.   [*They sing:*

JUNO.   Honor, riches, marriage-blessing,
                 Long continuance, and increasing,
                 Hourly joys be still upon you!
                 Juno sings her blessings on you.

CERES.   Earth's increase, foison plenty,
                 Barns and garners never empty;
Vines with clustering bunches growing;
Plants with goodly burthen bowing;
Spring come to you at the farthest
In the very end of harvest!
Scarcity and want shall shun you;
Ceres' blessing so is on you.

FERDINAND. This is a most majestic vision, and
Harmonious charmingly. May I be bold
To think these spirits?

PROSPERO.   Spirits, which by mine art
I have from their confines call'd to enact
My present fancies.

FERDINAND.   Let me live here ever;
So rare a wonder'd father and a wise
Makes this place Paradise.

                       [JUNO *and* CERES *whisper, and send*
                                IRIS *on employment.*

PROSPERO.   Sweet, now, silence!
Juno and Ceres whisper seriously;

    There 's something else to do: hush, and be mute,
    Or else our spell is marr'd.

IRIS. You nymphs, call'd Naiads, of the windring brooks,
    With your sedged crowns and ever-harmless looks,
    Leave your crisp channels, and on this green land
    Answer your summons; Juno does command:
    Come, temperate nymphs, and help to celebrate
    A contract of true love; be not too late.

Enter certain Nymphs.]

    You sunburn'd sicklemen, of August weary,
    Come hither from the furrow, and be merry:
    Make holiday; your rye-straw hats put on,
    And these fresh nymphs encounter every one
    In country footing.

Enter certain REAPERS, *properly habited; they join
      with the* NYMPHS *in a graceful dance; towards
      the end whereof* PROSPERO *starts suddenly, and
      speaks; after which, to a strange, hollow, and
      confused noise, they heavily vanish.*]

PROSPERO. [*Aside*] I had forgot that foul conspiracy
    Of the beast Caliban and his confederates
    Against my life: the minute of their plot
    Is almost come. [*To the* SPIRITS.] Well done! avoid; no
    more!

FERDINAND. This is strange: your father 's in some passion
    That works him strongly.

MIRANDA.   Never till this day
    Saw I him touch'd with anger so distemper'd.

PROSPERO. You do look, my son, in a moved sort,
    As if you were dismay'd: be cheerful, sir.
    Our revels now are ended. These our actors,
    As I foretold you, were all spirits, and
    Are melted into air, into thin air:
    And, like the baseless fabric of this vision,
    The cloud-capp'd towers, the gorgeous palaces,
    The solemn temples, the great globe itself,
    Yea, all which it inherit, shall dissolve,
    And, like this insubstantial pageant faded,

   Leave not a rack behind. We are such stuff
As dreams are made on; and our little life
Is rounded with a sleep. Sir, I am vex'd;
Bear with my weakness; my old brain is troubled:
Be not disturb'd with my infirmity:
If you be pleased, retire into my cell,
And there repose: a turn or two I 'll walk,
To still my beating mind.

FERDINAND, MIRANDA.   We wish your peace.   [*Exeunt.*

PROSPERO. Come with a thought. I thank thee, Ariel: come.
Enter ARIEL.]

ARIEL. Thy thoughts I cleave to. What 's thy pleasure?

PROSPERO.   Spirit,
   We must prepare to meet with Caliban.

ARIEL. Aye, my commander: when I presented Ceres,
I thought to have told thee of it; but I fear'd
Lest I might anger thee.

PROSPERO. Say again, where didst thou leave these varlets?

ARIEL. I told you, sir, they were red-hot with drinking;
So full of valor that they smote the air
For breathing in their faces; beat the ground
For kissing of their feet; yet always bending
Towards their project. Then I beat my tabor;
At which, like unback'd colts, they prick'd their ears,
Advanced their eyelids, lifted up their noses
As they smelt music: so I charm'd their ears,
That, calf-like, they my lowing follow'd through
Tooth'd briars, sharp furzes, pricking goss, and thorns,
Which enter'd their frail shins: at last I left them
I' the filthy-mantled pool beyond your cell,
There dancing up to the chins, that the foul lake
O'erstunk their feet.

PROSPERO.   This was well done, my bird.
   Thy shape invisible retain thou still:
The trumpery in my house, go bring it hither,
For stale to catch these thieves.

ARIEL.   I go, I go.   [*Exit.*

PROSPERO. A devil, a born devil, on whose nature
  Nurture can never stick; on whom my pains,
  Humanely taken, all, all lost, quite lost;
  And as with age his body uglier grows,
  So his mind cankers. I will plague them all,
  Even to roaring.

Re-enter ARIEL, *loaden with glistering apparel, etc.*]
  Come, hang them on this line.

PROSPERO *and* ARIEL *remain, invisible. Enter* CALIBAN,
  STEPHANO, *and* TRINCULO, *all wet.*]

CALIBAN. Pray you, tread softly, that the blind mole may not
  Hear a foot fall: we now are near his cell.

STEPHANO. Monster, your fairy, which you say is a harmless
  fairy, has done little better than played the Jack with us.

TRINCULO. Monster, I do smell all horse-piss; at which my nose
  is in great indignation.

STEPHANO. So is mine. Do you hear, monster? If I should take
  a displeasure against you, look you,—

TRINCULO. Thou wert but a lost monster.

CALIBAN. Good my lord, give me thy favor still.
  Be patient, for the prize I'll bring thee to
  Shall hoodwink this mischance: therefore speak softly.
  All's hush'd as midnight yet.

TRINCULO. Aye, but to lose our bottles in the pool,—

STEPHANO. There is not only disgrace and dishonor in that,
  monster, but an infinite loss.

TRINCULO. That's more to me than my wetting: yet this is
  your harmless fairy, monster.

STEPHANO. I will fetch off my bottle, though I be o'er ears for
  my labor.

CALIBAN. Prithee, my king, be quiet. See'st thou here,
  This is the mouth o' the cell: no noise, and enter.
  Do that good mischief which may make this island
  Thine own for ever, and I, thy Caliban,
  For aye thy foot-licker.

STEPHANO. Give me thy hand. I do begin to have bloody
  thoughts.

TRINCULO. O King Stephano! O peer! O worthy Stephano! look what a wardrobe here is for thee!

CALIBAN. Let it alone, thou fool; it is but trash.

TRINCULO. O, ho, monster! we know what belongs to a frippery. O King Stephano!

STEPHANO. Put off that gown. Trinculo; by this hand, I 'll have that gown.

TRINCULO. Thy grace shall have it.

CALIBAN. The dropsy drown this fool! what do you mean
To dote thus on such luggage? Let 's alone,
And do the murder first: if he awake,
From toe to crown he 'll fill our skins with pinches,
Make us strange stuff.

STEPHANO. Be you quiet, monster. Mistress line, is not this my jerkin? Now is the jerkin under the line: now, jerkin, you are like to lose your hair, and prove a bald jerkin.

TRINCULO. Do, do: we steal by line and level, an 't like your grace.

STEPHANO. I thank thee for that jest; here 's a garment for 't: wit shall not go unrewarded while I am king of this country. 'Steal by line and level' is an excellent pass of pate; there 's another garment for 't.

TRINCULO. Monster, come, put some lime upon your fingers, and away with the rest.

CALIBAN. I will have none on 't: we shall lose our time,
And all be turn'd to barnacles, or to apes
With foreheads villainous low.

STEPHANO. Monster, lay-to your fingers: help to bear this away where my hogshead of wine is, or I 'll turn you out of my kingdom: go to, carry this.

TRINCULO. And this.

STEPHANO. Aye, and this.

*A noise of hunters heard. Enter divers Spirits,
in shape of dogs and hounds, hunting
them about;* PROSPERO *and* ARIEL *setting them on.*]

PROSPERO. Hey, Mountain, hey!

ARIEL. Silver! there it goes, Silver!

PROSPERO. Fury, Fury! there, Tyrant, there! hark, hark!

    [CALIBAN, STEPHANO, *and* TRINCULO *are driven out.*

  Go charge my goblins that they grind their joints
  With dry convulsions; shorten up their sinews
  With aged cramps; and more pinch-spotted make them
  Than pard or cat o' mountain.

ARIEL.   Hark, they roar!

PROSPERO. Let them be hunted soundly. At this hour
  Lie at my mercy all mine enemies:
  Shortly shall all my labors end, and thou
  Shalt have the air at freedom: for a little
  Follow, and do me service.   *[Exeunt.*

ACT V

SCENE I — *Before the cell of* PROSPERO.

Enter PROSPERO *in his magic robes, and* ARIEL.]

PROSPERO. Now does my project gather to a head:
  My charms crack not; my spirits obey; and time
  Goes upright with his carriage. How 's the day?
ARIEL. On the sixth hour; at which time, my lord,
  You said our work should cease.
PROSPERO.   I did say so,
  When first I raised the tempest. Say, my spirit,
  How fares the king and 's followers?
ARIEL.   Confined together
  In the same fashion as you gave in charge,
  Just as you left them; all prisoners, sir,
  In the line-grove which weather-fends your cell;
  They cannot budge till your release. The king,
  His brother, and yours, abide all three distracted,
  And the remainder mourning over them,
  Brimful of sorrow and dismay; but chiefly
  Him that you term'd, sir, 'The good old lord, Gonzalo';
  His tears run down his beard, like winter's drops
  From eaves of reeds. Your charm so strongly works 'em,
  That if you now beheld them, your affections
  Would become tender.
PROSPERO.   Dost thou think so, spirit?
ARIEL. Mine would, sir, were I human.
PROSPERO.   And mine shall.
  Hast thou, which art but air, a touch, a feeling
  Of their afflictions, and shall not myself,
  One of their kind, that relish all as sharply,
  Passion as they, be kindlier moved than thou art?
  Though with their high wrongs I am struck to the quick,
  Yet with my nobler reason 'gainst my fury

Do I take part: the rarer action is
In virtue than in vengeance: they being penitent,
The sole drift of my purpose doth extend
Not a frown further. Go release them, Ariel:
My charms I 'll break, their senses I 'll restore,
And they shall be themselves.

ARIEL.   I 'll fetch them, sir.   [*Exit.*

PROSPERO. Ye elves of hills, brooks, standing lakes, and groves;
And ye that on the sands with printless foot
Do chase the ebbing Neptune, and do fly him
When he comes back; you demi-puppets that
By moonshine do the green sour ringlets make,
Whereof the ewe not bites; and you whose pastime
Is to make midnight mushrooms, that rejoice
To hear the solemn curfew; by whose aid—
Weak masters though ye be—I have bedimm'd
The noontide sun, call'd forth the mutinous winds,
And 'twixt the green sea and the azured vault
Set roaring war: to the dread rattling thunder
Have I given fire, and rifted Jove's stout oak
With his own bolt; the strong-based promontory
Have I made shake, and by the spurs pluck'd up
The pine and cedar: graves at my command
Have waked their sleepers, oped, and let 'em forth
By my so potent art. But this rough magic
I here adjure; and, when I have required
Some heavenly music,—which even now I do,—
To work mine end upon their senses, that
This airy charm is for, I 'll break my staff,
Bury it certain fathoms in the earth,
And deeper than did ever plummet sound
I 'll drown my book.   [*Solemn music.*

Re-enter ARIEL *before: then* ALONSO, *with a frantic ges-*
       ture, attended by GONZALO; SEBASTIAN *and* AN-
       TONIO *in like manner, attended by* ADRIAN *and*
       FRANCISCO: *they all enter the circle which*
       PROSPERO *had made, and there stand charmed;*
       which PROSPERO *observing, speaks:*

A solemn air, and the best comforter
To an unsettled fancy, cure thy brains,
Now useless, boil'd within thy skull! There stand,
For you are spell-stopp'd.
Holy Gonzalo, honorable man,
Mine eyes, even sociable to the show of thine,
Fall fellowly drops. The charm dissolves apace;
And as the morning steals upon the night
Melting the darkness, so their rising senses
Begin to chase the ignorant fumes that mantle
Their clearer reason. O good Gonzalo,
My true preserver, and a loyal sir
To him thou follow'st! I will pay thy graces
Home both in word and deed. Most cruelly
Didst thou, Alonso, use me and my daughter:
Thy brother was a furtherer in the act.
Thou art pinch'd for 't now, Sebastian. Flesh and blood,
You, brother mine, that entertain'd ambition,
Expell'd remorse and nature; who, with Sebastian,—
Whose inward pinches therefore are most strong,—
Would here have kill'd your king; I do forgive thee,
Unnatural though thou art. Their understanding
Begins to swell; and the approaching tide
Will shortly fill the reasonable shore,
That now lies foul and muddy. Not one of them
That yet looks on me, or would know me: Ariel,
Fetch me the hat and rapier in my cell:
I will discase me, and myself present
As I was sometime Milan: quickly, spirit;
Thou shalt ere long be free.

ARIEL *sings and helps to attire him.*]

　　　　Where the bee sucks, there suck I:
　　　　In a cowslip's bell I lie;
　　　　There I couch when owls do cry.
　　　　On the bat's back I do fly
　　　　After summer merrily.
　　　　Merrily, merrily shall I live now
　　　　Under the blossom that hangs on the bough.

PROSPERO. Why, that 's my dainty Ariel! I shall miss thee;
But yet thou shalt have freedom: so, so, so.
To the king's ship, invisible as thou art:
There shalt thou find the mariners asleep
Under the hatches; the master and the boatswain
Being awake, enforce them to this place,
And presently, I prithee.

ARIEL. I drink the air before me, and return
Or ere your pulse twice beat.   [Exit.

GONZALO. All torment, trouble, wonder and amazement
Inhabits here: some heavenly power guide us
Out of this fearful country!

PROSPERO.   Behold, sir king,
The wronged Duke of Milan, Prospero:
For more assurance that a living prince
Does now speak to thee, I embrace thy body;
And to thee and thy company I bid
A hearty welcome.

ALONSO.   Whether thou be'st he or no,
Or some enchanted trifle to abuse me,
As late I have been, I not know: thy pulse
Beats, as of flesh and blood; and, since I saw thee,
The affliction of my mind amends, with which,
I fear, a madness held me: this must crave—
An if this be at all—a most strange story.
Thy dukedom I resign, and do entreat
Thou pardon me my wrongs.—But how should Prospero
Be living and be here?

PROSPERO.   First, noble friend,
Let me embrace thine age, whose honor cannot
Be measured or confined.

GONZALO.   Whether this be
Or be not, I 'll not swear.

PROSPERO.   You do yet taste
Some subtilties o' the isle, that will not let you
Believe things certain. Welcome, my friends all!
[Aside to SEBASTIAN and ANTONIO] But you, my brace of
    lords, were I so minded,

I here could pluck his highness' frown upon you,
And justify you traitors: at this time
I will tell no tales.

SEBASTIAN. [*Aside*] The devil speaks in him.

PROSPERO. No.

For you, most wicked sir, whom to call brother
Would even infect my mouth, I do forgive
Thy rankest fault,—all of them; and require
My dukedom of thee, which perforce, I know,
Thou must restore.

ALONSO. If thou be'st Prospero,
Give us particulars of thy preservation;
How thou hast met us here, who three hours since
Were wreck'd upon this shore; where I have lost—
How sharp the point of this remembrance is!—
My dear son Ferdinand.

PROSPERO. I am woe for 't, sir.

ALONSO. Irreparable is the loss; and patience
Says it is past her cure.

PROSPERO. I rather think
You have not sought her help, of whose soft grace
For the like loss I have her sovereign aid,
And rest myself content.

ALONSO. You the like loss!

PROSPERO. As great to me as late; and, supportable
To make the dear loss, have I means much weaker
Than you may call to comfort you, for I
Have lost my daughter.

ALONSO. A daughter?
O heavens, that they were living both in Naples,
The king and queen there! that they were, I wish
Myself were mudded in that oozy bed
Where my son lies. When did you lose your daughter?

PROSPERO. In this last tempest. I perceive, these lords
At this encounter do so much admire,
That they devour their reason, and scarce think
Their eyes do offices of truth, their words
Are natural breath: but, howsoe'er you have

Been justled from your senses, know for certain
That I am Prospero, and that very duke
Which was thrust forth of Milan; who most strangely
Upon this shore, where you were wreck'd, was landed.
To be the lord on 't. No more yet of this;
For 'tis a chronicle of day by day,
Not a relation for a breakfast, nor
Befitting this first meeting. Welcome, sir;
This cell 's my court: here have I few attendants,
And subjects none abroad: pray you, look in.
My dukedom since you have given me again,
I will requite you with as good a thing;
At least bring forth a wonder, to content ye
As much as me my dukedom.

Here PROSPERO *discovers* FERDINAND *and* MIRANDA
       playing at chess.]

MIRANDA. Sweet lord, you play me false.

FERDINAND.   No, my dear'st love,
I would not for the world.

MIRANDA. Yes, for a score of kingdoms you should wrangle,
And I would call it fair play.

ALONSO.   If this prove
A vision of the island, one dear son
Shall I twice lose.

SEBASTIAN.   A most high miracle!

FERDINAND. Though the seas threaten, they are merciful;
I have cursed them without cause.   [*Kneels.*

ALONSO.   Now all the blessings
Of a glad father compass thee about!
Arise, and say how thou camest here!

MIRANDA.   O, wonder!
How many goodly creatures are there here!
How beauteous mankind is! O brave new world,
That has such people in 't!

PROSPERO.   'Tis new to thee.

ALONSO. What is this maid with whom thou wast at play?
Your eld'st acquaintance cannot be three hours:

Is she the goddess that hath sever'd us,
And brought us thus together?

FERDINAND.   Sir, she is mortal;
But by immortal Providence she 's mine:
I chose her when I could not ask my father
For his advice, nor thought I had one. She
Is daughter to this famous Duke of Milan,
Of whom so often I have heard renown,
But never saw before; of whom I have
Received a second life; and second father
This lady makes him to me.

ALONSO.   I am hers:
But, O, how oddly will it sound that I
Must ask my child forgiveness!

PROSPERO.   There, sir, stop:
Let us not burthen our remembrances with
A heaviness that 's gone.

GONZALO.   I have inly wept,
Or should have spoke ere this. Look down, you gods,
And on this couple drop a blessed crown!
For it is you that have chalk'd forth the way
Which brought us hither.

ALONSO.   I say, Amen, Gonzalo!

GONZALO. Was Milan thrust from Milan, that his issue
Should become kings of Naples? O, rejoice
Beyond a common joy! and set it down
With gold on lasting pillars: In one voyage
Did Claribel her husband find at Tunis,
And Ferdinand, her brother, found a wife
Where he himself was lost, Prospero his dukedom
In a poor isle, and all of us ourselves
When no man was his own.

ALONSO. [*To* FERDINAND *and* MIRANDA] Give me your hands:
Let grief and sorrow still embrace his heart
That doth not wish you joy!

GONZALO.   Be it so! Amen!

Re-enter ARIEL, *with the* MASTER *and* BOATSWAIN
          amazedly following.]

O, look, sir, look, sir! here is more of us:
I prophesied, if a gallows were on land,
This fellow could not drown. Now, blasphemy,
That swear'st grace o'erboard, not an oath on shore?
Hast thou no mouth by land? What is the news?

BOATSWAIN. The best news is, that we have safely found
Our king and company; the next, our ship—
Which, but three glasses since, we gave out split—
Is tight and yare and bravely rigg'd, as when
We first put out to sea.

ARIEL.   [*Aside to* PROSPERO.] Sir, all this service
Have I done since I went.

PROSPERO.   [*Aside to* ARIEL.] My tricksy spirit!

ALONSO. These are not natural events; they strengthen
From strange to stranger. Say, how came you hither?

BOATSWAIN. If I did think, sir, I were well awake,
I 'ld strive to tell you. We were dead of sleep,
And—how we know not—all clapp'd under hatches;
Where, but even now, with strange and several noises
Of roaring, shrieking, howling, jingling chains,
And mo diversity of sounds, all horrible,
We were awaked; straightway, at liberty;
Where we, in all her trim, freshly beheld
Our royal, good, and gallant ship; our master
Capering to eye her:—on a trice, so please you,
Even in a dream, were we divided from them,
And were brought moping hither.

ARIEL.   [*Aside to* PROSPERO] Was 't well done?

PROSPERO. [*Aside to* ARIEL] Bravely, my diligence.
Thou shalt be free.

ALONSO. This is as strange a maze as e'er men trod;
And there is in this business more than nature
Was ever conduct of: some oracle
Must rectify our knowledge.

PROSPERO.   Sir, my liege,
Do not infest your mind with beating on
The strangeness of this business; at pick'd leisure

Which shall be shortly, single I'll resolve you,
Which to you shall seem probable, of every
These happen'd accidents; till when, be cheerful,
And think of each thing well. [*Aside to* ARIEL] Come hither,
    spirit:
Set Caliban and his companions free;
Untie the spell. [*Exit* ARIEL.] How fares my gracious sir?
There are yet missing of your company
Some few odd lads that you remember not.

Re-enter ARIEL, *driving in* CALIBAN, STEPHANO, *and*
    TRINCULO, *in their stolen apparel.*]

STEPHANO. Every man shift for all the rest, and let no man take
    care for himself; for all is but fortune.—Coragio, bully-
    monster, coragio!

TRINCULO. If these be true spies which I wear in my head,
    here's a goodly sight.

CALIBAN. O Setebos, these be brave spirits indeed!
How fine my master is! I am afraid
He will chastise me.

SEBASTIAN.   Ha, ha!
What things are these, my lord Antonio?
Will money buy 'em?

ANTONIO.   Very like; one of them
Is a plain fish, and, no doubt, marketable.

PROSPERO. Mark but the badges of these men, my lords,
Then say if they be true. This mis-shapen knave,
His mother was a witch; and one so strong
That could control the moon, make flows and ebbs,
And deal in her command, without her power.
These three have robb'd me; and this demi-devil—
For he's a bastard one—had plotted with them
To take my life. Two of these fellows you
Must know and own; this thing of darkness I
Acknowledge mine.

CALIBAN.   I shall be pinch'd to death.

ALONSO. Is not this Stephano, my drunken butler?

SEBASTIAN. He is drunk now: where had he wine?

ALONSO. And Trinculo is reeling ripe: where should they

Find this grand liquor that hath gilded 'em?—
How camest thou in this pickle?

TRINCULO. I have been in such a pickle, since I saw you last,
that, I fear me, will never out of my bones: I shall not fear
fly-blowing.

SEBASTIAN. Why, how now, Stephano!

STEPHANO. O touch me not;—I am not Stephano, but a cramp.

PROSPERO. You 'ld be king o' the isle, sirrah?

STEPHANO. I should have been a sore one, then.

ALONSO. This is a strange thing as e'er I look'd on.

                                  [Pointing to CALIBAN.

PROSPERO. He is as disproportion'd in his manners
  As in his shape. Go, sirrah, to my cell;
  Take with you your companions; as you look
  To have my pardon, trim it handsomely.

CALIBAN. Aye, that I will; and I 'll be wise hereafter,
  And seek for grace. What a thrice-double ass
  Was I, too take this drunkard for a god,
  And worship this dull fool!

PROSPERO.   Go to; away!

ALONSO. Hence, and bestow your luggage where you found it.

SEBASTIAN. Or stole it, rather.

              [Exeunt CALIBAN, STEPHANO, *and* TRINCULO.

PROSPERO. Sir, I invite your Highness and your train
  To my poor cell, where you shall take your rest
  For this one night; which, part of it, I 'll waste
  With such discourse as, I not doubt, shall make it
  Go quick away: the story of my life,
  And the particular accidents gone by
  Since I came to this isle: and in the morn
  I 'll bring you to your ship, and so to Naples,
  Where I have hope to see the nuptial
  Of these our dear-beloved solemnized;
  And thence retire me to my Milan, where
  Every third thought shall be my grave.

ALONSO.   I long
  To hear the story of your life, which must
  Take the ear strangely.

PROSPERO.   I 'll deliver all;
  And promise you calm seas, auspicious gales,
  And sail so expeditious, that shall catch
  Your royal fleet far off. [*Aside to* ARIEL] My Ariel, chick,
  That is thy charge: then to the elements
  Be free, and fare thou well! Please you, draw near.
                                 [*Exeunt.*

Epilogue

Spoken by PROSPERO.

Now my charms are all o'erthrown,
And what strength I have 's mine own,
Which is most faint: now, 'tis true,
I must be here confined by you,
Or sent to Naples. Let me not,
Since I have my dukedom got,
And pardon'd the deceiver, dwell
In this bare island by your spell;
But release me from my bands
With the help of your good hands:
Gentle breath of yours my sails
Must fill, or else my project fails,
Which was to please. Now I want
Spirits to enforce, art to enchant;
And my ending is despair,
Unless I be relieved by prayer,
Which pierces so, that it assaults
Mercy itself, and frees all faults.
As you from crimes would pardon'd be,
Let your indulgence set me free.

GLOSSARIES

GLOSSARY

FOR

A Midsummer Night's Dream

ABRIDGMENT, an entertainment to while away the time; V. i.

ABY, pay for; III. ii.

ADAMANT, loadstone; II. i.

ADDRESS'D, ready; V. i.

ADMIRABLE, to be wondered at; V. i.

ADVISED, "be advised" = "consider what you are doing"; I. i.

AGAINST, in preparation for; V. i.

AGGRAVATE, Bottom's blunder for "decrease"; I. ii.

ALL, fully; II. i.

AN, if; I. ii.

AN IF, if; II. ii.

ANTIQUE, strange; V. i.

APPROVE, prove; II. ii.

APRICOCKS, apricots; III. i.

ARGUMENT, subject of story; III. ii.

ARTIFICIAL, skilled in art; III. ii.

AS, that as; I. i.

ASK, require; I. ii.

AUNT, old dame; II. i.

AUSTERITY, strictness of life; I. i.

BARM, froth, yeast; II. i.

BARREN, empty headed; III. ii.

BATED, excepted; I. i.

BEARD, the prickles on the ears of corn; II. i.

BELIKE, very likely; I. i.

BELLOWS-MENDER, mender of the bellows of organs; I. ii.

BERGOMASK DANCE, a rude clownish dance such as the people of the town Bergamo or of the province Bergamasco were wont to practice. "Bergamo, a town in the Venetian territory, capital of the old province Bergamasco, whose inhabitants used to be ridiculed as clownish"; V. i.

BETEEM, accord, permit; I. i.

BILL, list; I. ii.

BLOOD, passion; I. i.; I. i.; birth, social rank; I. i.

BOLT, arrow; II. i.

BOOTLESS, in vain, uselessly; II. i.

BOSOM, heart; I. i.

BOTTLE, bundle, truss; IV. i.

BOUNCING, imperious; II. i.

BRAVE TOUCH, noble action; III. ii.

BREATH, voice, notes; II. i.

BRIEF, short statement; V. i.

BRISKY, brisk; III. i.

BROACH'D, stabbed, spitted; V. i.

BULLY, comrade; III. i.

BUSKIN'D, wearing the buskin, a boot with high heels, worn by hunters and huntresses; II. i.

CANKER-BLOSSOM, the worm that eats into blossoms; III. ii.

CANKERS, worms; II. ii.

CAPACITY, "to my c." *i. e.* "so far as I am able to understand"; V. i.

CAVALERY, cavalero, cavalier; IV. i.

CENTAURS, "battle with the c." an allusion to the attack made on

341

Hercules by the Centaurs when he was in pursuit of the Erymanthian boar; the battle referred to is not their famous contest with the Lapithæ; V. i.

CHANCE, "how c." *i. e.* "how chances it"; I. i.

CHANGELING, a child substituted by the fairies for the one stolen by them; II. i.

CHEEK BY JOLE, *i. e.* cheek to cheek, side by side; III. ii.

CHEER, countenance; III. ii; V. i.

CHIDING, barking; IV. i.

CHILDING, productive, fertile; II. i.

CHURCH-WAY, leading to the church; V. i.

CHURL, boor, peasant; II. ii.

CLERK, scholars; V. i.

COIL, confusion, ado; III. ii.

COLLIED, dark, black; I. i.

COMPACT, composed, formed; V. i.

COMPARE WITH, try to rival; II. ii.

CON, learn by heart; I. ii.

CONCERN, accord with, befit; I. i.

CONDOLE, probably one of Bottom's blunders, unless perhaps used in the sense of lament; I. ii.

CONFUSION, ruin; I. i.

CONSECRATE, consecrated; V. i.

CONSTANCY, consistency; V. i.

CONTAGIOUS, pestilential; II. i.

CONTINENTS, banks; II. i.

COURAGEOUS, happy, fortunate; IV. ii.

COY, fondle; IV. i.

CRAZED, "c. title," *i. e.* "a title with a flaw in it"; I. i.

CREATE, created; V. i.

CRITICAL, censorious; V. i.

CRY, pack of hounds; IV. i.

CUPID'S FLOWER, the pansy, "love-in-idleness"; IV. i.

CURST, shrewish; III. ii.

CUT THREAD AND THRUM = cut everything, good and bad (*vide* THREAD AND THRUM); V. i.

DANCES AND DELIGHT = delightful dances; II. i.

DARKLING, in the dark; II. ii.

DEAD, deadly, death-like; III. ii.

DEAR, "dear expense," a privilege dearly bought; I. i.

DEBATE, contention; II. i.

DEFEATED, cheated; IV. i.

DEFECT, Bottom's bunder for "effect"; III. i.

DERIVED, "as well derived," as well-born; I. i.

DEVICES, plans, projects; I. ii.; performance; V. i.

DEWBERRIES, the fruit of the dewberry bush; III. i.

DEWLAP, the loose skin hanging from the throat of cattle; here used for "neck"; II. i.; dewlapp'd; IV. i.

DIAN'S BUD, probably the bud of the Agnus Castus or Chaste-tree; "the vertue of this herbe is that he wyll kepe man and woman chaste"; IV. i.

DISCHARGE, perform; I. ii.; IV. ii.

DISFIGURE, to obliterate; I. i.

DISFIGURE, Quince's blunder for "figure"; III. i.

DISTEMPERATURE, disorder of the elements; II. i.

DOLE, grief; V. i.

DONE, "when all is done," = when all is said and done; III. i.

DOWAGER, a widow with a jointure; I. i.

DRAWN, with drawn sword; III. ii.

EARTHLIER, "earthlier happy," happier as regards this world; I. i.

EAT, ate; II. ii.

EGLANTINE, sweetbriar; II. i.

EGYPT, "brow of E." = the brow of a gypsy (*i. e.* an Egyptian); V. i.

EIGHT AND SIX, alternate verses of four and three feet; the common ballad meter of the time; III. i.

EMBARKED TRADERS, traders embarked upon the sea; II. i.

ENFORCED, forced, violated; III. i.

ENOUGH, "you have enough," *i. e.* you have heard enough to convict him; IV. i.

ERCLES = HERCULES, whose twelve labors had often formed the subject of dramatic shows, the hero resembling Herod in his ranting; I. ii.

EREWHILE, a little while ago; III. ii.

ESTATE UNTO, bestow upon; I. i.

EVER, always; I. i.

EXPOSITION, Bottom's blunder for "disposition"; IV. i.

EXTENUATE, mitigate, relax; I. i.

FAINT, pale; I. i.

FAIR, fairness, beauty; I. i.

FAIR, kindly; II. i.

FALL, let fall, drop; V. i.

FANCY, love; I. i.; IV. i.

FANCY-FREE, free from the power of love; II. i.

FANCY-SICK, sick for love; III. ii.

FAVOR, features; I. i.

FAVORS, love-tokens; II. i.; nosegays of flowers; IV. i.

FELL, "passing fell," extremely angry; II. i.

FELLOW, match, equal; IV. i.

FIGURE, typify; I. i.

FIRE, will of the wisp; III. i.

FLEW'D, having an overhanging lip on the upper jaw; IV. i.

FLOODS, waters; II. i.

FLOUT, mock at; II. ii.

FOND, foolish; II. ii.

FOR, "for the candle," *i. e.* "because of"; V. i.

FORCE, "of force" = perforce; III. ii.

FORDONE, exhausted; V. i.

FORGERIES, idle inventions; II. i.

FORTH, out of, from; I. i.

FOR THAT, because; II. i.

FORTY, used as an indefinite number; II. i.

FRENCH CROWN COLOR, light yellow, the color of the gold of the French crown; I. ii.

GALLANT = "gallantly" (which the Folios read); I. ii.

GAWDS, trifles, trinkets; I. i.

GENERALLY, Bottom's blunder for "severally"; I. ii.

GLANCE AT, hint at; II. i.

GLEEK, jest, scoff; III. i.

GO ABOUT, attempt; IV. i.

GOSSIP'S BOWL, originally a christening cup; thence applied to a drink usually prepared for christening feasts; its ingredients were ale, spice, sugar, and roasted *crabs* (*i.e.* crab-apples); II. i.

GOVERNMENT, control; "in government" = under control; V. i.

GRACE, favor granted; II. ii.

GRIM-LOOK'D, grim-looking; V. i.

GROW, "grow to a point," come to the point; I. ii.

HANDS, "give me your hands," applaud by clapping; V. i.

HEAD, "to his head" = to his face; I. i.

HEARTS, good fellows; IV. ii.

HELEN, a blunder for "Hero"; V. i.

HEMPEN HOME-SPUNS, coarse fellows (rude mechanicals); III. i.

HENCHMAN, page, attendant; II. i.

HIGHT, is called; V. i.

HORNED MOON, used perhaps quibblingly with reference to the material of Moonshine's lanthorn; V. i.

HUMAN, humane, courteous; II. ii.

HUMAN MORTALS, men as distinguished from fairies, who were considered *mortal*, though not *human;* II. i.

IMBRUE, stain with blood; V. i.

IMMEDIATELY, purposely; I. i.

IMPEACH, bring into question; II. i.

IN = on; II. i.

INCORPORATE, made one body; III. ii.

INJURIOUS, insulting; III. ii.

INTEND, pretend; III. ii.

INTERCHAINED, bound together; II. ii.

JUVENAL, juvenile, youth; III. i.

KIND, "in this kind," in this respect; I. i.

KNACKS = knick-knacks; I. i.

KNOT-GRASS, "hindering k." was formerly believed to have the power of checking the growth of children; III. ii.

LAKIN; by 't lakin, *i. e.* by our ladykin, or little lady, *i. e.* the Virgin Mary; III. i.

LATCH'D, moistened, anointed; III. ii.

LEAVE, give up; II. i.

LEVIATHAN, whale; II. i.

LIMANDER, a blunder for "Leander"; V. i.

LION-FELL, lion's skin; V. i.

LOB, buffoon, clown; II. i.

LODE-STAR, the leading star, the polar star; I. i.

LORDSHIP, "unto his lordship, whose," etc., = unto the government of him to whose, etc.; I. i.

LOSE, forget; I. i.

LOVE-IN-IDLENESS, the heartsease, or pansy, called "Cupid's flower"; II. i.

LOVES; "of all loves," for love's sake; II. ii.

LUSCIOUS, delicious, sweet; II. i.

MAKE MOUTHS UPON = "make face at, mock at"; III. ii.

MAY, can; V. i.

MAZED, perplexed; II. i.

MAZES, "figures marked out on village greens for rustic sports, such as the game called *running the figure of eight";* II. i.

MEANS, moans; V. i.

MECHANICALS, working-men; III. ii.

MIMIC, actor; III. ii.

MINDING, intending; V. i.

MINIMUS, tiny creature; III. ii.

MISGRAFFED, grafted on a wrong tree; I. i.

MISPRISED, mistaken; III. ii.

MISPRISION, mistake; III. ii.

MOMENTANY, momentary, lasting a moment; I. i.

MORNING'S LOVE, *i. e.* Cephalus; III. ii.

MOUSED, torn in pieces, as a cat worries a mouse; V. i.

MOUTH, sound; IV. i.

MURRION = infected with murrain, a disease among cattle; II. i.

MUSK-ROSE, described in Gerarde's *Herbal* as "a flower of a white colour," with "certaine yellow seedes in the middle . . . of most writers reckoned among the wilde Roses"; II. i.

NAUGHT, "a thing of naught," a worthless thing; IV. ii.

NEAF, fist, IV. i.

NEARLY, "nearly that concerns" = that nearly c.; I. i.

NEEZE = sneeze; II. i.

NEXT, nearest, first; III. ii.

NIGHT-RULE, night revel; III. ii.

NINE MEN'S MORRIS, "a plat of green turf cut into a sort of chess board, for the rustic youth to exercise their skill upon. The game was called 'nine men's morris' (or 'merrils,' i. e. 'counters' or 'pawns') because the players had each nine men which they moved along the lines cut in the ground—a diagram of three squares, one within the other —until one side had taken or penned up all those on the other"; II. i.

NINUS, the supposed founder of Nineveh, the husband of Semiramis, Queen of Babylon; V. i.

NOLE, noddle, head; III. ii.

NONE, "I will none," i. e. "nothing to do with her, none of her"; III. ii.

OBSCENELY, Bottom's blunder for (?) seemly; I. ii.

OBSERVANCE, "to do o. to a morn of May," i. e. "to observe the rights of May-day"; I. i.

OBSERVATION = observance of May-day; IV. i.

OF, by; II. ii.; for; III. i.

ON, "fond on," i. e. "doting on"; II. i.

ON = of; V. i.

ORANGE-TAWNY, dark yellow; I. ii.

ORBS, rings of rich green grass thought to be caused by the fairies; II. i.

ORIGINAL = originators; II. i.

OTHER, others; IV. i.

OUNCE, a kind of lynx; II. ii.

OUSEL, blackbird; III. i.

OVERBEAR, overrule; IV. i.

OWE, own; II. ii.

OXLIPS, a kind of cowslip not often found wild; II. i.

PAGEANT, show, exhibition; III. ii.

PALPABLE-GROSS, palpably gross; V. i.

PARD = leopard; II. ii.

PARLOUS = perilous; III. i.

PARTS, qualities; III. ii.

PAT, PAT, exactly, just as it should be; III. i.

PATCHED, wearing a coat of various colors; "patched fool," i. e. "a motley fool"; IV. i.

PATCHES, clowns; III. ii.

PATENT, "virgin patent," privilege of virginity; I. i.

PELTING, paltry; II. i.

PENSIONERS, retainers; II. i.

PERIODS, full stops; V. i.

PERT, lively; I. i.

PHIBBUS = Phœbus; I. ii.

PILGRIMAGE, "maiden pilgrimage," a passing through life unwedded; I. i.

PLAIN-SONG, used as an epithet of the cuckoo, with reference to its simple, monotonous note; a "plain-song" is a melody without any variations; III. i.

POINTS, "stand upon points," used quibblingly (1) "mind his stops," and (2) "be over-scrupulous"; V. i.

POSSESS'D, "as well possess'd," possessed of as much wealth; I. i.

PREFERRED, submitted for approval; IV. ii.

PREPOSTEROUSLY, perversely; III. ii.

PRESENTLY = immediately; IV. ii.

PREVAILMENT, weight, sway; I. i.

PREY, the act of preying; II. ii.

PRINCESS, paragon, perfection; III. ii.

PRIVILEGE, safeguard, protection; II. i.

PROCRUS, a blunder for "Procris," the wife of Cephalus; V. i.

PRODIGIOUS, unnatural; V. i.

PROLOGUE, speaker of the prologue; V. i.

PROPER, fine, handsome; I. ii.

PROPERTIES, a theatrical term for all the adjuncts of a play, except the scenery and the dresses of the actors; I. ii.

PROTEST, vow; I. i.

PUMPS, low shoes; IV. ii.

PURPLE-IN-GRAIN, dyed deep red; I. ii.

QUAIL, quell, overpower; V. i.

QUELL, kill; V. i.

QUERN, a mill for grinding corn by hand; II. i.

QUESTIONS, arguing; II. i.

RECORDER, a kind of flageolet; V. i.

RENT, rend; III. ii.

RERE-MICE, bats; II. ii.

RESPECT, "in my r.," *i. e.* "in my estimation"; II. i.

RESPECTS, regards; I. i.

RIGHT MAID, true maid; III. ii.

RINGLETS, the circles on the greensward, supposed to be made by the fairies (*cp.* ORBS); II. i.

RIPE, grow ripe; II. ii.

RIPE, ready for presentation; V. i.

ROUND, a dance in a circle; II. i.

ROUNDEL, dance in a circle; II. ii.

RUN THROUGH FIRE, a proverbial expression signifying "to do impossibilities"; II. ii.

SAD, serious; IV. i.

SANDED, sandy colored; IV. i.

SAVORS, scents, fragrance; II. i.

SCHOOLING, instructions; I. i.

SCRIP, "scroll," *i. e.* list of actors; I. ii.

SEAL, pledge; III. ii.

SEETHING, heated, excited; V. i.

SELF-AFFAIRS, my own business; I. i.

SENSIBLE, capable of feeling; V. i.

SERPENT'S TONGUE, *i. e.* hissing, as a sign of disapproval; V. i.

SHAFALUS, a blunder for "Cephalus," who remained true to his wife Procris notwithstanding Aurora's love for him; V. i.

SHEEN, brightness; II. i.

SHORE = shorn; V. i.

SHREWD, mischievous; II. i.

SIMPLENESS, simplicity; V. i.

SINISTER, left; V. i.

SISTERS THREE, *i. e.* the Fates; V. i.

SLEEP, sleeping; IV. i.

SMALL, in a treble voice like a boy or a woman; I. ii.

SNUFF, used equivocally; "to be in snuff" = "to be offended"; V. i.

So, in the same manner; IV. i.

SOLEMNITIES, nuptial festivities; I. i.

SOLEMNLY, with due ceremony; IV. i.

SOOTH, truth; II. ii.

SORT, company, crew; III. ii.

SORTING, "not s. with," not befitting; V. i.

SPHERY, star-like; II. ii.

SPLEEN, sudden passion; I. i.

SPLIT, "to make all split," a proverbial expression used to denote violent action; originally used by sailors; I. ii.

SPOTTED, polluted; I. i.

SPRING, "middle summer's spring," the beginning of midsummer; II. i.

SQUARE, wrangle, squabble; II. i.

STAY = to stay; II. i.

STEALTH, stealing away; III. ii.

STEPPE (so Quarto 1), probably an error for "steep" (the reading of the Folios and Quarto 2); hence Milton's "Indian steep" (*Comus*, 139); it is doubtful whether Shakespeare was acquainted with this Russian term; II. i.

STILL, always, ever; I. i.

STOOD UPON, depended upon; I. i.

STREAK, touch softly; II. i.

STRETCH'D, strained; "extremely s." *i. e.* "strained to the utmost"; V. i.

STRINGS, to tie on false beards with; IV. ii.

SUPERPRAISE, overpraise; III. ii.

TARTAR'S BOW, the Tartars or Parthians were famous for their skill in archery; in the old maps Tartary included the ancient Parthia; III. ii.

TEAR, "to tear a cat in," a proverbial phrase = to rant violently; I. ii.

THICK-SKIN, dolt; III. ii.

THRACIAN SINGER, *i. e.* Orpheus; "His grief for the loss of Eurydice led him to treat with contempt the Thracian women, who in revenge tore him to pieces under the excitement of their Bacchanalian orgies"; V. i.

THREAD, the warp; V. i.

THROWS, throws off, sheds; II. i.

THRUM, the loose end of a weaver's warp; V. i.

'TIDE, betide; V. i.

TIRING-HOUSE, dressing-room; III. i.

TOWARD, in progress; III. i.

TOYS, trifles; "fairy toys," fanciful tales; V. i.

TRACE, traverse; II. i.

TRANSLATED, transformed; I. i.; III. i.

TRANSPORTED, removed, carried off; IV. ii.

TRIPLE HECATE, *i. e.* ruling in three capacities—as Luna or Cynthia in heaven, Diana on earth, and Hecate in hell; V. i.

TRIUMPH, public show; I. i.

TROTH, truth; II. ii.

TUNEABLE, tuneful; I. i.

UNBREATHED, unexercised; V. i.

UNHARDEN'D, impressionable; I. i.

UPON, by; II. i.

VANTAGE, "with vantage," having the advantage; I. i.

VAWARD = vanguard; IV. i.

VILLAGERY, a collective word, meaning either (1) village population, or (2) villages; II. i.

VIRTUE, "fair virtue's force," *i. e.* the power of thy fairness; III. i.

VOICE, approval; I. i.

VOTARESS, a vestal vowed to virginity; II. i.

WANDERING KNIGHT = knight errant; I. ii.

WANT, lack; II. i.

WANTON, luxuriant, thick; II. i.

WASTED, consumed; V. i.

WAYS, "all ways," in all directions; IV. i.

WEED, robe; II. i.

WHERE (dissyllabic); II. i.

WHERE = wherever; IV. i.

WHETHER (monosyllabic); I. i.

WITHERING OUT, delaying the enjoyment of; I. i.

WITHOUT, outside of; I. i.; beyond the reach of; IV. i.

WODE, mad (with a play upon "wood"); II. i.

WOODBINE, honeysuckle; II. i. probably convolvulus or bindweed; IV. i.

WORM, serpent; III. ii.

WRATH, wrathful; II. i.

YOU (ethic dative); I. ii.

GLOSSARY

FOR

As You Like It

ABUSED, deceived; III. v.

ACCORD, consent; V. iv.

ADDRESS'D, prepared; V. iv.

ALL AT ONCE, all in a breath; III. v.

ALLOTTERY, allotment, allotted share; I. i.

ALL POINTS = at all points; I. iii.

AMAZE, confuse; I. ii.

AN, if; IV. i.

ANATOMIZE, expose; I. i.

ANSWERED, satisfied; II. vii.

ANTIQUE, ancient, old; II. i.; II. iii.

ANY, any one; I. ii.

ARGUMENT, reason; I. ii.

ARM'S END, arm's length; II. vi.

As, to wit, namely; II. i.

ASSAY'D, attempted; I. iii.

ATALANTA'S BETTER PART, variously interpreted as referring to Atalanta's "swiftness," "beauty," "spiritual part"; probably the reference is to her beautiful form; III. ii.

ATOMIES, motes in a sunbeam; III. ii.

ATONE TOGETHER, are at one; V. iv.

BANDY, contend; V. i.

BANQUET, dessert, including wine; II. v.

BAR, forbid; V. iv.; "bars me," *i.e.* excludes me from; I. i.

BATLET = little bat, used by laundresses; II. iv.

BEHOLDING, beholden; IV. i.

BESTOWS HIMSELF, carries himself; IV. iii.

BETTER, greater; III. i.

BLOOD, affection; II. iii.; passion; V. iv.

BOB, rap, slap; II. vii.

BONNET, hat; III. ii.

BOTTOM, "neighbor b.," the neighboring dell; IV. iii.

BOUNDS, boundaries, range of pasture; II. iv.

Bow, yoke; III. iii.

BRAVERY, finery; II. vii.

BREATHED, "well breathed," in full display of my strength; I. ii.

BREATHER, living being; III. ii.

BREED, train up, educate; I. i.

BRIEF, in brief; IV. iii.

BROKE, broken; II. iv.

BROKEN MUSIC, "Some instruments such as viols, violins, etc., were formerly made in sets of four, which, when played together, formed a 'consort.' If one or more of the instruments of one set were substituted for the corresponding ones of another set, the result is no longer a 'consort,' but 'broken music'" (Chappell); I. ii.

BRUTISH, animal nature; II. vii.

BUCKLES IN, surrounds; III. ii.

BUGLE, a tube-shaped bead of black glass; III. v.

BURDEN, the "burden" of a song

348

was the base, foot, or under-song, III. ii.

BUTCHERY, slaughter-house; II. iii.

CALLING, appellation; I. ii.

CAPABLE, sensible, receivable; III. v.

CAPON LINED, alluding to the customary gifts expected by Elizabethan magistrates, "capon justices," as they were occasionally called; II. vii.

CAPRICIOUS, used with a play upon its original sense; Ital. *capriccioso*, fantastical, goatish; *capra*, a goat; III. iii.

CARLOT, little churl, rustic; III. v.

CAST, cast off; III. iv.

CENSURE, criticism; IV. i.

CHANGE, reversal of fortune; I. iii.

CHANTICLEER, the cock; II. vii.

CHARACTER, write; III. ii.

CHEERLY, cheerily; II. vi.

CHOPT, chapped; II. iv.

CHRONICLERS (Folio 1 "chroniclers") perhaps used for the "jurymen," but the spelling of Folio 1 suggests "coroners" for "chroniclers"; IV. i.

CHURLISH, miserly; II. iv.

CICATRICE, a mere mark (not the scar of a wound); III. iv.

CITY-WOMAN, citizen's wife; II. vii.

CIVIL, "c. sayings," sober, grave maxims, perhaps "polite"; III. ii.

CIVILITY, politeness; II. vii.

CLAP INTO 'T, to begin a song briskly; V. iii.

CLUBS, the weapon used by the London prentices, for the preservation of the public peace, or for the purposes of riot; V. ii.

CODS, strictly the husks containing the peas; perhaps here used for "peas"; II. iv.

COLOR, nature, kind; I. ii.

COMBINE, bind; V. iv.

COME OFF, get off; I, ii.

COMFORT, take comfort; II. vi.

COMMANDMENT, command; II. vii.

COMPACT, made up, composed; II. vii.

COMPLEXION, "good my c.," perhaps little more than the similar exclamation "goodness me!" or "good heart!"; possibly, however, Rosalind appeals to her complexion not to betray her; III. ii.

CONCEIT, imagination; II. vi.; mental capacity; V. ii.

CONDITION, mood; I. ii.

CONDUCT, leadership; V. iv.

CONNED, learnt by heart; III. ii.

CONSTANT, accustomed, ordinary; III. v.

CONTENTS, "if truth holds true c." *i. e.* "if there be truth in truth"; V. iv.

CONTRIVER, plotter; I. i.

CONVERSED, associated; V. ii.

CONVERTITES, converts; V. iv.

CONY, rabbit; III. ii.

COPE, engage with; II. i.

COPULATIVES, those desiring to be united in marriage; V. iv.

COTE, "*cavenne de bergier;* a shepherd's cote; a little cottage or cabin made of turfs, straw, boughs, or leaves" (*Cotgrave*); II. iv.

COULD, would gladly; I. ii.

COUNTENANCE, "his countenance" probably = "his entertainment of me, the style of living which he allows me"; I. i.

COUNTER, worthless wager; originally pieces of false money used as a means of reckoning; II. vii.

COURTSHIP, court life; III. ii.

COUSIN, niece; I. iii.

COVER, set the table; II. v.

CROSS, used equivocally in the

sense of (1) misfortune, and (2) money; the ancient penny had a double cross with a crest stamped on, so that it might easily be broken into four pieces; II. iv.

CROW, laugh heartily; II. vii.

COURTLE-AXE, a short sword; I. iii.

DAMNABLE, worthy of condemnation; V. ii.

DEFIED, disliked; Epil.

DESPERATE, bold, daring, forbidden; V. iv.

DEVICE, aims, ambitions; I. i.

DIAL, an instrument for measuring time in which the hours were marked; a small portable sundial; II. vii.

DISABLE, undervalue; IV. i.

DISABLED, disparaged; V. iv.

DISHONEST, immodest; V. iii.

DISLIKE = express dislike of; V. iv.

DISPUTABLE, fond of disputing; II. v.

DIVERTED, diverted from its natural course; II. iii.

DOG-APES, baboons; II. v.

DOLE, grief; I. ii.

DUCDAME, burden of Jaques' song, variously interpreted by editors, e. g. "duc ad me," "huc ad me;" probably, however, the word is an ancient refrain, of Celtic origin; Halliwell notes that dus-adam-me-me occurs in a MS. of Piers Plowman, where ordinary texts read How, trolly, lolly (C. ix. 123); it is probably a survival of some old British game like "Tom Tidler," and is said to mean in Gælic "this land is mine"; according to others it is a Welsh phrase equivalent to "come to me." Judging by all the evidence on the subject the Gælic interpretation seems to be most plausi-

ble; n. b. 1. 61, "to call fools into a circle"; II. v.

DULCET DISEASES, [? an error for "dulcet discourses"] perhaps "sweet mortifications," alluding to such proverbial sayings as "fool's bolt is soon shot," &c.; V. iv.

EAST, eastern; III. ii.

EAT, eaten; II. vii.

EFFIGIES, likeness; II. vii.

ENCHANTINGLY, as if under a spell; I. i.

ENGAGE, pledge; V. iv.

ENTAME, bring into a state of tameness; III. v.

ENTREATED, persuaded; I. ii.

ERRING, wandering; III. ii.

ESTATE, bequeath, settle; V. ii.

ETHIOPE, black as an Ethiopian; IV. iii.

EXEMPT, remote; II. i.

EXPEDIENTLY, expeditiously; III. i.

EXTENT, seizure; III. i.

EXTERMINED, exterminated; III. v.

FAIR, beauty; III. ii.

FALLS, lets fall; III. v.

FANCY, love; III. v.

FANCY-MONGER, love-monger; III. ii.

FANTASY, fancy; II. iv.

FAVOR, aspect; IV. iii.; countenance; V. iv.

FEATURE, shape, form; used perhaps equivocally, but with what particular force is not known; "feature" may have been used occasionally in the sense of "verse-making"; III. iii.

FEED, pasturage; II. iv.

FEEDER, servant ("factor" and "fedary" have been suggested); II. iv.

FEELINGLY, by making itself felt; II. i.

FELLS, woolly skins; III. ii.

FLEET, make to fly; I. i.

FLOUT, mock at, jeer at; I. ii.

FOND, foolish; II. iii.

FOR, for want of; II. iv.; II. vi.; because; III. ii.; as regards; IV. iii.

FORKED HEADS, *i. e.* "fork-heads," which Ascham describes in his *Toxophilus* as being "arrows having two points stretching forward"; II. i.

FORMAL, having due regard to dignity; II. vii.

FREE, not guilty; II. vii.

FREESTONE-COLOR'D, dark colored, of the color of Bath-brick; IV. iii.

FURNISHED, apparelled; Epilogue.

GARGANTUA'S MOUTH; alluding to "the large-throated" giant of Rabelais, who swallowed five pilgrims, with their pilgrims' staves, in a salad; though there was no English translation of Rabelais in Shakespeare's time, yet several chap-book histories of Gargantua were published; III. ii.

GENTILITY, gentleness of birth; I. i.

GESTURE, bearing; V. ii.

GLANCES, hits; II. vii.

GOD BUY YOU = "God be with you"; hence, "good-bye"; III. ii.

GOD 'ILD YOU = "God yield (reward) you"; III. iii.

GOD YE GOOD EVEN = God give you good even (often represented by some such form as "Godgigoden"); V. i.

GOLDEN WORLD, golden age; I. i.

"GOOD WINE NEEDS NO BUSH," alluding to the bush of ivy which was usually hung out at Vintners' doors; Epil.

GOTHS (evidently pronounced very much like "goats," hence Touchstone's joke); the Getæ (or Goths) among whom Ovid lived in banishment; III. iii.

GRACE, gain honor; I. i.

GRACE ME, get me credit, good repute; V. ii.

GRACIOUS, looked upon with favor; I. ii.

GRAFF, graft; III. ii.

GRAVELLED, stranded, at a standstill; IV. i.

HARM, misfortunes; III. ii.

HAVE WITH YOU, come along; I. ii.

HAVING, possession; III. ii.

HE = man; III. ii.

HEADED, grown to a head; II. vii.

HEART, affection, love; I. i.

HERE MUCH, used ironically, in a negative sense, as in the modern phrase "much I care!"; IV. iii.

HIM = he whom; I. i.

HINDS, serfs, servants; I. i.

HOLLA, "cry holla to"; restrain; III. ii.

HOLY, sacramental; III. iv.

HONEST, virtuous; I. ii.

HOOPING, "out of all hooping," beyond the bounds of wondering; III. ii.

HUMOROUS, full of whims, capricious; I. ii.; II. iii.; fanciful; IV. i.

HURTLING, din, tumult; IV. iii.

HYEN, hyena; IV. i.

ILL-FAVORED, ugly in face, bad looking; V. iv.

ILL-FAVOREDLY, ugly; I. ii.

IMPRESSURE, impression; III. v.

INCISION, "God make in." *i. e.* "give thee a better understanding"; a reference perhaps to the cure by blood-letting; it was said of a very silly person that he ought to be cut for the simples; III. ii.

INCONTINENT, immediately; V. ii.

INQUISITION, search, inquiry; II. ii.

INSINUATE WITH, ingratiate myself with; Epil.

INSOMUCH = in as much as; V. ii.

INTENDMENT, intention; I. i.

INVECTIVELY, bitterly, with invective; II. i.

IRISH RAT, Irish witches were said to be able to rime either man or beast to death; berimed rats are frequently alluded to in Elizabethan writers; III. ii.

IRKS, grieves; II. i.

JARS, discordant sounds; II. vii.

JUDAS'S, "browner than J."; he was usually represented in ancient painting or tapestry with red hair and beard; III. iv.

JUNO'S SWANS, probably an error for Venus, represented as swan-drawn in Ovid (Meta. x. 708); I. iii.

JUST, just so; III. ii.

JUSTLY, exactly; I. ii.

KIND, nature; IV. iii.

KINDLE, enkindle, incite; I. i.

KINDLED, brought forth; used technically for the littering of rabbits; III. ii.

KNOLL'D, chimed; II. vii.

LACK, do without; IV. i.

LEARN, teach; I. ii.

LEAVE, permission; I. i.; I. ii.

LEER, countenance; IV. i.

LIEF, gladly; I. i.; III. ii.

LIMN'D, drawn; II. vii.

LINED, drawn; III. ii.

LIVELY = life-like; V. iv.

LOOSE, let loose; III. v.

LOVER, mistress; III. iv.

MAKE = make fast, shut; IV. i.

MANAGE, training or breaking in of a horse; I. i.

MANNISH, male; I. iii.

MATTER, sound sense; II. i.; sense, meaning; V. iii.

MEASURE, a court dance; V. iv.

MEED, reward; II. iii.

MEMORY, memorial; II. iii.

MIGHT, may; I. ii.

MINES, undermines; I. i.

MISPRISED, despised, thought nothing of; I. i.; I. ii.

MOCKABLE, liable to ridicule; III. ii.

MOCKS, mockeries; III. v.

MODERN, commonplace, ordinary; II. vii.; IV. i.

MOE, more; III. ii.

MOONISH, variable, fickle; III. ii.

MORAL, probably an adjective, moralizing; II. vii.

MORALIZE, discourse, expound; II. i.

MORTAL, "mortal in folly"; a quibble of doubtful meaning; perhaps = "excessive, very," i. e. "extremely foolish" (? = likely to succumb to folly); II. iv.

MOTLEY, the parti-colored dress of domestic fools or jesters; II. vii.; (used adjectively); II. vii.; fool; III. iii.

MUTTON, sheep; III. ii.

NAPKIN, handkerchief; IV. iii.

NATURAL, idiot; I. ii.

NATURE, "of such a nature," whose special duty it is; III. i.

NATURE'S SALE-WORK = ready-made goods; III. v.

NAUGHT, "be n. awhile," a proverbial expression equivalent to "a mischief on you"; I. i.

NEEDLESS, not needing; II. i.

NEW-FANGLED, fond of what is new; IV. i.

NICE, trifling; IV. i.

NURTURE, good manners, breeding; II. vii.

OBSERVANCE, attention; III. ii.; reverence, respect; V. ii. (the repetition is probably due to the compositor; "endurance," "obedience," "deservance," have been suggested.)

OCCASION, "her husband's o." = an opportunity for getting the better of her husband; IV. i.

OF, "searching of" = a-searching of; II. iv.; "complain of," *i. e.* of the want of; III. ii.; by; III. ii.; III. iii.

OFFER'ST FAIRLY, dost contribute largely; V. iv.

OLIVER, "O sweet O." the fragment of an old ballad; III. iii.

PAINTED CLOTH, canvas painted with figures, mottoes, or moral sentences, used for hangings for rooms; III. ii.

PANTALOON, a standing character in the old Italian comedy; he wore slippers, spectacles, and a pouch, and invariably represented as an old dotard; taken typically for a Venetian; St. Pantaleon was the patron saint of Venice; II. vii.

PARCELS, detail; III. v.

PARD, leopard; II. vii.

PARLOUS, perilous; III. ii.

PASSING, surpassing, exceedingly; III. v.

PATHETICAL, probably "affection-moving," perhaps used with the force of "pitiful"; IV. i.

PAYMENT, punishment; I. i.

PEASCOD, literally the husk or pod which contains the peas, used for the plant itself; "our ancestors were frequently accustomed in their love-affairs to employ the divination of a peascod, and if the good omen of the peas remaining in the husk were preserved, they presented it to the lady of their choice"; II. iv.

PEEVISH, wayward, saucy; III. v.

PERPEND, reflect; III. ii.

PETITIONARY, imploring; III. ii.

PHŒNIX, "as rare as p."; the phœnix, according to Seneca, was born once only in 500 years; IV. iii.

PLACE = dwelling-place; II. iii.

PLACES, topics, subjects; III. viii.

POINT-DEVICE, *i. e.* at point device, trim, faultless; III. ii.

POKE, pocket; II. vii.

POOR, "p. a thousand crowns," the adjective precedes the article for the sake of emphasis, and probably also because of the substantial force of the whole expression "a thousand crowns"; I. i.

PORTUGAL, "bay of P." "still used by sailors to denote that portion of the sea off the coast of P. from Oporto to the headland of Cintra"; IV. i.

PRACTICE, plot, scheme; I. i.

PRACTICES, plots, schemes; II. iii.

PRESENT, being present; III. i.

PRESENTATION, representation; V. iv.

PRESENTLY, immediately; II. vi.

PREVENTS, anticipates; IV. i.

PRIZER, prize-fighter; II. iii.

PRIVATE, particular, individual; II. vii.

PRODIGAL, "what p. portion have I spent," *i. e.* "what portion have I prodigally spent"; I. i.

PROFIT, proficiency; I. i.

PROLOGUES, "the only p.," *i. e.* only the p.; V. iii.

PROPER, handsome; I. ii.

PROPERER, more handsome; III. v.

PUISNY, unskilled, inferior; III. iv.

PULPITER (Spedding's emendation for "Jupiter," the reading of the Folios); III. ii.

PURCHASE, acquire; III. ii.

PURGATION, vindication; I. iii.; proof, test; V. iv.

PURLIEUS, the grounds on the borders of the forest; IV. iii.

PYTHAGORAS' TIME, an allusion to that philosopher's doctrine of the transmigration of souls; III. ii.

QUAIL, slacken; II. ii.

QUESTION, conversation; III. iv.

QUINTAIN, a figure set up for tilting at in country games, generally in the likeness of a Turk or Saracen, bearing a shield upon his left arm, and brandishing a club with his right, which moved round and struck a severe blow if the horseman made a bad aim; I. ii.

QUINTESSENCE, the extract from a thing, containing its virtues in a small quantity; originally, in medieval philosophy, the fifth essence, or spirit, or soul of the world, which consisted not of the four elements, but was a certain fifth, a thing above or beside them; III. ii.

QUIP, a smart saying; V. iv.

QUIT, acquit; III. i.

QUOTIDIAN, a fever, the paroxysms of which return every day, expressly mentioned in old writers as a symptom of love; III. ii.

RAGGED, rough, untuneful; II. v.

RANK, row, line; IV. iii.; "butterwomen's rank" ["rate," "rack," "rant (at)," "canter," have been proposed] = file, order, jogtrot; III. ii.

RANKNESS, presumption; I. i.

RASCAL, technical term for lean deer; III. iii.

RAW, ignorant, inexperienced; III. ii.

REASON, talk, converse; I. ii.

RECKS, cares; II. iv.

RECOUNTMENTS, things recounted, narrations; IV. iii.

RECOVER'D, restored; IV. iii.

RELIGIOUS, belonging to some religious order; III. ii.

REMEMBRANCE, memory; I. i.

REMORSE, compassion; I. iii.

REMOVED, remote; III. ii.

RENDER, describe; IV. iii.

RESOLVE, solve; III. ii.

REVERENCE, "his reverence," the respect due to him; I. i.

RIGHT, downright; III. ii.; true; III. ii.

RIPE, grown up; IV. iii.

ROUNDLY, without delay; V. iii.

ROYNISH, rude, uncouth; II. ii.

SAD, serious; III. ii.

SAD BROW, serious face; III. ii.

SAWS, maxims; II. vii.

SCHOOL, (probably) university; I. i.

SCRIP, shepherd's pouch; III. ii.

SEEKS (used instead of the singular); V. i.

SEEMING, seemly; V. iv.

SE'NNIGHT = seven-night, a week; II. ii.

SENTENTIOUS, pithy; V. iv.

SHADOW, shady place; IV. i.

SHALL, must; I. i.

SHE, woman; III. ii.

SHEAF, gather into sheaves; III. ii.

SHOULD BE, came to be, was said to be; III. ii.

SHOULDST = wouldst; I. ii.

SHOW, appear; I. iii.

SHREWD, evil, harsh; V. iv.

SIMPLES, herbs used in medicine; IV. i.

SIR, a title bestowed on the inferior clergy, hence Sir Oliver

Martext, the country curate; probably a translation of "Dominus," still applied to "Bachelors" at the University; III. iii.

SMIRCH, besmear, darken; I. iii.

SMOTHER, "from the smoke into the s."; thick suffocating smoke; I. ii.

SNAKE, used as a term of scorn; IV. iii.

So, if, provided that; I. ii.

SORTS, kinds, classes; I. i.

SOUTH-SEA OF DISCOVERY, a voyage of discovery over a wide and unknown ocean; the whole phrase is taken by some to mean that a minute's delay will bring so many questions that to answer them all will be like a voyage of discovery. Perhaps the reference is to Rosalind's discovery of her secret, of the truth about herself; III. ii.

SPEED, patron; I. ii.

SPLEEN, passion; IV. i.

SQUANDERING, random; II. vii.

STAGGER, hesitate; III. iii.

STAY, wait for; III. ii.

STICKS, strikes, stabs; I. ii.

STILL, continually; I. ii.

STILL MUSIC, i. e. soft, low, gentle music; V. iv.

STRAIGHT = straightway, immediately; III. v.

SUCCESSFULLY, likely to succeed; I. ii.

SUDDENLY, quickly, speedily; II. ii.

SUIT, used quibblingly, (1) petition, (2) dress; II. vii.

SUITS = favors (with a play upon "suit," "livery"); I. ii.

SUN, "to live i' the s." i. e. to live in open-air freedom; II. v.

SURE, firmly joined; V. iv.

SWASHING, swaggering; I. iii.

SWIFT, keen of wit; V. iv.

TA'EN UP, made up; V. iv.

TAXATION, censure, satire; I. ii.

TEMPERED, composed, blended; I. ii.

THATCHED HOUSE, alluding to the story of Baucis and Philemon; III. iii.

THAT THAT = that which; V. iv.

THOUGHT, melancholy; or perhaps "moody reflection"; IV. i.

THRASONICAL, boastful (from Thraso the boaster, in the *Eunuchus* of Terence); V. ii.

THRICE-CROWNED QUEEN, ruling in heaven, earth, and the underworld, as Luna, Diana, and Hecate; III. ii.

THRIFTY, "the th. hire I saved," i. e. "that which by my thrift I saved out of the hire"; II. iii.

TO, as to; II. iii.

TOUCHES, characteristics; III. ii.

TOWARD, at hand; V. iv.

TOY, bagatelle, trifling affair; III. iii.

TRAVERSE, crossways; III. iv.

TROW YOU, know you; III. ii.

TURN'D INTO, brought into; IV. iii.

UMBER, brown pigment, brought from Umbria; I. iii.

UNCOUTH, unknown, strange; II. vi.

UNEXPRESSIVE, inexpressive, unable to be expressed; III. ii.

UNKIND, unnatural; II. vii.

UNQUESTIONABLE, unwilling to be conversed with; III. ii.

UNTO, in addition to; I. ii.

UNTUNEABLE (Theobald and other editors "untimeable," *cp.* the page's reply), out of tune, perhaps also "out of time"; V. iii.

UP, "kill them up"; used as an intensive particle; II. i.

VELVET, delicate ("velvet" is the

technical term for the outer covering of the horns of a stag in the early stages of its growth); II. i.

VENGEANCE, mischief; IV. iii.

VILLAIN, bondman, serf; with play upon the other sense; I. i.

VOICE, "in my voice," *i. e.* as far as my vote is concerned; II. v.

WARE, aware; II. iv.; cautious; II. iv.

WARP, turn, change the aspect of, twist out of shape; II. vii.

WAYS, "come your ways" = come on; I. ii.

WEAK EVILS, evils which cause weakness; II. vii.

WEAR, fashion; II. vii.

WEARING, wearying; II. iv.

WEEK, an indefinite period of time, perhaps = "in the week," *cp.* the phrase "too late in the day"; II. iii.

WHEREIN WENT HE, how was he dressed? III. ii.

WHERE YOU ARE = what you mean; V. ii.

WIT, WHITHER WILT, an exclamation of somewhat obscure meaning, used evidently when anyone was either talking nonsense or usurping a greater share in conversation than justly belonged to him; IV. i. *cp.* "Wit! whither wander you"; I. ii.

WOEFUL, expressive of woe; II. vii.

WOMAN OF THE WORLD, *i. e.* married; V. iii.

WORKING, endeavor; I. ii.

WRATH, passion, ardor; V. ii.

WRESTLER (trisyllabic); II. ii.

YOU = for you; II. v.

YOUNG, inexperienced; I. i.

GLOSSARY

FOR

Twelfth Night

ABUSE, deceive; III. i.

ACCOSTED, addressed; III. ii.

A DEGREE, one step; III. i.

ADHERES, accords; III. iv.

ADMIRE, wonder; III. iv.

ADVERSE, hostile; V. i.

ADVISE YOU, take care; IV. ii.

AFFECTIONED, affected; II. iii.

AGONE, ago; V. i.

ALLOWED, licensed; I. v.

ALLOW ME, make me acknowledged; I. ii.

ALONE, pre-eminently; I. i.

AN = one; II. i.

ANATOMY, body, used contemptuously; III. ii.

AND, used redundantly, as in the old ballads; V. i.

ANTIQUE, quaint; II. iv.

APT, ready; V. i.

ARBITREMENT, decision; III. iv.

ARGUMENT, proof; III. ii.

AS YET, still; V. i.

ATTENDS, awaits; III. iv.

BACK-TRICK, a caper backwards; I. iii.

BAFFLED, treated with contempt; V. i.

BARFUL, full of impediments; (Pope, "O baneful"; Daniel, "a woeful"); I. iv.

BARREN, dull; I. v.

BARRICADOES, fortifications made in haste, obstructions; IV. ii.

BAWBLING, insignificant, trifling; V. i.

BAWCOCK, a term of endearment; always used in masculine sense; III. iv.

BEAGLE, a small dog; II. iii.

BEFORE ME, by my soul; II. iii.

BELIKE, I suppose; III. iii.

BENT, tension; II. iv.

BESHREW, a mild form of imprecation; IV. i.

BESIDES, out of; IV. ii.

BESPAKE YOU FAIR, spoke kindly to you; V. i.

BIAS, originally the weighted side of a bowl; V. i.

BIBBLE BABBLE, idle talk; IV. ii.

BIDDY, "a call to allure chickens"; III. iv.

BIRD-BOLTS, blunt-headed arrows; I. v.

BLAZON, "coat-of-arms"; I. v.

BLENT = blended; I. v.

BLOODY, bloodthirsty; III. iv.

BLOWS, inflates, puffs up; II. v.

BOSOM, the folds of the dress covering the breast, stomacher; III. i.

BOTCHER, mender of old clothes; I. v.

BOTTLE-ALE, bottled ale; II. iii.

BOTTOM, ship, vessel; V. i.

BRABBLE, brawl, broil; V. i.

BRANCHED, "adorned with needlework, representing flowers and twigs"; II. v.

BREACH, surf; II. i.

BREAST, voice; II. iii.

BRED, begotten; I. ii.

BROCK, badger, a term of contempt; II. v.

357

BROWNIST, a member of a Puritan sect; III. ii.

BUM-BAILY, bailiff; III. iv.

BUT = than; I. v.

BUTTERY-BAR, *buttery*, place where drink and food were kept; *bar*, place where they were served out; I. iii.

BY THE DUELLO, by the laws of duelling; III. iv.

CANARY, wine from the Canary Isles; I. iii.

CANTONS = cantos; I. v.

CASE, body, skin; V. i.

CASTILIANO VULGO, "Spanish of Sir Toby's own making"; perhaps it may mean, "Be as reticent as a Castilian now that one of the common herd is coming"; I. iii.

CATIAN, Chinese; used here as a term of reproach; II. iii.

CATCH, "a song sung in succession"; II. iii.

CHAIN, the chain of office which stewards were accustomed to wear; II. iii.

CHANTRY, a private chapel; IV. iii.

CHECKS, "to check" is "a term in falconry, applied to a hawk when she forsakes her proper game, and follows some other of inferior kind that crosses her in her flight"; II. v.; III. i.

CHERRY-PIT, "a game consisting in pitching cherry-stones into a small hole"; III. iv.

CHEVERIL, roe-buck leather; symbol of flexibility; III. i.

CHUCK, chicken, a term of endearment; III. iv.

CIVIL, polite, well-mannered; III. iv.

CLODPOLE, blockhead; III. iv.

CLOISTRESS, inhabitant of a cloister, nun; I. i.

CLOYMENT, surfeit; II. iv.

COCKATRICE, an imaginary creature, supposed to be produced from a cock's egg, and to have so deadly an eye as to kill by its very look; III. iv.

COLLIER, "the devil was called so because of his blackness"; *cp.* the proverb: *"like will to like, quoth the devil to the collier"*; III. iv.

COLORS, "fear no colors," fear no enemy; I. v.

COMFORTABLE, comforting; I. v.

COMMERCE, conversation; III. iv.

COMPARE, comparison; II. iv.

COMPETITORS, confederates; IV. ii.

COMPLEXION, external appearance; II. iv.

COMPTIBLE, sensitive; I. v.

CONCEITED, has formed an idea; III. iv.

CONCLUSIONS TO BE AS KISSES, *i. e.* "as in a syllogism it takes two premises to make one conclusion, so it takes two people to make one kiss" (Cambridge edition); V. i.

CONDUCT, guard, escort; III. iv.

CONSEQUENTLY, subsequently; III. iv.

CONSIDERATION, "on carpet c." = "a mere carpet knight"; III. iv.

CONSTANT, consistent, logical; IV. ii.

CONVENTS, is convenient; V. i.

CORANTO, a quick, lively dance; I. iii.

COUPLET, couple; III. iv.

COXCOMB, head; V. i.

COYSTRILL, a mean, paltry fellow; I. iii.

COZIERS, botchers, cobblers; II. iii.

CREDIT, intelligence; IV. iii.

CROSS-GARTERED, alluding to the custom of wearing the garters crossed in various styles; II. v.

CROWNER, coroner; I. v.

CRUELTY, cruel one; II. iv.

CUBICULO (one of Sir Toby's "affectioned" words), apartment; III. ii.

"CUCULLUS NON FACIT MONACHUM" = a cowl does not make a monk; I. v.

CUNNING, skillful; I. v.

CURST, sharp, shrewish; III. ii.

CUT, a docked horse; II. iii.

CYPRESS, probably "a coffin of cypresswood"; (others explain it as a shroud of *cypress;* Cotgrave mentions *white cipres*); II. iv.

CYPRESS, crape; III. i.

DALLY, play, trifle; III. i.

DAY-BED, couch, sofa; II. v.

DEADLY, death-like; I. v.

DEAR, heartfelt; V. i.

DECEIVABLE, delusive; IV. iii.

DEDICATION, devotedness; V. i.

DELIVER'D, set at liberty; V. i.

DENAY, denial; II. iv.

DENY, refuse; V. i.

DESPERATE, hopeless; II. ii.; reckless; V. i.

DESPITE, malice; III. iv.

DETERMINATE, fixed; II. i.

DEXTERIOUSLY, dexterously; I. v.

DILUCULO SURGERE (saluberrimum est), to rise early is most healthful; II. iii.

DIMENSION, bodily shape; I. v.; V. i.

DISCOURSE, reasoning; IV. iii.

DISMOUNT, draw from the scabbard; III. iv.

DISORDERS, misconduct; II. iii.

DISSEMBLE, disguise; IV. ii.

DISTEMPER, make ill-humored; II. i.

DISTEMPERED, diseased; I. v.

DRY, insipid; I. v.

EGYPTIAN THIEF, an allusion to Thyamis, a robber chief in the Greek Romance of *Theagenes and Chariclea* (trans. into English before 1587; the thief attempted to kill Chariclea, whom he loved, rather than lose her; by mistake he slew another person; V. i.

ELEMENT, sky and air; I. i.; sphere; III. i.

ELEPHANT, the name of an inn; III. iii.

ENCHANTMENT, love-charm; III. i.

ENCOUNTER, go towards; used affectedly; III. i.

ENDEAVOR THYSELF, try; IV. ii.

ENLARGE, release; V. i.

ENTERTAINMENT, treatment; I. v.

ESTIMABLE WONDER, admiring judgment; II. i.

EXCEPT, BEFORE EXCEPTED, alluding to the common law-phrase; I. iii.

EXPENSES, a tip, douceur; III. i.

EXPRESSURE, expression; II. iii.

EXTENT, conduct, behavior; IV. i.

EXTRACTING (later Folios "exacting"), "drawing other thoughts from my mind"; V. i.

EXTRAVAGANCY, vagrancy; II. i.

FADGE, prosper; II. ii.

FALL, strain, cadence; I. i.

FANCY, love; I. i.; V. i.

FANTASTICAL, fanciful, creative; I. i.

"FAREWELL, dear heart, since I must needs begone," etc., altered from *Corydon's Farewell to Phillis* (Percy's *Reliques*); II. iii.

FAVOR, face, form; II. iv.; III. iv.

FEATURE, external form, body; III. iv.

FEELINGLY, exactly; II. iii.

FELLOW, companion; III. iv.

FIRAGO, corruption of virago; III. iv.

FIRE-NEW, brand-new; III. ii.

FIT, becoming, suitable; III. i.

FLATTER WITH, encourage with hopes; I. v.

FLESHED, "made fierce and eager for combat, as a dog fed with flesh only"; IV. i.

FOND, dote; II. ii.

FORGIVE, excuse; I. v.

FOR THAT, because; III. i.

FOURTEEN YEARS' PURCHASE, *i. e.* "at a high rate," the current price in Shakespeare's time being twelve years' purchase; IV. i.

FRAUGHT, freight; V. i.

FREE, careless (or perhaps graceful, comely; *cp.* "fair and free"); II. iv.

FRESH IN MURMUR, began to be rumored; I. ii.

FRIGHT, affright; V. i.

FROM, "f. Candy," *i. e.* "on her voyage from Candy"; V. i.

FULSOME, gross, distasteful; V. i.

GALLIARD, a lively French dance; I. iii.

GASKINS, a kind of loose breeches; I. v.

GECK, dupe; V. i.

GENTLENESS, kindness, good-will; II. i.

GIDDILY, negligently; II. iv.

GIN, snare; II. v.

GINGER, a favorite spice in Shakespeare's time, especially with old people; frequently referred to by Shakespeare; II. iii.

GOES EVEN, agrees, tallies; V. i.

GOOD LIFE, jollity, with a play upon the literal meaning of the word, "virtuous living"; II. iii.

GOODMAN (Folios "good man"), a familiar appellation, sometimes used contemptuously; IV. ii.

GRACE, virtue; V. i.

GRACIOUS, full of graces; I. v.

GRAIN, "in grain," natural; I. v.

GRATILLITY, clown's blunder for "gratuity"; II. iii.

GREEK, "foolish Greek," *i. e.* jester, merrymaker (*cp.* "Matthew Merrygreek" in *Ralph Roister Doister*); "the Greeks were proverbially spoken of by the Romans as fond of good living and free potations" (Nares); IV. i.

GRIZE, step, degree; III. i.

GRIZZLE, a tinge of gray (perhaps a grizzly beard); V. i.

GUST = gusto, enjoyment; I. iii.

HAGGARD, a wild untrained hawk; III. i.

HALE, draw; III. ii.

HAPLY, perhaps; IV. ii.

HAVING, possessions; III. iv.

HEAT, course; I. i.

"HEY ROBIN, JOLLY ROBIN," etc., an old ballad (to be found in the *Reliques*, Percy); IV. ii.

HIGH = highly; I. i.

HOB NOB, "have or have not, hit or miss, at random"; III. iv.

"HOLD THY PEACE, THOU KNAVE," an old three-part catch, so arranged that each singer calls the other "knave" in turn; II. iii.

HONESTY, "decency, love of what is becoming"; II. iii.

HORRIBLE, horribly; III. iv.

HULL, float; I. v.

HUMOR OF STATE, "capricious insolence of authority"; II. v.

IDLENESS, frivolousness; I. v.

IMPETICOS, to impocket, or impetticoat; one of the clown's nonsense words; II. iii.

IMPORTANCE, importunity; V. i.

IMPRESSURE, impression; II. v.

INCENSEMENT, exasperation; III. iv.

INCREDULOUS, incredible; III. iv.

INGRATEFUL, ungrateful; V. i.

INTERCHANGEMENT, interchange; V. i.

INTO, unto; V. i.

JEALOUSY, apprehension; III. iii.

JETS, struts; II. v.

JEWEL, a piece of jewelry; III. iv.

JEZEBEL, used vaguely as a term of reproach; II. v.

JOINDER, joining; V. i.

JUMP, tally; V. i.

KICKSHAWSES = kickshaws; I. iii.

KINDNESS, tenderness; II. i.

LAPSED, surprised; III. iii.

LATE, lately; I. ii.; III. i.

LEASING, lying; I. v.

LEMAN, lover, sweetheart; II. iii.

LENTEN, scanty, poor; I. v.

LETS, hinders; V. i.

LIES, dwells; III. i.

LIGHTER, inferior in position; V. i.

LIMED, caught with bird-lime, ensnared; III. iv.

LIST, boundary, limit; III. i.

LITTLE, a little; V. i.

LIVER, popularly supposed to be the seat of the emotions; II. iv.; III. ii.

LOVE-BROKER, agent between lovers; III. ii.

LOWLY, mean, base; III. i.

LULLABY, "good night"; V. i.

MAIDENHEAD = maidenhood; I. v.

MALAPERT, saucy, forward; IV. i.

MALIGNANCY, malevolence; II. i.

MAUGER, in spite of; III. i.

MEDDLE, fight; III. iv.

METAL (Folio 1, "mettle"; Folio 2, "nettle"); "metal of India" = "my golden girl, my jewel"; (others explain "nettle of India" as the *Urtica marina,* a plant of itching properties); II. v.

MINION, favorite, darling; V. i.

MINX, a pert woman; III. iv.

MISCARRY, be lost, die; III. iv.

MISPRISION, misapprehension; I. v.

MISTRESS MALL, probably "a mere personification," like "my lady's eldest son" in *Much Ado;* I. iii.

MOLLIFICATION, "some m. for your giant," *i. e.* "something to pacify your gigantic (!) waiting maid"; I. v.

MONSTER, unnatural creature; II. ii.

MORTAL, deadly; III. iv.

MOUSE, a term of endearment; I. v.

NAYWORD, by-word; II. iii.

NEWLY, lately; V. i.

NICELY, sophistically, subtilely; III. i.

NON-REGARDANCE, disregard; V. i.

NOT, used pleonastically after "forbid"; II. ii.

NOTE, "come to note," *i. e.* "become known"; IV. iii.

NOTORIOUS, notable; V. i.

NUMBERS, measures of the verses; II. v.

NUNCIO, messenger; I. iv.

OF = on; III. iv.; for the sake of; V. i.

ON = at; II. ii.

OPAL, a precious stone supposed to change its colors; II. iv.

OPEN, openly; III. iii.

OPPOSITE, opponent; III. ii.; III. iv.

OPPOSITE, hostile; II. v.

ORB, earth; III. i.

ORBED CONTINENT, the sun; V. i.

OTHER GATES, in another way; V. i.

"O, THE TWELFTH DAY OF DECEMBER," the opening of some old ballad now lost; II. iii.

OVER-SWEAR, repeat, swear over again; V. i.

OWE = own; I. v.

PARISH-TOP, alluding to the large top kept in every village, for the peasants to whip in frosty weather, for the purpose of keeping themselves warm and out of mischief; I. iii.

PART, in part, partly; III. iv.

PASSAGES, acts; III. ii.

PASS UPON (literally, to thrust), to make a push in fencing; make sallies of wit; III. i.

PEDANT, schoolmaster; III. ii.

PEEVISH, silly, willful; I. v.

"PEG-A-RAMSAY," the name of an old ballad now unknown; II. iii.

PENTHESILEA, the queen of the Amazons; II. iii.

PERCHANCE, by chance; I. ii.

PERDY, a corruption of *par Dieu;* IV. ii.

PERPEND, attend, listen; V. i.

PERSONAGE, personal appearance; I. v.

PERSPECTIVE, deception; V. i.

PILCHARD, a fish strongly resembling the herring; III. i.

PIPE, voice; I. iv.

"PLEASE ONE, AND PLEASE ALL"; the title of an old ballad (entered on the Stationers' Registers in Jan. 18, 1591-92; printed in Staunton's *Shakespeare*); III. iv.

PLUCK ON, excite; V. i.

POINT-DEVISE, exactly; II. v.

POSSESS US, put us in possession, tell us; II. iii.

POST, messenger; I. v.

PRACTICE, plot; V. i.

PRAISE = appraise; (perhaps (?) with a play upon the two senses of *praise*); I. v.

PRANKS, adorns; II. iv.

PREGNANT, clever, expert; II. ii.; III. i.

PRESENT, *i. e.* present wealth; III. iv.

PRESENTLY, immediately; III. iv.

PREVENTED, anticipated; III. i.

PRIVATE, privacy; III. iv.

PROBATION, examination; II. v.

PROOF, "vulgar p." common experience; III. i.

PROPER, handsome; III. i.; own; V. i.

PROPER-FALSE, "well-looking and deceitful"; II. ii.

PROPERTIED, taken possession of; IV. ii.

PROPRIETY, individuality, thyself; V. i.

PURE, purely; V. i.

QUESTION, "in contempt of q." past question; II. v.

QUICK, living, lively; I. i.

QUINAPALUS, an imaginary philosopher; I. v.

QUIRK, humor, caprice; III. iv.

RECEIVING, understanding, quick wit; III. i.

RECOLLECTED, variously interpreted to mean, (1) studied; (2) refined; (3) trivial; "recollected terms" perhaps = popular refrains (? "terms" = "turns" or "tunes"); II. iv.

RECORD, memory; V. i.

RECOVER, win; II. iii.

REGARD, look, glance; V. i.

REINS, is governed by the bridle; III. iv.

RELIQUES, memorials; III. iii.

RENOWN, make famous; III. iii.

REVERBERATE, reverberating, echoing; I. v.

ROUND, plain; II. iii.

RUB WITH CRUMS, to clean; II. iii.

RUBIOUS, red, rosy; I. iv.

RUDESBY, blusterer; IV. i.

RULE, behavior; II. iii.

SACK, Spanish and Canary wine; II. iii.

SAD, serious; III. iv.

SAINT BENNET, probably St. Bennet's, Paul's Wharf, London, destroyed in the great fire; V. i.

SCAB, a term of reproach or disgust; II. v.

SCOUT, watch; III. iv.

SELF, self-same (perhaps with the force of "exclusive," "absolute"); I. i.

SEMBLATIVE, seeming, like; I. iv.

"SHAKE YOUR EARS," an expression of contempt, "grumble at your pleasure"; II. iii.

SHE, woman; I. v.

SHEEP-BITER, a cant term for a thief; II. v.

SHENT, chidden; IV. ii.

SHERIFF'S POST, alluding to the custom of sheriffs setting up posts at their doors, upon which to place notices and proclamations; I. v.

SHREWISHLY, pertly; I. v.

SILLY SOOTH, simple truth; II. iv.

SIR, gentleman, lord; III. iv.; title formerly applied to the inferior clergy; IV. ii.

SKILLESS, inexperienced; III. iii.

SKILLS, matters; V. i.

SKIPPING, wild, mad; I. v.

'SLID, a corruption of "by God's lid"; III. iv.

'SLIGHT, a corruption of "God's light"; II. v.; III. ii.

SNECK UP, an exclamation of contempt; go and be hanged; II. iii.

SOPHY, Shah of Persia; II. v.; III. iv.

SOUND, clear; I. iv.

SOWTER, name of a hound; II. v.

SPINSTERS, female spinners; II. iv.

SPOKE, said; I. iv.

SQUASH, an immature peascod; I. v.

STABLE, steady; IV. iii.

STANDING WATER, between the ebb and flood of the tide; I. v.

STANIEL (Folios, "stallion," corrected by Hammer), a kind of hawk; II. v.

STATE=condition, fortune; I. v.; V. i.

STATE, chair of State; II. v.

STITCHES, a sharp pain; III. ii.

STOCK, stocking; I. iii.

STONE-BOW, "a cross-bow, from which stones or bullets were shot"; II. v.

STOUP, a drinking vessel; II. iii.

STRANGE, estranged; V. i.

STRANGE, STOUT, reserved and proud; II. v.

STRANGENESS, reserve; IV. i.

STRANGLE, suppress; V. i.

STUCK, stoccato, a thrust in fencing; III. iv.

SUBSTRACTORS, Sir Toby's blunder for "detractors"; I. iii.

SUITED, clad; V. i.

SUPPORTANCE, upholding; III. iv.

SWABBER, one who scrubs the ship's deck; I. v.

SWARTHS, swaths; II. iii.

SWEETING, a term of endearment; II. iii.

TABOR, an instrument used by professional clowns; III. i.

TAFFETA, a fine smooth stuff of silk; II. iv.

TAINTING OF, bringing discredit upon; V. i.

TAKE UP, acknowledge; V. i.

TALL, used ironically; I. iii.

TANG, twang; II. v.

TARTAR, Tartarus; II. v.

TASTE, put to use, try; III. i.

TAXATION, tax, demand; I. v.

TENDER, hold dear; V. i.

TERMS, words, vide "recollected terms"; II. iv.

TESTRIL, sixpence; II. iii.

"THERE DWELT A MAN IN BABYLON," a line from the old ballad of Susanna; II. ii.

"THREE MERRY MEN BE WE," a fragment of an old song; frequently quoted by the dramatists (*cp.* Chappell's *Popular Music*); II. iii.

THROW, a throw with the dice, hence "cast, or venture"; V. i.

TILLYVALLY, an exclamation of contempt; II. iii.

TIME-PLEASER, time-server, flatterer; II. iii.

TINKERS, menders of old brass; "proverbial tipplers and would-be politicians"; II. iii.

TRADE, business; III. i.

TRAVEL OF REGARD, looking about; II. v.

TRAY-TRIP, a game like backgammon; II. v.

TROUBLE, "your tr." the trouble I have caused you; II. i.

TRUNKS, alluding to the elaborately carved chests in use in Shakespeare's time; III. iv.

TUCK, rapier; III. iv.

UNAUSPICIOUS, inauspicious; V. i.

UNCHARY, heedlessly; III. iv.

UNGIRD, relax; IV. i.

UNHATCHED, "unhacked, not blunted by blows"; III. iv.

UNPRIZABLE, invaluable; V. i.

UNPROFITED, profitless; I. iv.

UPON, because of, in consequence of; V. i.

USE, usury; III. i.

VALIDITY, value; I. i.

VENERABLE, worthy of veneration; III. iv.

VICE, the buffoon of the old morality plays; IV. ii.

VIOL-DE-GAMBOYS, Sir Toby's blunder for *viol da gamba*, a base-viol or violoncello, a fashionable instrument of that time; I. iii.

VOUCHSAFED, vouchsafing; III. i.

WAINROPES, wagon-ropes; III. ii.

WARE, "Bed of Ware"; a huge bed, capable of holding twelve persons; formerly at the Saracen's Head Inn at Ware, and now at the Rye-House; III. ii.

WAS, had been; IV. iii.

WATERS, "I am for all waters," *i. e.* "I can turn my hand to anything; like a fish, I can swim equally well in all waters"; IV. ii.

WEAVER, alluding perhaps to the psalm-singing propensities of the weavers; II. iii.

WEEDS, garments; V. i.

WELKIN, sky; II. iii.; III. i.

WELL-A-DAY, an exclamation expressive of grief; "welaway," alas! IV. ii.

WERE BEST, had better; III. iv.

WERE BETTER, had better; II. ii.

"WESTWARD-HO!" an exclamation often used by the boatmen on the Thames; III. i.

WHAT, at which; IV. iii.

WHAT'S SHE = who is she; I. ii.

WHILES = while; III. iii.; until; IV. iii.

WHIPSTOCK, whip-handle; II. iii.

WINDY, safe; III. iv.

WITH, by; I. v.

WITS, "five wits," *viz.* "common wit, imagination, fantasy, estimation, and memory"; IV. ii.

WOODCOCK, a bird popularly supposed to have no brains, hence the word was commonly used for a fool; II. v.; IV. ii.

WORTH, substance, wealth; III. iii.

YARE, ready, active; III. iv.

"YEOMEN OF THE WARDROBE," a regular title of office in Shakespeare's time; II. v.

ZANIES, "subordinate buffoons whose office was to make awkward attempts at mimicking the tricks of the professional clown"; I. v.

GLOSSARY
FOR
The Tempest

A = on; II. i.

ABUSE, deceive; V. i.

ACHES (dissyllabic, pronounce "aitches," like the letter H); I. ii.

ADMIRE, wonder; V. i.

ADVANCE, raise, lift up; I. ii.

ADVENTURE, to risk; II. i.

AFTER, afterwards; II. ii.

AGAIN, again and again; I. ii.

A-HOLD, "to lay a ship a-hold," *i. e.*, "to bring a ship close to the wind so as to hold or keep her to it"; I. i.

AMAZEMENT, anguish; I. ii.

AMEN, used probably in the sense of "again!" or perhaps merely with the force of "many"; others render it "hold, stop!"; II. ii.

AN, if; II. i.

ANGLE, corner; I. ii.

ARGIER, Algiers; I. ii.

AS, as if; II. i.

ASPERSION, sprinkling of rain or dew (with an allusion perhaps to the ceremony of sprinkling the marriage-bed with holy water); IV. i.

ATTACHED, seized; III. iii.

AVOID, begone; IV. i.

BACKWARD, distant, past; I. ii.

BADGES, "household servants usually wore on their arms, as part of their livery, silver 'badges' whereon the shield of their masters was engraved"; V. i.

BAREFOOT (used adjectively); II. ii.

BARNACLES, barnacle geese; IV. i.

BASS, utter in a deep bass; III. iii.

BAT-FOWLING, a term used for catching birds by night; thence the name of a thieves' trick for plundering shops about dusk by pretending to have lost a jewel near; II. i.

BEAK, bow (of a ship); I. ii.

BEAR UP, *i. e.*, take your course, sail up; III. ii.

BERMOOTHES, *i. e.*, Bermudas; "said and supposed to be inchanted and inhabited with witches and deuills, which grew by reason of accustomed monstrous thunder, storme, and tempest," &c. Stow's *Annals;* I. ii.

BERRIES (? = Coffee); I. ii.

BLUE-EYED, with blueness about the eyes; I. ii.

BOMBARD, "black jack" of leather; II. ii.

BOOTLESS, profitless; I. ii.

BOSKY, wooded; IV. i.

BOURN, boundary; II. i.

BRAVE, fine; I. ii.

BRING TO TRY, "to lay the ship with her side close to the wind, and lash the tiller to the lee side"; I. i.

365

BROOM-GROVES, groves in which broom (*Spartium scoparium*) abounds; or perhaps woods overgrown with *genista*, pathless woods; IV. i.

BUDGE, stir; V. i.

BURTHEN, undersong; I. ii.

BUT, except that; I. ii.; otherwise than; I. ii.

BY AND BY, immediately; III. ii.

CAN, is able to make; IV. i.

CANDIED, converted into sugar, sweetened; II. i.

CAPABLE, retentive; I. ii.

CAPERING, jumping for joy; V. i.

CARRIAGE, burden; V. i.

CASE, condition; III. ii.

CAST, to throw up; perhaps with a play upon "cast" in the sense of "to assign their parts to actors"; II. i.

CAT (with reference to the old proverb that good liquor will make a cat speak); II. ii.

CATCH, a part-song; III. ii.

CERTES, certainly; III. iii.

CHALKED FORTH, *i. e.*, chalked out; V. i.

CHERUBIN, a cherub; I. ii.

CHIRURGEONLY, like a surgeon; II. i.

CLEAR, blameless; III. iii.

CLOSENESS, retirement; I. ii.

CLOUDY, gloomy; II. i.

COCKEREL, the young cock; II. i.

COIL, turmoil; I. ii.

COME BY, to acquire; II. i.

CONFEDERATES, conspires; I. ii.

CONSTANT, self-possessed; I. ii. "my stomach is not c." *i. e.* "is qualmish"; II. ii.

CONTENT, desire, will; II. i.

CONTROL, contradict; I. ii.

CORAGIO, couragel; V. i.

COROLLARY, a supernumerary, a surplus; IV. i.

CORRESPONDENT, responsive, obedient; I. ii.

COURSES, the largest lower sails of a ship; I. i.

CRABS, crab-apples; II. ii.

CRACK, to burst (with reference to magic bands, or perhaps to the crucibles and alembics of magicians); V. i.

DEAR, zealous; I. ii.

DEAREST, most precious object; II. i.

DEBOSHED, debauched; III. ii.

DECKED, sprinkled; I. ii.

DEEP, profound, wise; II. i.

DELIVER, relate; V. i.

DEMANDED, asked; I. ii.

DEW-LAPPED, having flesh hanging from the throat (a reference probably to the victims of "goitre"); III. iii.

DIS, Pluto; IV. i.

DISCASE, undress; V. i.

DISCHARGE, performance, execution; used probably as a technical term of the stage; II. i.

DISTEMPERED, excited; IV. i.

DISTINCTLY, separately; I. ii.

DOIT, the smallest piece of money; eighty doits went to a shilling; II. ii.

DOLLAR, used quibblingly with "dolor"; II. i.

DOWLE, a fiber of down; III. iii.

DRAWN, having swords drawn; II. i.; having taken a good draught; II. ii.

DREGS (with reference to the "liquor of the bombard,"); II. ii.

DROLLERY, puppet-show; III. iii

DRY, thirsty; I. ii.

DULLNESS, stupor; I. ii.

EARTH'D, buried in the earth; II. i.

EBBING, "ebbing men," *i. e.*, "men whose fortunes are declining"; II. i.

ECSTASY, mental excitement, madness; III. iii.

ENDEAVOR, laborious effort; II. i.

ENGINE, instrument of war, military machine; II. i.

ENTERTAINER, perhaps quibblingly interpreted by Gonzalo in the sense of "inn-keeper"; II. i.

ENVY, malice; I. ii.

ESTATE, to grant as a possession; IV. i.

EYE, tinge; II. i.

FALL, to let fall; II. i.

FEARFUL, timorous; I. ii.

FEATER, more becomingly; II. i.

FEATLY, deftly; I. ii.

FELLOWS, companions; II. i.

FEW, "in few," in few words, in short; I. ii.

FISH, to catch at, to seek to obtain; II. i.

FLAT, low level ground; II. ii.

FLAT-LONG, as if struck with the side of a sword instead of its edge; II. i.

FLESH-FLY, a fly that feeds on flesh and deposits her eggs in it; III. i.

FLOTE, flood, sea; I. ii.

FOIL, disadvantage; III. i.

FOISON, plenty; II. i.

FOUNDER'D, disabled by overriding, footsore; IV. i.

FORTH-RIGHTS, straight paths; III. iii.

FRAUGHTING, freighting; I. ii.

FRESHES, springs of fresh water; III. ii.

FRIPPERY, a place where old clothes are sold; IV. i.

FRUSTRATE, frustrated; III. iii.

GABERDINE, a long coarse outer garment; II. ii.

GALLOWS, cf. "He that is born to be hanged will never be drowned"; I. i.

GAVE OUT, i. e., gave up; V. i.

GENTLE, high-born (and hence "high-spirited"); I. ii.

GILDED, made drunk (an allusion to the *aurum potabile* of the alchemists); V. i.

GINS, begins; III. iii.

GLASSES, hour-glasses. i. e., runnings of the hour-glass; I. ii.

GLUT, to swallow up; I. i.

GRUDGE, murmur; I. ii.

HEAVY, "the heavy offer"; i. e., the offer which brings drowsiness; II. i.

HELP, cure; II. ii.

HESTS, behests; I. ii.

HINT, theme; I. ii.; occasion, cause; II. i.

HIS, its; II. i.

HOIST, hoisted (past tense of "hoise" or "hoist"); I. ii.

HOLLOWLY, insincerely; III. i.

HOME, to the utmost, effectively; V. i.

HONEYCOMB, cells of honeycomb; I. ii.

IGNORANT, appertaining to ignorance, "i. fumes" = "fumes of ignorance"; V. i.

IMPERTINENT, irrelevant; I. ii.

INCH-MEAL, inch by inch; II. ii.

INFEST, vex; V. i.

INFLUENCE (used in its astrological sense); I. ii.

INFUSED, endowed; I. ii.

INHERIT, take possession; II. ii.

INLY, inwardly; V. i.

INQUISITION, enquiry; I. ii.

INVERT, change to the contrary; III. i.

JACK, "played the Jack," i. e. the knave = "deceived"; IV. i.

JERKIN, a kind of doublet; IV. i.

JUSTIFY, prove; V. i.

KEY, tuning-key; I. ii.

KIBE, heel-sore; II. i.

KNOT (folded arms); I. ii.

LAKIN, "Ladykin," or the Virgin Mary; III. iii.

LASS-LORN, forsaken by his lass; IV. i.

LAUGHTER, possibly used with a double meaning; "lafter" was perhaps the cant name of some small coin; still used provincially for the number of eggs laid by a hen at one time; II. i.

LEARNING, teaching; I. ii.

LIEU, "in lieu of," i. e., in consideration of; I. ii.

LIFE, "good life," i. e., "life-like truthfulness"; III. iii.

LIKE, similarly; III. iii.

LIME, bird-lime; IV. i.

LINE, lime-tree (with punning reference to other meanings of "line" in subsequent portion of the scene); IV. i.

LINE-GROVE, lime-grove; V. i.

LIVER, regarded as the seat of passion; IV. i.

LOATHNESS, reluctance; II. i.

LORDED, made a lord; I. ii.

LUSH, luscious, luxuriant; II. i.

LUSTY, vigorous; II. i.

MAID, maid-servant; III. i.

MAIN-COURSE, the main sail; I. i.

MAKE, to prove to be; II. i.

MAKE A MAN, i. e., make a man's fortune; II. ii.

MANAGE, government; I. ii.

MARMOSET, small monkey; II. ii.

MASSY, massive, heavy; III. iii.

MATTER, an important matter; II. i.

MEANDERS, winding paths; III. iii.

MEASURE, pass over; II. i.

MEDDLE, to mingle; I. ii.

MERCHANT, merchantman ("the masters of some merchant"); II. i.

MERELY, absolutely; I. i.

METTLE, disposition, ardor; II. i.

MINION, favorite; IV. i.

MIRACULOUS, "the miraculous harp" of Amphion, the music of which raised the walls of Thebes; II. i.

MISS, to do without; I. i..; to fail in aiming at, not to hit; II. i.

MO, more; II. i.

MOMENTARY, instantaneous; I. ii.

MOON-CALF, abortion; II. ii.

MOP, grimace; IV. i.

MORSEL, remnant, "a piece of a man" (contemptuously); II. i.

MOUNT, raise; II. ii.

MOW, grimace; IV. i.

MOW, make grimaces; II. ii.

MUCH, "to think it much," to reckon it as excessive, to grudge; I. ii.

MUM, hush; III. ii.

MUSE, wonder at; III. iii.

NATURAL, idiot; III. ii.

NATURE, natural affection; V. i.

NEAT, horned beast; II. ii.

NERVES, sinews; I. ii.

NIMBLE, excitable; II. i.

NINNY, simpleton; III. ii.

NOBODY, an Elizabethan sign; probably a direct allusion to the print of No-body, prefixed to the anonymous comedy of No-body and Somebody (printed before 1600), or to the engraving on the old ballad, called the Well-Spoken No-body; III. ii.

NOOK, bay; I. ii.

NOTE, information; II. i.

NOTHING, nonsense; II. i.

OBSERVATION, attention to detail; III. iii.

OCCASION, critical opportunity; II. i.

ODD, out-of-the-way; I. ii.

O'ER, over again; "trebles thee o'er," i. e., makes thee three times as great"; II. i.

O'ERPRIZED, surpassed in value; I. ii.

OF, as a consequence of; or = on, i. e., "of sleep" = "asleep"; V. i.

OMIT, neglect; I. ii.; II. i.

ON, of; I. ii.; IV. i.

OOZE, bottom of the sea; I. ii.

OR, ere; "or ere" (a reduplication); I. ii.

OUT, completely; I. ii.

OVERBLOWN, blown over; II. ii.

OVERTOPPING, outrunning; I. ii.

OWED, owned; III. i.

OWES, owns; I. ii.

OWN, "no man was his o." i. e., "master of himself, in his senses"; V. i.

PAINFUL, laborious; III. i.

PAINS, tasks; I. ii.

PAPHOS, a city in Cyprus, one of the favorite seats of Venus; IV. i.

PASS, thrust (a term of fencing), sally; IV. i.

PASSION, suffering, grief; I. ii.

PASSION, to feel pain or sorrow; V. i.

PATCH, fool, jester; III. ii.

PATE, "pass of pate" = "sally of wit"; IV. i.

PAUNCH, run through the paunch; III. ii.

PAY, repay; "to pay home" = "to repay to the utmost"; V. i.

PERTLY, briskly; IV. i.

PIECE, "perfect specimen"; I. ii.

PIED, motley-coated; III. ii.

PIG-NUTS, earth-nuts; II. ii.

PIONED, (?) "overgrown with marsh-marigold" (still called "peony" in the neighborhood of Stratford); IV. i.

PLANTATION, colonization; interpreted by Antonio in the ordinary sense; II. i.

PLAY, act the part of; "play the men," i. e. behave like men; I. ii.

POINT, detail; "to point," in every detail; I. ii.

POLE-CLIPT, with poles clipt, or embraced, by the vines; IV. i.

POOR-JOHN, a cant name for hake salted and dried; II. ii.

PREMISES, conditions; I. ii.

PRESENTED, represented; IV. i.

PRESENTLY, immediately; I. ii.; IV. i.

PROFESS, to make it one's business; II. i.

PROFIT, to profit; I. ii.

PROVISION, foresight; I. ii.

PURCHASED, acquired, won; IV. i.

PUTTER-OUT, "p. of five for one," one who invests, puts out, a sum of money before leaving home, on condition of receiving five times the amount on his return, i. e., "at the rate of five for one"; III. iii.

QUAINT, adroit, trim, excellent; I. ii.

QUALITY, skill; I. ii.

QUICK, living, fresh; III. ii.

QUICKENS, gives life to; III. i.

RABBLE, company, crowd (not used slightingly); IV. i.

RACE, breed; I. ii.

RACK, floating cloud; IV. i.

RATE, estimation; I. ii.; reckoning; II. i.

RAZORABLE, ready for shaving; II. i.

REAR, raise; II. i.

REASON, what is reasonable; III. ii.

REASONABLE, "reasonable shore," i. e., "shore of reason"; V. i.

RECOVER, restore; II. ii.

REELING-RIPE, "in a state of

intoxication sufficiently advanced for reeling"; V. i.

RELEASE, "till your release" = till you release them; V. i.

REMEMBER, commemorate; I. ii.; remind; I. ii.

REMEMBRANCE, the faculty of remembering; II. i.

REMORSE, pity; V. i.

REQUIT, requited; III. iii.

RESOLVE, explain to; V. i.

RID, destroy; I. ii.

ROOM, sea-room; I. i.

ROUNDED, "the whole round of life has its beginning and end in a sleep"; IV. i.

SACK, a name applied to certain white wines of Spain; II. ii.

SANCTIMONIOUS, holy; IV. i.

SANS, without; I. ii.

SCAMELS, probably some kind of bird, but not yet satisfactorily explained; II. ii.

SCANDAL'D, scandalous; IV. i.

SECURING, guarding; II. i.

SEDGED, made of sedges; IV. i.

SENSE, feelings; II. i.

SENSIBLE, sensitive; II. i.

SETEBOS, the god of Sycorax (said to be the chief god of the Patagonians); I. ii.; V. i.

SETS OFF, i. e., shows to the best advantage; III. i.

SEVERAL, separate; III. i.

SHAK'D, shook; II. i.

SHROUD, take shelter; II. ii.

SIEGE, stool, excrement; II. ii.

SINGLE, (1) solitary, (2) feeble; I. ii.

SKILLESS, ignorant; III. i.

SOCIABLE, companionable, being in close sympathy; V. i.

SOMETHING, somewhat; I. ii.

SOMETIME, sometimes; I. ii.

SORE (used quibblingly); V. i.

SORT, possibly a punning allusion to "sort" = "lot"; II. i.

SOT, fool; III. ii.

SOUNDLY, thoroughly, smartly; II. ii.

SOUTH-WEST, "a south-west," i. e., a south-west wind (charged with the noxious breath of the Gulf-Stream); I. ii.

SPEAK, to proclaim; II. i.

SPHERE, orbit; II. i.

SPOON, "long spoon," an allusion to old proverb that "he must have a long spoon that must eat with the devil"; II. ii.

SPIRITING, the service done by a sprite; I. ii.

STAIN, to disfigure; I. ii.

STANDARD, standard-bearer, ensign; III. ii.; (quibble on "standard" and "stander"); III. ii.

STANDING, "standing water," i. e. water neither ebbing nor flowing; II. i.

STEADED, stood in good stead; I. ii.

STILL-CLOSING, constantly closing again; III. iii.

STILL-VEXED, ever troubled; I. ii.

STOCK-FISH, dried cod; III. ii.

STOMACH, courage; I. ii.; appetite, inclination; I. i.

STOVER, fodder for cattle; IV. i.

STRANGE, rare; III. iii.

STRANGELY, wonderfully; IV. i.

STUDY, to give thought and attention to, to wonder; II. i.

SUBSTITUTION, deputyship; I. ii.

SUBTILTIES, the word "subtilty" was borrowed from the language of cookery, and denoted a device in pastry, hence "illusion"; V. i.

SUDDEN, swift; II. i.

SUFFERED, i. e., suffered death; II. ii.

SUGGESTION, prompting, hint (cf. villainy); II. i.

SUSTAINING, bearing (them) up; I. ii.

SWABBER, one who sweeps or *swabs* the deck of a ship; II. ii.

TABOR, a small drum used for festivities; IV. i.

TABORER, a player on a tabor; III. ii.

TACKLE, ropes; I. ii.

TALKING, saying; II. i.

TANG, shrill sound; II. ii.

TASTE, experience; V. i.

TEEN, grief; I. ii.

TELL, to count (the strokes of the clock); II. i.

TEMPERANCE, temperature; Temperance, like Charity, used as a proper name; II, i.

TEND, attend; I. i.

TENDED, to regard; II. i.

THATCHED, covered, strewn; IV. i.

THRID, thread; IV. i.

THROE, to cause pain; II. i.

THROUGHLY, thoroughly; III. iii.

TILTH, tillage; II. i.

TO, for, as; II. i.; in comparison with; II. i.

TRASH, to check the speed of hounds when too forward; I. ii.

TREBLES, "tr. thee o'er," *i. e.,* "makes thee thrice what thou art"; II. i.

TREMBLING, the *"tremor"* which is represented to be a sign of being possessed by the devil; II. ii.

TRICE, "on a tr.," *i. e.,* "in an instant"; V. i.

TRICKSY, sportive; V. i.

TRIFLE, phantom; V. i.

TROLL, run glibly over (perhaps "sing irregularly"); III. ii.

TWILLED, (?) covered with reeds or sedges; IV. i.

TWINK, a twinkling; IV. i.

UNDER THE LINE, probably a term in tennis; "to strike (the ball) under the line" = "to lose the game"; IV. i.

UNDERGOING, enduring; I. ii.

UNICORN (with allusion to its proverbial ferocity); III. iii.

UNSTANCHED, incontinent; I. i.

UP-STARING, standing on end; I. ii.

URCHINS, hedgehogs, hobgoblins; I. ii.

URCHIN-SHOWS, elfin apparitions; I. ii.

USE, to be accustomed; II. i.

VANITY, illusion; IV. i.

VAST, silent void, or vacancy (of night); I. ii.

VERILY, true; II. i.

VIRGIN-KNOT, alluding to the girdle worn by maidens in ancient times; IV. i.

VISITATION, affliction (as of a plague); III. i.

VISITORS, priestly visitant, "consolator"; II. i.

VOUCHED, warranted; II. i.

WAIST, the part of a ship between the quarter-deck and the forecastle; I. ii.

WARD, attitude of defense; I. ii.

WEATHER, storm; I. i.

WEATHER-FENDS, defends from the weather; V. i.

WEIGHED, considered, pondered; II. i.

WENCH (used as term of endearment); I. ii.

WEZAND, windpipe; III. ii.

WHEN (an exclamation of impatience); I. ii.

WHILE-ERE, short time since; III. ii.

WHIST, hushed, silent; I. ii.

WICKED, baneful; I. ii.

WIDE-CHAPPED, opening the mouth wide; I. i.

WINK, the act of closing the eye; II. i.; (a short distance measured by a "wink"; II. i.).

WINK, to close the eyes; II. i.

WISEST, "after the wisest," *i. e.*, "in the wisest fashion"; II. ii.

WOE, sorry; V. i.

WORKS, affects; IV. i.

WOUND, twined about; II. ii.

WRANGLE, contend, quarrel; V. i.

WRONG, "to do oneself wrong," *i. e.*, "to be much mistaken"; I. ii

YARE, ready; I. i.

YARELY, alertly; I. i.

YOND, there; I. ii.

YOUR (= subjective genitive); V. i.

ZENITH, the highest point of one's fortune; I. ii.